Focus on Secondary Education

Focus on Secondary Education

an introduction to principles and practices

E. DALE DAVIS Southern Methodist University

SCOTT, FORESMAN AND COMPANY GLENVIEW, ILLINOIS · Atlanta · Dallas · Palo Alto · Oakland, N.J.

This book is dedicated to

LOU NOWELL DAVIS

for her valuable assistance in editing and typing the manuscript and for one thousand and one other reasons.

Preface

Focus on Secondary Education is concerned with the development of secondary education in the United States, its present status, and significant trends that are already manifesting themselves to the point of reshaping the secondary schools. The story of the development of secondary education is briefly considered in order that the reader may understand the factors that have produced the American secondary school. The programs and practices of today's schools are discussed in detail so that an understanding and appreciation of the current situation may be grasped. Finally, consideration also is given to those significant innovations that are influencing secondary school teaching.

Focus on Secondary Education is a textbook in teacher education for courses that are usually referred to as "Secondary Education" or "Principles of Secondary Education." In determining its content, I have surveyed past and present textbooks and have sought the guidance of numerous individuals now teaching such courses. By visiting with teachers at their schools, by seeking them out at national and state meetings, and by corresponding with them, I have selected topics that seemed to be of greatest concern to the instructors of courses dealing with the secondary school in American society. After the topics were researched and carefully studied, the chapters were written.

The point of view dominating the entire book is that the best educational experiences must be provided for American youth. The text is divided into five parts. Part One deals with the historical development of the American secondary school. In order that a better historical perspective might be given, three chapters, dealing with the development of secondary education in the United States, the objectives of secondary education in this country, and the students enrolled in secondary education, are presented.

Part Two is devoted to a study of the curriculum found in American secondary schools. Chapter 4 provides an overview of the curriculum, and the next five chapters give specific information on the major areas in the curriculum. Chapter 5 discusses general education and the major methods by which it is provided. The major subjects, procedures, and activities that are primarily concerned with specialized education are explored in Chapter 6. Chapter 7 examines the crucial issues in planning an appropriate curriculum for a heterogeneous student population, and Chapter 8 pinpoints the major trends in the curriculum which transcend subject lines. Chapter 9 deals with the important role of extraclass activities —the so-called "third curriculum."

Part Three consists of four chapters dealing with guidance and counseling, planning and directing classroom instruction, the teacher's role, and the organizational and administrative framework of secondary education. The chapters on teaching methods, guidance, and administration are presented as introduction to these areas; they are not intended as substitutes for textbooks on methods of teaching, guidance, and administration.

Part Four provides a condensed comparative analysis of private and parochial secondary schools with public schools in one chapter and of American secondary education with European education in two others. Most textbooks on secondary education furnish little or no information about nonpublic schools; but it is important for the student of education to be aware of the role that these schools play in American education and to inform himself concerning their organization, curriculums, and procedures. The chapters on European education are necessary because of the tremendous amount of interest on the part of American educators in education abroad and because of the tendency of recent critics to urge that the American secondary school copy European practices.

Part Five consists of one chapter, which discusses critics, criticisms, and accomplishments of American secondary education. It is not intended as a comprehensive treatment of the subjects but rather as a provocative introduction to an area that demands careful study by a future teacher.

The author has served both as teacher and principal in secondary schools. He has also taught courses in undergraduate and graduate teacher education programs for many years. In this book he has tried to present the current picture of secondary education in light of historic perspective.

It is his opinion that no one text can provide enough material for an entire course in an area such as secondary education. Students and teachers are therefore urged to supplement this text with appropriate collateral and supplementary reading.

E.D.D.

Contents

The secondary school in perspective

PART I

Historical development
of secondary education

1

chapter

History sets forth examples of man dealing with old and new problems; man improving old devices and institutions; man creating new devices and institutions to solve his problems and meet new demands and forces. Much in secondary education today had its beginnings in the past.

A brief consideration of some of the more significant developments in the history of secondary education in this country will better enable the individual to know and understand the secondary schools of today.

Definition of secondary education

What is meant by *secondary education?* It is possible to define it in terms of grade levels — generally, grades seven through twelve or grades seven through twelve plus junior college. Such a definition, however, leaves much to be desired. It does not throw any light on the type of curriculum offered. It tells nothing about the pupils involved. It gives no indication of the objectives and functions of the school.

There are some who define secondary education as the educational opportunities available to adolescents. But opinions vary as to what constitutes an adolescent. Some define adolescence as the period of life from fourteen to eighteen; others refer to it as the span between twelve and twenty. Actually, adolescence has no fixed age limits.

Some educators attempt to define secondary education in terms of curriculum. French, for example, defines it in the European sense as "organized, in-school, post-elementary education of a reasonable degree of intellectual difficulty."[1]

Many individuals define secondary education in functional terms. Perhaps the classic definition in this vein is that set forth by the Committee on the Orientation of Secondary Education of the Department of Secondary-School Principals of the National Education Association:

Secondary education denotes the education provided by schools for the purpose of guiding and promoting the development of normal individuals for whom on the one hand the elementary school no longer constitutes a satisfactory environment, and who on the other hand are either not yet prepared to participate effectively in society unguided by the school, or are not ready for the specialized work of the professional schools or the upper division of the liberal arts college.[2]

As we look at the earlier stages in the development of secondary education, we shall find that not all the forms of education provided for adolescents were offered in schools; primarily, however, secondary education shall be considered here as that schooling which demands and follows an acceptable degree of elementary schooling and is offered in a formal, organized setting.

Beginnings of secondary education in America

It was only natural that the early settlers should bring with them to the New World the form of schooling prevalent in England at the time. This was the Latin grammar school. The first of these schools had been founded in the mother country in 1510 by John Colet, Dean of the Cathedral, at St. Paul's Cathedral in London. After the Reformation, many of the old monastic and cathedral schools were converted into this kind of school, and many new ones were established. Historians disagree on the number of Latin schools in England at the time of the American colonization, but it

[1]William Marshall French, *American Secondary Education* (New York: The Odyssey Press, Inc., 1957), p. 25.

[2]*Bulletin of the Department of Secondary-School Principals*, Bulletin 59, Report of the Committee on the Orientation of Secondary Education Issues of Secondary Education, National Education Association (Chicago: NEA, January 1936), p. 22.

is safe to say that there were at the least three hundred and at the most five hundred.[3] Many of the colonists had attended this type of institution.

Growth of the Latin grammar school

As early as 1621 the Virginia Company of London proposed to establish a Latin grammar school in Virginia. A portion of land was set aside and some gifts were received, but an Indian massacre stopped all plans for the venture.

This unfortunate event gave the early settlers of Massachusetts the distinction of establishing the first Latin schools in the New World. In 1635, only fifteen years after the landing at Plymouth, the Boston Latin Grammar School was opened. This school has had a continuous existence until the present and is today part of the secondary school system of Boston. The town records show that in April of 1635 the citizens not only voted to establish such a school but also set up rules to help the school achieve its purposes, to govern its curriculum offerings, to determine the qualifications of its teachers, and to regulate tuition and teachers' salaries. Other towns followed this early example.

Little is known about these early schools. From information found in old town records, early correspondence, and old newspapers, scholars know that a considerable number were established. Manuscripts tell of Latin schools existing very early in such towns as Charlestown, Ipswich, Salem, Dorchester, Newbury, and Roxbury—all in Massachusetts. Others were established at an early date in Connecticut in such towns as New Haven, Hartford, and Guilford. There were also early Latin schools at New Amsterdam in New Netherlands, at Newport in Rhode Island, and at several places in Virginia and the other Southern colonies.

The Latin grammar school was a public school, open to all the children of the community. Families that could afford to pay tuition for their children were expected to do so; children of indigent parents were admitted free. (The same policy existed in England at the time.) Since the Latin school was not entirely free, it was not a "public" school in the current sense of the word. Instead, these schools were part public and part private, for even though most of the towns used public lands and/or tax money for the Latin school, some citizens agreed among themselves to give certain sums of

---

[3]R. Freeman Butts, *A Cultural History of Western Education,* 2nd ed. (New York: McGraw-Hill Book Company, Inc., 1955), p. 210.

money annually for the support of the schools, and some of these schools received endowments.[4]

The curriculum of the schools consisted principally of Latin, but other elementary subjects such as reading, writing, arithmetic, and spelling were offered in some of the Latin schools, and Greek was taught in many schools. After 1789 the seven-year course of study was reduced to four years, and entrance requirements were established—for example, that students be at least ten years of age and be "previously well instructed in English Grammar." Some people have seen in this four-year school the origin of the four-year pattern of secondary education that was dominant in this country until the appearance of the junior high school. Inglis gives the four-year curriculum offered in 1789 by the Boston Latin School:

1st Class: Cheever's "Accidence"
             Corderiu's "Colloquies"—Latin and English
             Nomenclator
             Aesop's Fables—Latin and English
             Ward's Latin Grammar, or Eutropius
2nd Class: Clarke's Introduction—Latin and English
             Ward's Latin Grammar
             Eutropius continued
             "Selectae e Veteri Testament Historiae," or Castilio's
                "Dialogues"
             The Making of Latin, from Garretson's "Exercises"
3rd Class: Caesar's "Commentaries"
             Tully's Epistles, or Offices
             Ovid's "Metamorphoses"
             Virgil
             Greek Grammar
             The Making of Latin, from King's "History of the
                Heathen Gods"
4th Class: Virgil continued—Tully's Orations
             Greek Testament—Horace
             Homer—"Gradus ad Parnassum"[5]

The above curriculum should make clear why this school was called the Latin grammar school. When one remembers that this school was designed primarily to prepare young boys for college and that the colleges of the day existed principally for the educa-

[4]French, op. cit., p. 45.
[5]Alexander James Inglis, The Rise of the High School in Massachusetts (New York: Teachers College, Columbia University, 1911), pp. 2–3.

tion of future ministers, it is not surprising to find so much emphasis placed on Latin and Greek.

The Latin schools had rugged schedules. The school day extended from seven or eight in the morning to four or five in the afternoon, with two hours off for lunch. There were no summer vacations and only an occasional holiday. The dominant method of teaching was memorization. President Charles Eliot of Harvard, recalling his experiences as a scholar in the Boston Public Latin School in 1844, said:

> At ten years of age I committed to memory many rules of syntax, the meaning of which I had no notion of, although I could apply them in a mechanical way. The rule for the ablative absolute, for instance — "A noun and a participle are put in the ablative, called absolute, to denote the time, cause, or concomitant of an action, or the condition on which it depends" — I could rattle off whenever I encountered a sample of that construction, but it was several years after I learnt the rule that I arrived at even the faintest conception of what it meant. The learning by heart of the grammar then preceded rather than accompanied as now exercises in translation and composition.[6]

From the records that have been preserved it can be gathered that the percentage of young people attending the Latin schools was always small. In 1738 the combined enrollment in the Boston Latin School and the North Latin Grammar School was just 202.

Laws of 1642 and 1647

A discussion of colonial education in general, and the Latin school in particular, is incomplete without mention of the Massachusetts Laws of 1642 and 1647. The Law of 1642 was set forth because it had become evident that many parents and masters were neglecting the education of their children and their apprentices. To remedy such conditions the town fathers were, under this law, "to take account from time to time of all parents and masters of their children . . . especially of their ability to read and understand the principles of religion and the capital laws of their country."[7] Parents and masters who refused to comply with the law or whose children were found to be lacking in the above requirements could be fined. The children could even be taken from such neglectful

---

[6]Quoted in Pauline Holmes, *A Tercentenary History of the Boston Latin School, 1635–1935* (Cambridge, Mass.: Harvard University Press, 1935), p. 377.

[7]Adolphe E. Meyer, *An Educational History of the American People* (New York: McGraw-Hill Book Company, Inc., 1957), p. 30.

parents and put out as apprentices. This law remained in effect until 1647, when it was amended by a more forceful law. Similar laws were passed throughout New England with the exception of Rhode Island.

While the law of 1642 provided for compulsory education, it did not establish schools as such, nor did it make any provisions for compulsory attendance. This was perhaps because of the still prevailing English practice of leaving the responsibility for the schooling of the young to parents and masters. In 1647 the General Court of Massachusetts set forth the most significant law of the colonial period as far as education is concerned. This law is known as the "Old Deluder, Satan Act."

It being one chief project of the old deluder, Satan, to keep men from the knowledge of the Scriptures . . . it is therefore ordered, that every township in this jurisdiction, after the Lord hath increased your number to 50 householders, shall then forthwith appoint one within their town to teach all such children as shall resort to him to write and read, whose wages shall be paid either by the parents or masters of such children, or by the inhabitants in general . . . Provided, those that send their children be not oppressed by paying much more than they can have them taught for in other towns; and it is further ordered, that where any town shall increase to the number of 100 families or householders they shall set up a grammar school, the master thereof being able to instruct youth so far as they shall be fitted for the university, provided that if any town neglect the performance hereof above one year, that every such town shall pay five pounds to the next school till they shall perform this order.[8]

This law, which called for definite provisions for education, became a model for other colonies in New England.

The laws of 1642 and 1647 are important milestones in the development of education in this country and, indeed, among the English-speaking people of the world. They set up the first system of public elementary and secondary schools in America. They had the authority of the government behind them, and in them the government established its right to prescribe education for children and, in effect, its right to establish schools. Furthermore, this education was to be compulsory, and it was to be supported at public expense. Some scholars attach very little importance to these laws because the government of Massachusetts was at that

[8]Quoted in Ellwood P. Cubberley, *Readings in Public Education in the United States* (Boston: Houghton Mifflin Company, 1934), pp. 16–17.

time controlled by the church. Most feel, however, that because the laws were copied on a large scale and because they provided for a system of elementary and secondary education at public expense, they were certainly significant, even though calling them "cornerstones" of the American public school system probably is not justified.

Outside the New England area the government had very little to do with education in colonial America. In the Middle Colonies religious diversity made it difficult for the colonial governments to assume an important role. In the South the leaders felt that parents should determine what education children should have and provide it as they saw fit.

Decline of the Latin grammar school

The Latin grammar school was the first step in the founding of secondary education in the United States, yet schools of this type often found it difficult to function, even in New England. The reasons for this are not hard to understand. This was a pioneer society; survival itself was often a great task, and most people had little time to devote to education.

During the early years of the nineteenth century the Latin school began a gradual decline. There were a number of reasons for this:

1. The younger generations differed from their predecessors in that they were more concerned with the practical and the present and less concerned with old-world traditions such as the Latin school.

2. Life in the wilderness was not conducive to education in general and especially to the type provided by the Latin school.

3. Social and economic conditions demanded a more practical type of education.

4. A shift in religious thinking from the harsh authoritarianism of the Puritans to a new emphasis on the innate worth of the free individual led to a shift in educational means and ends.

5. The appearance of private-venture schools (see page 10) created even greater demands for schools that would provide education in the practical affairs of business and life in this new country.

Credit due the Latin grammar school

The Latin grammar school did the job it was created to do; it prepared leaders for church and state. Many eighteenth- and nine-teenth-century leaders received their education in this type of school, among them Cotton Mather, Benjamin Franklin, John Hancock, Edward Everett, Ralph Waldo Emerson, Charles Sumner, Henry Ward Beecher, Edward Everett Hale, Charles Eliot, and Phillips Brooks.

Certainly the Latin school represented an important phase in the development of our system of secondary education. It helped keep the tradition of secondary education alive in a new country, and it established precedents—for example, the right of the government to provide education and the tradition of lay control. It is true that this institution was highly selective, but most parents had not received a secondary education and did not desire one for their children. It should also be remembered that a lack of such education was not a serious handicap in those days.

Despite relatively small enrollments, the Latin school enjoyed considerable prestige, especially in New England. There were several reasons for this:

1. It carried on the type of education that many of the early settlers had received in England.

2. It was the school attended by local and national leaders.

3. It was considered a bulwark of religion.

4. It was the school of Latin and Greek, the traditional languages of religion and learning in the Western world.

5. It prepared students for institutions of higher learning.

6. It attracted teachers of high caliber.

Other forms of colonial secondary education

There were at least two forms of secondary education in early colonial America besides the Latin grammar school. The first of these was apprenticeship training, a European practice transplanted to the New World. It was a widespread custom in all the colonies for boys and girls from homes of the "poorer sort" to be bound out to some master for a certain period of years to learn a trade. Most apprenticeships lasted seven years. The masters were supposed to teach, or see that someone else taught, their apprentices reading and writing and to give them religious training.

The other early form of secondary education was tutorial instruction. This form of education was very popular among the upper classes in some of the Southern colonies, especially Virginia. Meyer indicates that in the wealthier Southern families the tutor was an integral part of the household, and that now and then smaller planters would consign their children to the charge of a neighbor's tutor.[9]

[9]Meyer, *op. cit.*, p. 54.

Rise of the academy

Essentially the same reasons that led to the decline of the Latin grammar school also led to the establishment of a new type of secondary school called the academy. Other factors were the growing feelings of hostility toward England and England's institutions and the great demands for preparing students for business, trades, and surveying. In short, the general public saw little value in the old "dead language" type of education and wanted a form of education more in keeping with the changing way of life. Many individuals were already teaching practical subjects on a private tutorial basis, and many private-venture schools, offering courses that would prepare the individual for the world of business and trade, were in operation.

There was a great demand for persons who were competent in navigation, accounting, and the modern foreign languages. Cubberley gives an example of the type of institution that was attempting to meet the demand:

Over against the Post Office in Second-Street, Philadelphia, is taught Writing, Arithmetick in whole numbers and fractions, Vulgar and Decimal, Merchants accounts, Algebra, Geometry, Surveying, Gauging, Trigonometry, Plain and Spherical, Navigation in all kinds of Sailing, Astronomy, and all other parts of the Mathematicks by Theophilus Grew. His Hours are this Winter from 9 to 12 in the morning; from 2 to 5 in the afternoon; and (for the conveniency of those who cannot come in the Day time) from 6 to 9 in the Evening. He teaches Writing and Arithmetick at the usual Rate of 10s. per Quarter. Merchants Accounts, Navigation &c., for 30s. per Quarter. And will undertake to furnish anyone with sufficient knowledge in any of the foregoing Branches, in three Months time, provided the person have a tolerable Genius and observes a constant application.[10]

Most of these private-venture schools—sometimes called "grammar schools," "English schools, or "English grammar schools"—were in New England and the cities in the Middle Colonies. They were free to offer what their students needed and desired without the restrictions of any group structuring their curriculum. They concentrated on equipping their students for the world of trade and business, though some made preparation for higher education part of their offerings.[11] The growing demand for practi-

[10]Quoted in Cubberley, *op. cit.*, pp. 87–99.
[11]William M. Alexander and J. Galen Saylor, *Modern Secondary Education* (New York: Holt, Rinehart & Winston, Inc., 1959), pp. 128–129.

cal knowledge and the rise of private-venture schools, which attempted to answer that demand, laid the foundations for a new type of secondary school—the academy.

Benjamin Franklin's academy

The academy, which was to dominate American secondary education during the latter part of the eighteenth century and throughout most of the nineteenth, was conceived by Benjamin Franklin, the first prominent American to see the value of a secondary education provided in a special school that was primarily concerned with the practical. Actually, it would be more correct to say that he conceived its adaptation to American society in his day, for Milton had proposed the establishment of such an "academy" in England in 1644. It is also worth mentioning that during and after the Renaissance the term *academy* was used to denote associations of learned men, formed for study and for the advancement of knowledge.

Although historians disagree as to the sources of Franklin's ideas about this new type of school, they probably grew out of the private-venture schools. In his *Proposals Relating to the Education of Youth in Philadelphia* (1749), Franklin set forth the theory that there should be a school which would teach—in addition to the classical languages—French, German, Spanish, rhetoric, literature, English grammar, history, science, and other such subjects of a useful nature. Franklin had tried as early as 1743 to establish a school that would carry out these ideas, but he had been unsuccessful in gaining support.

In 1751, however, Franklin's ideas resulted in the opening of an academy in Philadelphia. This school had three departments: the English, the mathematical-scientific, and the classical. Later, in 1754, a philosophical department was added. In 1755 the academy was rechartered as the College, Academy, and Charitable School of Philadelphia. Later the school developed into the University of Pennsylvania. The reader can best understand what Franklin had in mind for his school by considering his own words:

As to their Studies, it would be well if they could be taught *every thing* that is useful, and *every thing* that is ornamental; But Art is long, and their Time is short. It is therefore propos'd that they learn those Things that are likely to be *most useful* and *most ornamental*. Regard being had to the several Professions for which they are intended.[12]

[12]Quoted in Edgar W. Knight and Clifton Hall, *Readings in American Educational History* (New York: Appleton-Century-Crofts, 1951), pp. 76–77.

Franklin had wanted the school to concentrate on the modern and the useful, but this was not to be the case. From the start, the academy glorified the classical and the traditional. After the school was rechartered in 1755, the classical side was emphasized even more. Franklin tried to eliminate this emphasis, but he was unable to do so; the hold of the conservatives was too great.

Nevertheless, Franklin's idea caught on. Academies were established in some of the colonies before the Revolution and in all the colonies after the Revolution. In Massachusetts the Dummer Academy was established in 1782 and the Phillips Academy at Andover in 1780. By the year 1800 there were seventeen academies in Massachusetts. By 1787 New York State also had academies.

In most cases these institutions were controlled by a board of trustees. Many of the academies were church schools, with trustees appointed by the sponsoring church. These boards set up their own rules and regulations governing the policies of the school, the teachers, and the subjects offered. Since most boards were responsible to no central authority, it was only natural that the institutions varied widely. Many were boarding schools; others were day schools. Despite the fact that there were many differences among them, the majority had two primary objectives: to prepare their students for the various social and vocational roles they were to play later in life and to prepare for higher education those who desired it.

Although the majority of these schools were controlled by boards of trustees who were not responsible to any central authority, this was not always true. Most of the academies in New York were under the supervision of, and considered part of, the University of the State of New York (the Board of Regents of the State of New York is not an institution of higher learning, but rather a strong state board of education).

Curriculum of the academies

Many of the academies offered subjects that today are considered material for the elementary school, but much of their curriculum can certainly be called secondary education. Some of the better academies offered instruction that then, even as now, could quite properly be labeled college subjects. In fact, some of the graduates of these schools were given advanced placement in the colleges of that day.

Paul Monroe gives a good description of the wide range of subjects available in academies as he discusses the offerings in the

academies in the state of New York during the first half of the
nineteenth century:

> Arithmetic, algebra, architecture, astronomy, botany, bookkeeping,
> Biblical antiquities, biography, chemistry, composition, conic sec-
> tions, constitution of the United States, constitution of New York,
> elements of criticism, declamation, drawing, dialing, English grammar,
> evidences of Christianity, embroidery, civil engineering, extempora-
> neous speaking, French, geography, physical geography, geology,
> plane geometry, analytic geometry, Greek, Grecian antiquities, Ger-
> man, general history, history of the United States, history of New York,
> Hebrew, Italian, Latin, law (constitutional, select revised statutes,
> criminal, mercantile, Blackstone's Commentaries), logic, leveling,
> logarithms, vocal music, instrumental music, mapping, mensuration,
> mineralogy, mythology, natural history, navigation, nautical astron-
> omy, natural theology, orthography, natural philosophy, moral phi-
> losophy, intellectual philosophy, penmanship, political economy,
> painting, perspective, physiology, English pronunciation, reading,
> rhetoric, Roman antiquities, stenography, statistics, surveying, Span-
> ish, trigonometry, topography, technology, principles of teaching.[13]

Because there were few restrictions from higher authorities and
because there were no traditions or antecedents to hinder innovation and originality, the curriculum was very diverse and included a
great variety of subjects.

Drill and memorization were favorite methods of instruction in
most academies. In most classes only one textbook was used.
There were many long lectures and much memorization of notes
taken on the lectures. The accepted theory of learning in that day
was mental discipline, and these methods were thought best to
ensure success in learning. Such approaches were also in keeping
with the popular notion that if learning was difficult, that proved it
was "good for you." In most cases libraries and laboratories were
lacking. School facilities and equipment were not yet extensive.

Admission of girls to the academy

The first academies were designed for boys only. As time went
by, however, special "female academies" made their appearance.
Later some of the regular academies developed "female departments." Much of the education provided for girls was the same as
that offered to the young gentlemen of the day, but many courses

---

[13]Paul Monroe, *Principles of Secondary Education* (New York: The Macmillan Company, 1912), p. 58. Used by permission.

were designed to train young ladies for their proper roles as host-
esses and mothers. This may not sound too enticing to the young
ladies of today, but it is perhaps more acceptable than the offerings
of certain other female academies of days past. Consider the curriculum of one such academy in Virginia:

> Petit Points in Flowers, Fruit, Landscapes and Sculpture, Nun's
> work, Embroidery in Silk, Gold, Silver, Pearls, or embossed, shading
> of all kinds, in the Various Works in Vogue, Dresden Point work, Lace
> Ditto, Catgut in different Modes, flourishing Muslin, after the Newest
> Taste, and most elegant Pattern Waxwork in figure, fruit, or flowers,
> Shell Ditto, or grotesque, Painting in Water Colours, and Mezzotinto;
> also the Art of taking Foliage, with several Embellishments necessary
> for the Amusement of Persons of Fortune who have Taste.[14]

In some academies the girls were taught in the same classes
with the boys; in others the girls received instruction from the
same teachers but not in the same classes. Thus in the academies is
found the beginning of coeducation in secondary schools.

Teachers in the academies

During the era of the academies there were no such requirements for entering the teaching profession as exist today. It was
not necessary to have a college degree, and there were, of course,
no state teachers' certificates. Local school officials set their own
standards—if they had any—and employed whom they desired.
Many teachers had received only an elementary education. Others,
however, had attended an academy and thus received the benefit
of at least a secondary education.[15] In many academies the headmasters were clergymen; however, the teachers in general, save in
the denominational schools, were not overly concerned with
religion.

New York gave state aid to some of its academies with the
understanding that in addition to their other work they prepare
prospective teachers. According to the educational historians, a
high percentage of the teachers of that day were educated in the
academies. Some academies eventually became normal schools
—the forerunners of the teachers' colleges. Even after some states
had established normal schools, the academy continued to produce
many teachers. Meyer points out that "because of the advanced

[14]Paul Monroe, *Cyclopedia of Education,* II (New York: The Macmillan Company, 1912),
p. 120.
[15]French, *op. cit.,* pp. 75–76.

nature of some of its subjects, [the academy] was able to present the lower schools with some of their best-educated masters."[16]

Contributions of the academies

The academy made significant contributions to the advancement of education in this country. It was a popular institution because it provided a more practical education than had its predecessor, the Latin school. It was not, however, this alone that made the academy so popular. There was an atmosphere of democracy about the academy. It appealed to the people in general—especially to the middle classes who were engaged in agriculture, commerce, manufacturing, and trades—and thus made secondary education more popular.

A second contribution was the large-scale admission of girls to secondary education in a formal setting. While it is true that some of the academies did not admit girls, the majority of them eventually did. The academy made a third contribution in that it offered secondary education entirely free from sectarian control. A fourth contribution of the academy was the enrichment and extension of subjects offered in secondary education.

A fifth major contribution was that the academy prepared the general public for universal secondary education, which was to become a reality later in the establishment of the high school. It bridged the transition from the Latin grammar school on the one hand to the public high school on the other. Perhaps the fact that it prepared so many of the teachers of the day, thus giving the elementary schools especially a supply of instructors with a reasonable background in education for the times, should be mentioned as still another contribution.

For about seventy-five years the academy was the dominant form of secondary education in the United States. For a considerable amount of that time it was the only form of secondary education in some sections of this country. Its influence remains, and some of the academies are still in existence and are healthy institutions.

Decline of the academy

The academy failed to keep pace with the times. Among the chief reasons for its decline was the growing feeling on the part of the general public that secondary education should be free just as elementary education was. The academies were not completely

---

[16]Meyer, *op. cit.*, p. 130.

democratic—they charged tuition and were often controlled by private boards. Also, college preparatory work was taking precedence over the "practical" subjects. As more and more high schools were established to meet the demands of a changing society, the academies became less and less popular.

Establishment of the American high school

The first high school was established in Boston in 1821. It was originally called the English Classical School of Boston; in 1824 this was changed to English High School of Boston. The term *high school* seems to have come from Scotland. There was near Edinburgh a famous secondary school called a high school, and accounts of this school had been published in America in the 1820's. John Griscom, a New York native who had traveled in Scotland, later established two high schools in New York.

The antecedents of the Boston English High School, however, go back much further than 1821. The citizens were interested in the idea of a secondary school that would offer subjects of interest to the young people from the lower and middle classes and prepare them for life. They were already familiar with a system of free public elementary schools. Furthermore, some of these elementary schools had a higher department called a "grammar school." The need for a new school was perhaps more pressing in Boston than in many other cities because it did not have an academy. A school board committee studied the situation and reported that the elementary schools were doing little or nothing for the bright boys who were approaching or had reached fifteen years of age, and that in many cases these schools were encouraging bad habits such as idleness rather than preparing adolescents for some vocation and for life. Thus in 1821 a new type of institution was opened in Boston.

This early high school seems to have been similar to an academy, but it charged no tuition and was controlled by a public school board. The following is the course of study offered in this first high school:

Studies for the First Class:
  Composition; reading from the most approved authors; exercises in criticism, comprising critical analyses of the language, grammar, and style of the best English authors, their errors and beauties; declamation; Geography; Arithmetic continued.
Studies for the Second Class:
  Composition, Reading, Exercises in Criticism, Declamation; Alge-

bra; ancient and modern History and Chronology; Logic; Geometry, plane Trigonometry, and its application to mensuration of heights and distances; Navigation; Surveying; Mensuration of surfaces and solids; Forensic Discussions.
Studies for the Third Class:
Composition; Exercises in Criticisms; Declamation; Mathematics; Logic; History, particularly that of the United States; Natural philosophy, including Astronomy; Moral and Political Philosophy.[17]

This first high school was so successful that in 1827 Massachusetts passed a law requiring every town of more than five hundred families to establish a high school. Many towns obeyed the law, but in the rural areas it was more often ignored than heeded. As this type of education became more valuable and public appreciation of this new institution spread, more and more high schools were created. By 1860 there were many high schools not only in Massachusetts and the other New England states but also in New York, Pennsylvania, Ohio, Illinois, Indiana, Iowa, and California.

There were, however, those who opposed the establishment of high schools at public expense, and in several states, the opposition carried its cause to the courts. The most important court case seems to be the Kalamazoo Case. In 1872 the City of Kalamazoo, Michigan, voted to set up a high school to be supported by taxation. This action was challenged by a local citizen, who took the issue to court. In 1874, the State Supreme Court ruled in favor of the City of Kalamazoo. The Court took the position that according to the Constitution education was a responsibility of the people of the state and this responsibility was not limited to elementary schools. Thus the people could make public secondary schools an integral part of their school system if they desired and could use public monies to support such schools.

Conceived as an extension of the public elementary school, the high school created the remaining necessary step on the American educational ladder. (The state universities were already a reality.) The high school is America's contribution to education. It was and is in keeping with American ideas of equality and democracy. The high school today still serves its original function, though it has also assumed the role of college preparation.

The first high schools were for boys only. In 1826 a high school for girls was established in Boston. This school had room for only 130 girls and was at once overcrowded. The number of girls seek-

---

[17]Cubberley, *op. cit.*, pp. 230–231. (Cubberley is quoting from Minutes of the Boston School Committee, 1821.)

ing admission was so large that after two years the town fathers decided things were getting out of hand, and they abolished the school. They immediately proceeded, however, to make more elementary education available to girls. Later, high schools for girls were established in Massachusetts and in other states. Most of the cities and smaller towns found that they could not afford to have special schools for girls; thus the high school began to develop as a coeducational institution.

Growth of the high school

It is difficult to present complete statistics on the growth of the high schools. During its early history no attempts were made to collect such data. By 1860 there were over 300 recognized high schools, and by the school year of 1889–1890 there were over 2500. By the end of 1905, more than 7200 public high schools had been established. Some of these offered only two- or three-year courses. More than 24,000 public secondary schools were in existence in the United States in 1965.

The phenomenal growth of the high school is evidenced not only by the number of new institutions established but also by the great increases in enrollment. In 1880 only about 110,277 students were enrolled in high schools. This was only 2.7 per cent of the youth population from fourteen to seventeen years of age. In 1900 there were about 520,000 of the same age group enrolled, and the percentage had increased to almost 9. By 1930 the enrollment was over 4 million. In 1940 more than 7 million students were enrolled in secondary education, but not all of them were in the above age classification. In the school year of 1954–1955 the enrollment was 6,290,000, a little less than the enrollment figure for 1940. This drop was due to three factors: (1) the low birth rate of the 1930's, (2) the greater number of jobs available to teen-agers in the early 1950's, and (3) the increasing number of marriages which took teen-agers out of school. The proportion of adolescents in school in the 1950's, however, was greater than it had been in 1940. The tendency for a higher percentage of young people of high school age to remain in school continues. In the school year 1962–1963 there were 13,633,082 students enrolled in grades nine through twelve in public schools and over 1 million in the same grades in private schools. During the 1964–1965 school year this figure had reached 15 million—over 90 per cent of the age group from fourteen to seventeen.

Close examination of enrollment figures for secondary schools between 1880 and 1920 reveals, as has been mentioned, that only a small percentage of the persons of high school age were enrolled. Why did so few individuals of high school age enroll in high school? There were many reasons; the important ones are listed below. Probably only a few of these reasons were operating to keep students out of school in any one community. In some communities, however, all or most of them were important influences.

1. Many communities could not support a high school.

2. High school attendance was not a tradition in many areas.

3. Many families could not afford to pay for books, school supplies, and lunches.

4. Because it was theoretical and academic, secondary education did not appeal to all boys and girls.

5. In certain areas high schools were pathetically poor and offered a very limited program.

6. Attendance laws did not, in most cases, make attendance compulsory beyond age fourteen or the completion of the eighth grade. Some states had no compulsory attendance laws before World War I. In other states such laws were not enforced.

7. Child-labor laws were ineffective or nonexistent; with all types of labor being sought by industry, many children were rushed into employment at an early age.

8. Preparatory departments were maintained by many of the state universities and denominational colleges. These retarded the establishment of high schools and thus helped deny educational opportunities to many who desired a secondary education for purposes other than preparation for college.

9. Because there were few good roads and no motor buses, it was not practical to think of providing secondary education for all adolescent youth in many rural areas.

10. The secondary school was a selective institution; students were frequently required to pass an examination before they were admitted.[18]

Curriculum of the early high school

The curriculum of the English Classical School of Boston has already been given; however, this does not indicate very much about the high school curriculum as it later developed. An examination of some of the offerings in high schools from 1860 to 1890 reveals that there was little uniformity among the various schools. This was true not only on a national basis but also within individual states. One reason for the establishment of the first high schools

[18]French, *op. cit.*, pp. 101–104.

was to provide courses that were not college preparatory. As the years went by, however, the preparation of students for college began to assume increasing importance in most high schools. By 1900 the college-preparatory subjects were the major offerings in many small high schools. The larger high schools did offer more work in other courses; but, during the 1890's—for reasons that shall be considered later—most of the attention of high-school personnel was turned toward the business of getting students ready for college.

Some high schools, especially in New York State, offered a four-year course to prepare students for college and a three-year course for those not going to college. During the 1880's the Board of Regents approved special programs in classical, mathematical, and scientific studies which would lead to graduation in three years but were not intended to prepare students for college. They were given on the theory that all students in secondary education needed them.

Some of the high schools divided their offerings into English departments and classical departments. In some cases they were divided into more departments. For example, high schools concerned with the preparation of teachers sometimes created a normal department.[19] Table 1 gives some idea of the wide range of subjects offered in the high schools between 1889 and 1910.

Committee of Ten

In 1892 the Committee of Ten, which was to have a great influence on secondary education, was appointed by the National Education Association to study secondary education with the idea of developing uniformity in college entrance requirements. This was the first committee appointed to study any area of education at the national level.

The committee also had to deal with the problem of college preparation. The academy in its day had developed into an institution whose major concern was college preparation. Later, as the academy declined, this role was assumed by the public high school. Yet, in many cases, the high schools were not suitable institutions for such work. This was due in most part, not to the lack of college-preparatory courses, but to differing practices as to the amount of time spent on the various subjects and the standards maintained within the various subjects. The problem of articulation between high school and college was much greater than it had been

---

[19]W. H. Well, "Public High School in Chicago," *American Journal of Education*, III (1857), 536.

table **1**   **Percentage of Pupils in Public Secondary Schools Enrolled in Certain Subjects**[20]

Subject	Per Cent Enrolled		
	1889 / 1890	1900 / 1901	1909 / 1910
Latin	34.69	50.45	49.05
Greek	3.05	2.63	0.75
French	5.84	8.29	9.90
German	10.51	15.45	23.69
Algebra	45.40	56.96	56.85
Geometry	21.33	27.83	30.87
Trigonometry	⊕	2.04	1.87
Astronomy	⊕	2.34	0.53
Physics	22.21	18.40	14.61
Chemistry	10.10	7.56	6.89
Physical Geography	⊕	22.83	19.34
Geology	⊕	3.44	1.16
Physiology	⊕	26.60	15.32
Zoology	⊕	⊕	8.02
Botany	⊕	⊕	16.83
Agriculture	⊕	⊕	4.66
Domestic economy	⊕	⊕	3.78
Psychology	⊕	2.19	0.96
Rhetoric	⊕	40.71	57.10
English Literature	⊕	45.08	57.09
History	27.31	38.91	55.03
Civics	⊕	20.97	15.55
Number of schools reporting	2,526	5,442	8,097

⊕Not included in original data; not known whether subjects were not taught or enrollments were not obtained by the Commissioner.

Original Source: U.S. Bureau of Education, Report of the Commissioner of Education for the year ending June 30, 1910 (Washington, D.C.: Government Printing Office, 1911), p. 1139.

between the better academies and the colleges. In fact, many colleges found it necessary to provide special preparation in certain areas for some of their students before they were capable of doing college work. Deficient students complicated the colleges' problems and in some cases prevented these institutions from maintaining the standards they felt to be necessary.

[20]Alexander and Saylor, *op. cit.*, p. 146.

As early as 1872 President Eliot of Harvard University had started an attack on this problem. Eliot discussed the situation in the report to his board of trustees during that year, pointing out that the high schools were just not adequately preparing students for higher education.

In 1870, two years earlier, the president of the University of Michigan had recommended that a group of examiners from the university visit high schools. These examiners were to evaluate the schools' curriculum, staff, and equipment and the general achievement of the students. A student from an approved school could be admitted to the university without taking an entrance examination if the examiners were satisfied with the quality of his work. This policy of accreditation was a great inducement to high schools to meet the qualifications of the institution of higher learning. By 1897 this method of accreditation was being used by 42 state colleges and universities and about 150 other institutions of higher learning.[21]

The policy of accreditation helped, but it did not solve the problem. Eliot and others continued to work for better articulation. The result of this labor, especially on the part of Eliot, was the appointment of the Committee of Ten in 1892 to study the situation and make recommendations. The committee was composed of Eliot, five other college and university representatives, a school principal, two headmasters of private schools, and William T. Harris, the United States Commissioner of Education. A subcommittee was also appointed, over half of whose members (forty-seven out of ninety) were connected with colleges either as teachers or administrators. Twenty-one were headmasters of private schools.

Two years later the committee presented its report, setting forth the theory that the secondary schools of the nation did not, as a whole, exist to prepare individuals for college. It then proceeded to recommend a program that it considered appropriate for the secondary schools. These recommendations were very influential in the development of a unified program of education for all pupils, with the high school serving as a connecting link between the elementary school and higher education. The committee specified that every subject taught in the high school should be taught in the same way and for the same length of time to every student so long as he pursued the course and regardless of his objectives beyond

[21]Nelson L. Bossing, *Principles of Secondary Education* (Englewood Cliffs, N.J.: Prentice-Hall, Inc., 1955), p. 49.

secondary education. It set forth no differentiation of the curriculum on any grounds.[22]

The committee suggested that languages be taught three to five years earlier than they were at that time. It urged that all subjects be taught at an earlier level, that elementary education be limited to six years, and that seventh and eighth grades be concerned with secondary education. These and other recommendations have caused some educators to credit the Committee of Ten with casting the high school into a uniform mold designed to prepare students for higher education. This generalization cannot be fully substantiated, however. It is true that most of the courses would be considered college preparatory today. The committee justified its recommendations on the need for better preparation for life and for college and on the "mental discipline" theory of learning. As something of an afterthought, it did concede that such subjects as bookkeeping and commercial arithmetic could be permitted as an optional substitution for algebra by students enrolled in a so-called "English curriculum."

For the next twenty-five years every major committee designed to study secondary education had as one of its major concerns the question: How can the secondary school better prepare students for college? Subsequent committees, which will be discussed in the following pages, included the following:

1. The Committee on College Entrance Requirements, 1899
2. The Committee on Economy of Time, 1908
3. The Committee on Articulation of the High School and College, 1911
4. A second Committee on Economy of Time, 1913

There were attempts to introduce some practical courses, and some of these attempts were successful; however, in many communities the high school from 1890 to 1930 was primarily a college-preparatory institution.

Developments in secondary education in the twentieth century

As is obvious from the list of committees presented above, the Committee of Ten did not solve all of the problems in secondary education. In fact, it did not entirely solve the problem of articulation between the high schools and the colleges. Despite the fact

[22]*Report of the Committee of Ten on Secondary School Studies,* Committee on Secondary School Studies, National Education Association (Washington, D.C.: Government Printing Office, 1894), p. 17.

that this committee carried great weight and exerted a powerful influence, some educators challenged its recommendations from the start. Consider, for example, the following early criticism which noted that the recommendations

provide no place for music, drawing, elocution, spelling, penmanship, etc. Such studies as stenography and manual training are coming into high schools and are coming to stay, and we might as well recognize the fact. Another and a very different class of subjects, such as political economy, psychology, and ethics has long been taught in secondary schools, and I am not prepared to recommend their abolition from the curriculum. Remembering that more than 90 per cent of high school pupils may not go to college, I consider such subjects far more valuable than astronomy, meteorology, or physiography.[23]

There were others who were especially displeased with the idea that the subjects prescribed by the committee were good for all students and that the freedom to choose different subjects had little value. High schools, especially large ones in cities, were aware that they must offer subjects developed along practical lines. The fact that 90 per cent of the students were not going to college prompted many people in secondary education to be concerned for a curriculum that would be related to the future objectives of this majority of students.

Committee on College Entrance Requirements
The Committee on College Entrance Requirements was appointed in 1895, only two years after the Committee of Ten made its report. This new committee suggested that the high school be organized into a six-year program; that it offer a limited number of elective courses; that it develop special accelerated programs for gifted students; and that science courses be developed into a better sequential program. It also recommended that more courses be deemed worthy of consideration as college preparatory subjects. English was used as an example of one of these subjects.

The chairman of this committee was Dr. A. F. Nightingale, superintendent of the Chicago Public Schools. He stated well the task that the public schools of the United States were facing at the beginning of the twentieth century:

[23]O. D. Robinson, "The Report from the Point of View of the Large Mixed High School," *Report of the Commissioner of Education for the Year 1892–1893*, U.S. Bureau of Education (Washington, D.C.: Government Printing Office, 1895), p. 1490.

The secondary schools are the schools of the people, and the people have demanded, and in still more effectual ways will demand, that their courses must be practical, beneficial, disciplinary. . . .

The public high school can become a link in the golden chain of our American system of education only when the colleges begin where the best high schools leave off; otherwise the gap between the common school and the college must be filled by the private schools, patronized by the children of the rich, and the sons and daughters of the great middle class must be deprived of the benefits of a higher education because, forsooth, they have failed to fulfill some specific requirement of the college they would otherwise enter. I have faith, however, that these conflicting requirements will be harmonized, their incongruities removed, so that we may in the near future have a unified system of education, from kindergarten to the graduate school of the university, which will give to every child, without let or hindrance, the right of way for such an education as will best develop the power with which, in a plastic state, he has been endowed by the Infinite Architect.[24]

This committee listed the subjects that it thought necessary for college preparation and even outlined the work to be considered in these courses:

Two units in English

Four units in foreign languages (no languages were to be accepted in less than two units)

Two units in mathematics

One unit in history

One unit in science

These subjects were to be required of all students; in other words, they were to be constants. It is worth remembering that this committee was recommending that only ten of the sixteen or more high school units be required. This left room for electives. It should be noted, however, that four units of foreign languages were required but only two of English. These recommendations provided for college preparation and for subjects of a practical nature. The high schools, in most cases, were happy with this arrangement. Most of their personnel wanted a unified system of education; not a system such as was and is in existence in Europe, where separate schools are provided for those students preparing for higher education and those going into trades and industry.

[24]"Report of the Committee on College Entrance Requirements," *NEA Journal of Proceedings and Addresses, 1899,* Committee on College Entrance Requirements, National Education Association (Washington, D.C.: NEA, 1899), p. 636.

An important element of this committee's work was its suggestion that there be a unit of measure to serve as a standard for determining the amount of secondary preparation in the various subjects that should be required for college admission. The term *units of credit* was widely used after this report was submitted. Later, in 1909, the Carnegie Foundation for the Advancement of Teaching defined a unit as constituting the work done in a high school subject for one class period a day, in a class meeting five times a week throughout a school year of thirty-six to forty weeks.

Committee on the Economy of Time in Education

Another important committee appointed early in the twentieth century was the Committee on the Economy of Time in Education. This committee was appointed in 1909 and made its main report in 1911. It, too, emphasized that elementary education was limited to six years in the other major countries of the world and should be in the United States. The committee went a step further by recommending that secondary education be extended not only downward into grades seven and eight but also upward into what had thus far been considered the first two years of college. In addition to these "progressive" proposals, it recommended the organization of junior high schools and junior colleges.

Committee on the Articulation of High School and College

The Committee on the Articulation of High School and College agreed with the idea of constants for all in the high school curriculum, but it voiced suspicion of the practice of colleges and universities exerting too much influence on what these elements should be.[25] Until this time college admission requirements had been formulated by the colleges themselves; this committee was the first group to recommend a standard program of college preparation for high schools to follow. The program it set forth was more liberal in the matter of subjects that were acceptable for entrance credit, and it reduced the entrance requirements in languages to one language. The recommended course of study was as follows:

Every high school course should include at least three units of English, one unit of social science (including history), and one unit of natural science.

Every high school course should include the completion of two majors of three units each and one minor of two units, and one of the majors should be English.

[25]Alexander and Saylor, *op cit.,* p. 157.

The requirements in mathematics should not exceed two units of mathematics and in foreign languages should not exceed two units other than English.

Of the total fifteen units, not less than eleven units should consist of English, foreign language, mathematics, social science (including history), natural science, or other work conducted by recitation and home study. The other four units should be left as a margin to be used for additional academic work, and any other kind of work that the best interests of the student appear to require.

In place of either two units of mathematics or two units of a foreign language, the substitution under proper supervision should be allowed of a second unit of social science (including history) and a second unit of natural science.

In other words, there should be allowed under proper supervision the selection of four units from the following:

(1) Two units of one foreign language

(2) Two units of mathematics

(3) Two units of a second unit of social science and a second unit of natural science.[26]

The unit requirements recommended by the committee are listed below; this plan allowed the student, "under proper supervision," to substitute the work in column B or C for the work in column A:

	A	B	C
English	3	3	3
Foreign Language	2	2	0
Mathematics	2	0	2
Social Studies	1	2	2
Natural Science	1	2	2
Total specified	9	9	9
To which must be added to make another major	1 or 2	1	1
Total	10	10	10

Commission on the Reorganization of Secondary Education

In 1918 the Commission on the Reorganization of Secondary Education issued one of the most important reports in the history

[26]"Committee of Nine on the Articulation of High School and College," *Proceedings of the National Education Association* (Washington, D.C.: NEA, 1911) pp. 559–567.

of secondary education in this country—the *Cardinal Principles of Secondary Education*. The student of American secondary education will constantly find references to this report in his preprofessional work and, later, in his professional reading.

The major areas treated in this report are the need for reorganization of the secondary school; the objectives of education in this country; the role of the school in reaching these objectives; the interrelation of the various goals of education; education as a process of growth; the need for explicit, immediate values in secondary education; the demand for high schools with varying curricula to serve the individual needs of a heterogeneous school population.[27]

This commission felt, as others had, that there was a great need for the reorganization of secondary education, growing out of the following conditions:

1. American society had changed from a predominantly simple, rural society to a more complex, industrial society.

2. The high school population had shifted from a small, select percentage of youth to a much larger percentage that was much less select in abilities, interests, and motivation.

3. Educational research had led to the development of new theories on individual differences, methods of teaching, and application of knowledge, as well as on the "laws of learning."

The commission stated the general objectives of secondary education in American society in the following terms:

The purpose of democracy is so to organize society that each member may develop his personality primarily through activities designed for the well-being of his fellow members and of society as a whole. . . .

Education in a democracy, both within and without the school, should develop in each individual the knowledge, interests, ideals, habits, and powers whereby he will find his place and use that place to shape both himself and society toward ever nobler ends.[28]

The commission set forth seven specific objectives, the achievement of which would ensure the accomplishment of the general purposes stated above. These objectives, known as the Seven Cardinal Principles, concerned (1) health, (2) command of

[27]French, *op. cit.*, p. 130.
[28]*Cardinal Principles of Secondary Education*, Department of the Interior, Bureau of Education Bulletin 1918, No. 35 (Washington, D.C.: Government Printing Office, 1937), p. 9.

fundamental processes, (3) worthy home membership, (4) vocation, (5) citizenship, (6) worthy use of leisure, and (7) ethical character. In the opinion of the commission these were the basic objectives to be achieved by the secondary schools in the United States.

From 1918 to the present many schools have attempted to implement the Seven Cardinal Principles. They have served as guides for the planning of programs in secondary education by many school systems.

Educational Policies Commission

It was not until 1935 that another commission to study secondary education was appointed. In that year the National Education Association appointed the Educational Policies Commission for the purpose of further defining and clarifying the task of public education in a democracy. In 1938 this commission set forth a statement of educational objectives. These were classified into four groups, based on the four areas with which the commission felt education should be concerned:

1. The objectives of self-realization.
2. The objectives of human relationship.
3. The objectives of economic efficiency.
4. The objectives of civic responsibility.

The Educational Policies Commission is still in existence. It consists of about twenty-five outstanding leaders in American education. Some of its more outstanding members have been Dwight D. Eisenhower, former president of Columbia University; James B. Conant, former president of Harvard; Alexander J. Stoddard, superintendent of schools in Philadelphia and in Los Angeles; and William Jansen, superintendent of schools in New York.

The commission has been responsible for many important reports and statements on education in this country. Some of the more important ones are listed below:

The Unique Function of Education in American Democracy (1937)

The Purposes of Education in American Democracy (1938)

Learning the Ways of Democracy (1940)

The Education of Free Men in American Democracy (1941)

Education for All American Youth (1944; revised in 1952)

Education for the Gifted (1950)

Education for All American Youth: A Further Look (1952)

Public Education and the Future of America (1955)

Manpower and Education (1956)

Higher Education in a Decade of Decision (1957)
The Contemporary Challenge to American Education (1958)

The most important of the above publications from the standpoint of the secondary school teacher were the studies entitled *Education for All American Youth* and *Education for All American Youth: A Further Look. Education for All American Youth* is the story of the school systems in two fictitious communities, Farmville and American City, U.S.A. These two communities were supposed to be typical of American communities in general, and the plans presented for these two school systems were to serve as models for systems throughout the country in their planning for better education.

The commission listed what it considered to be the ten imperative needs of youth which should be filled by secondary education:

1. All youth need to develop salable skills and those understandings and attitudes that make the worker an intelligent and productive participant in economic life. To this end, most youth need supervised work experience as well as education in the skills and knowledge of their occupations.

2. All youth need to develop and maintain good health and physical fitness and good mental health.

3. All youth need to understand the rights and duties of the citizens of a democratic society and to be diligent and competent in the performance of their obligations as members of the community and citizens of the state and nation and people of the world.

4. All youth need to understand the significance of the family for the individual and society and the conditions conducive to successful family life.

5. All youth need to know how to purchase and use goods and services intelligently, understanding both the value received and the economic consequences of their acts.

6. All youth need to understand the methods of science, the influence of science on human life, and the main scientific facts concerning the nature of the world and of man.

7. All youth need opportunities to develop their capacities to appreciate beauty in literature, art, music, and nature.

8. All youth need to be able to use their leisure time well and to budget it wisely, balancing activities that yield satisfaction to the individual with those that are socially useful.

9. All youth need to develop respect for other persons, to grow in this insight into ethical values and principles, and to grow in the moral and spiritual values of life.

10. All youth need to grow in their ability to think rationally, to express their thoughts clearly, and to read and listen with understanding.[29]

National Survey of Secondary Education
In 1929 the North Central Association of Colleges and Secondary Schools conceived the idea of a national survey of secondary education. The United States Office of Education agreed to direct the survey, which was concerned with the following areas of secondary education: organization, legal provisions, administration and supervision, selection and appointment of teachers, population, reorganization, provisions for individual differences, guidance, research, libraries, and the various subject-matter fields.

The survey attempted to determine where this country stood in secondary education by an examination of those schools which appeared to be outstanding in their practices and provisions. Five hundred fifty schools in forty-one states and the District of Columbia were selected for the study. A careful examination of their practices was made, including visitation of the schools. The results of the study were then tabulated and digested. Some of the major findings of this national survey were as follows:

1. Small high schools, with good administrative leadership, could make improvements.

2. States should encourage schools to develop more flexible programs and to attempt more experiments in curriculum.

3. Progress was being made in the area of better student articulation between high school and college.

4. There was much confusion among school people regarding the terminology related to the various methods being used. This was especially true of the term *unit assignment*.

5. The study and revision of curriculums was making a worthwhile contribution to the professional growth of teachers.

6. The junior high school curriculum manifested a definite trend toward "general" courses.

7. Experiments with special classes for slow and gifted students, classes employing the unit method, and homogeneous grouping were promising approaches toward providing for individual differences.

8. Secondary schools with good library facilities were doing a better job than schools without such facilities. It was predicted that

---

[29]*Education for All American Youth*, Educational Policies Commission, National Education Association (Washington, D.C.: NEA, 1944), p. 216.

the library would soon become a major feature in junior and senior high schools.[30]

Eight-Year Study of the Progressive Education Association

In 1930 the Progressive Education Association created the Commission on the Relation of School and College. This commission asked representatives of selected colleges to work with it in an experimental study that would extend over an eight-year period. The colleges were asked to receive the graduates of a small group of high schools located throughout the country which would be engaged in experimental work, whether the students had taken the usual college-preparatory subjects or not. Over 250 colleges and universities agreed to work with the commission and the selected high schools. The principals of the thirty high schools selected to engage in the study were required to furnish statements to the colleges on the students' school activities, life outside of school, and interests, as well as their scores on scholastic, aptitude, and other diagnostic tests.

Over 10,000 graduates of the selected schools had been admitted to the cooperating colleges by 1941. A careful study was made of the records of over 2000 of these experimental graduates. The records of 1475 were then matched with graduates of traditional high schools. The students were compared, student by student, with other students who were of the same age, sex, home background, scholastic aptitude, and interests, insofar as was possible. Below are some of the more important results of the comparison:

1. Graduates of the thirty selected schools were more concerned with current world happenings than graduates of the conventional high school programs.

2. Graduates of the experimental schools showed a higher degree of intellectual curiosity and drive.

3. Graduates of the experimental schools made better grades than did the graduates of traditional schools.

4. Graduates of the experimental schools did not perform quite so well as the graduates of the traditional schools in the area of foreign language.

5. Graduates of the experimental schools did not differ from the graduates of the traditional schools in the number of times they were placed on probation.

6. Graduates of the experimental schools majored in the same academic areas as did the graduates of the conventional programs.

[30]J. Minor Gwynn, *Curriculum Principles and Social Trends,* 3rd ed. (New York: The Macmillan Company, 1960), pp. 342–343.

7. Graduates of the experimental schools received more honors each year.

8. Graduates of the experimental schools were judged by their teachers to be superior in objective thinking.

9. Graduates of the experimental schools participated in more student activities.

10. Graduates of the experimental schools used their time better.

11. Graduates of the experimental schools read more widely than did the graduates of the conventional school programs.

12. Graduates of the experimental schools showed greater ability in making decisions concerning the choice of a vocation.[31]

In short, the Eight-Year Study indicated that students could do well in college even though they had not followed the traditional plan of college preparation. It also pointed out that there was great value in the high school personnel's knowing their students well and giving them intelligent counseling based on information received as a result of a great many tests and complete records.

This study has encouraged experimentation in the high school curriculum, and it has also acted as a stimulus for the in-service training of teachers.

Cooperative Study of Secondary School Standards

In 1933 the Commission on Secondary Schools of the North Central Association of Colleges and Secondary Schools appointed a committee to study the ways in which accrediting standards were being administered. Representatives from the five other accrediting associations were invited to participate in the study. The others accepted the invitation and in the same year a national committee was organized under the direction of the United States Commissioner of Education, George F. Zook. The General Education Board agreed to provide financial assistance, and a central office was established in Washington, D.C. The national committee was concerned with answering four key questions:

1. What are the characteristics of a good school?

2. What practicable means may be employed to evaluate the effectiveness of a school in terms of its objectives?

3. How does a good school develop into a better one?.

4. How can regional associations help secondary schools continue to improve?[32]

[31]W. M. Aiken, *The Story of the Eight-Year Study with Conclusions and Recommendations,* Vol. II (New York: Harper & Row, Publishers, Inc., 1942).

[32]*How to Evaluate a Secondary School,* The Cooperative Study of Secondary School Standards (Washington, D.C., 1938), pp. 27–31.

For a period of five years the national committee studied the process of accreditation and evaluation of secondary schools. The results of its labors was a series of proposals and methods that were then used on an experimental basis in two hundred school systems. After these original tryouts, the criteria and the techniques were revised and published as the *Evaluative Criteria.* Along with this document a manual, *How to Evaluate a Secondary School,* was produced.

Now, how does a school use these publications? The local school contacts its regional accrediting association, making known its desire to be accredited. Then, using the *Evaluative Criteria,* the school administrators and their staff make a careful study of their school. Special areas of concern are the school's educational philosophy, the community served by the school, the curriculum, the student activities, the school library, the guidance program and personnel, the methods of instruction used, the pupil population, the teaching personnel, the administrative staff, and the physical plant. When this study is completed, the results are sent to the regional accrediting association.

Then the school invites a committee of educators to visit and study the school on behalf of the regional association. This committee compares its judgments with the study made by the local personnel. The results are charted on bar graphs which show whether the school has been judged superior, good, average, poor, or inferior on specific points. An evaluation report is sent to the school seeking accreditation, pointing out its favorable and unfavorable characteristics. Emphasis is placed on suggested improvements. If the visiting committee feels that the school measures up to acceptable standards, it is accredited.

Such an evaluation concerns not only local administrative and instructional personnel but also parents, students, and other individuals in the community. Most individuals who have participated in such an evaluation have found it to be a very educative and stimulating experience. The *Evaluative Criteria* has made a very important and significant contribution to secondary education in this country.

Development of the junior high school
A discussion of the development of secondary education in the twentieth century is incomplete without mention of the junior high school. Although this form of school organization will be treated more fully in a later chapter, its development and some of the reasons for its existence will be considered here.

Most authorities give credit to Berkeley, California, and Columbus, Ohio, for the establishment of the first junior high schools. Both Saginaw, Michigan, and Richmond, Indiana, have also claimed to be first in the field, however, and the City of Los Angeles had a junior high school at an early date. These schools were at first referred to as *intermediate schools,* but later the term *junior high school* was used.

For years such educators as President Charles W. Eliot of Harvard, President William Rainey Harper of the University of Chicago, and John Dewey had concerned themselves with the idea of reorganizing the American school system to shorten the period of elementary education to six years and extend the period of secondary education to six years. (This was, of course, the form of school organization advocated by the Committee on the Economy of Time.) It was felt that a great deal of repetition existed in the eight-year elementary school and that six years would be sufficient time for students to acquire the fundamental skills necessary for advancement in the various fields of knowledge. Students would then be taught more advanced material and a greater variety of subject matter in the six-year secondary school.

The form of organization that evolved, however, was not a six-year high school. Instead it was the junior high school and, in most cases, the three-year senior high school. This form of organization is commonly referred to as the "six-three-three plan."

Among the more important reasons behind the movement for reorganization was the feeling that the eight-four plan did not provide appropriate schooling for students in the seventh and eighth grades, many of whom were already in early adolescence. The four-year secondary school had not been planned; it had merely developed out of tradition. It had little, if any, relationship to the students' patterns of mental, physical, or emotional development. Many educators felt that a much better job could be done for students of early adolescent age if they were removed from the elementary school and given a school of their own. This would provide a better psychological environment for these young adolescents. Advancement to the new school would give them a feeling of accomplishment, and they would feel that the adults in their world—teachers, parents, and administrators—were aware that they were no longer little children. A more suitable curriculum could be planned for them, and better facilities for such courses as science, home economics, and industrial arts could be provided, as well as a better program and more adequate facilities for physical education. The students could have the opportunity to develop, under intelligent school supervision, a more meaningful program of activities.

Widespread research had indicated that the prolonged period of elementary education was to a great extent responsible for the large number of students who failed to enter high school, the drop-out rate being highest at the end of the seventh and eighth grades. It was felt that the junior high school would help solve this problem by providing a gradual transition from elementary to secondary education.

Educators were also concerned with the fact that graduates of American secondary schools were inferior in attainments to their European counterparts. They did not wish to shape our secondary schools along European lines, but rather to concentrate on areas that could rightly be considered secondary material and thus provide a more challenging education for high school students in this country.

At first the spread of the junior high school was slow, but after 1922 the movement grew rapidly. It should be noted, however, that there were forms of organization other than the six-three-three plan. For example, many systems were organized on a six-two-four plan, and others on an eight-two-four plan.

After World War II, many school systems found that reorganization could help solve their building shortage. In systems where the elementary schools and the traditional high school were overcrowded, the administration and the local school board realized that they could temporarily provide space for all students at a reduced cost by constructing one new building to house the seventh and eighth grades from the elementary school and the ninth grade from the high school. The solution of a system's building problem is not, however, an adequate reason for reorganization. The junior high school demands teachers who are specially prepared to work at this level, and it demands a program designed for young adolescents.

Development of the junior college

There has long been considerable controversy over whether education offered in the junior or community college should be considered secondary education or higher education. If one looks at the laws authorizing the establishment of such schools and considers the traditional practices in American education, it seems that the junior college is looked upon as a form of higher education. Yet in many school systems it is considered a part of secondary education. In such districts grades thirteen and fourteen are established as a separate school—often referred to as the community college—and offer a program in technical education as well as the academic subjects offered in the first two years of a four-year college. A few communities have organized their secondary schools on a four-four basis. This provides for a high school composed of grades seven through ten and a community college made up of grades eleven through fourteen. The question of whether courses in junior or community colleges should be classified as secondary education or higher education can apparently be settled only by looking at each particular institution and its curriculum. In most cases in this country the junior college will probably remain a separate institution offering courses considered a part of higher education.

Today, there are over five hundred junior colleges in the United States, enrolling over 15 per cent of the students who are pursuing a higher education. Although approximately half of these schools are private institutions, they account for less than one fourth of the junior college enrollment. From 1951 to 1959 enrollments in junior colleges under public control increased by 128.3 per cent, while the junior colleges under private control showed an increase of only 24.7 per cent.[33]

The basic purposes of the junior or community colleges are to prepare students for more advanced study, to provide an extension of general education, to render a community service to students who do not wish to or cannot leave the community for educational opportunities, and to provide adult education.

Conant report on the high school

In 1959 Dr. James B. Conant published his report on the high school, which has been carefully studied by millions of Americans. This report was the result of a widespread study made by Conant and his staff using a grant from the Carnegie Corporation of New York to the Educational Testing Service of Princeton, New Jersey.

Many educators have objected to the report's title, *The American High School Today,* pointing out that Conant visited only fifty-five schools in eighteen states and was concerned mainly with grades nine through twelve. These critics further charge that Conant showed too little concern for city and suburban schools, that

---

[33]By "public" is meant those institutions under city, county, state or federal governments. "Private" institutions are those under nonpublic auspices such as private corporations or church groups.

he overemphasized large schools in his recommendations, and that he was concerned only with comprehensive schools.

In all fairness it should be stated that Dr. Conant did not intend his study to be considered all-inclusive, and that his recommendations were set forth as suggestions for improvement — not as ironclad rules. The reader is urged to study his twenty-one recommendations carefully. Some of the more important recommendations were concerned with the following:

The counseling system
Individualized programs
Required programs for all
Ability grouping
English composition
Diversified programs for the development of marketable skills
Special consideration for the very slow readers
Programs for the academically talented
Highly gifted pupils
The academic inventory
Summer school
Foreign languages
Science courses
Twelfth-grade social studies

Actually there are three important recommendations made in Dr. Conant's report that are not found among the twenty-one he listed. These recommendations are more general and are implied at many points in the report:

1. Do not establish specialized high schools for academic students, but rather maintain and improve the American comprehensive high school.

2. Do away with as many small high schools as possible through the process of consolidation.

3. Continue and improve the policy of local control of education.

Conant report on junior high schools

In the fall of 1960 Dr. Conant issued a second report, *Recommendations for Education in the Junior High School Years*. The report was based on a study similar to that made in the senior high schools. The recommendations were along the same lines as those for the high school; indeed, some of them were almost identical. Essentially, these recommendations were designed to promote the education of the gifted. Many of the recommendations, just as in the case of the high schools, are already standard practices in many of the better junior high schools. Most junior high schools, however, are not large enough to carry out some of the recommendations.

Other developments

Several other major developments will be mentioned only briefly here, since they will be elaborated on in later chapters. In 1954 the Supreme Court of the United States decided that segregation of races in public schools was unconstitutional. This decision resulted in much controversy in many areas that provided separate schools and facilities for the education of Negro and white students. This controversy is still alive, despite the fact that most states and hundreds of school districts have made progress toward desegregation.

The White House Conferences on education during the 1950's and 1960's served to bring to the attention of the nation many of the accomplishments and needs in the area of secondary education.

The National Defense Education Act, passed in 1958, has been and still is an important influence on the secondary school curriculum and the education of teachers, especially in the areas of mathematics, science, and foreign languages. Just what influence the launching of Sputniks I and II played in bringing about the Act is a question that can be debated but not ignored.

In the late fifties and early sixties enrollments in public secondary schools began to increase greatly. There have been many attempts on the part of educators to adjust to these increases. Two important attempts, which will be discussed at length in a later chapter, are team teaching and programed learning. These two approaches to teaching and learning have offered some promising possibilities, and they have also created quite a bit of controversy as to their value and place in secondary education.

Recent years have seen a marked increase in the number of cities requiring high school teachers to have five years of college and university preparation. Several states are now making this a statewide requirement for secondary school certification.

There has been a great increase in the emphasis given to instruction in economics in secondary schools. Greater attention is also being given to theories and philosophies of government. Many secondary schools have introduced the study of Russian, while others have added third- and fourth-year courses in other foreign languages. World geography, history of non-Western nations, and courses in world cultures have been and are still being introduced into the high school curriculum. There has been much more attention given to the academically talented student, as well as a greater emphasis on general education. This emphasis, however, is now being accompanied by increased concern for the culturally deprived student, who is usually a product of a depressed neighborhood and a home that provides little or no motivation toward success in school.

In 1964 Congress passed the antipoverty bill, which is affecting education in many ways. This bill sets up a job corps that eventually is to enroll 100,000 young people in remedial education and job training programs. It also established work training designed to discourage teen-agers from dropping out of school.

The late 1950's and early 1960's saw a definite acceleration of the trend to replace the eight-four plan of vertical school organization with the six-three-three plan in larger cities and the six-six plan in smaller communities.

In 1959 the National Education Association established the Project on the Instructional Program of the Public Schools, since known as the Project on Instruction. This Project was given the task of making careful and creative recommendations which would serve as guidelines to the teaching profession and the public in their cooperative efforts to evaluate and improve American education. A national committee and a headquarters staff were selected to carry on the work of the Project. The recommendations of this committee were published in a series of four reports in 1963: *Schools for the Sixties, Deciding What to Teach, Planning and Organizing for Teaching,* and *Education in a Changing Society.*[34]

The Project identified twelve crucial issues facing education in the 1960's, and it set forth thirty-three specific recommendations. At this point it is impossible to state what the impact of these reports will be on American secondary education, but they are receiving careful consideration by many educators and responsible citizens interested in the schools.

Selected references

ALEXANDER, WILLIAM M. AND J. GALEN SAYLOR. *Modern Secondary Education.* New York: Holt, Rinehart & Winston, Inc., 1959.

---

[34]The reader is urged to look at all of these reports, but he should by no means fail to read *Schools for the Sixties.*

BUTTS, R. FREEMAN AND LAWRENCE A. CREMIN. *A History of Education in American Culture.* New York: Holt, Rinehart & Winston, Inc., 1953.

DOUGLASS, HARL R. *Secondary Education in the United States,* 2nd ed. New York: The Ronald Press Company, 1964.

FRENCH, WILLIAM MARSHALL. *American Secondary Education.* New York: The Odyssey Press, Inc., 1957.

MCKEAN, ROBERT C. *Principles and Methods in Secondary Education.* Columbus, Ohio: Charles E. Merrill, Inc., 1962.

MEYER, ADOLPHE E. *An Educational History of the American People.* New York: McGraw-Hill Book Company, Inc., 1957.

REPORT OF THE COMMITTEE OF TEN ON SECONDARY SCHOOL STUDIES. Committee on Secondary School Studies (Committee of Ten), National Education Association. Washington, D.C.: Government Printing Office, 1894.

Schools for the Sixties. Project on Instruction, National Education Association. New York: McGraw-Hill Book Company, Inc., 1963.

TAYLOR, L. O., DON R. MCMAHILL, AND BOB L. TAYLOR. *The American Secondary School.* New York: Appleton-Century-Crofts, 1960.

The Nat.

Objectives of secondary education

chapter **2**

The people of the United States want schools that are free, that will reflect the needs and desires of local communities, and that will provide universal education for adolescents.[1] They have committed themselves to these ideas in secondary education by words and deeds. Public schools require no tuition; they are controlled by individuals at the local level; they accept practically all young people who want to attend.

In tracing the development of secondary schools in the United States in the previous chapter, it was necessary to present information reflecting changes that have come about through the years in philosophy and objectives in education. The present discussion is directed toward an understanding of the objectives that have been and are shaping the programs offered at the secondary level. Educational goals determine the types of institutions a society will sponsor and the programs such institutions will provide. Much learning takes place outside of school, but schools offer an organized program designed to provide education in predesignated, crucial areas that are considered important to society and the individual. The purposes and objectives held by a people and by those they entrust with the education of their youth will determine what is taught in these strategic areas.

---

[1]Edward A. Krug, *The Secondary School Curriculum* (New York: Harper & Row, Publishers, Inc., 1960), p. 1.

The types of programs that might be offered are many; it is the responsibility of teachers, administrators, and the public to select the learning experiences most helpful to students in reaching the goals that society considers most appropriate. At the present time there is no clear and complete list of objectives for secondary education acceptable to all. In fact, some educators believe that one of the major shortcomings of education today is that "secondary schools have not properly defined their basic functions and purposes."[2] Since the nature of the school and its curriculum are determined by educational objectives, it is pertinent that individuals who plan to teach in secondary schools give close attention to the purposes governing their efforts.

Educational purposes and objectives may be thought of at three levels: goals for secondary education in general, goals for a specific school, and goals for a specific teacher as he works with a certain class. Chapter 11 furnishes information on the selection and use of goals at the third level. The goals for education in a specific school should be formulated by the people of the local community and the educators in charge of that particular school. The present discussion will deal with goals for secondary education in general.

Historical development of objectives

The colonial Latin grammar schools were governed by three major objectives: preparation for college, knowledge of religion, and development of educated leaders for public service and the church. Although they were primarily European institutions transplanted to the New World, the Latin grammar schools constituted the foundation of American secondary education.

Colonial private-venture schools, conducted by teachers as a business enterprise, were established to provide a practical education that would enable citizens to carry on their growing shipping and commercial activities. These schools undoubtedly contributed to the rise of the academy.

The major objective of the academies was to offer a more practical education than that given in the Latin grammar schools. To fulfill this function, writing, history, English, mathematics, science, modern foreign languages, agriculture, bookkeeping, commerce, geography, and similar subjects were taught. Academies also taught Latin and Greek, and they eventually took over the college-preparatory function of the Latin grammar schools. The

[2]William M. Alexander and J. Galen Saylor, *Modern Secondary Education* (New York: Holt, Rinehart & Winston, Inc., 1959), p. 103.

academies were regarded as being more democratic than were the Latin schools and as offering greater equality of educational opportunities. Many educators believe that they helped prepare the way for the American public high school.

The high school was founded to make available to young people a free secondary education that would prepare them for life. It represented an effort to offer equality of educational opportunity to those who could not afford to pay for an academy education. A better understanding of the reasons for the creation of this new institution and the purposes it was to serve can be gained by considering the report calling for its establishment, as recorded in the minutes of a town meeting in Boston:

A parent who wishes to give a child an education that shall fit him for active life, and shall serve as a foundation for eminence in his profession, whether Mercantile or Mechanical, is under the necessity of giving him a different education from any which our public schools can now furnish. Hence, many children are separated from their parents and sent to private academies in this vicinity, to acquire that instruction which cannot be obtained at the public seminaries. . . .

The Committee, for these and many other weighty considerations that might be offered, and in order to render the present system of public education more nearly perfect, are of the opinion that an additional school is required. They therefore, recommend the founding of a seminary which shall be called the English Classical School. . . .[3]

The function of this school was clarified further in the regulations promulgated in 1833 which declared that it was designed to furnish the young men of Boston who had enjoyed the usual advantages of the public elementary schools, but did not intend to follow a collegiate course of study, with a good English education to prepare them for life and eminence in private or public service.[4] The high school was not at this time considered a college-preparatory institution; that purpose was still reserved for the Latin grammar schools and the academies.

At first the high school developed slowly, especially in the original thirteen states where the academies were firmly entrenched. During the last half of the nineteenth century and the first half of the twentieth century, however, the growth of the high

---

[3]Quoted in Elmer E. Brown, *The Making of Our Middle Schools,* 3rd ed. (New York: Longmans, Green and Co., 1907), p. 547.

[4]Alexander J. Inglis, *The Rise of the High School in Massachusetts* (New York: Teachers College, Columbia University, 1911), p. 166.

school in the United States was phenomenal. The great increase in enrollment forced educators to consider what objectives this institution should seek to fulfill. The objectives of public high school education were arrived at primarily between 1892 and 1918.

In 1894 the Committee on Secondary School Studies, also referred to as the Committee of Ten, believed the major objective of the high school should be to prepare for the duties of life that small proportion of pupils capable of profiting from attendance. The program of studies, however, consisted principally of the traditional college-preparatory subjects, a program defended by the committee as the best possible preparation for life.

The work and recommendations of this group were extremely important factors in the shaping of the high school curriculum during the ensuing decades. In effect, if not in words, the committee gave its approval to the high school's assuming the responsibility for preparing students for higher education. The general public also readily adopted this feeling — that, in addition to providing a program of studies that would prepare students for life, a free public high school should provide sufficient background for those who wanted to attend an institution of higher learning. In fact, an examination of the curriculums of most high schools between 1894 and 1920 might readily lead one to believe that those responsible for planning programs for secondary education considered preparation for college more important than preparation for life.

Many high school principals and school superintendents, sensitive to the demands of the people in their own communities, objected to the emphasis on the humanistic, classical curriculum which was demanded by the colleges. These and other groups, including professors of education, vigorously declared that the high school must serve a function broader than that of college preparation. They maintained that practical courses and the sciences should be given more emphasis than the Committee of Ten had been willing to recommend or the schools had been willing to provide. Even Charles W. Eliot, president of Harvard and chairman of the Committee of Ten, later raised his voice in demanding a broader secondary school curriculum.

Objectives developed by national commissions

As has been mentioned earlier, some educators consider the fact that secondary schools have not properly defined their basic functions and purposes to be one of the major shortcomings in education today. If this is true, it is not for lack of effort on the part of national committees and commissions. The work of several of the more important national groups that have tried to clarify the goals of the junior and senior high schools will be considered here.

Commission on the Reorganization of Secondary Education

The major contribution of the Commission on the Reorganization of Secondary Education (see p. 27) was that it gave full expression at the national level to the demand for a broad secondary school curriculum. In order to ensure such a curriculum, the commission set forth the Seven Cardinal Principles, which grouped the objectives of the secondary school under the major headings of health, command of fundamental processes, worthy home membership, vocation, citizenship, worthy use of leisure, and ethical character.

The commission, meeting only twenty-five years after the Committee of Ten, obviously took quite a different view on the purposes of secondary education. One reason for this major shift in opinion was the intensive debate and discussion that had taken place during the intervening years. Although the Commission on the Reorganization of Secondary Education did not reject the preparation of students for college as a legitimate responsibility of the public secondary schools, it did emphasize that their essential task was to educate all adolescents of the nation in order that they could effectively participate in all major aspects of living. Another reason for the shift in stated objectives for secondary education was the practical, utilitarian temper of the populace.

Attempts to redefine these goals since 1918 have done little to improve upon the Seven Cardinal Principles.

Educational Policies Commission

During the 1930's American educators continued their evaluation of the function of public education. Significant work in this area was done by the Educational Policies Commission of the National Education Association and the American Association of School Administrators. This commission stated that any set of educational goals must take into consideration the changing society in which the schools are to function, the nature of students in school, and the values held by the social group. After considering the social setting of the United States at that time, the commission then proposed a classification of goals into four groups, based upon the four areas with which education is concerned. The significance of the commission's presentation can be best understood by considering the introduction of the objectives it recommended:

Education Is Concerned with the Development of the Learner.

The first role, or phase of total behavior, is that of the educated person. Conduct in this field is centered on the personal development, growth, and learning of the individual. It includes his use of the fundamental tools of learning, his health, his recreation, his personal philosophy. The placing of these objectives first in the list is not accidental. They deal with the development of the individual himself. In a democracy this field is of supreme importance. Success in this role conditions one's success in every other phase of life's activities. The purposes of education which fall under this section of total behavior will be referred to as *the objectives of self-realization.*

Education Is Concerned with Home, Family, and Community Life.

A second area is that of home and family relationships with their immediate and natural extensions to neighbors and community. Educationally the home is the most powerful, as it is perhaps the oldest, of all social institutions. Good homes and good communities are the basic units of democracy. The activities of the educated individual which relate to these immediate, person-to-person contacts are, therefore, grouped together in a section on *the objectives of human relationship.*

Education Is Concerned with Economic Demands.

The next aspect of the activities of the member of a democratic society includes the economic sphere—the creation and satisfaction of material wants. Here we consider the education of the individual as a producer, a consumer, an investor. The importance of such education in providing the indispensable material basis for comfort, safety, and even life itself is clear. The objectives within this general area will be classified under the heading of *the objectives of economic efficiency.*

Education Is Concerned with Civil and Social Duties.

Finally, there are the activities of the educated citizen. They involve his dealings with his government—local, state, and national—his relationships with the peoples of other nations, and his other "long-distance" contacts in large-scale collective enterprises. This field of activity is served by education through *the objectives of civic responsibility.*[5]

These classifications have been widely quoted and have frequently been used as a basis for secondary school programs at the

[5]*The Purposes of Education in American Democracy,* Educational Policies Commission, National Education Association (Washington, D.C.: NEA, 1937), pp. 45–47.

local level. (It should be remembered, however, that the objectives recommended by this group were not for public secondary education alone, but for public education in general.) Under each of the four general classifications the committee listed a number of specific objectives, which clarified the general statement and provided the basis for a more detailed plan in educating adolescents.

The complete list of objectives recommended by the Educational Policies Commission is summarized below:

THE OBJECTIVES OF SELF-REALIZATION

The Inquiring Mind. The educated person has an appetite for learning.
Speech. The educated person can speak the mother tongue clearly.
Reading. The educated person reads the mother tongue efficiently.
Writing. The educated person writes the mother tongue effectively.
Number. The educated person solves his problems of counting and calculating.
Sight and Hearing. The educated person is skilled in listening and observing.
Health Knowledge. The educated person understands the basic facts concerning health and disease.
Health Habits. The educated person protects his own health and that of his dependents.
Public Health. The educated person works to improve the health of the community.
Recreation. The educated person is participant and spectator in many sports and other pastimes.
Intellectual Interests. The educated person appreciates beauty.
Character. The educated person gives responsible direction to his own life.

THE OBJECTIVES OF HUMAN RELATIONSHIP

Respect for Humanity. The educated person puts human relationships first.
Friendships. The educated person enjoys a rich, sincere, and varied social life.
Cooperation. The educated person can work and play with others.
Courtesy. The educated person observes the amenities of social behavior.
Appreciation of the Home. The educated person appreciates the family as a social institution.
Conservation of the Home. The educated person conserves family ideals.

Homemaking. The educated person is skilled in homemaking.
Democracy in the Home. The educated person maintains democratic family relationships.

THE OBJECTIVES OF ECONOMIC EFFICIENCY

Work. The educated producer knows the satisfaction of good workmanship.
Occupational Information. The educated producer understands the requirements and opportunities for various jobs.
Occupational Choice. The educated producer has selected his occupation.
Occupational Efficiency. The educated producer succeeds in his chosen vocation.
Occupational Adjustment. The educated producer maintains and improves his efficiency.
Occupational Appreciation. The educated producer appreciates the social value of his work.
Personal Economics. The educated consumer plans the economics of his own life.
Consumer Judgment. The educated consumer develops standards for guiding his expenditures.
Efficiency in Buying. The educated consumer is an informed and skillful buyer.
Consumer Protection. The educated consumer takes appropriate measures to safeguard his interests.

THE OBJECTIVES OF CIVIC RESPONSIBILITY

Social Justice. The educated citizen is sensitive to the disparities of human circumstance.
Social Activity. The educated citizen acts to correct unsatisfactory conditions.
Social Understanding. The educated citizen seeks to understand social structures and processes.
Critical Judgment. The educated citizen has defenses against propaganda.
Tolerance. The educated citizen respects honest differences of opinion.
Conservation. The educated citizen has a regard for the nation's resources.
Social Application of Science. The educated citizen measures scientific advance by its contribution to the general welfare.
World Citizenship. The educated citizen is a cooperating member of the world community.
Law Observance. The educated citizen respects the law.

Economic Literacy. The educated citizen is economically literate. *Political Citizenship.* The educated citizen accepts his civic duties. *Devotion to Democracy.* The educated citizen acts upon an unswerving loyalty to democratic ideals.[6]

In a later publication, *Education for All American Youth,* the Educational Policies Commission indicated that the goal of general education in the secondary school should be to help all youth in the following areas:

1. Civic responsibility and competence.
2. Understanding of the operation of the economic system and of the human relations involved therein.
3. Family relationships.
4. Intelligent action as consumers.
5. Appreciation of beauty.
6. Proficiency in the use of language.[7]

Although these purposes are described as pertaining to general education, the context does not limit them to so-called "general education" or "common learnings" courses. In a more recent publication the commission listed the following additional objectives for the required courses in the curriculum:

1. Growth in the ability to think rationally and in respect for truth which is arrived at by rational processes.
2. Growth in respect for other people and the ability to work cooperatively with others.
3. Growth in insight into sound ethical values and principles.
4. Growth in ability to use their time well and to budget it efficiently.
5. Growth in ability to plan their own lives, as individuals and with groups.[8]

In these two later publications the Educational Policies Commission was obviously elaborating on the goals it had established in 1937. The major objectives that have been formulated by this commission through the years are captured and condensed in the statements known as the Ten Imperative Needs of Youth, which are presented on pages 30–31.

Commission on life adjustment education

In 1945 educators attending a conference on "Vocational Education in the Years Ahead" in Washington, D.C., stated that they

[6]*Ibid.,* summarized from pp. 50–123.

[7]*Education for All American Youth,* Educational Policies Commission, National Education Association (Washington, D.C.: NEA, 1944). Adapted from the entire publication.

[8]*Education for All American Youth: A Further Look,* Educational Policies Commission, National Education Association (Washington, D.C.: NEA, 1952), pp. 50–232.

believed the secondary schools of the United States were capable of doing a creditable job in preparing about 20 per cent of the youth for entrance into skilled occupations and another 20 per cent for entrance into college. They maintained, however, that the remaining 60 per cent were not receiving the "life adjustment" education they needed and would not receive it unless the public schools provided a better program for this purpose. The members of the conference then requested that the United States Commissioner of Education call a conference or conferences to deal with the problem.

The result was the creation of the First Commission on Life Adjustment Education. The work of this and subsequent commissions was pertinent to the needs of American education in the 1950's and still is today. The term *life adjustment* was popular until the mid 1950's, but since that time many critics have abused the term in attacking the intellectual achievements of secondary schools. Although the problems that life adjustment education commissions sought to solve are still present, it is important to consider their proposals. The goals which they felt should govern programs in secondary schools can be inferred from the answer of the first commission to the question: What is life adjustment education?

It is concerned with ethical and moral living and with physical, mental, and emotional health.

It recognizes the importance of fundamental skills since citizens in a democracy must be able to compute, to read, to write, to listen, and to speak effectively. . . .

It is concerned with the development of wholesome recreational interests of both an individual and social nature.

It is concerned with the present problems of youth as well as with their preparation for future living.

It is for all American youth and offers them learning experiences appropriate to their capacities.

It recognizes the importance of personal satisfactions and achievements for each individual within the limits of his abilities.

It respects the dignity of work and recognizes the educational values of responsible work experience in the life of the community.

It provides both general and specialized education but, even in the former, common goals are to be attained through differentiation both as to subject matter and experience.

It has many patterns. For a school, a class, or a pupil, it is an individual matter. . . . It must make sense in each community in terms of the goals which are set and the resources which are available.

It emphasizes deferred as well as immediate values. . . .

It recognizes that many events of importance happened a long time ago but holds that the real significance of these events is their bearing upon life of today.

It emphasizes active and creative achievements as well as adjustment to existing conditions; it places a high premium upon learning to make wise choices, since the very concept of American democracy demands the appropriate revising of aims and the means of attaining them.

It is education fashioned to achieve desired outcomes in terms of character and behavior. It is not education which follows convention for its own sake or holds any aspect of the school as an end in itself rather than a means to an end.

Above all, it recognizes the inherent dignity of the human personality.[9]

Recent publications such as James B. Conant's *Slums and Suburbs* and George W. Burchill's *Work-Study Programs for Alienated Youth* indicate that the concepts stated above are not outdated. Neither are they responsible for anti-intellectualism in the schools. While the commission did not mention college preparation as such, it can certainly be inferred from items four through twelve. Thoughtful consideration of the current scene in the United States makes clear the bearing of the commission's work on the formulation of appropriate goals for American secondary education. Consider, for example, the following observation on continuing problems facing secondary school personnel:

Rising in our midst is a problem so serious no sober schoolman can ignore it. Mary Conway Kohler puts the finger on one aspect: "A *million* youngsters have no useful place in our country. They have nothing to do; they are going nowhere. Next year there will be more." By 1970, the number will be pressing *two* million.

So part of the problem is youth unemployment. In 1962, with total unemployment at 5.5 per cent, the rate for ages 16–21 was 14 per cent; even for the age 20–24 group it was 9 per cent. The statistics are twice as bad for dropouts as for graduates—and still worse for those who are not white—but even the graduates have a hard time. Especially the males; "men's work" of some types has leveled off or is

[9]*Life Adjustment Education for Every Youth,* U.S. Office of Education Bulletin 22 (Washington, D.C.: Government Printing Office, 1951), p. 16.

falling. In the 60's total employment will rise about 20 per cent; but jobs for laborers and miners won't rise at all, and farm jobs will drop a fifth. While this goes on a flood of youngsters will hit the market: 26 million, of whom 7.5 million may be dropouts and millions more will lack what the market most wants.

Responsible economists fear that many will never hold a regular job—will have to be "pensioned off." Nobody knows how many, but private speculation often turns on a figure of 10–15 per cent. Displaced persons, wandering aimlessly down the years!

But jobs are only one element. There is the deadly disease called alienation, which Havighurst and others estimate to be gnawing at the heart of 15 per cent—even 40–50 per cent in some schools. It is a dreadful thing to be walled off from the grown-up world just when one should be busily growing into it. Our society is a hard one to grow into—maybe the hardest in all history. It lacks easy gradients into the world of work and the whole of adult life. Adolescence craves significance and responsibility, and we offer only childhood. So delinquency and crime keep rising year by year—even in "good" neighborhoods and rural areas; so adolescents "clam up," form their private subculture, model on one another instead of real adults, and join a formless rebellion against the world they yearn to belong to.

Then there is the rising tide of cultural deprivation. One authority estimates that, from one in five culturally deprived a while back, we are moving relentlessly to one in two. Whether or not that figure is exact, the general fact is inescapable: a growing proportion of our families is falling so far behind the swift pace as to be essentially out of things. The problem is worst in the urban slum, in the lower classes, and above all among the minority groups—but it is not just a slum or minority problem. Our youth as well as our adults are separating on two sides of a wall: on one side the sunny future of a bright new world; on the other the dismal gray of what Andrew Hacker has called "the second America," "a society of losers. . . ."

We must go to work. . . . As we go to work let's remember there is a bright side, too. The future was never so good for those who do move toward high-level competence. Let's remember, too, that the problems and responsibility aren't ours alone. The whole society must tackle the problems that grow out of swift automation and mass urbanization; of an economy that creates new jobs too slowly, leveling off at higher levels of unemployment—especially for youth—in the boom after each recession; and of homes too barren to send us children ready to learn.[10]

[10]*NASSP Spotlight*, ed. Fred T. Wilhelms (Washington, D.C.: National Association of Secondary-School Principals, November-December 1963), pp. 1–2.

The work of other commissions and groups, such as the White House Conferences on Education, could be quoted here, but this would only prove repetitious and overlapping. Indeed, repetition and overlapping are already evident in the material presented above; but these very elements are indications of validity—that is, they support the thesis that there is widespread agreement among educators in the United States on what the objectives of secondary education should be. A careful study of these and other objectives formulated by commissions would reveal that the essence of most such statements is found in the Ten Imperative Needs of Youth and the Seven Cardinal Principles.

It is essential, however, that these statements not be taken either as lists to be memorized or as statements planned for mere show. They have not been developed for such purposes, and they have not been presented here for such ends. Instead, they should serve to help the individual interested in education decide which objectives he accepts as valid and, if he teaches, which goals he should strive for in his own courses.

Education cannot be constructed like a building by simply adding brick after brick in grade after grade.[11] Instead, it is a complicated process of gradual growth and development. Educational objectives, such as those discussed here, are guides to the type of individual that schools should aim to produce. The teacher's concern is with the selection of educational experiences that contribute to desirable growth toward appropriate objectives.

Objectives that have found general acceptance

There is no agreement on any one list of objectives for education in this country; however, there are objectives that have received wide acceptance from educators and the general public. This statement, of course, is subject to certain qualifications:

1. There exist many publics in this country.

2. Formal lists of objectives for education may or may not reflect the opinions of citizens.

3. Agreement on a statement of objectives does not imply agreement on the relative importance of the stated goals.

4. Schools do not have a monopoly on educational goals.

With these qualifications in mind, an attempt will be made to formulate a statement of those objectives for secondary education that seem to have gained general acceptance.

[11]J. Murray Lee and Dorris May Lee, *The Child and His Curriculum* (New York: Apple-ton-Century-Crofts, 1950), p. 11.

1. *Secondary education should provide for the development of each personality to the fullest realization of inborn capacities.* The secondary school program should promote the conditions fostering full realization of a student's individual capacities. Most Americans express a belief in the merit and dignity of the individual. It follows then that their schools should provide those conditions necessary for the greatest creative and intellectual development. This comprehensive objective—which covers many specific goals—should become the standard by which the worth and significance of secondary education are judged.

2. *Secondary education should provide for the maximum development of each student's intellect.* Not all pupils in American secondary schools are capable of profiting from a strict, rigid academic program; however, a program of studies should be designed to promote the best intellectual development of each individual. No curriculum should be offered which is based on an anti-intellectual philosophy. Instead, the objective should be to provide learning experiences appropriate for students with different abilities and goals. This means an education grounded in the advanced academic disciplines for some and a utilitarian program involving general education and marketable skills for others, but it does not imply a watered-down curriculum for any pupil.

3. *Secondary education should provide for the development of good citizenship on the part of students.* Secondary schools should strive to develop loyalty to the United States, to produce individuals who know the structure and function of their government, and to develop in young citizens the realization that Americans should apply themselves to the intelligent solution of civic problems.

4. *Secondary education should provide for the development of understanding and knowledge about life that will lead to good physical and mental health.* The school must be concerned with more than a physical fitness program. It must use its physical education department—and other areas such as the social studies and the natural sciences—to educate students in desirable physical and mental health.

5. *Secondary education should provide for the desirable moral development of its students.* This does not mean that the public secondary school should engage in verbal indoctrination of sectarian religious precepts; but rather that it should provide knowledge of moral and ethical principles, an environment conducive to the development of these principles, and opportunities "to relate ethical principles to specific situations calling for decisions."[12]

[12]Krug, *op. cit.*, pp. 103–104.

What values are developed through education will determine the kinds of behavior patterns we exhibit as a nation. For example, if schools were to sponsor values of passive resistance to violence, this could very well influence the future course of governmental policy. Or if schools engendered the belief that the individual should be subservient to the state, future citizens would most likely make decisions in terms of this value. The framework of values developed through education could determine the direction this nation would take in the generations to come. No function in society is more important.[13]

6. *Secondary education should provide education in family living.* Secondary schools should be concerned with educational experiences that will result in a greater appreciation for and skill in family living. This concern might well manifest itself in three major approaches in secondary school programs: (1) instruction in desirable family relationships; (2) instruction on such topics as family finance, clothing, and food; (3) instruction dealing with sex education. All instruction in family living should help the student develop healthy boy-girl relationships; acquire information concerning courtship, marriage, and family relationships; and develop an understanding of the place of the home in American society.

7. *Secondary education should provide educational experiences that will help students equip themselves with the skills, knowledge, understandings, and attitudes necessary for earning their own living.* This objective applies to all students, not just to those in business and trades courses. The notion that only terminal students should be prepared for occupational competence is fictitious; college-bound students are, in most cases, concerned with earning their own living or at least being capable of earning it. Certainly secondary education should help these students acquire the traits and qualities needed in gaining a college or university education, but it should not fail to develop those characteristics necessary for working with people.

Occupational competence as an objective in the secondary school may be broken down into the following specific functions or objectives: (1) to provide vocational guidance for all students; (2) to help every student develop skills and understandings relevant to success in many occupational fields; (3) to help every student develop the personal qualities generally needed in work relationships; (4) to provide some students with essential preparation for advanced profes-

[13]Mario Fantini, "Education and the National Purpose," *Bulletin of the National Association of Secondary-School Principals*, XLVII (December 1963), 78.

sional study; and (5) to provide to some students under some circumstances specific training in the skills and techniques of particular occupations.[14]

8. *Secondary education should help students live a better, more enriched, enjoyable life.* Education should focus directly on the individual student and his search for answers to such appropriate questions as: "Who am I?" "What is important in life?" "What can I and what should I do with my life?" Many school subjects — music, the social studies, science, literature, languages — can enrich the lives of learners. Teachers should lead students to the exploration of the cultural resources that can enable them to get more enjoyment from life.

The various lists of objectives discussed in this chapter are in many ways quite similar. Achieving such goals involves the offering of a comprehensive program on the part of the American secondary school. Educational objectives, when well conceived and developed, can provide a helpful set of guides for educational planning. As educational programs continue to change, it will become increasingly important for a school to have sound objectives that can serve as guideposts. If the goals of secondary education are well conceived and defined, it will be possible for the schools to make the necessary adaptations in response to new and insistent demands and still allow the orderly processes of education to continue without major dislocations.

Selected references

BILLETT, ROY O. *Teaching in Junior and Senior High Schools.* Dubuque, Iowa: William C. Brown Company, Publishers, 1963.

CHASE, FRANCIS S., HAROLD A. ANDERSON, AND OTHERS, EDS. *The High School in a New Era.* Chicago: University of Chicago Press, 1959.

Education for All American Youth. Educational Policies Commission, National Education Association. Washington, D.C.: NEA, 1944.

Education for All American Youth: A Further Look. Educational Policies Commission, National Education Association. NEA, 1952.

[14]Krug, *op. cit.*, pp. 119–120.

FANTINI, MARIO. "Education and the National Purpose," *Bulletin of the National Association of Secondary-School Principals,* XLVII (December 1963), 74–79.

The Purposes of Education in American Democracy. Educational Policies Commission, National Education Association. Washington, D.C.: NEA, 1937.

Schools for the Sixties. Project on Instruction, National Education Association. New York: McGraw-Hill Book Company, Inc., 1963.

STILES, LINDLEY J., LLOYD E. MCCLEARY, AND ROY C. TURNBAUGH. *Secondary Education in the United States.* New York: Harcourt, Brace & World, Inc., 1962.

Students in secondary education

What is the nature of the high school population today? How does it differ from the student population of the past? In what respects are the students in American secondary schools different from those in European secondary schools? What factors cause students to drop out of high school? What are the trends in secondary school enrollments? These are some of the questions that occupy the minds of individuals interested in secondary education in this country today. If one is to think and talk intelligently about secondary education, he must be familiar with the answers to the above questions. Above all, those who plan secondary school curriculums or teach in secondary schools must know the answers to these questions if they are to plan and teach effectively.

Public secondary schools are designed to serve all youth and the nation in general. The school must provide the type of organization, curriculum, and instruction that will be functional. If they are to develop proper programs of study, the people who serve in the secondary schools must be well acquainted with the individuals who are enrolled in these schools. Dewey points out that the fundamental factors in the educational process are students and social aims, meanings, and values.[1] Other chapters of this book deal with the social aims, meanings, and values—in other words,

[1] John Dewey, *The Child and the Curriculum* (Chicago: University of Chicago Press, 1902), pp. 7–8.

the curriculum. This chapter will be concerned with the student population of American secondary schools and the extent to which adolescents are availing themselves of secondary education.

This discussion is not comprehensive. Research is plentiful on these topics, and although the statistical data is the most recent available, it is' subject to change each year. The following resource materials will provide up-to-date information:

1. *Biennial Survey of Education.* This publication is released every two years by the United States Office of Education. The information found in it provides the basis for an analysis of school enrollments and attendance.

2. *The Encyclopedia of Educational Research.* This publication, edited by Chester W. Harris and published in 1960, is an excellent source of information on recent research dealing with major phases of education.

3. *Publications by the United States Office of Education.* The United States Office of Education each year publishes many pamphlets and brochures giving up-to-date information and statistics on trends and practices in the schools.

4. *The United States Census.* The data found in the census is basic and reliable. Although this information is quickly dated, it is nevertheless of great value in providing an understanding of general trends and conditions.

5. *Studies made by individual and state school systems.* The student is urged to study the research undertaken by his own state and its department of education and to compare such research with that done in other states.

6. *Individual research by educators.* Much research is carried on by educators within their own institutions and by graduate students in the various universities. Very often this research spotlights areas of special interest, such as drop-outs and hidden costs in secondary education.

7. *Individual study and observation.* The student of secondary education will find it helpful to do some observing and study on his own. This approach not only informs but also helps develop an attitude basic for growth in any area.

The secondary school population

Secondary education is generally considered to consist of instruction and experiences offered in grades seven through twelve. Most students enrolled in these grades are between the ages of twelve and seventeen, although there are, of course, exceptions.

Secondary education enrollment

Public secondary school enrollment in the United States during the school year 1964–1965 was about 15 million. This number was largely a result of the great rise in the birth rate after 1946. The school age population (ages five through seventeen) increased 63.2 per cent from 1950 to 1965.[2] In the late 1950's the rise in the birth rate was beginning to be reflected in the secondary school enrollments. In the school year 1951–1952 there were only 7 million enrolled in public secondary education. Ten years later, in 1961–1962, there were almost 13 million—actually 12,632,691 —pupils enrolled in public secondary schools. During the following four-year period this total climbed another 2 million.[3]

Despite the fact that the number of young people under the age of twenty is increasing, the ratio of youth to the total population of the United States is decreasing. In 1900 young people under twenty years of age made up 44.4 per cent of the population of the nation. By 1950 individuals in this age group represented 34.1 per cent of the total population. Today the number of young people in the same category comprises a little over 10 per cent of the total population. This means that while the secondary school enrollments have increased and are increasing and more and more money is needed and will be needed for secondary schools and teachers, there is a greater percentage of adults in society to help provide education for young people.

Figures also show that a majority of the young people in the secondary school age group attend school. While a much smaller number actually complete their secondary school education, over 90 per cent of the young people in that age group are enrolled in secondary school. This is a much larger proportion than was enrolled in the past. Table 2 gives a historical picture of enrollments.

The secondary schools of the United States are unusual in that such a large percentage of young people from the general population of the country attend them. Unlike major secondary schools in most other countries, American schools enroll students of varying abilities and backgrounds. Secondary schools in most European countries—with exceptions in such countries as England, Sweden, Norway, and Russia—are designed to serve minority groups. Only about 20 per cent of the students from sixteen to seventeen years of age are enrolled in the secondary schools of Western Europe.

[2]*NEA Research Bulletin,* XL:1 (Washington, D.C.: Research Division, National Education Association, February 1962), p. 4.
[3]These statistics are based on the information given in *Statistics of Education in the United States* and various NEA publications.

table **2**   **Enrollments in Public Secondary School
Grades, 1890 – 1965**

Year	Pupils in Grades 7 – 12⊕
1965	15,000,000
1962	12,632,692
1959	11,105,400
1952	7,693,140
1946	6,861,030
1938	7,458,045
1930	5,212,179
1920	1,999,106
1910	915,061
1900	519,251
1890	202,963

⊕The figures for Alaska and Hawaii are not complete for the year 1959. They are complete for the year 1962. Figures for these states are not included for the years before 1959.

Sources: U.S. Office of Education, *Statistics of State School Systems* and *Statistical Summary of Education,* for years listed (Washington, D.C.: Government Printing Office, 1962).
   The figure for 1965 is based on statistics found in educational journals such as the *NEA Journal* of November 1964.

It is often said that Americans waste the talents of many of their young people because educators do not make their programs in secondary education as difficult as those found in most European schools. No doubt many American schools should be concerned with more challenging programs. Yet it is also true that much talent is being wasted in Europe and other areas because the vast majority of students are not allowed to continue in academic secondary education programs. The American secondary schools have almost as many students in their honor societies as there are students at every level of achievement in all the European secondary schools combined.[4]

[4]Vernon E. Anderson and William T. Gruhn, *Principles and Practices of Secondary Education* (New York: Ronald Press Company, 1962), pp. 83 – 84. Copyright © 1962, The Ronald Press Company.

Increased mobility of the high school population

Still another important factor to be considered in a discussion of the secondary school population is mobility. There is, of course, great mobility on the part of the population in general in the United States today. Secondary school personnel are keenly aware of the effect of this mobility on enrollments, since in many cases it creates problems for the student and the school. Because there is a great movement from rural to urban areas, many students are moving from small to large schools, and they are likely to have problems of adjustment. Sometimes these are emotional problems; the student has difficulty finding new friends and adjusting to a large student body and many new teachers. Sometimes they are academic problems. If a student transfers from a school that is academically poor, chances are he will not be prepared to make satisfactory progress in a school system where high achievement is emphasized. In many cases this causes the student to fail subjects or to drop out of school.

The 1960 census reveals that about 18 per cent of the individuals in the nation under twenty years of age had moved from the houses in which they lived during the previous year. It also shows that from 6 to 11 per cent of the population of high school age had moved to a new county during the school year 1959–1960. Some of the students who moved during the year probably made only short moves; many, no doubt, still attended the same school. The ones who moved from one county to another would not, in most cases, be attending the same school.

Students in small and large secondary schools

About 60 per cent of the young people of high school age live in urban areas. This, of course, is a reflection of the great trend toward urbanization on the part of the population in general. Large metropolitan areas having a population of one million or more people contain one of every five individuals of high school age. About 20 per cent of the individuals in this age group live on farms, and about 20 per cent live in small towns and villages. Here again, however, these statistics are changing as increasing numbers of people continue to move to the metropolitan areas.

During the school year 1959–1960 there were just over 24,000 public secondary schools in the nation. About 70 per cent of these schools had enrollments of less than five hundred students each; these schools enrolled less than one third of the secondary school population. At this time, almost 4000 public secondary schools enrolled less than one hundred students. Despite the fact that the median enrollment has increased significantly in recent years, in 1960 it was still less than three hundred students.

It is evident from these statistics that most secondary school students are enrolled in large schools. It is also clear, however, that the small high school cannot be ignored. Educators for years have been concerned with the problem of the small high schools, many of which are not able to provide the educational program needed by their students.

Marriage and the secondary school population

Not too long ago it was considered proper for students to withdraw from high school if they decided to marry before they were graduated.[5] In fact, until World War II marriage for most high school students was strictly taboo, and a married student was automatically barred from attending many high schools. During World War II, however, early marriage was looked upon as a normal outgrowth of wartime living. Young men of eighteen and nineteen were called into service and some of them married girls of sixteen, seventeen, and eighteen who were still in high school. These young women wanted to be graduated, and high schools accepted them as regular students. When the war ended, there was no abatement in the practice of early marriage, and many schools continued to allow married students to complete their education.

Most of the married students in high schools have been girls, but in recent years a considerable number of boys have married and remained in school. At the present time about 6 per cent of the girls and about 1 per cent of the boys in high school are married

These changes have created some real problems for school personnel and parents. In most cases these married students are not financially independent, yet they resent being treated as immature adolescents. Many parents object to having their single offspring in school with married students, particularly with married girls who are pregnant. In some cases secondary school teachers resent the presence of married students in their classes. Recently some of the schools in the Dallas, Texas, metropolitan area have passed regulations barring married boys from participating on their athletic teams.

The presence of married students has had considerable influence on the instructional program and routine of the school. Many married students want more practical courses and fewer academic courses, and this in itself creates problems in some

[5]L. O. Taylor and others, *The American Secondary School* (New York: Appleton-Century-Crofts, 1960), p. 99.

schools. Nevertheless, many high schools have recognized that they must attempt to serve these young people. They are providing more courses in homemaking, commercial subjects, retail sales, and consumer economics. Some secondary schools are urging married students to avoid having children until they have finished school and are encouraging many of them to go on to college.

Some schools have a guidance program that attempts to show the unmarried student the advantages of delaying marriage until he completes his education. While this seems to be the most promising approach, it seems mandatory that the school provide for the needs of those students who do marry. Surely they should not be treated as juvenile delinquents or deviates who must be eliminated from school.

Students who drop out of secondary education

There is a gradual reduction in the number of students remaining in high school from one year to another. While it is no doubt true that special circumstances in the lives of many students cause them to drop out, it is also true that the school itself often does not meet the needs of its students; some of them drop out because they do not have appropriate programs to pursue. During the school year 1960–1961 approximately one fourth of the individuals sixteen and seventeen years of age were not enrolled in any type of school program. In some areas of the nation as many as one half of the students in school drop out of grades nine, ten, and eleven.[6]

Why do so many students drop out of school? There is no *one* answer, but some of the reasons are given below.

Some students drop out because of financial reasons. Students must have money for textbooks, workbooks, lunches, special publications, materials, student tickets, yearbooks, newspapers, dances, uniforms, fees, class rings, and field trips. Research has shown that the amount needed varies from a few dollars to hundreds of dollars. Many children who come from the lower economic levels of society drop out of school because they cannot afford these expenses or cannot get spending money.

Some students drop out because they are members of ethnic and racial groups that are not given equal opportunity to attend school or equality of opportunity at school. Such discrimination is found in more than one section of the country, and it affects more than one group. Inequalities in education exist in parts of the

[6]James B. Conant, *Slums and Suburbs* (New York: McGraw-Hill Book Company, Inc., 1961).

South; in some sections of the Southwest; and in many Northern cities, as Conant has pointed out in *Slums and Suburbs*. It should be acknowledged, however, that most school systems are making great efforts to remedy the situation and that progress is being made in solving the problem of equality of opportunity in secondary education.[7]

Many students drop out of secondary education because the programs in their schools are too limited. Schools with very limited programs cannot meet the needs of a large heterogeneous student body. All students have many needs in common; yet as individuals they have many specific and special needs because of their varying abilities, interests, and backgrounds. Therefore, many elective courses and other special programs, such as remedial reading courses and provision for ability grouping, must be available if the school is to serve the youth and the community well.

In order to provide proper programs, secondary schools must be adequately financed. Money will not solve all of the problems in education, but quality education is possible only where adequate facilities and competent teachers are provided. The amount of money spent for the education of students on a per pupil basis varies considerably from state to state and from district to district within states, and the states with less wealth available to support education have the most children to educate.

Statistics reveal that the Northeast has the smallest number of secondary school students per one thousand adults between the ages of twenty and sixty-four; the Western states have next fewest; the North Central states are next in order; and the South has the largest number of students of secondary school age to educate per one thousand adults. In the South, which has the most young people to educate in proportion to the number of adults to help pay for schools, one finds the lowest percentage of youth enrolled in the secondary schools. The school age population in South Carolina in 1960 equaled 30.8 per cent of the total population, while in Massachusetts the school age population equaled only 21.5 per cent of the total population. These two states represent the highest and lowest percentages of school age population in the fifty states.

According to the 1960 census, the average personal income in the United States was $2223. In Delaware it was $3013, the highest in the nation. Mississippi was at the bottom with only $1173. Such statistics are often cited by individuals who call for more effort on the part of the federal government in the field of educa-

[7]Anderson and Gruhn, *op. cit.*, p. 88.

tion. They argue that since the ability to finance schools is not equally distributed among the various sections of the nation, the federal government should step in and provide sufficient funds to equalize opportunity for all the youth in the country.

The area of the nation in which a young person happens to reside affects his opportunity of attending a secondary school and his chances of being graduated. This can, of course, be inferred from the previous discussion, but it should be emphasized as one of the special reasons why students drop out of secondary schools. For example, an adolescent between fourteen and seventeen years of age who lived in Virginia in 1950 was not as likely to be enrolled in a secondary school as he would have been if he were living in the state of Washington. In Georgia in 1956 only 46.5 per cent of the students who had entered the ninth grade four years earlier were graduated from high school. In the same year 93.1 per cent of the students who had entered the ninth grade in Wisconsin four years previously were graduated from high schools.

Students with average or below-average intelligence are less likely to complete a secondary education than are students with above-average intelligence. Students with low intelligence find it difficult to keep up with class work and thus often drop out of school, a situation educators are trying to remedy. The public, in general, believes that all pupils can profit from a secondary education intent upon developing character, competence in the areas of general education, citizenship, and vocational training. Secondary schools throughout the country, however, have not yet developed a program of general education supplemented by proper elective courses and activities for all youth. Many large schools offer a great variety of subjects and also provide good guidance services for their students, but very few of these schools have programs that are adaptable to all types of students.

Most educators believe that students of below-average intelligence can and should have an opportunity to finish high school. They also know that it is necessary for the school to provide such students with a curriculum revised to meet their varying needs and abilities. However, responsible educators do not advocate a program that would allow these students to "get by" without serious effort on their part. In fact, they believe that slower students will have to show greater application of their abilities than do many average or above-average students in order to profit from the general education or special elective program.

Low cultural and social backgrounds cause many students to drop out of high school. Students who come from the lower cultural and social levels very often do not have high academic interests. Their parents and friends probably do not emphasize success in school. In many cases the parents themselves received little education. The values stressed by the home and the peer group definitely influence adolescents. It is only natural that many young people in an environment where education is not held in high regard will be uninterested in completing the secondary school. It is also true, however, that some students use their adverse environment as a spur to greater achievement.

Low cultural and economic levels are closely related to the dropping out of school at sixteen years of age, the upper limit of compulsory attendance in most states. Parents from average or high cultural and economic levels seldom allow their children to stop school simply because they are sixteen and want to quit. Parents from lower levels are more likely to allow their children to drop out and, in some cases, are impatient for them to begin earning their own money.

The following quotation sums up the picture:

The average drop-out is 16 years old; often he has been marking time, waiting to reach the age when he may legally quit school. He is most likely to quit between the ninth and tenth, or between the tenth and eleventh grades. It is especially likely that he will not return after a summer vacation.

As a rule, the drop-out has shunned participation in extracurricular activities, and he may have failed to become part of a social group within the school.

Usually his relationships with his teachers and with many of his fellow students indicate tension, suspicion, and strain. His poor attendance record, lack of interest, and failure to cooperate have contributed to his being retarded by about two years. Before leaving school, he may have spent as many years there as one who graduates, but because he has probably been held back rather than promoted regularly, he will not have completed the full program by the end of his attendance period.

The typical drop-out's parents are unimpressed with the value of education; often they openly scorn "book learning." In addition, the family is likely to regard school as a financial burden; not only does it cost something to keep a child in school, but the family is deprived of the money which the boy or girl could be contributing to the budget.[8]

[8]"High-School Drop-outs," NEA *Research Bulletin,* XXXVIII:11 (Washington, D.C.: Research Division, National Education Association, February 1960), p. 2.

In 1955 the St. Paul, Minnesota, school system made a study of their high school drop-outs, students who entered the ninth grade in the fall of 1950 and were thus expected to be graduated from high school in the spring of 1954. The study included information on students who transferred from one high school to another within the St. Paul system and those who transferred to other school systems; students who transferred from other systems during this time were not included. During the four-year period 23.3 per cent of the students dropped out of school. This was below the national drop-out rate, which was about 30 per cent. There was, however, great variation among the ten high schools in the system—from 48.3 per cent for one school to 9 per cent for another. As was true in the nation as a whole, more boys dropped out than girls. The major reasons given by students and by school officials for withdrawals from school were as follows:

Preferred work to being in school
Little or no interest in school
No special reason
Getting married or already married
Going into armed forces
Excessive absences
Must earn money to help the family
Must earn own spending money
Placed in a correctional institution[9]

In 1954 the New York State Department of Education made a study to determine some of the reasons why students were dropping out of school. Its primary source of information was secondary school principals. The principals in this study gave the following as primary reasons:

Desire to get a job
Failing subjects and grades
Intelligence too low
Poor home situation—parents unconcerned
Little interest in school
Broken home
Excessive absences[10]

The high percentage of students dropping out of school continued into the 1960's, and the drop-out is now recognized as a national problem. One of the major reasons for the 1964 antipov-

---

[9]*Drop-Out Study*, St. Paul Public Schools (St. Paul, Minn.: Available at the Office of Secondary and Vocational Education, St. Paul Schools, 1955).
[10]*Drop-Outs: The Cause and Cure*, New York State Department of Education (Albany, N.Y., 1954).

erty bill was to help keep students in school by providing work experience and more vocational training. It was estimated by the *NEA Journal* in September 1964 that the provisions of this bill would help keep as many as 200,000 teen-agers from dropping out of school.

Secondary school graduates and college attendance

During the past decade there has been a great increase in the number of young people enrolled in higher education in the United States. The "G.I. Bill of Rights" was responsible for a big increase in college enrollments in the late 1940's and very early 1950's. This bill gave many veterans an opportunity which they otherwise would not have had. During the middle and late 1950's interest in higher education increased, and there was a growing need for professionally and technically trained people. As a result, the colleges are reflecting the enrollment increases that hit elementary and secondary schools in the recent past.

In the 1930's and early 1940's only 10 to 20 per cent of high school graduates went on to college. A study made in Kansas in 1955 revealed that over 50 per cent of the graduates of high schools with enrollments totaling above 475 were going on to college.[11]

Perhaps the most complete study of college enrollments of the secondary school graduates of a particular state was that undertaken by the School of Education of the University of Wisconsin. The study included about 95 per cent of the students completing high school in Wisconsin in 1957. It was found that almost one half of these high school graduates were enrolled in some form of education beyond the secondary school.

Other studies completed before 1958 showed that over 50 per cent of the graduates from many high schools in the United States were attending college. In some situations 80 to 90 per cent of the graduating class entered college. During the fall of 1965 over 50 per cent of the young people who had been graduated from secondary schools that spring were enrolled in some form of post-secondary education.

Characteristics and needs of adolescents

Our schools exist to provide educational opportunities for the young people of the nation. The first concern of the good second-

[11]Alex A. Daughtry, *A Report on the Post-Graduation Activities of the 1956 Kansas High School Graduates,* The Emporia State Research Studies, Vol. 2 (Emporia, Kansas: Kansas State Teachers College, 1956).

ary school teacher, therefore, should be the adolescent boys and girls with whom he works. He must be aware of their characteristics and needs in order to plan worth-while opportunities for them and to direct their learning activities into channels that will lead to desirable mental and social growth. He must try to lead each student into active participation in instructional activities, for effective learning consists of the individual's organizing and reorganizing meaningful experiences into new patterns of action and understanding. Adolescents who are inactive or bored in class are going to be discipline problems and, more important, are going to waste their time in school.

The adolescent in American society

In American society today adolescents are dependent upon adults longer than they have been in any society known to history. Most of them, whether married or single, are not financially independent. They reach physical maturity long before they are recognized as adults, and such drives as the sex drive and the desire to be independent often cause great frustration. Whereas fifty years ago a boy and girl eighteen years of age might be married, farming their own land, or holding jobs, they are now standing in line to get permission slips for the library. Young people are caught in a no-man's land. They are too old to be treated as children but not ready to play the role of adults. Such forces as the necessity for more education, military service, and extreme emphasis on material goods are constantly at work on them. They have their own individual goals that they are striving to realize.

Although adolescence has always been a critical period in the development of the individual, society today makes it even more complex. But adolescence is not necessarily a stage of great difficulties. It can be simply a period in which dependence upon older people is gradually replaced by independence. Many adolescents find their problems no more complex and difficult than those they faced in childhood and those they will face as adults. In fact, adolescence is more often an orderly development toward adulthood than a period of violent change.

Physical characteristics of adolescents

Adolescence is the stage during which the physical process of becoming an adult takes place. It is a period of rapid, continuous growth. Although this growth is at times uneven, it should not be thought of as consisting of sudden, sharp breaks. The individual does not move from childhood to adolescence or adulthood overnight.

Physically, adolescence starts when the sex organs begin to develop rapidly as a result of secretion of sex hormones, and it ends when there is complete development of the sex organs and achievement of adult stature. Although there is wide variation among individuals as to the time this development begins, eleven years of age usually marks the beginning of adolescence. There are great differences among girls of this age. Some are well on the way toward sexual maturity; others are still children. Boys of this age show little or no signs of sexual maturation and are more uniform in physical development. Boys and girls, in most cases, know about reproduction and sexual intercourse. Girls are very much concerned with menstruation. Some girls become interested in boys; others are neutral or dislike boys. In most cases, boys are uninterested in girls except as rivals in school. Both groups are very active physically, and in school they tend to show off, push one another, and make noise.

Girls of twelve are, in most cases, growing fast in weight and height. Menarche usually occurs the twelfth or thirteenth year. Their physical development is more obvious than that of boys. The girls are more aware of sex than before and are very conscious of their bodies and their appearance. They desire a great amount of physical activity and get angry easily. Boys of twelve begin to drop their antigirl attitudes. They are, however, still very much interested in other things, such as outdoor sports. Boys and girls of this age are full of exuberance.

Many girls slow down in physical growth when they reach thirteen. They are less open in their interest in sex. Boys are experiencing voice change and more rapid physical development.

The fourteen-year-old girl is typically more a young woman than a child. Even the boys are beginning to seem less like children. They continue to grow rapidly, and their voices become much deeper. Many boys have masturbated, and these experiences, along with "wet dreams," cause them to worry and have guilt feelings. Girls and boys are very interested in the many aspects of heterosexual relationships, including reproduction.

At fifteen, girls are well rounded and relatively mature. Boys are still far from being sexually mature but are more like men than children. They continue to grow in height and in physical strength. Both boys and girls are still seeking more information on the complex factors associated with sex, social relationships with the opposite sex, and reproduction.

During years sixteen, seventeen, and eighteen, physical development is still taking place for most girls, but at a much slower rate. Boys grow rapidly at sixteen and seventeen, and most of them catch up with girls in physical maturity at the age of eighteen. During these three years both groups are attempting to understand and accept their own physiques. They strive hard to play what they consider the desirable masculine or feminine role and to achieve new and more mature relationships with their peers of both sexes.

Mental and emotional characteristics of adolescents

Parents and teachers should take a cautious approach to generalizations concerning physical, mental, or emotional characteristics associated with adolescents. It is fuzzy thinking to type and classify any or all of them with a limited group of general statements. For example, many theories are advanced concerning the emotional strain or great feelings of uncertainty experienced by adolescents. It is true that some adolescents run the entire gamut of emotional experiences, but adolescence can also be a time of comparatively peaceful development. There are, however, sound reasons for studying emotional and mental characteristics of individuals in this period of life; a parent or teacher who is aware of these characteristics can work with young people more successfully.

It is natural for the eleven-year-old to be stormy and violent in his reactions at times. He is competitive, jealous, often wants to get even, and cries frequently. He is attempting to find himself.

The twelve-year-old is also quick to respond to an emotional situation with anger or tears; however, his outbreaks are usually more verbal and less tearful than they were at eleven. Twelve-year-olds worry a great deal about school, peer groups, and their physical development. Research indicates that at twelve the individual has more problems than he does at any other age between ten and sixteen.[12] The problem that bothers the twelve-year-old most is school, and he finds it difficult to get along with his parents and with brothers and sisters. He worries about friends; he does not argue as much as he did at eleven; he is more reasonable.

Gesell and others give an excellent description of the adolescent between the ages of thirteen and sixteen:

Such adjectives as sophisticated, more inhibited, calmer, conscientious, all give some idea of a real inwardizing change that is occurring at Thirteen years. The rapid, almost pell-mell enthusiasm of

[12]William Van Til and others, *Modern Education for the Junior High School Years* (New York: The Bobbs-Merrill Co., Inc., 1961), p. 161.

Twelve is now withheld and concentrated in more organized and sustained eagerness to learn. Thirteen stands off as he watches the antics of the 12-year-olds, chasing each other up and down the halls, snatching any loose pieces of clothing they can grab from each other to produce further chase and interplay. . . .

Thirteen is basically happier in school than he has been. . . .

Fourteen is ready for a change, in school as in other things—a sizable change that will satisfy his expansiveness. His decrease in suspicious belligerence especially readies him for new territory. He is quieter within himself, even though, compared with Thirteen, he is both less inwardized, and more noisy with the group. His greater inner quietness is linked with a paradoxical development—an increase in interest in himself, yet a decrease in "self-consciousness." His contemplation of his own personality is becoming less uneasy, dissatisfied, and defensive, more calm and judicious. . . .

When Fifteen expresses a hostile attitude toward school, as he often does, he does not become the easiest person to teach. The very expression "the 15-year-old slump" suggests that an inner change has occurred in Fifteen, that something isn't quite right. Teachers are often surprised by this "slump" and may not take it into sufficient consideration. Many conflicts arise between teachers and students. The rise in drop-outs from school following this year, especially among the boys, indicates the crucial aspect of this year and the failure of the school to meet the challenge. But it is no wonder that teachers speak of Fifteen as an "enigma." Many teachers would welcome any light of understanding about Fifteen or help about ways to handle him.

Fifteens tend to move in groups, almost in crowds, but the clique or close circle of friends may not be as important to him as they were at fourteen. . . .

The integrating forces working within Sixteen can make him both a responsive and an interesting person to teach. He often speaks of his junior year as being "better than last year." And he also reports that he is getting a lot out of school.

This is the age when it becomes more evident in what direction he is heading. Those who are interested in college are now ready to buckle down to show that they can do the work, that they can grasp a subject and achieve well in it. Those who are drawn toward the more active, practical direction desire training in specific techniques of commercial or skilled trades. . . .[13]

[13]Arnold Gesell and others. *Youth: The Years from Ten to Sixteen* (New York: Harper & Row, Publishers, Inc., 1956), pp. 165, 204, 251, 270. Copyright © 1956 by Gesell Institute of Child Development, Inc.

Adolescents at one time or another will show most of the physical, emotional, and mental characteristics described above, although there will be wide variations among individuals in any particular group. The extent of the variations found in a given school will depend to some degree on the size of the school and on the experiences of the boys and girls themselves.

The boy or girl who was a slow student in elementary school will probably be a slow student in high school. In all but a very few instances, the relationship between mental age and chronological age remains relatively constant when all other factors of growth and general well-being are equal. Of course, some students who were slow learners in elementary school, and even a few who were considered far below normal in mental ability, were merely the victims of slow development, and they often catch up during adolescence. The student who was a bright child in the elementary school will retain his ability during adolescence.

At the present time there is no evidence to support the generalization that there is a sudden spurt in mental development at the beginning of pubescence. It is true that during the years twelve to seventeen mental abilities become much more evident in many individuals than they were during childhood; yet adolescents show great variations in the ability to concentrate on academic subject matter, to memorize, or to engage in problem-solving activity. Concentration, however, is closely connected with interests and meaning. The typical adolescent does develop a greater attention span.[14]

The secondary schools must provide appropriate encouragement, challenge, and stimulation for adolescents with varying degrees of mental ability, motivation, and alertness. In the latter part of the nineteenth century and the early part of this century, the secondary school program was geared to the superior pupil; most students of average or below-average ability were eliminated from school. Furthermore, schools in general were unconcerned with the emotional and social development of their students. Today secondary schools must be concerned with the education of all, and there is a growing realization that they must provide adolescents with desirable experiences that will result in good social and emotional development. At times this increased responsibility on the part of the school has resulted in a program that failed to provide an intellectually challenging education for superior students. Modern teachers, parents, and school administrators are alert to this dan-

[14]Lester D. Crow and others, *Education in the Secondary School* (New York: American Book Company, 1961) pp. 90–91.

ger, and they are striving to provide greater motivation, increased challenge, and an appropriate educational program for those students who possess special talents and superior intellectual ability.

Adolescent needs as guideposts

Although adolescents have physical, mental, personal, and social needs, the present discussion is concerned with their social and personal needs which can be met in full or in part by the school. A social or personal need is here considered as one which must be successfully fulfilled if an individual is to experience desirable and rewarding mental, emotional, and physical growth and development.

In 1953 Havighurst published what is perhaps the most significant publication, within the past two decades, on human needs. Although he was concerned with developmental tasks or needs of individuals throughout life, he devoted a considerable amount of his discussion to adolescence.[15] His famous ten developmental tasks of adolescence are as follows:

1. Developing new and more mature relationships with age-mates of both sexes.

2. Achieving a masculine or feminine social role.

3. Accepting one's physique and using the body effectively.

4. Gaining emotional independence of parents and other adults.

5. Achieving assurance of economic independence.

6. Selecting and preparing for an occupation or field of work.

7. Preparing for marriage and family life.

8. Developing intellectual skills and concepts necessary for civic competence.

9. Desiring and achieving socially responsible behavior.

10. Acquiring a set of conscious values and an ethical system by which to live.

The reader will note that Havighurst used the term *developmental tasks* rather than *needs*. He defined a developmental task as one which manifests itself at or about a certain time in the life of each individual and which must be achieved if the individual is to be successful with later tasks. Failure in these tasks, he indicated, leads to unhappiness for the individual and to the possible disapproval of society, as well as to difficulty with later tasks.[16]

Today the secondary schools of the United States are concerned not only with the transmission of the major portions of

[15]Robert J. Havighurst, *Developmental Tasks and Education* (Chicago: University of Chicago, 1953).
[16]*Ibid.*, p. 8.

knowledge called the cultural past but also with helping students live at their best in the present and with helping them prepare for the future. This is necessary if the school is to help young people grow into mental, social, and emotional maturity.

The extent to which the secondary school assists young people in their developmental tasks or basic needs is in reality a measure of how well it serves the society that has created it. The adolescent needs or developmental tasks can help the teacher understand young people better and can serve as guideposts in planning a school's educational program.

Developing new and more mature relationships with one's peers.　The adolescent wants to be accepted by friends of his own age group. He wants to belong and to be a part of the gang or peer group. In a healthy social group he learns the value of sportsmanship, fair play, and the give and take of associations with others. The school can shape and direct group activities in desirable social channels. This responsibility is shared, of course, with the home, religious groups, and other agencies.

The need to belong is urgent and intense during adolescence; gaining the acceptance of their peers is far more important to many, if not most, young people than mastery of subject matter or even respect for the school or other authorities. Yet many young people are shy, socially unskilled, or possess undesirable physical characteristics that hinder them in their bid for acceptance. School authorities must be aware of this fact and attempt to plan experiences in the classroom and in student activities that will enable adolescents to become acquainted with other young people and to gain the friendship they seek.

Achieving a masculine or feminine social role.　It is often difficult for a young person to identify the proper roles of men and women in society today. The separate roles of the sexes, usually clear in past generations, are today not so evident. The problem of identification is complicated by the fact that young people often find themselves in conflict with what adults consider the proper role of the teen-age boy or girl, and the resentment thus created on the part of the adolescents tends to bind them together in the formation of their own codes of behavior. These codes are primarily concerned with dating, dressing, going steady, and being attractive to the opposite sex. While it is possible for the secondary school to ignore these things, a good school will attempt to help students analyze themselves and their social situation. It will assist them in setting desirable standards for grooming and boy-girl relationships. A sympathetic and intelligent approach on the part of the school will not only help adolescents make progress toward maturity; it will also reduce antagonism between young people and their parents, their teachers, and the adult world in general.

Accepting one's physique and using the body effectively. Within certain limits, heredity determines the physique of the adolescent. Many times this physique does not meet the popular concept of the ideal body. Failure to meet what the teen-ager considers the standard can be a serious cause of frustration. The school should provide information on growth and development that will promote understanding on the part of its students. It is important that neither teachers nor students be allowed to ridicule individuals who are victims of extreme variations.

Gaining emotional independence of parents and other adults. For satisfactory adjustment to adult life an individual must be emotionally independent of parents and other adults. The mature person is one who is capable of making and carrying out his own decisions. In many homes, as well as in many schools, adolescents are overdominated. Although parents should provide protection and have affection for the adolescent, overprotection can hinder proper development. Parents should discuss problems with their children and set proper limits as behavior guides; they should also provide opportunities for the adolescent to grow gradually from dependency to responsibility. The school can help in this area of development by providing opportunities and activities that will help the adolescent develop skill in making and carrying out his own decisions.

Achieving assurance of economic independence. Secondary school students find that they need a considerable amount of spending money if they are to date, keep up with the gang, take trips, and meet the many other expenses of school and social life. Young people often find it difficult to have the friends they would like because they do not possess the clothes, car, or money that would enable them to associate with certain groups. Sometimes these things are so serious to the teen-ager that he will stop school if he is old enough and go to work in order to get the money he needs or feels he needs.

Society does not expect the adolescent to be financially independent, but it does expect him to make progress toward this end.

In most cases such progress can best be made through thorough application to schoolwork and through some work experiences at home and perhaps on a part-time basis outside the home. In addition to helping the individual toward economic independence, these experiences give him valuable opportunities in learning to get along with people, in using his own abilities, and in evaluating himself and others.

The school should attempt to relate its instruction to life in the whole society, to help students see the importance of their day-to-day tasks. The secondary school must provide a guidance program that will enable a student to gain valuable information about himself and to realize the many vocational opportunities available. This means the school must provide general and special educational programs and must stress quality in the curriculum.

Selecting and preparing for a field of work. This need, of course, cannot be divorced from the need to develop economic independence; yet it deserves special emphasis. Schools are becoming better equipped to help students know their aptitudes and competencies. Through a cooperative guidance program involving parents, teachers, and guidance experts, students can be provided with the necessary information and assistance to make an intelligent choice of vocation.

Preparing for marriage and family life. As the school attempts to meet the other needs, it is also helping the teen-ager prepare for marriage and family life. Yet the school should also provide specific guidance and information directed toward this goal.

Developing intellectual skills and concepts necessary for civic competence. Society looks to the school to provide information and experiences that will enable young men and women to become competent citizens. Young people need to understand their local community and the nation, and they must learn the meaning of democracy and how it works. These things can best be learned through direct experiences and face-to-face relationships. The high school, assisted by civic clubs, adults, and local government leaders, can assist adolescents in their attempts to participate in community life.

Desiring and achieving socially responsible behavior. The adolescent must realize that society accepts and follows standards and guidelines for proper behavior in order that group life can continue.

He must learn to evaluate his course of action and to be responsible for his own conduct. The school can and should help in this area.

Acquiring a set of values and an ethical system as a guide to behavior. During adolescence many young people become intensely religious. Most adolescents are searching for a set of values that will give life meaning. Oftentimes they are critical of the inconsistencies in the creeds and actions of adults, and sometimes this leads to rebellion and disgust.

Joint effort of the home, religious institutions, and school is needed. As students deal with literature, science, history, current events, and a study of society itself, the school can emphasize moral and spiritual values without resorting to the teaching of sectarian religion.

Selected references

ALEXANDER, WILLIAM M. AND J. GALEN SAYLOR. *Modern Secondary Education.* New York: Holt, Rinehart & Winston, Inc., 1959.

ANDERSON, VERNON E. AND WILLIAM T. GRUHN. *Principles and Practices of Secondary Education.* New York: The Ronald Press Company, 1962.

BILLETT, ROY O. AND J. W. YEO. *Growing Up,* 2nd ed. Boston: Heath & Company, 1958.

COLE, L. *Psychology of Adolescence,* 5th ed. New York: Holt, Rinehart & Winston, Inc., 1959.

CONANT, JAMES B. *Slums and Suburbs.* New York: McGraw-Hill Book Company, Inc., 1961.

DOUGLASS, HARL R. *Secondary Education in the United States,* 2nd ed. New York: The Ronald Press Company, 1964.

Freeing Capacity to Learn. Association for Supervision and Curriculum Development. Washington, D.C.: National Education Association, 1960.

GARRISON, KARL C. *Psychology of Adolescence,* 5th ed. Englewood Cliffs, N.J.: Prentice-Hall, Inc., 1956.

GESELL, ARNOLD, FRANCES L. ILG, AND LOUISE BATES AMES. *Youth: The Years from Ten to Sixteen.* New York: Harper & Row, Publishers, Inc., 1956.

A study
of the secondary school curriculum

The secondary school curriculum

chapter **4**

The curriculum is the heart of the secondary school — its reason for existence. Philosophies of education may be written and goals may be listed, but it is the curriculum that determines what is really accomplished in a school. Schools cannot be successful unless they offer pertinent educational opportunities for students under the direction of competent, well-educated teachers. The most important concern of educators today is the provision of a meaningful, challenging, well-balanced curriculum involving appropriate selection of content, intelligent planning and organization, and effective teaching.

Schools are established to serve the needs of society and of the individual students. The curriculum is the means by which the school meets these needs.

In today's world a sound secondary school curriculum is more important than ever before. The schools must provide for students with great variations in abilities, interests, and objectives; they must afford opportunities in established areas of knowledge that have increased in complexity as well as in those that are new and different. Students must have a curriculum that will not only acquaint them with their cultural heritage and prepare them for a job or profession but also enable them as adults to solve the many problems that confront their nation and a world "grown small" by advances in communication and transportation.

It is not enough for the schools to do as good a job today as they did twenty or thirty years ago. The curriculum must not and cannot remain static. It must constantly change to meet new demands; yet, it must also retain the "essentials" and do an even better job in teaching those elements which are recognized as basic. This task is not a small one.

But just what is meant by "the curriculum"? The Latin word *curriculum* originally meant a race course. Through the years the word evolved to mean the subjects that were offered by the schools. The modern educator does not think of the curriculum in terms of subject matter alone; rather he conceives of it as also including activities, guidance, relationships between students and teachers and among students themselves, and opportunities for students to practice self-discipline. In fact, the modern educator thinks of subject matter not as a body of knowledge to be mastered for its own sake but as material that can help students grow and develop mentally; that can provide necessary experiences for youth in their quest for self-realization in the present and can enable them to acquire the experiences, skills, and competencies necessary for vocational success in the future. Educators recognize that subject matter has a key role to play in helping students grow toward good social adjustment; yet they realize that mastery of subject matter alone will not be sufficient. Students must have opportunities to learn to live and work with others; lessons in respect and responsibility cannot be learned from books alone.

While the modern definition of *curriculum* does not include all student experiences — conversations and disputes with other students in the halls or on the way to school, for example — it is broad enough to include such school-sponsored activities as guidance, student activities, physical education, and school services.

Major aspects of the secondary school curriculum

To understand the modern secondary school curriculum, one must study, classify, and describe the major areas and aspects of the curriculum. Before this can be done properly, it is important to arrive at a common understanding of terms which are generally used in discussing the secondary school curriculum:

Curriculum — All the experiences offered to students under the guidance and sponsorship of the school.

Course of study — A plan used by teachers in guiding and directing the learning experiences of students. It is a planned arrangement of materials and activities that are to be used by a teacher or teachers in a particular subject or field. It may be an individual teacher's plan or one designed by a school system, arranging activities and materials for a subject by topics, units, and, in some cases, day-by-day lesson plans.

Program of studies — A list of the subjects offered by a school, including all the courses of study. For example, science is a subject, and Biology I is a course of study within that subject; mathematics is a subject, and Algebra II is a course of study.

General education — Education deemed necessary because it meets needs common to all students. This includes English, mathematics, social studies, and science, which are required of all students. It should be noted, however, that not all courses in general education are constants, and many elective courses provide experiences that involve general education.

Constants (required courses) and variables (electives) — Constants are courses that are required of all students in a certain school or, in the case of schools which offer track programs, of all students in a particular group. Sometimes the constants offered by a school are referred to as common learnings or the general education curriculum. Variables, or electives, are courses that students may choose to take because of their special interests or needs.

Unit of credit — A standard for measuring various credits earned in high school. A unit of credit is awarded a student who attends a class that meets five days a week for an entire school year if he successfully fulfills the course requirements. Actually, the technical requirement for a unit's credit is successful completion of a course that meets 120 sixty-minute hours.

Core program — That part of the curriculum which is built around broad areas of learning that deal with personal and social competencies considered necessary for all students. Most core programs have thus far been organized around problem situations which are planned to teach these needed competencies. Core programs are usually given large blocks of time in the school schedule.

Unit of instruction — An area of subject matter that is organized around a central theme or point of view for the purpose of teaching and may or may not cut across subject-matter lines. More than one class period's work, it is usually planned for several weeks or a month. Units may also be classified as resource or teaching units. A resource unit is designed to be used as a resource for teachers. A teaching unit is planned by an individual teacher for use in his class; it may be an adaptation of a single resource unit or of materials and activities from several.

Integration of the curriculum — The practice of combining material from various subject areas. In an integrated course, subject-matter lines are disregarded; in most cases such a course is organized around major problems that are to be solved.

Correlation — The practice of relating two or more subjects to one another as they are being taught. The subjects are not combined — in fact, they may be taught by different teachers in separate classrooms — but a special effort is made to stress the significant relationships between them.

Fusion — Fusion, unlike correlation, involves combining two or more subjects into a single course. In some junior high schools, for example, science and health are taught as a fused course.

Curriculum planning — The continuous shaping of the curriculum to fit the needs, · interests, and desires of a heterogeneous student body. It is a process designed to make learning more efficient and teaching more effective. This term replaced two older ones, *curriculum construction* and *curriculum reorganization;* it is more appropriate since it does not imply either that there is no curriculum at present or that the existing one is in need of complete revision.

Learning experiences and learning activities — The opportunities provided by which students can learn; anything that students and teachers do to further the learning process. Included are such areas as problem solving, studying, experimenting, reading, discussions, writing, or taking field trips.

Schedule — The list of subjects and activities offered, the time they will be taught, and, in most cases, where they will be taught.

Scope and sequence of the curriculum — The scope of the curriculum means the breadth and inclusiveness of the experiences and activities offered. The sequence is the order in which classes or experiences will take place by grade levels and within the various levels themselves.

Broad-fields curriculum — The combining of single subjects into a larger area. For example: English, spelling, composition, and speech may be fused into an area called language arts; history, geography, economics, and government into social studies; and zoology, biology, and physiology into life sciences or biology.

Motives producing today's curriculum

The motives and factors that have operated through the years to determine the curriculum of the junior and senior high schools are easy to identify and are well documented.[1] Many of the motives that have operated to produce the secondary schools found in the United States today have been mentioned earlier in this book; it is important to examine them more thoroughly if one is to acquire a genuine understanding of the modern curriculum.

Religious motive (1635 – 1770).   The religious motive is accepted as the most important influence on secondary education in this country from 1635 to 1770. It was responsible for the system of Latin grammar schools established at an early date in New England and other colonies and for the systems of parochial schools established in the Middle Colonies. It also played a fairly important role in the South. While other motives, such as the economic and political, were in operation, the religious motive was the most compelling.

Cubberley identifies three types of education in colonial America, each the result of the religious motive: (1) the church-state type, found in Puritan New England; (2) the parochial type, found in the Middle Colonies; and (3) the philanthropic or charity type, found in the South.[2] He indicates that these types were determined by the various cultures transplanted to the New World by the colonists and by their religious backgrounds. These secondary schools reflected the traditions of Europe, and, to a great extent, were class schools for boys only. Their major purpose was to provide an education for ministers and other community leaders who would carry on the faith and doctrines of the religious groups that sponsored them.

Political motive (1770 – 1860). The religious motive continued to operate between 1770 and 1860, but it was no longer dominant. After the United States had won its independence, the trade and commerce that had developed before the Revolution began to flourish on a grand scale. There were demands for a practical type of education and a reaction against many of the European influences.

The founding fathers, though they intentionally or unintentionally neglected to mention education in the Constitution, realized that it was necessary if the new nation were to survive. They spoke

---

[1]Two of the most recent books which discuss these motives are J. Minor Gwynn's *Curriculum Principles and Social Trends* and *The American Secondary School* by Taylor and others. See the suggested references at the end of this chapter for complete bibliographical data.

[2]Ellwood P. Cubberley, *Public Education in the United States*, rev. ed. (Boston: Houghton Mifflin Company, 1934), Chapter 2.

on its behalf; they set aside land for education; they established schools in their various states. These early leaders stressed education for the preservation of liberty and the new government, as many of the earlier colonists had emphasized it for the perpetuation of their religions. The political motive was encouraged by the development of two other powerful influences: (1) the belief in the equality of all citizens with the demand for equal rights for all, and (2) the spirit of "rugged individualism," strengthened by the system of free enterprise, the frontier, and the rise of the common man in the Jacksonian Era.

Restrictions on the right of white men to vote were abolished, and a great wave of humanitarianism swept the nation during the first half of the nineteenth century resulting in, among other things, a demand for free public education. The United States was looked upon as the "land of opportunity," and that opportunity was thought to include the right to obtain an education.

During this period secondary schools became concerned with the education of girls. Some academies began to admit girls as well as boys, and separate female academies were established. The 1820's saw the establishment of the first coeducational public high schools.

Despite the fact that education was a responsibility and privilege of the state and local area, it was influenced by the spirit of nationalism. Millions of immigrants were coming to this country; the schools were looked upon as agencies which could prepare their children for American citizenship. Many citizens felt that the schools were serving as a bulwark of democracy. (The many problems of government faced today by some of the newer, undeveloped countries illustrate the validity of this early belief in education as the foundation of democracy.)

Utilitarian motive (1860–1890). Although the secondary curriculum was certainly very restrictive and enrollments relatively small, it can be argued that the utilitarian motive was dominant in the rise of the free public high school. For many years after the establishment of the high school, the academy remained the traditional college-preparatory institution, and only when the academy declined did the high schools begin to emphasize college preparation.

During the first half of the nineteenth century the high school curriculum was designed to continue the general education of the elementary schools, the main purpose of which was to prepare students for life. To this end scientific courses, modern foreign languages, and laboratory courses in science were introduced on a wide scale between 1860 and 1890. Courses in manual training and home economics were introduced and developed. Table 3 lists the subjects offered in secondary schools in the 1890's.

From 1890 to 1920, as will be shown later, college preparation overshadowed life preparation as the main purpose of the secondary school curriculum. However, in the last two decades the latter motive has regained much of its original position.

Looking back on the development of the American school curriculum from 1860 to 1890, the utilitarian motive is found to be predominant in American secondary education, and one can see that it is also a leading motive up to the present time. Ample evidence of this is found in (1) the establishment of the high school at public expense, with emphasis upon its function of preparation for life as well as preparation for college; (2) federal grants to the several states for vocational education on both collegiate and secondary levels; (3) the establishment of specialized schools, such as commercial and technical high schools, to prepare boys and girls for life; and (4) the emphasis upon economy of time in education, pointing toward training youth effectively for life work in a shorter period of time.[3]

College-preparatory motive (1890–1920). From 1890 to 1920 the traditional high school was primarily a college-preparatory institution. There were some subjects offered in high schools, especially the larger ones, that were not college preparatory; but most of the courses offered were academic and were taught to students with college entrance as the primary objective. Almost every major committee concerned with education from 1890 to 1918 devoted most of its work to streamlining the high school curriculum for college preparation.

The curriculum was designed primarily for students of above-average ability and the gifted. As late as 1900 only about 10 per cent of all adolescents were in school, and the fact that most of the courses were strictly academic is considered one of the major reasons keeping many out of the secondary school. Studies by the American Youth Commission and the Board of Regents of the State of New York showed that as late as 1938 this was still a major reason for students' either dropping out of the secondary schools or failing to enter.

[3]J. Minor Gwynn, *Curriculum Principles and Social Trends*, 3rd ed. (New York: The Macmillan Company, 1960), p. 34.

table **3**   **Subjects of Study in Public High Schools, 1891**

1. English, including both literature and composition and the elements of Rhetoric	14. Physical geography
	15. Geology
	16. Botany
	17. Zoology
2. History (Ancient, Medieval, and Modern)	18. Physiology
	19. Physics
3. Civil government	20. Chemistry
4. French	21. Astronomy
5. German	22. Psychology
6. Latin	23. Moral philosophy
7. Greek	24. International law
8. Arithmetic	25. Political economy
9. Algebra	26. Science of education
10. Plane geometry	27. Music
11. Solid geometry	28. Drawing
12. Trigonometry	29. Stenography
13. Analytic geometry	30. Bookkeeping

Source: Adapted from C. W. Eliot's "Undesirable and Desirable Uniformity in Schools," *Addresses and proceedings of the National Education Association* (October, 1892), p. 93.

Mass-education motive (1920–1960's). By the 1920's all states had passed compulsory attendance laws resulting in a very heterogeneous student body. It was evident to educators and public alike that the old curriculum was not appropriate for all students and would have to undergo great modifications. There was a growing determination to make a secondary education meaningful to all, not simply by providing a free institution, but also by offering real opportunities from which all students could profit.

Perhaps the greatest breakthrough came in 1918 when the Commission on the Reorganization of Secondary Education published the *Cardinal Principles of Secondary Education* (see page 28). This report served to remind educators that the public secondary schools existed to prepare students for life and that a curriculum must be offered from which all students—and, in turn, society—could profit.

The mass-education motive has done much to produce the present system of secondary schools based on the awareness that all adolescents must be educated; that the school must do more than *keep* young people; and that a program involving academic, commercial, trade, and technical subjects as well as general education must be provided.[4]

Equality thus came to mean for . . . Americans not only political equality but also equality of opportunity. . . .

The percentage of youth attending a college or university has jumped from 4 to 35 [Conant is here referring to the changes in the first half of the twentieth century], and, at the same time, the percentage enrolled in grades eleven to twelve of the high school has about doubled. In 1910 only 35 per cent of the seventeen-year-olds were in school; today, the corresponding figure is over 70 per cent. These changes could easily have been predicted in 1900 by a student of American education. He would have seen how enormous was the power of the twin ideals of equality of opportunity and equality of status; it was evident that the American people had come to believe that education provided the means by which these ideals were to be realized. . . .

With few exceptions, for the most part in large eastern cities, the public high school is expected to provide education for all the youth living in a town, city, or district. Such a high school has become known as a "comprehensive" high school in contrast to the "specialized" high schools which provide vocational education or which admit on a selective basis and offer only an academic curriculum.[5]

The American secondary school is intended to provide education for all—to offer a course of study for every adolescent capable of profiting from instruction. There are those in this country who do not approve of these ideals, who would make secondary education more selective along European lines. The great majority of United States citizens, however, want a public secondary school open to all.[6]

The desire of the American people to provide for mass education has been the most important influence in American secondary education since 1920. It has led to the establishment of thousands of high schools, the reorganization of other thousands, changes in the curriculum, and the development of many student activities. In addition, the mass-education motive has promoted the rapid rise of the public junior college and the community college.

[4]Franklin J. Keller, *The Comprehensive High School* (New York: Harper & Row, Publishers, Inc., 1955), pp. 31–32.
[5]James B. Conant, *The American High School Today* (New York: McGraw-Hill Book Company, Inc., 1959), pp. 5–8.
[6]*Ibid.*, p. 8.

Other factors determining today's curriculum

The factors discussed above are the controlling motives that influenced secondary school curriculums at various periods in the history of this country. We should not, however, lose sight of the other factors that have operated to modify the curriculum.

Tradition.   Tradition is a great force in almost any institution; the American secondary school is no exception. There is a great similarity between the present-day high school curriculum and that of thirty, forty, and even fifty years ago. Once a course or activity gets into the curriculum, it tends to remain. Many elements in such secondary school courses as English literature, Latin, algebra, geometry, and grammar are in the curriculum, not because they have important values for young people, but because they have "always" been a part of the curriculum.

Tradition often gives to certain courses values which are not deserved. The best safeguard against this is to evaluate constantly the curriculum of the individual secondary school, determining the goals of each course and what it has to offer students today.

College-entrance requirements.   It will be recalled that the early secondary schools, both in this country and in Europe, were established primarily to prepare individuals for college. During the first forty years of the present century, the curriculums of many secondary schools consisted primarily of subjects that were considered college preparatory despite the fact that a large percentage of the students were not going to college.

Since the 1940's, and in some cases earlier, the larger high schools have developed curriculums with broad offerings, but college-entrance requirements continue to dictate most of the elective courses for students who plan to go on to college. In small schools arrangements must first be made for the college-preparatory courses and teachers hired to teach them; then the school adds courses in commercial subjects, industrial arts, and other areas as best it can.

Very often subjects that are considered college-entrance requirements are retained because of tradition. For example, some colleges state in their requirements for admission that a student must have three units of mathematics to be prepared properly for college; yet these same colleges will graduate students who have not taken a single course in mathematics.

Pressure from individuals and groups.   Many pressure groups and individual laymen influence the secondary school curriculum, some concerned with religious teachings or Bible study, Americanization or patriotism, the evil effects of alcohol and tobacco, or other "causes." Many individuals feel that certain subjects they studied in school, or the methods used in teaching these subjects, should still be stressed in secondary schools. Although these individuals should be allowed to make their wishes known, educators generally feel the curriculum should not be reorganized constantly on the basis of all the pressures brought to bear upon school administrators. For example, great pressure has been exerted recently on secondary schools to place more emphasis on the teaching of science, mathematics, and foreign languages. Many educators agree with the laymen who are concerned with the defense of the nation and with a technological society, and they feel that these subjects should be emphasized in the curriculum if the schools are really to prepare young people for life. At the same time others are very much concerned that proper emphasis be given to the language arts and the social studies.

Secondary school administrators should welcome suggestions and respect the wishes of individuals and groups; however, they should not forget that some of those who bring pressure to bear are seeking to protect vested interests and attempting to use the schools to gain their own ends rather than to further the welfare of the students and society. Some groups do not view the curriculum objectively as a whole, and they must not be allowed to handicap the schools' efforts to provide the best opportunities for all students.

Activities of the federal government. Since 1917 the federal government has influenced the secondary school curriculum by providing special grants for vocational education programs and more recently by providing special funds for the education of teachers of mathematics, science, and foreign languages. It has also made available to schools special free or inexpensive materials through the United States Office of Education. This federal department has helped shape the secondary school curriculum by making the results of its own research and that of others available to the schools and by providing consultant help to those who seek it. Public schools which serve the children of military personnel and of persons engaged in defense projects have been able to provide better curriculums than they otherwise could have in their impacted situations because they receive special funds.

Requirements of state authorities. Various state authorities, such as departments of education, school boards, and legislatures, frequently establish curriculum requirements for the schools under their jurisdiction. In most cases these have been kept to a minimum and have not worked hardships or harm on the schools. In fact, such requirements are sometimes absolutely necessary to ensure even a low standard or level of curriculum offerings, particularly in small schools.

A 1958 study of large and small high schools in one state indicated that while the larger high schools were going far beyond state regulations in their programs, many of the smaller ones failed to meet the state requirements in some basic areas; and even when the latter met the requirements, the quality of instruction frequently left much to be desired.[7] It was evident that if it were not for the state requirements, conditions in some of these schools would have been much worse.

There is always the possibility, of course, that a state can put too many regulations in its constitution or that its legislature will list too many minute requirements and practices. The states should be concerned with broad policies and adequate financing of schools. They should prescribe minimum standards, then leave curriculum planning of the local schools to the local people and educators.

Regional accrediting associations. The regional accrediting associations of this country were at first more concerned with quantitative than qualitative factors. This was due to practical considerations rather than to a lack of concern for quality. Today these associations are also interested in the conditions affecting the quality of a school's educational program, and they are very much concerned that good schools develop into better schools.

Regional associations have been accused of working along with college-entrance requirements to keep a strangle hold on secondary school curriculum, but the evidence does not support this point of view. These groups have set requirements, but they have also been leaders in encouraging experimentation. No doubt certain schools have felt at times that they were being limited in some way by their regional associations; yet the associations have made important contributions to American secondary education.

Educational theories. Educational theories have had an important influence on the secondary school curriculum. Until the early part of the present century the theory of mental discipline and the

---

[7]Elwood Dale Davis, "A Study of Objective Differences Existing in Selected Small and Large Union Schools in North Carolina" (unpublished University of North Carolina doctoral dissertation, 1958).

transfer of training controlled the thinking and practices of most secondary school educators. They felt that, to be worth-while, learning should be difficult and, in many cases, unpleasant. They believed that the mind was made of separate "faculties" — such as memory, judgment, and reason — which could be trained by mastering difficult subject matter. It was believed that the mental training students received in studying classical languages, mathematics, and modern foreign languages could be "transferred" to other learning situations. No attempt was made to make the subjects interesting; indeed, it was felt that this might lessen their disciplinary value.

Psychologists have since subjected these theories to objective and critical observation and proved them false. There is such a thing as transfer of training, but it is the result of identifying similar elements and applying generalizations rather than discipline of mental faculties. Today educators think of learning as the modification of behavior and know that it involves the entire nervous system. Interest and motivation are considered to be of supreme importance for effective learning, and much attention is also directed to recognition of individual differences. All of these elements influence what a secondary school decides to teach and how it is taught.

Major areas in today's curriculum

A program of studies was defined earlier as a complete listing of the subjects or classes offered by an individual school. Many of these courses are required for graduation; others may be elected by the students. The program of studies is the most important part of the secondary school curriculum. It consists of two major areas — general and specialized education.

Since over 90 per cent of the adolescents in this country today are in some type of secondary school, the student body is very heterogeneous. These adolescents must be in school, according to the law, until they are sixteen — or, in some states, eighteen — years of age. Although they have many different individual needs, they all have certain common needs which usually are included in an area called the *need for socialization*. This broad term includes mastery of general mathematics; ability to speak, write, and read in a correct and efficient manner; ability to work and cooperate with others; acceptance of the values held by society; and loyalty to state and nation. The content of courses designed to meet these common needs is called *general education*.

These courses are planned to help students develop an understanding and appreciation of their cultural heritage and skill in such fundamental areas as English usage, basic mathematics, and reading. Most general education subjects, such as general science, English, general mathematics, social studies, and various broad fields and core programs, are usually required of all students. Special consideration is given to these areas in the next chapter.

By *specialized areas* are meant primarily the vocational programs and the college-preparatory programs which high school students may elect in addition to their general education courses. These specialized areas sometimes overlap with general education, but their major purpose is to provide for study in areas of special interest.

The advanced courses in academic subjects, such as advanced English and composition, geometry, chemistry, and physics, must be elected by students who plan to go to college. Those who are not planning further formal learning are required to have some of these courses for graduation, and they may elect more if they desire; however, they usually take most of their electives in commercial, trade, or other vocational courses. The most important subjects in the vocational areas are agriculture, home economics, business education, and industrial arts.

Constants, or required courses, demand over half of a student's time in most high schools. To illustrate, the required courses for all students in the secondary schools of Texas, which are typical of those found throughout the nation, are listed in Table 4. Individual schools within a state often add requirements of their own.

The unit system of determining requirements for high school graduation and college entrance was developed early in this cen-

table **4**   **Graduation Requirements in Texas Public Schools, 1963**

All pupils who enter the ninth grade must complete at least 16 units plus two units of health and physical education. This must include the following:

    English (3 units) (many schools require 4 units)
    World History (1 unit)
    American History (1 unit)
    Science (2 units)
    Mathematics (2 units)
    Government (1/2 unit)

---

tury by the Carnegie Foundation for the Advancement of Teaching. It has persisted and has brought about some uniformity — some educators would say too much uniformity — in the accounting system of secondary schools. Many schools are now using "hours" as the basic unit of their accounting system.[8]

Even though most high schools prescribe courses that occupy only about one half of a student's time, it should not be assumed that he is free to elect all of his other units. He often is required to "elect" courses which are specified for the particular track or curriculum that he is pursuing.

Junior high school curriculum

Most of the material presented above applies to the three- or four-year high school. The curriculum of the junior high school, which is usually the first stage of secondary education, is made up primarily of required general education courses. In most cases no electives are permitted in the seventh grade and only one in the eighth grade. Many junior high schools do not allow any electives until the ninth grade and then only one or two. The ninth grade is hard to separate from the senior high school and is, of course, a part of those four-year high schools that have not been reorganized into junior and senior high school patterns. Many three-year high schools include ninth grade courses in their requirements for graduation.

There is wide variation in the organization and curriculums of junior high schools throughout the country. The most common form of organization includes grades seven through nine; other forms consist of grades seven and eight only or grades seven through ten. In some of these schools the curriculum is very similar to that found in the seventh and eighth grades of the unreorganized elementary school (a school which still has eight grades); in others there is a system of departmentalization almost identical with that of senior high school.

The junior high school curriculum at its best will provide educational opportunities that are not offered in the traditional elementary or high school. Its purposes are different from those of the senior high school, though, of course, there are common elements. Both the junior and senior high school curriculums provide experiences in general education; however, the junior high is mainly concerned with general education and with offering the student an

---

[8]William M. Alexander and J. Galen Saylor, *Modern Secondary Education* (New York: Holt, Rinehart & Winston, Inc., 1959), p. 320.

opportunity to explore a number of areas; it is less involved with specialization than is the senior high.

Guidance should receive much emphasis at this level. The student is moving away from elementary school experiences; he must soon elect an area of specialization and therefore should have opportunities to become acquainted with the various areas of knowledge such as mathematics, science, social studies, practical arts, and music. The adolescent also needs guidance in understanding and adjusting to the physical and psychological changes that are taking place within him.

Most of the core programs and those involving large blocks of time are found in the junior high school. Educators believe that a student at this educational level needs the opportunity to develop a close relationship with at least one teacher. They feel that if a student spends enough time in a core program or in a general education class such as social studies, he will feel increasingly free to converse with and confide in his teacher, and that this faculty member can come to know the student well enough to advise him in light of his abilities and interests. More information on core programs is given in the next chapter.

The fact that many junior high schools allocate an extended period of time each day for a general education program involving guidance opportunities on the part of a teacher does not mean that guidance specialists are not used. They are used and they work very closely with the teachers, but in good guidance programs the teacher plays the key role. Junior high school teachers need special professional preparation that will help them provide incidental guidance and counseling; teachers thus trained can be much more effective in helping the student make the transition from the non-departmentalized elementary school to the senior high school—one of the major justifications for the existence of junior high schools.

The junior college curriculum

As has been mentioned, in some school systems the offerings of junior or community colleges are considered a part of secondary education. The major functions of such a school are considered to be guidance, terminal education, preparatory work for senior college, and the popularization of higher education by making it available locally to more high school graduates.

Junior college curriculums include general education, courses leading to a college degree, professional courses leading to more advanced specialization, and courses that will equip individuals to go immediately into vocational work.

Student activities

The modern curriculum is considered to be composed of all the experiences and activities offered to students under the guidance and supervision of the school. This, of course, emphasizes the fact that the activities which were once called extracurricular are not "extra" at all but a vital part of the school curriculum. Student publications, bands, social affairs, special clubs, and athletics are today called student activities and are recognized for the valuable contributions they make toward the education of adolescents. Many that were once only "extracurricular" are now a part of the regular curriculum and carry units of credit. The many activities sponsored by the secondary school and something of their history and governing principles are treated in a later chapter.

Community resources

To make many of the experiences offered in the secondary school more vivid and realistic, to provide many learning experiences that cannot take place in the school itself, and to enrich the curriculum in general, the modern secondary school utilizes community resources such as factories, businesses, newspapers, radio and television studios, points of historical interest, farms and dairies, units of civic government, and individuals who have special skills or have had unique experiences. The use of community resources by junior and senior high schools involves special planning and preparation on the part of students and teachers, but it can result in many effective learning experiences.

Types of curriculum organization

An attempt to identify and explain very briefly some of the major types of curriculum organization will be made here, although classifying curriculums into types has many limitations and is, at best, an arbitrary approach. For example, some curriculums that are classified as separate-subject organizations involve many elements, such as experiments and field trips, which would be considered a vital part of core programs. The teacher determines, to a great extent, what the curriculum will be as he uses textbooks, reference books, and various types of experiences and activities in his course. It is also true that no learning takes place in any subject unless the student really "experiences" the various elements.

Separate-subject organization

The separate organization of the various subjects is by far the most widely used form of curriculum organization. Even though the junior high schools have experimented with a wider variety of programs than have the senior high schools, they still adhere mainly to the separate-course organization. In this method of curriculum organization, subjects are taught as separate entities. Students take four or five subjects, each usually taught by a different teacher in the larger high schools; in the smaller schools the same teacher will often teach several subjects. Often no attempt is made to relate special subject fields to any other subject or fields of knowledge.

Most authorities feel the separate-subject approach is necessary because the different fields of knowledge have become so large and complex that teachers must specialize in their academic preparation and on the job if they are to be really competent in their chosen areas. There is much to be said for this point of view since the vast accumulation of knowledge and the rapid rate of change in many fields make it impossible for most teachers to be qualified to do an excellent job in several areas.

The separate-subject type of organization can have a serious fault, however, if an individual teacher's methods stress memorization of facts and definitions with little attention to understanding of basic principles, analysis, and problem solving. Important relationships among areas of knowledge are often ignored. Many educators feel that the separate-subject organization too often makes superficial mastery of the subject matter an end in itself rather than a means to an end — the growth and development of the student. Critics insist that this form of organization does not follow the proven laws of learning and that it ignores many of the ideas of sound psychology. They claim, for example, that it fails to consider the principle of readiness and the fact that students must relate new information to that already known, which results in passive learning — learning that is not really meaningful and does not become a lasting experience for the student. Critics also emphasize that the subject-matter approach fails to establish goals that are accepted by the student as being worthy of his best efforts.

Advocates of the separate-subject type of organization dismiss these arguments by pointing out that prospective teachers are required to pursue a varied college curriculum which provides for majors and minors plus other courses in the liberal arts. This, they contend, should enable the teacher of a special subject to be aware of relationships among his specialized area and related fields. They also maintain that under this form of curriculum organization a teacher can clearly distinguish his areas of responsibility and can concentrate on doing a good job in these areas, whereas unless the separate-subject approach is followed, many fundamental elements will not be taught to students, and they will be handicapped in further education and in life. Teachers who advocate the separate-subject curriculum believe there is another strong argument in its favor — that it gives a logically sound basis for learning and teaching, thus helping avoid confusion and overlapping of subject matter.

Regardless of the position taken on the separate-subject-matter approach, one must accept the fact that this method of curriculum organization has existed for a long time and is going to be around for many years to come. It is the most common type of organization, and the continued increase in human knowledge may make it increasingly necessary. This being the case, American educators must evaluate what they are doing in the secondary schools and find ways to overcome the weaknesses of this form of curriculum organization.

Correlated, fused, and broad-fields curriculums

The major weakness attributed to the separate-subject curriculum — that it fails to show important relationships among different subjects and between subject matter and life — has led to efforts and experiments aimed at avoiding such a situation.

In the first attempts, known as correlation of subjects, educators endeavored to articulate the major relationships existing among two or more subjects and still maintain the separate-subject divisions. The idea was to stress the natural relationships of the one subject with another. Most popular subjects for such experiments were history and literature, science and mathematics, and history and geography. While this approach usually involved some joint planning by teachers, they continued to teach their separate subjects.

Later attempts at correlation went further and fused two or more courses, thus breaking down traditional subject divisions and actually combining the material of two or more subjects into one course. For example, instead of trying to interrelate botany and zoology or history and geography while being taught by separate teachers in separate classrooms, those who favored fusion would combine botany and zoology into biology and history and geography into social studies.

Today one can realize how important the experiments in fusion have been by looking at many secondary school curriculums. Courses such as English, biology, civics, and social studies are composed of areas that were once taught as separate subjects.[9]

[9]Nelson L. Bossing, *Principles of Secondary Education,* 2nd ed. (Englewood Cliffs, N.J.: Prentice-Hall, Inc., 1955), p. 374.

When fusion is given an even broader subject-matter base, by combining two or more subjects, it results in what is known as a broad-fields organization of the curriculum. For example, a school science department may organize beginning science courses such as zoology, botany, biology, and physiology into one course called life science; and chemistry, physics, astronomy, geology, and physical geography into a single course entitled natural sciences.[10]

It can be readily noted that correlation, fusion, and the broad-fields approach are all based on categories of knowledge and skills and are still primarily concerned with subject matter. In fact, they are usually thought of as separate-subject areas once they are admitted to the curriculum.[11]

Unit method

In order to increase interest and promote transfer of training and experience, many secondary schools use the unit method of curriculum organization. (The unit method can also be applied within any of the other types of curriculum organization.) Units are conceived of as broad and significant aspects of the curriculum, organized about a center of interest, a point of view, or a central theme.

After selecting a central theme for a unit, the teacher establishes objectives to be accomplished by him and by the students. A unit consists of the following parts: a topic, a brief introduction or overview, a statement of objectives, an outline of materials and activities, a list of resources and references, and a section dealing with evaluation. All materials and activities should result in the students' and teacher's reaching their goals—factual knowledge, desirable habits, skills, attitudes, and appreciations.

English and social studies in some junior high schools are organized around units. These schools furnish their teachers with resource units that have been planned by curriculum experts and groups of experienced teachers. Using this material and any other sources they feel are appropriate, the teachers then design teaching units for their classes. Teachers who are most effective in using this approach recommend that the selection of units be based on the student's interest, elements that are and will be a part of the student's life, and areas that involve subject matter from many different fields.

[10]*Ibid.,* p. 375.
[11]Edward A. Krug, *The Secondary School Curriculum* (New York: Harper & Row, Publishers, Inc., 1960), p. 202.

Many senior high school teachers also employ the unit method in both general and specialized courses. Here, again, many school systems furnish their teachers with resource units and urge them to develop their own teaching units. Generally, the school officials encouraging this approach believe that by so doing they can avoid many of the weaknesses found in the separate-subject curriculum.

Core programs

Core programs — often referred to as "core classes," "common learnings," "general education," and "basic learnings" — are based on large problems, activities, and common needs and experiences, not on subject matter as such. This does not mean that those who advocate core programs disregard subject matter and fundamental skills; instead they recommend classes that are organized around problems to be solved or activities considered basic to all students. Most of the core programs that have been developed thus far involve only a part of the school day.[12]

Organizing core programs often presents many problems for the school. They must be carefully planned and introduced if the school is to avoid serious mistakes and many criticisms. It is sometimes very difficult for the general public and even teachers themselves to grasp the philosophy behind core programs and even harder for many to make the core class an effective vehicle of that philosophy. There is always the fear of the new and different as opposed to the known and the traditional; many people, both teachers and the lay public, dislike change, especially in the area of education. In fact, since most teachers have not received training and preparation for core classes, they sometimes become bitter opponents of core programs.

Challenges in the area of curriculum

Educators in the American secondary school are now faced with several crucial challenges, the most important being that of providing a curriculum appropriate for all educable youth. Schools are charged with the responsibility of preparing young people for effective participation in society as well as helping each student develop his individual interests and abilities to the maximum. Providing a curriculum that will achieve these two major goals is a task of great magnitude.

Another important challenge is that of maintaining a proper balance between general and specialized education. In other words,

[12]*Ibid.*, p. 221.

how can American secondary education, within a unified program, provide education for individual diversity and social unity?

The relative emphasis given to various subjects within the curriculum — always a matter of concern — is becoming increasingly important. In recent years such hard-core subjects as mathematics and science have been getting the most attention, but many educators are making strong pleas for more work on foreign languages. Others fear that the social studies and English will be neglected. To further complicate the picture, many educators and laymen are demanding more opportunities for students to develop "marketable skills" when they do not plan to continue their education. Balance in the curriculum can be achieved only by providing the individual student with the program from which he can profit most in light of his ability, special interests, and present situation.

Providing a flexible curriculum is a third major challenge. The student must not be prematurely committed to a program which precludes change. Since students do change their plans, the school must offer a course of study that meets their changing needs.

Inherent in this third challenge is a fourth one — providing sufficient variety in the curriculum. In recent decades the number of secondary school subjects has increased considerably; however, there is evidence that the program of studies in many schools is still provided for only a particular portion of the students.[13]

A final challenge is that of providing quality in secondary education. This fifth challenge can certainly not be separated from the four already mentioned. Perhaps the most serious weakness in the curriculums of many schools is the quality of the programs. Just as the American people in the past were pressed with the problem of making education available to all, they must now apply themselves to the task of making it challenging and suitable to all. This is being accomplished through improved teacher-education programs, ability grouping, increased emphasis on independent study, new teaching materials and devices, and new teaching methods. Yet increasing enrollments, expanding fields of knowledge, and a more complex society require continued improvement.

Selected references

ALCORN, MARVIN D. AND JAMES M. LINLEY, EDS. *Issues in Curriculum Development.* New York: Harcourt, Brace & World, Inc., 1959. Chapter 1.

[13]Lindley J. Stiles and others, *Secondary Education in the United States* (New York: Harcourt, Brace & World, Inc., 1962), p. 224.

BEREDAY, GEORGE Z. F. AND JOSEPH A. LAUWERYS, EDS. *The Secondary School Curriculum.* The Yearbook of Education, 1958. London: Evans Brothers Ltd., 1958.

CONANT, JAMES B. *The American High School Today.* New York: McGraw-Hill Book Company, Inc., 1959.

Deciding What to Teach. Project on Instruction, National Education Association. Washington, D.C.: NEA, 1963. All chapters of this publication.

GWYNN, J. MINOR. *Curriculum Principles and Social Trends,* 3rd ed., New York: The Macmillan Company, 1960.

KRUG, EDWARD A. *The Secondary School Curriculum.* New York: Harper & Row, Publishers, Inc., 1960.

Schools for the Sixties. Project on Instruction, National Education Association. New York: McGraw-Hill Book Company, Inc., 1963. Chapters 1–4.

TAYLOR, L. O., DON R. MCMAHILL, AND BOB L. TAYLOR. *The American Secondary School.* New York: Appleton-Century-Crofts, 1960. Chapter 6.

VENABLE, TOM C. *Patterns in Secondary School Curriculum.* New York: Harper & Row, Publishers, Inc., 1958. Part 1.

What Shall the High Schools Teach? 1956 Yearbook. Association for Supervision and Curriculum Development, National Education Association. Washington, D.C.: NEA, 1956. Chapter 3.

General education
in the secondary school program

chapter **5**

The American secondary school is a unique institution. It has the responsibility of educating all of the children of all of the people. This would be a challenge of great magnitude in a simple society; it is almost staggering in our present society. Some students are academically gifted, while others are slow learners. Many come from homes that are stable, cultured, and vitally interested in education; some come from homes that provide little security, encouragement, and motivation for learning. Yet the American secondary school must accept all of these students and give them an opportunity to develop the abilities and talents they possess.

The secondary school's responsibility does not stop there. It must take these individuals and equip them with the skills necessary for effective citizenship in a democratic society; it must help all students develop an appreciation for their heritage as free Americans and an understanding of and love for the American way of life. In other words, while individuals differ, they also have common needs which must be met — for the sake of both the individual and society.

If the secondary school is to meet students' needs and accomplish its own purposes, educators must possess certain convictions:

1. All individuals must be respected and accepted.

2. Every individual must be taught in such a way that he can develop to the height of his ability.

3. The individual's total personality is involved in learning.

4. Individuals must have experiences in school that will enable them to grow in self-discipline and self-direction.

5. Individuals are best prepared for their roles by teaching them, as adolescents, to have effective relationships with their peers and adults and to work toward meaningful goals in and out of school.

These convictions, however, will result in very little that is worthwhile unless they lead to certain provisions in the school curriculum:

1. Provision for individual differences—the school must take the student at his present stage of development and do what it can for him as an individual. This means an intelligent program of guidance, grouping by ability and interest, and some heterogeneous grouping.

2. Provision of a variety of methods and materials—these must be suitable for the slow, the average, and the superior student.

3. Provision for students to work in a problem-solving, learning situation using a laboratory approach—this means that the student must be concerned with the "why" as well as the "what" in learning and that both students and teachers must establish intelligent and meaningful goals toward which to work.

4. Provision for students to participate—this includes allowing them to help make decisions concerning goals to be achieved, areas to be studied, problems to be solved, and activities in which to engage.

5. Provision for all students to make a contribution—they must learn to speak, to write, to question, and to discuss in order that they will be able to establish and maintain effective relationships in the school and later in adult life.

Outcomes sought in general education

If secondary level educators possess the convictions and make the provisions mentioned above, a general education program capable of producing self-sufficient adults can be achieved. What are some of these desirable outcomes?

1. The ability to read, speak, write, and understand one's native language effectively.

2. Basic computational skills needed for successful participation in society.

3. Basic understanding of one's government and effective citizenship.

4. The ability to identify problems and, through intelligent application of the problem-solving method and past learning, to produce an intelligent solution or course of action.

5. The ability to understand the environment and man's relationship to it through one's experiences in science and social studies.

6. The ability to use one's leisure time wisely.

7. The ability to develop and maintain good health and physical fitness.

8. The ability to perform effectively on a job or in a profession.

Granted that these outcomes are not only desirable but also necessary for all, what materials can be used to help achieve such objectives? Granted that teachers must plan with students, must recognize individual differences and adapt instruction to individuals, and must use a problem-solving approach, what subject areas can and must be used?

The most important subject areas in general education are English, social studies, mathematics, science, health and physical education, homemaking, industrial arts, fine arts, and music. While some schools stress subject matter per se in their general education programs, many other schools feel that it should be used as a means toward desirable ends. In many general education classes and core programs, subject matter is used only as it contributes to the solution of broad problems that have been identified by the teacher and the class. Some schools make a study of the needs of youth and then, either through a problem-solving approach or a flexible approach within the separate subjects, attempt to meet these needs. Even in schools which have made no formal attempts to identify the needs of youth, many teachers are aware that these needs exist. It is often true, however, that teaching in general education programs does not provide many of the meaningful, lifelike learning situations.

Approaches used to provide general education

Schools use various approaches to provide the learning opportunities considered necessary for all students. Several of the more important methods are discussed below.

Required subjects

The most popular method is the policy of requiring students to take a certain number and type of courses. Students in grades seven and eight are usually required to take a fixed program in

English, social studies, science, mathematics, health, and music. They may be allowed one elective, such as band, orchestra, art, speech, industrial arts, or homemaking. Ninth-graders can often elect two courses, and as students progress through the grades, they may elect more subjects because fewer courses are required. In most cases, by the time the student has reached his senior year, he needs to take only one required subject. The methods used and the nature of these subjects vary, but such courses are taken from the curriculum areas previously listed.

Multiple program of studies

Secondary schools have developed different programs of studies, often referred to as tracks, such as college preparatory, commercial, industrial, and general. Students in such programs are required to take general education courses and certain other subjects considered necessary for graduation in a particular program. The purpose of this plan is not only to provide experiences in general education courses but also to provide for common needs and interests of large portions of the student body. To supplement the special tracks, schools offer additional elective courses, such as consumer education, family living, typing, and driver education.

Student activities

Because many educators feel that no one subject nor any combination of required subjects in the secondary school can supply all the needs of today's adolescents, most schools offer a program of student activities. Not all of these are concerned with providing opportunities in general education. However, the all-school student activities listed below are concerned with this objective:

1. School assemblies.
2. Use of service facilities such as the school lunchroom, the library, guidance services.
3. Social activities – parties, dances, dinners, camping trips.
4. Student elections and student government.
5. School publications.

Student activities will not have valuable educational results unless they have definite and well-defined goals. These major activities are briefly considered here because of their relationship to the general education program of the school. An extended discussion of activities is presented in Chapter 9.

School assemblies. The following are some of the more important purposes of different types of school assemblies held in secondary schools:

1. Presentation of awards to outstanding students.

2. Speeches on important topics of local, state, national, or international importance that are of interest and value to students.

3. Talks by visiting speakers on topics that are of special interest to most students.

4. Student-prepared programs commemorating special days or events.

5. Special music and drama programs presented by students and by outsiders with the purpose of developing esthetic appreciation.

6. Presentation of various forms of entertainment with the idea of developing a variety of interests on the part of the students.

7. Activities that give students the opportunity to participate, such as pep rallies, group singing, and election speeches.

Special secondary school facilities. As secondary school students make use of the school gymnasium, lunchroom, library, and shops, they are engaging in common activities that offer excellent opportunities for growth in basic skills. Students learn to share, to respect one another, and to be good citizens as they compete in the gymnasium and on the playing field; they get numerous experiences in learning the value of teamwork and the importance of group participation. In the lunchroom they have opportunities to reinforce learning concerned with nutrition and acceptable table manners and to practice courtesy and desirable social behavior. In special facilities such as visual-aids rooms, laboratories, music rooms, and auditoriums, students get good training for citizenship and self-discipline. The school library provides materials to furnish information commensurate with both the common and special interests and needs of students. Thus, by proper use of these facilities, students develop social, citizenship, library, and other personal skills.

Guidance services involve more than special facilities, but special tests, homeroom programs, and interviews in special counseling rooms are valuable opportunities for students to develop themselves to their highest potential ability.

Social activities. Secondary school students need to have experiences that will help them develop wholesome boy-girl relationships, social leadership among their peers, and interests and skills which will lead to worthy use of their leisure time in desirable recreational activities. The school can offer many opportunities for gaining valuable experiences in these areas—for example, dances and parties. A majority of schools allow after-school affairs such as dinners, camping trips, picnics, suppers, dances, and class parties, which students plan and carry out under faculty supervision.

Student government. Most large secondary schools and a high percentage of small and medium-sized schools have student councils or some form of student government. The plans for student government differ greatly, but most of them involve the students to a considerable extent. The better schools not only provide opportunities for the election of student council officers but also have well-defined areas of responsibility within which the student council can function. Such schools assign worth-while functions to the student government and provide assistance and directions for the council when needed. The student body is constantly kept informed of council action and is given an opportunity to be a vital part of the entire program through membership in constituent units such as the homeroom.

Some of the more desirable educational results that can be brought about through a good plan of student government include the following:

1. An understanding of democratic processes.

2. A greater spirit of group unity and better morale.

3. Proper recognition of worth-while efforts and achievements by students.

4. Acceptance of responsibility for results of the students' own plans and actions.

5. A greater understanding of democratic principles and procedures.

Student publications. Student publications are usually produced by juniors and seniors with other students sharing in the responsibilities. Since publication experience often counts as credit toward graduation, students are allowed to substitute such experience for part of the course requirements in English or journalism. While only a few students are actually involved in their production, good publications can help build school spirit and develop unity among students in desirable projects and activities.

Some of the other important school activities that affect most of the students and satisfy common needs are music, drama, and service and hobby clubs.

General education class or programs approach

The general education class, or core program (see definition on page 86), is a method of organizing the general education, or common learnings curriculum. This plan still leaves room for a program of elective as well as required subjects.

Although many individuals recognize that the separate-subject plan and the all-school activities programs can accomplish much in general education, they maintain that more is to be desired. What, then, are some of the reasons why secondary schools should provide general education classes? The following are suggested as worthy of consideration.[1]

1. Democratic processes and ideals can be acquired better in the functional setting and the longer period of time found in a general education class. Some educators believe that democratic processes can be experienced more effectively and thus learned more thoroughly when students are freed from the rigid time and subject requirements most often found in a curriculum organized on the separate-subject basis.

2. In a general education class, greater use can be made of community resources, field trips, supplementary reference materials, and consultants—whether specialists or lay people. Such a class gives students adequate time and maximum opportunities to study community problems. Since the general education class is not limited by conventional subject-matter boundaries and restrictions, teachers and students can explore areas of interest and importance to youth in the present and those of significance for the future. Many of these areas, especially those of great importance in shaping personality and character, are too often not considered or left only to chance in the traditional classroom setting.

What are some of these areas? Some of them are the ones upon which the American way of life and its value systems are established; for example, human relationships—relationships in the home, with adults, with members of the opposite sex, and with individuals of differing creeds, races, and opinions.

3. In a general education class, adolescents have a better opportunity to develop the ability to be self-directive, one of the big objectives of education. Schools should be, and are, concerned with developing in adolescents the ability to use discussion, arbitration, and reason, rather than brute force and strife in the solution of problems. If students are to develop the ability to be self-directive, they must have opportunities to plan and help structure the areas to be studied, and they must learn the real meaning of responsibility by actually being responsible for choices they make and activities they help plan.

---

[1]Compare Louise E. Hock and Thomas J. Hill, *The General Education Class in the Secondary School* (New York: Holt, Rinehart & Winston, Inc., 1960), Chapter 2.

4. The skills and the areas of knowledge necessary for all can be taught better in the laboratory atmosphere of a general education class. The information presented is related to the experiences of adolescents; it is given personal meaning. Open discussions are used more often than is possible in a highly structured class where a teacher lectures most of the time.

Opinions vary concerning the place, purpose, and objectives of the general education class. Smith, Stanley, and Shores see in the general education class, or core program, an opportunity for intense study of the social and cultural values of society. They point out that the universal elements of a culture give the society its stability and unity and that these values should constitute the heart of the general education class.[2] They feel that the core of the secondary school curriculum should consist largely of the socio-moral rules comprising the culture. Schools, according to these authors, should place great emphasis upon a deliberate study of the moral content of the culture.

Caswell advocates a program that would provide for a "core" which would center around carefully planned "personal-social problems." The more important elements in his program are as follows:

1. Students should receive understanding and helpful guidance in their personal and educational problems.

2. Students should be given opportunities which will aid them in meeting the demands of citizenship.

3. Students should be taught how to maintain good health.

4. Students should be afforded opportunities to study the basic areas of family life.

5. Students should be taught skills of communication and computation which are of general significance to all.[3]

In 1952 the Educational Policies Commission advocated a common course that would provide experiences designed to enable all young people to live happily and usefully while they were still young and at the same time to help equip them for the full responsibilities of adult life. The commission stated the following six aims as the chief purposes of such a course:

1. To help all youth grow in knowledge of their community, their nation, and the world of nations; in understanding of the rights and duties of citizens of the American democracy; and in diligent and

[2]B. Othanel Smith and others, *Fundamentals of Curriculum Development*, rev. ed. (New York: Harcourt, Brace & World, Inc., 1950), pp. 468–469, 471–472.

[3]Hollis L. Caswell and others, eds., *The American High School*, John Dewey Society Eighth Yearbook (New York: Harper & Row, Publishers, Inc., 1946), p. 143.

competent performance of their obligations as members of the community and as citizens of the state and nation.

2. To help all youth grow in knowledge of the operations of the economic system and in understanding of the human relations and problems in economic activities, particularly of the relations between management and employees.

3. To help all youth grow in understanding of personal relations within the family, of the conditions which make for successful family life, and of the importance of the family in society.

4. To help all youth grow in ability to purchase and use goods and services intelligently, with accurate knowledge of values received by the consumer and with understanding of the economic consequences of one's acts.

5. To help all youth grow in appreciation and enjoyment of beauty in literature, art, music, and nature.

6. To help all youth grow in ability to listen and read with understanding and to communicate their thoughts with precision and clarity.[4]

It is important to consider at this point some of the specific topics that could be used as the central theme, or problem, of a general education class. Among such topics are these identified by Van Til:

1. Choosing, buying, and using goods and services intelligently.
2. Keeping healthy.
3. Home, school, and friends.
4. Ways of living in other countries.
5. Recreation and leisure.
6. Obtaining an education.
7. Racial, religious, ethnic, and social-economic relationships.
8. Personal development and psychological understanding.
9. Domestic economy.
10. War—its causes and effects.
11. Propaganda and public opinion.
12. The government's role in labor and management.
13. Vocations.
14. Peace and world views.[5]

Regardless of the emphasis of any given general education class, certain characteristics must be evident if the best results are to be achieved:

[4]*Education for All American Youth: A Further Look.* Educational Policies Commission, National Education Association (Washington, D.C.: NEA, 1952), p. 238.

[5]William Van Til, "A Social Living Curriculum for Post-War Secondary Education" (unpublished Ohio State University doctoral dissertation, 1946), p. 217.

1. There must be a problems approach to content and procedures.

2. Content must be meaningful to all students.

3. The development of self-direction and self-discipline in the learner is a major goal of the class.

4. The student must be involved in the complete learning process — planning, organizing, carrying out, and evaluating his learning experiences.

5. Individual differences must be respected, utilized, and developed in constructive ways.[6]

Subject areas in general education

Although the special general education class, or core program, is organized around the common interests, needs, and experiences of young people, it should not be assumed that this type of curriculum organization makes special subject courses unnecessary. Educators do not believe that the general education class can provide all the desirable experiences and all the knowledge needed in general education. Although the general education class provides a unifying core so that subject matter can be used in a lifelike situation to solve meaningful problems, the secondary school curriculum must provide opportunities for students to deal with subject areas that are important enough to be presented separately. This does not mean that the material is not or should not be related; it does mean that students must have opportunities to make concentrated attacks on certain necessary subject areas.

While subjects that are of greatest importance in general education will be considered separately here, it is understood that good teachers will organize and present learning experiences that transcend subject-matter lines.

English

The study of English in the secondary schools was started in the days of the academy. Before this time such subjects as rhetoric and grammar occupied a large place in the curriculum but were not studied in the vernacular. High schools established in the first half of the nineteenth century developed programs involving areas that are referred to today as English; however, even in these schools English was not considered a first-rate subject. It was not until the present century that English, as such, was given a respectable place in the curriculum.

[6]Hock and Hill, *op. cit.,* pp. 30–31.

This can better be realized by considering one of the protests made on behalf of English by the Committee on College Entrance Requirements in 1899:

> The Committee presents first the proposition that the study of the English language and its literature is inferior in importance to no study in the curriculum. It offers all, or nearly all, the opportunities for mental training afforded by the study of any languages, and introduces the pupil to the literature of his own tongue, which must always be the chief source of his own thought, inspirations, ideals, and aesthetic enjoyment, and must also be the vehicle of his communication with his fellow-men. Hence this study should be placed in a position at least not inferior to that allotted other languages.[7]

At one time what is known as English was taught as separate subjects entitled composition, rhetoric, literature, and grammar. Today English incorporates all of these and is really a broad, unified field within the curriculum. The English program in the secondary schools is concerned with meeting common needs of all youth, which are skill in reading, writing, speaking, and listening.

English has become the most universally required of all subjects; students must study English in the junior high school and also take three, and sometimes four, additional units in grades nine through twelve. In addition to required English courses, many schools offer such related electives as speech, debate, journalism, creative writing, dramatic art, advanced composition, world literature, college preparatory English, and remedial English.

Most of the required English courses and the special related electives combine oral and written experiences with language and literature. Some unify elements of grammar, correct usage, and literature; others provide separate treatment of these elements in different semesters. In both cases, however, the objective is to develop proficiency in the oral and written use of the language, which is fundamental for all students, irrespective of future vocational or professional aspirations.

Although all teachers, regardless of their teaching areas, should be concerned with English usage, it is still necessary to provide special teachers and course work in English. Communication skills can be developed in any subject, a fact that has led to the dangerous generalization that every teacher is an English teacher. Op-

---

[7]*Report of the Committee on College Entrance Requirements*, National Education Association (Chicago: University of Chicago Press, 1899), pp. 12–13.

posed to this point of view is the cliché that everybody's business becomes nobody's business.[8]

Grammar and usage. Educators and the lay public consider correctness in speaking and in writing as one of the more important goals of general education. The modern secondary school attempts to teach grammar, proper use of word forms, and word order that shows logical relationships between words. It is even more concerned that students master acceptable usage in oral and written English. The terms *grammar* and *usage* should not be confused. *Grammar* is the structure of a language; *usage* is a matter of custom and convention. The English program in the secondary school is concerned with a study and description of good usage leading to competency on the part of the student.

It is the school's responsibility to provide an environment in which students will have opportunities to observe good examples of English usage; that is, the teachers themselves should speak and write acceptable English. The school, however, must do more than provide a good environment. It must teach proper usage by a formal and functional study of grammar that will acquaint the student with sound practice — with what forms of usage are correct and what forms are incorrect. Today the better English teachers are teaching grammar by selecting from traditional grammar those elements which are closely related to the students' speaking and writing practices. They are attempting to teach forms that are and will be used.

As early as 1917 Hosic pointed out that English teachers should concentrate on the construction of sentences and the function of words within a sentence, not on a study of grammar that emphasized classification and rote memory.[9] In 1956 the National Council of Teachers of English felt that six major elements were most necessary to correct grammar usage in speech and writing: sentence structure, modification and subordination, agreement, nouns and pronouns, verbs, and adjectives and adverbs.[10]

Despite the fact that most secondary schools are attempting to make the study of grammar a more selective and functional process, many of the larger high schools are finding that they have

[8]Edward A. Krug, *The Secondary School Curriculum* (New York: Harper & Row, Publishers, Inc., 1960), p. 237.

[9]James Fleming Hosic, *Reorganization of English in Secondary Schools,* Report by the National Joint Committee on English representing the Commission on the Reorganization of Secondary Education, National Education Association and the National Council of Teachers of English (Washington, D.C.: Department of the Interior, Bureau of Education, 1917), p. 37.

[10]Krug, *op. cit.,* p. 242.

enough students interested in an advanced study of grammar to justify a special course. In smaller schools where there may not be enough students for a special class, English teachers can work with interested students, helping them master advanced abstract concepts.

Literature. Historically, secondary schools have used several approaches to the teaching of literature. The first, used when English was just beginning to be accepted in the curriculum, was similar to that used in teaching Greek and Latin literature. This may have been due to the desire of English teachers to imitate teachers of classical subjects; however, it was undoubtedly aimed also at gaining respectability for the English program among other educators. This approach led to the selection of works considered to be classic, many of which soon became standard requirements. Colleges added to their entrance examination questions taken from these so-called English classics. From time to time the lists were revised by committees representing both colleges and high schools. Major selections listed around 1900 were *Ivanhoe, Merchant of Venice, Vision of Sir Launfal, Julius Caesar, Last of the Mohicans, Silas Marner, Vicar of Wakefield, Paradise Lost* (Books I and II), *Rime of the Ancient Mariner, Macbeth,* Carlyle's *Essay on Burns,* Tennyson's *Princess,* and Macaulay's essays on *Milton* and *Addison.* Many of these are still part of the secondary school literature program.

While this approach has often been criticized, it has value in that students should be familiar with some of the enduring works which are an important part of America's cultural heritage. The fact that many teachers have spent too much time with detailed analyses of such classics, as well as more recent selections, may in part account for the dislike many students acquire for literature.

As English became more firmly established in the secondary school and as the formal discipline theory of learning became open to suspicion, English teachers started stressing the moral and character values of these classics. Soon other approaches to the teaching of literature developed, such as literary types, themes, literary history, and a problems approach.

Today most teachers combine these approaches and integrate a study of good usage. Many schools have found that in grades seven, eight, and nine the themes approach works very well in the development of tastes and interests; attention is also paid to literary types, but not in technical or complex analyses. Most high schools introduce tenth-grade students to world literature, usually organized along geographical or regional lines within a broad framework of history.[11] The historical approach is popular with teachers of American literature in the eleventh grade and of English literature in the twelfth grade, although a study of literary types is also generally continued.

Ability to read and the literature program. Great variations in reading ability are found among secondary school students. For example, some seventh-grade students read at a third- or fourth-grade level; yet others in the same grade may be reading at tenth- and eleventh-grade levels. Schools must attempt to meet the problems that these varying abilities create by grouping pupils according to achievement and academic ability and by providing suitable materials. This means that the English teacher must provide a variety of materials and use many different approaches; otherwise, students will find little value or satisfaction in the literature program. Secondary school teachers are beginning to realize that they must constantly provide a developmental reading program that is concerned with all students — the slow, average, and rapid learner.

Developing skills. The English teacher helps students develop skill in reading, writing, speaking, and listening through literature, the study of grammar, and other kinds of subject matter. The unit approach seems to be especially appropriate for the development of language arts skills. In 1965 the National Council of Teachers of English had the following to say on the subject:

Unit teaching . . . provides a natural setting for well-motivated learning. It places the skills of communication where they belong — in purposeful activity in a social setting. It demands orderly planning and assumption of responsibility for carrying out the plans. It furnishes opportunity for extensive group work and for individualized procedures to meet the needs, the interests, and the capacities of all members of the class. It stimulates curiosity and creativeness, giving those with unusual powers of self-direction a chance to forge ahead on their own. Yet it keeps the entire class working together on a common problem. It permits the use of all types of literature — new and old, prose and poetry, easy and mature — and the development of skill in reading each of them. It recognizes the place of the library in the learning activities of the classroom and teaches economical use of the facilities available. It takes advantage of the natural relationships be-

[11]*Ibid.,* p. 243.

tween speaking and listening and writing and reading in the normal pursuit of well-integrated problems. It gives opportunity for enjoyment of literary selections by the class as a whole and at the same time develops personal standards of literary appreciation and personal habits of reading to suit individual interests. It gives opportunity for careful evaluation of progress by the students themselves and for the planning of the next steps in learning.[12]

Some secondary schools are arranging for English teachers to have the time necessary to work individually with students in helping them master basic English skills. Many schools are developing a team-teaching approach that results not only in more efficient teaching but also in more individual instruction. Teachers must offer specific, detailed criticisms of what students write. Students must be allowed to practice oral communication. A developmental reading program demands individual attention for students; therefore, the English teacher's student load should be no more than one hundred students.

Reading. Problems in reading affect the student's work in all academic areas and in his adjustment in life. In junior and senior high schools having developmental reading programs, students are usually grouped as slow readers, normal readers, and superior readers. Such grouping enables a teacher to work more effectively with all students.

Many schools have found that reading clinics, where students work individually, can produce excellent results; however, the reading clinic does not replace the work of the individual classroom teacher. Developmental reading should be a concern of all teachers in the secondary school.

A special curriculum guide for study in English language arts prepared for the State Board of Education of North Carolina emphasizes the fact that reading is a serious problem, but one that can be solved:

. . . The more effective the developmental program, the less need for a remedial one. Actually, it is possible for most language deficiencies to be corrected in the regular classroom, only the complex disabilities needing clinical help from experts.

There is no simple answer to the question of why we have a remedial reading problem. Yet the fact remains that 5% to 10% of

[12]*The English Language Arts in the Secondary School,* Commission on the English Curriculum, National Council of Teachers of English (New York: Appleton-Century-Crofts, 1956), p. 112.

students are retarded. Since poor vision and hearing are generally blamed, it is surmised that the difficulties of the poor reader can be prevented or corrected. Sometimes other factors are at work: low intelligence, poor diet, ineffectual instruction, and psychological problems. If home conditions are at fault, the teacher must offset them by attractive books and an atmosphere of acceptance and affection.

In a junior high school where remedies are not possible within the regular classroom, it is advisable to set up more than one hour for the language arts disciplines. This is a notion which needs more research than has been given it.

In a senior high school, it is often necessary to establish Practical English Courses in the 12th grade for those having difficulty with one or more phases of English. In it, a student gets at least one day per week for improving his rate and comprehension or reading, in addition to constant repetition of spelling words and the like.

But within the classroom, a remedial program can be effective if it is individualized. For instance, a student must be encouraged to select his own books based on his own interests. And more than ever in a remedial class, the teacher must motivate the reading by giving students something to look for.[13]

It is quite common for secondary schools to employ reading comprehension and diagnostic tests—such as Gray's *Oral Reading Test,* the Crow-Kuhlmann-Crow *Reading Comprehensive Test,* the *Stanford Achievement Test in Reading,* and the *Metropolitan Reading Test*—in order to determine the reading levels of the students.

The slow reader—Students who read two or three grades below their grade level are generally considered slow readers. In order to care for their needs, an increasing number of secondary schools are developing reading clinics conducted on an individual basis; others are developing programs of small corrective reading classes. Slow readers spend two or more hours per week in these special remedial classes in addition to their other school work.

Dealing with slow readers in the secondary school is complicated by the fact that they must be supplied with materials which are easy to read but which, at the same time, deal with subjects that are of interest to adolescents. Special basal readers have been prepared for secondary school students who are slow readers. Some schools use these readers plus *The Weekly Reader,* a special, well-illustrated publication; others provide a wide selection of

[13]Carl F. Brown and Richard Walser, *A Guide to Curriculum Study* (Raleigh, N.C. State Board of Education, 1959), pp. 43–44.

books and pamphlets designed for slow readers. Many classroom teachers collect materials on topics related to the students' fields of interest and written with an easy vocabulary.

In 1959 Conant suggested some ways of working with slow readers in the high school:

Those in the ninth grade of the school who read at a level of the sixth grade or below should be given special consideration. These pupils should be instructed in English and the required social studies by special teachers who are interested in working with such students and who are sympathetic to their problems. Remedial reading should be part of the work and special types of textbooks should be provided. The elective programs of these pupils should be directed toward simple vocational work, and they should be kept out of the regular vocational programs for boys, the distributive education program, and the regular commercial program for girls. These students should not be confused with mentally retarded students. The education of the mentally retarded is a special problem which in some states is also handled in the regular high school through special instruction and the use of special state funds.[14]

The superior reader — The modern secondary school provides special sections of various required subjects for its superior students. The homogeneous grouping involved affords the teacher opportunities to furnish capable students with materials that will be challenging and that will enable them to develop their capacities to a greater extent. These courses furnish many opportunities in oral and written communication, grammar, speech, and reading. In addition to these special required courses, students may elect courses designed especially for superior readers. Some of these courses are college-preparatory English, journalism, debate, dramatic art, speech, creative writing, modern literature, American literature, world literature, and advanced composition.

Attempts to help superior readers should not involve simply providing some of the same material that the average student is expected to master. Instead special sections should offer material dealing with more mature concepts and generalizations. If the school does not provide special sections and does not employ homogeneous grouping, the teacher must enrich the program for the superior student within the regular classroom.

[14]James B. Conant, *The American High School Today* (New York: McGraw-Hill Book Company, Inc., 1959), p. 55.

The average reader — The secondary school must not ignore the fact that a developmental reading program is important for all, including the average reader. Secondary school teachers must constantly strive to develop the reading vocabulary, speed, and comprehension of the average student. Indeed, since every major academic field has its own special vocabulary and skills, all teachers must, to some extent, be teachers of reading.

Practice in the English program.   The approach and the methods employed many times in English practice or drill result in boring learning experiences; yet, it is necessary to have intelligent, meaningful practice opportunities if students are to master basic English skills. Such areas as correct usage, knowledge of the formal structure of the language, syntax, enunciation, pronunciation, and oral expression demand drill. These exercises should be brisk, meaningful, and closely related to the students' everyday use. This type of individualized drill should involve the rules of grammar and a knowledge of the use of the various parts of speech, but it should avoid long, monotonous sessions that often have little meaning for students — especially those in junior high school.

Social studies

The term *social studies* covers a broad field; it refers to history, economics, geography, civics, sociology, and such areas as problems in American democracy or contemporary problems. The term is often severely criticized by individuals who interpret it to mean that history, geography, economics, and government have been either eliminated from the curriculum or watered down. This is not the case, however, for the secondary schools are still teaching these subjects as part of the general education program and as elective courses in special education.

The subjects called social studies found their way into the secondary school curriculum in the nineteenth century. The most important single subject was, and is, history. In many ways history is like English; it is a unifying subject that draws on many areas of human experience. History is a very broad field in itself, and the teacher of history must be very selective in the organization of materials.

Early secondary schools, such as the Latin grammar schools, looked on history as a sort of by-product or special activity that could be considered, if time permitted, along with the study of the classical languages. History was established as a separate course by the early academies and was later welcomed as an area from which special courses should be developed in high schools. In 1892 the Committee of Ten approved it as one of the major fields of the high school curriculum and also approved some of the related courses such as government, geography, and political economy. Today history is one of the three most required subjects in the secondary school curriculum, and some educators believe the requirements in it and in the social studies should be increased. The Conant report in 1959 recommended that students take three or four years of social studies and that two of these years should be spent in history.

Objectives in the social studies.   One of the more important objectives in teaching social studies is the development of good citizenship; in fact, all areas of the curriculum are concerned with this objective. Good citizenship is not limited to conformity to laws and the responsibilities of voting and paying one's taxes; it includes realization that while these responsibilities are important, good citizenship also involves constructive and intelligent action of the citizen in helping develop better laws and communities so that society as a whole may be improved. This implies several other objectives which social studies teachers must strive to develop within their students:

1. The ability to think reflectively.
2. The ability to work with others in arriving at decisions and formulating constructive policies.
3. The ability to relate policies and actions to the value systems of society.
4. The ability to gather information on a problem in order that intelligent decisions can be made.

It should be acknowledged once again that these objectives are also the concern of teachers in other fields; for example, the ability to think reflectively is certainly an objective of mathematics and science teachers. The ability to work with others in groups and the ability to gather information are objectives that pertain to most areas of the curriculum.

Objectives that are of major importance to the social studies field, especially the area of history, are the following:

1. To help students know and understand the past.
2. To help students understand the present and the problems with which individuals must deal.
3. To help students make better decisions for the future, especially in political, social, and economic areas.

4. To give students a good background for the understanding of cultural materials discussed in other classes, such as music and literature.

5. To help all students develop a greater appreciation of their cultural heritage.

Status of the social studies. In most schools social studies are still taught as separate subjects, although some are using the general education class for a portion of the work and thereby achieving a much higher degree of integration. A few schools are using a program of correlation which points out significant relationships among the various social studies areas.

Regardless of the plan used, educators know that it is important to have a good sequential relation of topics in social studies. Most secondary schools use the following sequence: seventh grade, state history and world geography or geography of one of the hemispheres; eighth grade, United States history; ninth grade, civics and government; tenth grade, world history; eleventh grade, United States history; twelfth grade, sociology and economics or a study of problems in American democracy. In many social studies programs it is necessary for the students to study United States history in the junior high school and again in the eleventh grade. Some states also require that schools teach the history of their state at a certain grade level, usually the seventh or eighth. A minimum of two years of social studies in grades nine through twelve is required by a majority of senior high schools.

A survey of many secondary schools and some of the leading authorities on secondary curriculum indicates that the following are representative of the major general practices and trends in the social studies field:

1. An attempt on the part of many secondary schools to develop their programs at the various grade levels around units or large problems.

2. An attempt to place great emphasis on citizenship.

3. An attempt to define and achieve certain definite objectives in the program offered.

4. An attempt on the part of most teachers to use a great variety of methods and approaches.

5. An attempt to teach the important areas of the past in such a way that the present can be better understood.

6. An attempt to integrate the social studies themselves and to correlate the social studies with other fields.

7. An attempt to broaden the scope of the social studies field.

Within the separate subjects themselves, the following practices seem to be common:

1. Geography is being required as usual in the seventh grade, but other courses in geography are being offered as electives above the seventh grade.

2. American history is being required in the eighth grade with major emphasis on basic facts and chronology.

3. American history is being required in the eleventh grade with less emphasis on elementary facts and chronology and more emphasis on movements, problems, and motives that have determined the course of American history and are affecting the United States today.

4. Courses in civics and government are beginning to deal with community problems, as well as with a study of the various levels of government.

5. In most schools, world history is still being offered as a ninth- or tenth-grade elective, but many schools are beginning to make it a graduation requirement.

6. Several schools are offering a two-year program in world history.

7. Many schools are offering courses in economics, government, and sociology as electives, but in most schools these courses are yielding to a twelfth-grade course that is usually called "Problems of American Democracy," "Senior Problems," or "Social Contemporary Problems."

Science

So important is science today that educators consider it one of the imperative needs of young people. Long before the present century a few deep thinkers grasped the importance of the study of science. Herbert Spencer, an English philosopher of the nineteenth century, had the following to say on the subject:

Thus to the question with which we set out—what knowledge is of most worth?—the uniform reply is—Science. This is the verdict on all the counts. For direct self-preservation, or the maintenance of life and health, the all-important knowledge is—Science. For that indirect self-preservation which we call gaining a livelihood, the knowledge of greatest value is—Science. For the due discharge of parental functions, the proper guidance is to be found only in—Science. For that interpretation of national life, past and present, without which the citizen cannot rightly regulate his conduct, the indispensable key is —Science. Alike for the most perfect production and highest enjoyment of art in all its forms, the needful preparation is still — Science. And for purposes of discipline — intellectual, moral, religious — the most efficient study is, once more — Science.[15]

Few educators today would see science as Spencer evidently did — as the solution for most problems. Yet, it would be hard to find the educator who does not believe that science is important in the school's general education program.

Historical development. Little science was taught in the Latin grammar schools. Some academies offered general courses in the area, but it was in the high schools that science became firmly established.[16] Natural philosophy, a forerunner of modern physics, was the first course taught in the high schools. Physiology, chemistry, geology, astronomy, natural philosophy, and botany were being offered by 1865. Zoology made great gains from 1865 to 1900, while geology and astronomy declined. Zoology, botany, and physiology were fused into biology early in the present century. A new subject, general science, made its appearance around 1922 and since then has been an important element in the secondary school curriculum.

General science, biology, chemistry, and physics are the most common science courses offered in the secondary school today. In most cases two science courses — general science and biology, or biology and chemistry or physics — are necessary for graduation from high school; however, many schools allow students to substitute for general science other courses such as agriculture, home economics, or conservation. Some schools urge the more academically capable students to take chemistry or physics instead of general science.

Objectives of science. The major objectives of science instruction in general education are as follows:

1. To help students learn more about the world around them and to help them understand the role science plays in solving and in creating problems in our society.

2. To furnish students with opportunities to acquire knowledge that will enable them to understand basic scientific concepts.

3. To help students understand the scientific method and how it works.

[15]Herbert Spencer, *Education: Intellectual, Moral, and Physical* (New York: Appleton-Century-Crofts, 1900), pp. 84–85.

[16]Rudyard K. Bent and Henry H. Kronenberg, *Principles of Secondary Education,* 4th ed. (New York: McGraw-Hill Book Company, Inc., 1961), p. 286.

4. To help students master the major generalizations of science and their importance for the average citizen in his daily life.

The science program today. General science is studied in all junior high grades including the ninth grade when it is included in the junior high school. Biology is required in the tenth grade of most secondary schools, and chemistry and physics are offered as electives in the eleventh and twelfth grades respectively.

Many times the ninth-grade general science course, which should make use of content materials to acquaint pupils with their environment, is simply a survey course organized into chapters or units on the specific sciences.

The tenth-grade biology course should attempt to develop a sound understanding of health and sanitation. The student should be given an opportunity to learn about his own body, good health habits, and sound health practices. Some educators, who feel the present biology course merely stresses meaningless terminology and classifications of the various forms of life, believe that the best way to achieve this would be to abolish biology as such and to continue a second year of general science. These educators would have tenth-grade students study such topics as communication, foods, pure water supply, transportation and safety, sanitation, animal life, plant life, and the physical world. The possibility that such a course will replace biology is very remote, however. In fact, there is a strong trend toward offering biology to capable ninth-graders in order that they may elect more advanced courses in the senior high school.[17]

Schools are definitely offering more science courses. Some schools are developing special sections for high academic achievers; others have established programs with a second year of chemistry, biology, or physics, an approach often made possible by offering biology in the ninth grade, chemistry in the tenth, and physics in the eleventh grade. In both programs students may qualify for advanced placement in college through the College Entrance Examination Board program.

A one-year physical science course consisting of chemistry, physics, and earth science, combined in a manner analogous to the botany-zoology approach in a one-year biology course, is also being used in some schools. Many students who find they do not have time in their schedule for two years of physical science after taking biology usually have to choose between chemistry and

[17]Krug, *op. cit.*, p. 332.

physics, thus getting a one-sided view of the physical science field as a whole. The one-year physical science course is one possibility for students who want more work in science but who cannot take both physics and chemistry.

Science teachers, however, often voice opposition to the physical science course because they believe it does not do justice to physics or chemistry and because it is used by some schools as a course for students with below-average ability. Most biology teachers, on the other hand, have accepted the fusion of botany and zoology as a better way of teaching the life sciences in high school than was done when the two were separate subjects.[18]

Mathematics

It is generally believed that all students should have basic instruction in number concepts and the elementary mathematical processes.[19] Professional educators and the public realize that the ability to think in quantitative terms is absolutely necessary for the citizen in today's society. Many students who complete the elementary school have mastered the mathematical knowledge and skills that are necessary in daily living, but others are often lacking in these areas even after the completion of junior high school. Some educators feel that in the areas of arithmetic and mathematics, just as in the areas of the language arts, all students who have the mental ability should be given the opportunity to master these subjects.

The seventh and eighth grade program should consist of an extension of arithmetic, of a large segment of intuitive geometry, and of an introduction to the ideas of algebra. The emphasis in arithmetic should be on its rationale and on increasing and maintaining the skills in computation, with much less stress on so-called business applications. This program should be so designed that highly capable pupils can complete it in one to one and one-half years of study, and then go on immediately to the four-year high-school program. The below-average and exceptionally slow pupils will pursue this program over a three-year period to the end of the ninth grade and even longer.[20]

[18]*The Scholars Look at the Schools,* Project on Instruction, National Education Association (Washington, D.C.: NEA, 1962), pp. 21–27.
[19]William M. Alexander and J. Galen Saylor, *Modern Secondary Education* (New York: Holt, Rinehart & Winston, Inc., 1959), p. 410.
[20]Howard F. Fehr, "High-School Mathematics for the Second Half of the 20th Century," *Bulletin of the National Association of Secondary-School Principals,* XLII (April 1958), 320.

Because mathematics is so important in today's technical civilization, instruction should not cease once students have mastered enough skill to function in routine business common to most citizens. They should be permitted to acquire more practical information and to use the knowledge from the various areas of mathematics to gain a better understanding of the universe and their cultural heritage.

Objectives of mathematics. Objectives in mathematics, as it is being taught in today's schools, fall into two closely related classifications — practical objectives and cultural objectives.

Practical objectives are as follows:

1. To enable all students to develop sufficient mathematical skills and enough mathematical knowledge to function effectively in everyday living.

2. To enable all students concerned with vocational fields demanding a certain efficiency in mathematics to reach that level of efficiency.

The cultural objectives stem from the fact that mathematics composes a great amount of one's cultural heritage; many things in man's environment can be understood or described only through their quantitative aspects. Examples are the exploration of space, the magnitude and complexity of the universe, the size of transportation and communication systems in today's world, geological formations, and the size of countries. There are many elements in nature, science, architecture, and even art that can be understood and appreciated only through a knowledge of mathematics.[21]

The status of mathematics. Arithmetic and mathematics are required in the seventh- and eighth-grade programs. In grades nine through twelve most schools used to require one year of mathematics for graduation.[22] Because many individuals feel that one unit of mathematics is far from adequate, two units are necessary for graduation in many secondary schools. These same educators point to the requirements in social studies and English, maintaining that mathematics is just as important in general education and should receive equal time.

The *Twenty-Second Yearbook* of the National Council of Teachers of Mathematics discusses this problem:

Gradually he [the writer] has arrived at the tentative judgment that there are four categories of secondary school mathematics pupils and

[21]Bent and Kronenberg, *op. cit.,* p. 297.
[22]Krug, *op. cit.,* pp. 280–281.

that there should be consequently four categories of curricular offerings. These offerings would be for: (a) the pupil who feels no interest in mathematics and would be studying it unwillingly and primarily or solely as a present and future consumer; (b) the pupil who has some interest and is studying it primarily as a part of a liberal education; (c) the pupil who may or may not have interest in mathematics, but who is studying it because he does have interest in applied mechanics and knows his need for it as a machinist, toolmaker, draftsman, or other such trades; (d) the pupil who has high interest in mathematics, and average or superior ability, and who expects to use mathematics as a professional worker in the field of teaching, chemistry, insurance, engineering, or other such professional fields.[23]

In many schools students are placed in sections that are appropriate to their achievement and aptitude levels. Those who possess high mathematical aptitudes and interests are given special opportunities for additional work on an elective basis.[24] It is not unusual for large schools to offer not only general mathematics and algebra in general education but also advanced algebra, geometry, trigonometry, and even calculus as special elective subjects. The better secondary schools are offering four or more units of work in mathematics to students who desire a challenging program in this area.

Many junior and senior high schools are now offering work in what is termed *modern mathematics,* which involves the use of a new approach and new materials in the teaching of mathematics. The approach centers on an understanding of mathematics and the relationships within arithmetic and mathematics. The new materials consist of such elements as sets, variables, numbers and operations, functions, mathematical systems, coordinates, proof, terminology, abstraction, and statistical thinking and machine computation. This new approach and many of the new concepts are being used in the required general education courses as well as the special elective courses.[25]

Other areas in general education
Attention has been given thus far to the four so-called traditional solid subject-matter fields. While these fields are of great importance, they do not meet all the general education needs of young people in American society. Areas such as health and phys-

[23]Douglas Brown, "The Mathematics Teacher's Part in Effective Guidance for Optimum Use of Differentiated Curriculums," *Emerging Practices in Mathematics,* Twenty-Second Yearbook (National Council of Teachers of Mathematics, 1954), pp. 95–96.

[24]Krug, *op. cit.,* p. 292.

[25]*The Scholars Look at the Schools, op. cit.,* pp. 19–21.

ical education, nonvocational home economics, industrial arts, music, and art have been established to meet these other needs. In this discussion home economics and industrial arts courses of a general, not a specialized, nature are being considered.

Health and physical education. Health and physical education courses are second only to English in the amount of time allotted to them in secondary schools. At one time schools provided only a recess or play period; at the present time health and physical education are highly organized and required areas of the school's curriculum.

As an individual subject, physical education has experienced greater recent growth than any other. In 1922 only 6 per cent of the public secondary school students were taking any physical education, but by 1950, 70 per cent of all students were taking this course. In many junior and senior high schools pupils receive health instruction in their physical education classes, but in most schools there are special courses in health.

The most important objectives of physical education are to develop strength, coordination, an appreciation of physical fitness, and an understanding of and skill in physical activities. Physical education teachers are also aware of other objectives, such as citizenship, effectiveness in group relations, and personality development. Nothing in the physical education program should contradict or nullify these general objectives of the school.[26] The most important objective of health instruction is to help students understand ways of achieving and maintaining good health. Wise use of leisure time for greater enjoyment of life is certainly one of the more important objectives of both health instruction and physical education.

According to Williams the six major areas of content in physical education and health are as follows: (1) games, sports, athletics; (2) aquatics; (3) dance; (4) self-testing activities; (5) camping and outdoor activities; and (6) body-guiding activities and adaptive physical education.[27] Some of the major topics considered in health instruction are proper foods for growth and development, narcotics and the human body, obtaining pure food and water, sanitation, vaccinations, and quarantine. Many of these topics are often included in the science program of the secondary school.

---

[26]Krug, *op. cit.,* p. 404.

[27]Jesse Feiring Williams, "Physical Education in the Curriculum," in Harl R. Douglass, *The High School Curriculum,* 3rd ed. (New York: The Ronald Press Company, 1964), pp. 566–568.

Home economics. Since most girls marry and become homemakers and mothers, the school has an obligation to its students and to society to help prepare them for their future role. Cooking and sewing, formerly taught in the home, are today often referred to the school, along with such other homemaking tasks as interior decorating, exterior beautification, home furnishings, and child care.

The home arts courses were able to make little progress until the year 1872 when Massachusetts made such courses a legal part of the school's curriculum. Later the federal government made great contributions to the vocational home economics program by providing funds for the promotion of extension work, the training of teachers, research, and help in paying the salaries of vocational home economics teachers.

At first the home economics program concentrated on nutrition, child care, and sewing and clothing. Family relationships, personal development, and other important areas have been added to the program in recent years. Dyer wrote as early as 1927 that "personal and family relationships, child growth and development, consumption as a primary function of the home, and the intangibles of home life are being stressed."[28] These intangibles today include family relationships, purchasing of goods for the home, housing, intelligent use of human resources, and child growth and development.

Several objectives toward which students and teachers should work in home economics are as follows:

1. Understanding what desirable family life is in terms of their own experimental background.

2. Understanding and appreciating the importance of family life.

3. Understanding what makes family living successful.

4. Understanding and appreciating the values in family living as they relate to changing family patterns.

5. Understanding and appreciating good family-community relations.

6. Understanding and appreciating the democratic relationships in family life.

7. Understanding the resources for family living existing in the community.

8. Understanding the abilities and skills needed for successful performance of homemaking activities.[29]

[28]Annie Robertson Dyer, *The Placement of Home Economics Content in Junior and Senior High Schools* (New York: Teachers College, Columbia University, 1927), p. 99.
[29]*Ibid.,* pp. 312–313.

Although many junior high schools require one year of home-making, others offer all work in this area on an elective basis. In general, the courses in grades nine through twelve are called Home-making I, II, III, and IV. Many courses are organized along general lines with a series of problem-type units extending from the first through the most advanced courses; others are general courses in the junior high with specialized areas in grades ten through twelve.

Industrial arts. The field of industrial arts is closely related to the field of home economics. The junior high school industrial arts program is designed to prepare students for worthy home membership rather than a vocational field, but the senior high elective courses are planned to prepare students in a general way for a vocation. As a result, the course content in the junior high school is very general while that of the senior high school is more technical and specialized.

Some of the more important objectives that educators in industrial arts are attempting to achieve are the following:

1. Offering opportunities for students to be creative in an area often neglected—manual skills.

2. Offering opportunities to acquire knowledge of industrial processes which transform raw materials into usable products.

3. Offering general experiences important to future consumers.

4. Offering opportunities to acquire knowledge that would provide an intelligent basis for the selection of an occupation without forcing students to make an early decision.

5. Offering a general foundation for entrance into and progress in certain vocations.

Most school systems offer exploratory courses in the junior high school and both general and specialized courses at the senior high school level. Some schools require at least one course in industrial arts at the junior high level.

No longer can industrial arts courses be justified if students make only a few objects of wood as they did several decades ago; today industrial arts should help the student understand the changing industrial order and economic life. Industrial arts courses should be as similar to industry procedures as the school shops and laboratories will permit; principles of production methods and the sources and uses of materials should be carefully studied.

However, industrial arts often includes work in arts and crafts—wood carving, basketry, sheet-metal molding, work with plastics, and leather tooling. The program "should include opportunities for pupils to develop individuality and the ability to use materials and tools as a means of self-expression.[30]

Art. Art as a secondary school subject is concerned with tangibles — drawing, painting, sculpture, and design. Thus it differs from art as literature, studied in English, and from art as music, dance, and drama, treated in other areas of the curriculum.

Art courses are offered under a variety of names. Some of the more common ones are freehand drawing, general art, commercial art, applied art, and art appreciation, or, simply, Art I, II, III, and IV.

Art educators feel that art education should be concerned with the development of abilities, appreciations, and understandings of art itself, as well as personal and social objectives of general education.[31] In general, most authorities mention the following as the major objectives of art education:

1. Opportunities for self-expression and creativity.
2. Opportunities for students to develop talents and learn skills in art.
3. Appreciation of good taste and judgment in art.
4. Cultural transmission.

Art is generally not required but is offered on an elective basis in both the junior and the senior high school. Some educators argue for a required course in the senior high school,[32] but others claim this is not desirable since students are required to study art in some junior high schools and can elect additional courses in the senior high school.[33] The most likely possibility for strengthening the secondary curriculum in the arts seems to be the development of a good program in the junior high school, where some art is required, accompanied by the development of an extensive program of electives in the senior high school.[34]

Music. Opinions vary about whether music should be required in the secondary school curriculum; nevertheless, a majority of educators are aware that music is important in the school's general education program.

[30]Bent and Kronenberg, *op. cit.,* pp. 324–325.

[31]Edward Warder Rannells, *Art Education in the Junior High School: A Study of Objectives,* Bulletin of the Bureau of School Service, College of Education, University of Kentucky, Vol. 18, No. 4 (June 1946), p. 11.

[32]Italo L. De Francesco, *Art Education: Its Means and Ends* (New York: Harper & Row, Publishers, Inc., 1958), p. 364.

[33]Krug, *op. cit.,* pp. 352–353.

[34]*Ibid.,* p. 358.

Dykema summarized the objectives of music education as being "(1) physical, (2) emotional, (3) aesthetic, (4) social, (5) skill developing, and (6) intellectual."[35]

Courses consisting chiefly of vocal music and music appreciation are sometimes required of all junior high students. Some schools insist that participation in vocal and instrumental activities be additional to the regular program in music; other schools allow these activities to be substituted for the required work in music. A high percentage of senior high students are enrolled in elective courses in music, chorus groups, band, and orchestra.

Music is frequently correlated with language arts and the social studies in the junior high; thus, the music of a particular culture may be studied along with other aspects of that culture being considered in those classes. This is accomplished by the music teacher and/or the teachers of the various classes. Recordings are often used to help develop appreciation of the esthetic aspects of the culture being studied.

The senior high school music program should provide a wide enough variety of courses to interest the average students and to offer advanced study for those with specialized interests and talents. Although small high schools cannot always do this, large schools can and should provide for general music courses, orchestra, band, and chorus. Very large high schools can offer "what is practically a music major or a vocational music program."[36]

Selected references

ALEXANDER, WILLIAM M. AND J. GALEN SAYLOR. *Modern Secondary Education.* New York: Holt, Rinehart & Winston, Inc., 1959.

BEREDAY, GEORGE Z. F. AND JOSEPH A. LAUWERYS, EDS. *The Secondary School Curriculum.* The Yearbook of Education, 1958. London: Evans Brothers Ltd., 1958.

DOUGLASS, HARL R., ED. *The High School Curriculum,* 3rd ed. New York: The Ronald Press Company, 1964.

FAUNCE, ROLAND C. AND NELSON L. BOSSING. *Developing the Core Curriculum,* 2nd ed. Englewood Cliffs, N.J.: Prentice-Hall, Inc., 1958.

[35]Peter W. Dykema, *Music for Public School Administrators* (New York: Teachers College, Columbia University, 1931), pp. 3–8.
[36]Krug, *op. cit.*

FRENCH, WILL. *Behavioral Goals of General Education in High School.* New York: Russell Sage Foundation, 1957.

HOCK, LOUISE E. AND THOMAS J. HILL. *The General Education Class in the Secondary School.* New York: Holt, Rinehart & Winston, Inc., 1960.

JONES, HOWARD M. *One Great Society: Humane Learning in the United States.* New York: Harcourt, Brace & World, Inc., 1959.

KRUG, EDWARD A. *The Secondary School Curriculum.* New York: Harper & Row, Publishers, Inc., 1960.

The Scholars Look at the Schools. Project on Instruction, National Education Association. Washington, D.C.: NEA, 1962.

Schools for the Sixties. Project on Instruction, National Education Association. New York: McGraw-Hill Book Company, Inc., 1963.

SPITZNAS, JAMES E. "General, Special, and Vocational Education: An Exploration of Distinctive Differences," *What Shall the High Schools Teach?* 1956 Yearbook. Association for Supervision and Curriculum Development, National Education Association. Washington, D.C.: NEA, 1956, pp. 176–211.

What Shall the High Schools Teach? 1956 Yearbook. Association for Supervision and Curriculum Development, National Education Association. Washington, D.C.: NEA, 1956.

WILES, KIMBALL. *The Changing Curriculum of the American High School.* Englewood Cliffs, N.J.: Prentice-Hall, Inc., 1963.

Specialized education
in the secondary school program

The secondary school curriculum can be divided into two large areas — general education and specialized education. In very broad terms one might say that all education is specialized because students must acquire knowledge at times and at rates suited to their varying abilities and needs. However, popular terminology usually places communication skills, general mathematics, and civics under general education and college-preparatory subjects, stenography, and business education under specialized education. While most specialized education consists of college-preparatory and vocational training courses, it also includes courses that provide for students' special interests, which are not always along vocational or college-preparatory lines.

Perhaps the most difficult problem in the area of specialized education is that of providing the proper type of special education for each individual. Guidance personnel can provide help, but some students are not sure at this early age for what they want to prepare, and many others change their minds regarding vocations. Nevertheless, most educators feel that the school must offer specialized programs providing introductory courses to academic and vocational opportunities.

The American high school has not always tailored its educational programs to the abilities and goals of all students. Historically, the secondary schools have provided much more specialized education for the professions than they have for vocations.

As a result of changes during the twentieth century, the high schools have developed terminal-education programs for students seeking employment immediately after completing high school, and during recent years they have, in theory and to a great extent in practice, offered a curriculum that would meet the demands of a heterogeneous student body having many different life objectives.

General education and special education have operated concurrently in the junior high schools, where educators consider their major task to be general education with educational opportunities in special education for the purpose of exploration rather than for vocational training. The senior high schools and junior colleges have the responsibility of continuing general education and specialization in accordance with the student's ability, maturity, and life goals. At these three levels—junior high school, senior high school, and junior college—the general education program is required of all students while each pupil elects his courses in special education.[1]

Since every effort made to provide for individual differences of students is a form of specialized education, what are the major ways that secondary schools provide organizationally, administratively, and functionally for large groups of pupils? The major approaches are special academic-elective courses, special vocational programs, special student activities, special administrative arrangements in grouping, guidance programs, and special schools.

Academic-elective courses

The major academic-elective courses are found in English, science, foreign languages, mathematics, fine arts, and music. They are classified here as special education because the advanced academic courses in these subjects are usually not taken by students unless they plan to go on to some type of higher education or unless they have special interests in these areas.

English

Most small and many large high schools have no special offerings in English for students going to college, but the better high schools offer college-bound students advanced courses in formal

---

[1]L. O. Taylor and others, *The American Secondary School* (New York: Appleton-Century-Crofts, 1960), p. 172.

grammar and composition. All students need an excellent program in English, but those going to college have specialized needs.

Science

Chemistry and physics are the two courses most often elected in high school science, but some secondary schools have been and are developing new science courses—for example, electricity, geology, photography, and aeronautics.

Foreign languages

It will be recalled that Latin and Greek at one time made up the most important areas of secondary schooling in the Western world. The academies and the high schools continued the study of these two languages and added modern foreign languages. The study of foreign languages maintained its important position into the early twentieth century.

The highest percentage of enrollments in the foreign languages was recorded in 1910, when the combined totals for modern and classical languages was 83.3 per cent of all students in public high schools. By 1915 the enrollment had dropped to 77.2 per cent, and by 1922, to 54.9 per cent. This was due largely to the fact that German was virtually abandoned during World War I. The decline from then on, however, became catastrophic; and by 1955 the teaching of languages in the American high school was near a state of collapse.[2] During that year combined enrollments came to only 20.6 per cent of the pupils in American high schools. Two interesting aspects of this situation are worth noting: (1) by 1955, 46 per cent of the public high schools in the United States did not offer any foreign language study whatsoever, and 54.6 per cent offered no modern foreign language; and (2) during this entire period, while the percentage of students in foreign language courses was decreasing, the actual number was not.

In general, until recent years most students did not elect a foreign language—with the great exception of Latin—unless they were planning to go to college. Many educators today emphasize that the election of a foreign language should not depend on whether a student intends to continue his education in college. Instead, they maintain, all qualified students should be urged to study a language for its cultural value and because of the present world situation. Some of the better schools in large city systems and suburban communities are offering four or more languages,

[2]Edward A. Krug, *The Secondary School Curriculum* (New York: Harper & Row, Publishers, Inc., 1960), pp. 258–259.

often with more than two years in a language so that students have time to become proficient in it.

Mathematics

General education provides many opportunities in mathematics, but college-bound students usually require algebra, geometry, and, in some cases, trigonometry. Most schools offer algebra, geometry, and business arithmetic as special electives, and many provide work in solid geometry, trigonometry, and calculus.

Schools generally are rapidly revising the mathematics programs in order to offer more courses and to improve the quality of existing ones. These new programs allow students with outstanding interests and abilities in mathematics to take four years of mathematics in grades nine through twelve. This can be done in the traditional algebra, geometry, trigonometry sequence or in new programs that call for the revision of some of the traditional material and a combination of some of the older approaches. For example, some schools are combining plane and solid geometry; others are offering algebra in the eighth grade, thus allowing students to finish four years of traditional mathematics by the end of the eleventh grade, so that they may participate in an advanced placement program in mathematics during their senior year. Follow-up studies indicate that the success of these students in college mathematics speaks for the wisdom of this practice.

Recognition by educators of the importance of mathematics not only in technology and science but also in the intellectual growth of students has made this a most creative field for curriculum study and improvement. Meaning and logic are considered the basis of the development of modern mathematics and the reorganization of the mathematics sequence in secondary schools. Included in this new approach is the realization that mathematics is a subject and language of unparalleled beauty, precision, and power, instead of a body of mechanical manipulations and routines.[3]

Fine arts and music

The secondary school generally provides elective courses in art and music for those individuals who desire more opportunities in these areas. Elective art courses should build on the foundation laid in general art courses and should be designed for students with special talents and interests. Many educators acknowledge that the chief difference between the general and specialized art and music

[3]Dorothy M. Fraser, *Current Curriculum Studies in Academic Subjects* (Washington, D.C.: National Education Association, 1962), pp. 27–42.

courses should be a shift in emphasis away from mere appreciation and intelligent consumption goals toward the development of skills essential for production.

It is generally understood that it is much easier to become successful in nonart vocations than it is in the arts since the arts require high ability if one is to be more than a mediocre success. However, an individual of only average ability can, with a reasonable amount of work, find much satisfaction in the arts as a leisure-time activity.

There is much subject matter in the field of art, including art history, criticisms and standards of taste, knowledge of various movements in art, types of art media and expression, and many other areas.

The framework of the music program offered in most secondary schools consists mostly of orchestra, chorus, harmony, and appreciation, but a first-rate high school music program will provide a variety of courses for students in general education and advanced specialized opportunities for students desiring such work. Schools with several hundred pupils or more can offer two years of general music, including some music history and music appreciation, and they can also sponsor an orchestra, band, and choral groups. A music major can be offered in large high schools. In fact, some of the larger high schools have at times offered so many courses in music that their personnel have become concerned lest students fail to receive sufficient instruction in other fields.

Vocational education

Occupational specialization has become increasingly commonplace, and the number of occupations from which young people may choose has increased into the thousands. Because parents generally feel that they are not in a position to advise their offspring about careers, it is necessary for today's high school to offer work in vocational education.

Parents, as the public, own the schools; they can and do expect the public secondary school to provide intelligent and informed counsel from which the students can benefit. The school does not take away the responsibility of the parent; it merely supplements the efforts of parents.[4]

The vocational programs offered in secondary schools are not designed to turn out specialists but rather to lay a good foundation

[4]Taylor and others, *op. cit.*, pp. 186–187.

for efficient learning and specialization after high school. Vocational educators realize that, in a time when changes are so rapid, many special skills and understandings acquired in high school may be out-of-date before the student has a chance to use them; thus vocational teachers stress flexibility and general skills. They seek to give the student a broad vocational education in an occupational area instead of in a special division of that area. For example, schools should try to acquaint the student with major areas and skills in business education as well as in a single area such as bookkeeping. Essential skills and understandings for a specific division of an occupational field can be acquired later in a junior college or on the job. In 1950 Prosser and Quiggley pointed out that from 75 to 95 per cent of the jobs available to high school graduates in vocational education require little or no preliminary training that could not be mastered quickly on the job.[5]

However, a new concept, that of fitting the individual to the job, has arisen, stressing that talent and aptitude are as important in business and industry as they are in the professions. More and more positions in industry and business are demanding people with ability on a par with those educated in academic areas.

The most important vocational education subjects in the high school program are industrial arts, homemaking, business education, and agriculture. Other vocational subjects offered in comprehensive high schools and in specialized high schools are as follows:

Aircraft engines	Machine shop
Baking	Pattern making
Bricklaying	Printing
Cabinet making	Painting
Carpentry	Radio repair
Dressmaking	Sheet metal
Electricity	Welding
General maintenance	Watch repair

Industrial arts, homemaking, business education, and agriculture have been in the high school curriculum longer than most other vocational subjects, and they are still the most popular and probably the best organized.[6]

Industrial arts

There are educators who claim that industrial arts is the interpreter of the machine age in the secondary school curriculum.

[5]Charles A. Prosser and Thomas A. Quiggley, *Vocational Education in a Democracy* (Chicago: American Technical Society, 1950), pp. 387–388.

[6]Louis V. Newkirk, quoted in Harl R. Douglass, *Secondary Education* (New York: The Ronald Press Company, 1952), Chapter 15.

Certainly its development has paralleled that of the machine age.

The major purposes of trade and industrial education in the high schools are listed below:

1. Knowledge of good workmanship and design.
2. Ability to select, use, and care for the products of industry.
3. Interest in industry and production.
4. Skill in the use of the tools and machines used in production.
5. Good work habits and an appreciation of efficiency.
6. Ability to understand blueprints and the ability to express ideas by the use of drawings.
7. Worthy leisure-time interests.
8. Knowledge and appreciation of health and safety.
9. Resourcefulness, self-reliance, and self-discipline.
10. Ability to work well with others.

Homemaking

Enrollments in vocational homemaking, currently offered in over two thirds of the public secondary schools, have been larger than those in any other vocational subject. Today boys also can be found in homemaking courses, especially since certain topics—for example, the operation and maintenance of electrical appliances in the home—are considered as important to boys as they are to girls. The homemaking programs in secondary schools have not only been very popular, they have also been very successful. The aid given by the federal government since 1917 has been of great importance to these programs, especially from the standpoint of providing well-qualified teachers and good equipment.

The following comprehensive list of activities provided in homemaking courses in the secondary schools illustrates the degree of specialization possible in the senior high school:

1. Maintaining good health in the home.
2. Selection and use of home appliances.
3. Good care of the home and its furnishings.
4. Taking care of and guiding children.
5. Rendering first aid.
6. Care of the sick at home.
7. Selection and care of clothing.
8. Selection, preparation, storage, and serving of food.
9. Purchase of food.
10. Planning budgets for the home.
11. Living together as a family.[7]

[7]Rudyard K. Bent and Henry H. Kronenberg, *Principles of Secondary Education*, 4th ed. (New York: McGraw-Hill Book Company, Inc., 1961), p. 349.

The nature of the homemaking program is determined, to a great extent, by the type of community in which the particular secondary school offering the program is located. However, because appliances are becoming commonplace in most homes and because even people living in cities are buying large quantities of vegetables and meats and storing them at home, the homemaking program is becoming more uniform throughout the United States.

Business education

Business education, which today comprises one of the most thriving and commanding areas in the secondary school program, is at present undergoing some major changes in its approach and emphasis. It is no longer considered an area designed to offer a few courses for people who want to be clerks. The importance of offering business education in the high schools of the United States can better be appreciated when one realizes that one out of every five employed Americans is working in an occupation for which business education offers training.[8]

Educators in business education are concerned that their students acquire basic skills in typewriting, bookkeeping, business arithmetic, and general business; but the objectives have broadened to become more social and to provide students with opportunities.

Writing in 1940, Tonne stated well the position taken by many people in business education:

The course which has been developed in the last decade, called elementary business training, everyday business, or introduction to business, is an admirable example of the possibilities in this field. Its purpose is to give an understanding of what business is, how it functions, and how it serves both the individual and the society as a whole. . . . Certainly business is at least as important a phase of present life as science. The problems of business are possibly even more important as far as human progress is concerned. Why not then give every pupil a non-technical understanding of the place of business in contemporary life, even as we give a course in general science to develop a realization of the contribution of science in our civilization?[9]

It should be acknowledged, however, that many teachers in the field of business believe that they should concentrate on specific

[8]William M. Alexander and J. Galen Saylor, *Modern Secondary Education* (New York: Holt, Rinehart & Winston, Inc., 1959), p. 493.
[9]Herbert A. Tonne, "The Senior High School Business Curriculum," *The Business Curriculum*, Sixth Yearbook (Washington, D.C.: National Commercial Teachers Federation, 1940), p. 77.

skills and understandings rather than on a broad, general approach. Their argument is that, in attempting to use a broad approach, business teachers overlap with elements considered as legitimate material for the social sciences. They further contend that the preparation needed by students seeking employment after finishing high school would be neglected. Since business education has been organized around a specific track or tracks or in special elective courses and since the student is limited in the amount of time available for specialization in this area, many authorities feel the secondary school should stress skills in a limited number of subjects rather than try a general approach.

In addition to typewriting, business arithmetic, general business, and bookkeeping, many schools offer such business courses as economics, business correspondence, business law, economic geography, salesmanship, shorthand, and office practice.

A study of the literature dealing with business education reveals these major objectives:

1. To equip students with the skills and understandings necessary for certain jobs in business.

2. To provide young people with the knowledge necessary for the role of intelligent consumers.

3. To provide young people with an understanding of the role of business in our civilization.

4. To provide young people with the opportunities necessary for exploration of some of the major areas of business.

One area of business education which deserves special consideration is distributive education, a program or course concerned with the coordination of instruction in a classroom situation with on-the-job experience. Such a program deals with occupations in which workers are directly engaged in merchandising, in direct sales, or in managing and operating a commercial service. Distributive education courses include salesmanship, advertising, human relations, product information, store organization, store operation, and channels of distribution.[10] Programs in distributive education are usually time-consuming since they include work at school and school-supervised on-the-job experience in the upper high school years.

Under the provisions of the George-Barden Act, the federal government helps pay vocational education teachers' salaries. The amount of money thus far invested in this area by the federal government has been small.

[10]Krug, *op. cit.,* p. 463.

Agriculture

Agriculture was the last of the major vocational fields to become established in the secondary schools, and it was largely developed through the Smith-Hughes Act of 1917 with its special provision of funds for vocational agriculture. In 1949 the *Biennial Survey of Education in the United States* stated that 6.7 per cent of the public secondary school students in grades nine through twelve were enrolled in vocational agriculture. This sequence demands no more than four units in most high school programs, a requirement most educators feel is adequate since students in this type of program need a good general education.

Secondary school personnel are aware of the fact that opportunities in agriculture are changing. If the present exodus of people from the rural areas to the city increases, most of the students taking courses in agriculture will not be engaged in farming when they finish high school. This should not be interpreted to mean that courses in vocational agriculture are useless unless one eventually farms. It does mean that secondary school people must take a realistic look at this area of the curriculum and give careful guidance to students who are planning to take agriculture courses and that these courses must be planned to give students experiences which are valuable regardless of their future vocation.[11]

Special student activities

The student activity program can be used to provide many educational opportunities for youth to develop their talents and interests in special areas. It is generally accepted that the major objective of student activities is to promote personal-social development; however, many activities contribute to the learning of academic subjects and skills. For example, clubs in the fields of science, English, and mathematics often provide the opportunity for a student to reach outstanding achievements. Similarly, opportunities for vocational exploration can be provided through student activities.

Special administrative arrangements for special education

The major administrative arrangements used to provide special educational opportunities for students are special classes, grouping, multiple-track plans, varying student loads, and acceleration.

[11]*Ibid.*, pp. 491–492.

Special classes

When a school is large enough to have a sufficient number of individuals with special abilities, interests, or disabilities, classes are often formed for them. Some of the major areas in which one can find special classes in large high schools are advanced placement programs, work for slow learners, provisions for physically handicapped students, programs in remedial reading, and special honors classes.

Grouping by ability

Ability grouping, first developed by the elementary schools for pupils with varying abilities, is becoming increasingly commonplace in all except the very small secondary schools. While it is true that homogeneous grouping has been criticized as being undemocratic, most parents and teachers today feel that it is best for the students, the school, and society. In fact, most educators look upon this as not only a more truly democratic approach to teaching but, even more important, the only efficient approach. Mental ability, achievement, and interests are the chief bases for grouping.

No system of grouping will ensure a truly homogeneous group. Ability grouping, however, does make it possible for teachers to work with students who are able, in general, to progress at a common rate. The repetition necessary for those lacking in ability or achievement can be avoided with students who do not need such work, thus allowing further learning and preventing boredom on the part of more capable students. Although teachers know that differences among students will quickly come to light in these special ability groups and that they still must plan for individual differences, these teachers also know that the range of abilities confronting them will be reduced.[12]

Multiple-track plans

Schools sometimes divide their students and their curriculum into special patterns or tracks, one organization of courses for students of below-average ability, another for the superior students, and still another for students of average ability. This practice often leads to pupils being typed and, therefore, is often criticized. If the school has a good guidance program, however, the plan can work well and much criticism can be avoided. The comprehensive high schools today are making it possible for students not only to

---

[12]Bent and Kronenberg, *op. cit.,* p. 340.

get their required courses in sections based on ability but also to elect subjects in keeping with their ability, interest, and future plans — a procedure which results in less typing of students.[13]

Adjusting pupil loads

One of the oldest and most popular methods of adjusting a student's educational experiences to his ability is by varying the amount of work he is to do in the school. This method enables the superior student to carry a heavier load in terms of number of courses, special assignments, and number and types of student activities. On the other hand, students who, because of lack of ability or some other reason, cannot make normal progress are allowed to take a lighter load. Some schools require students having trouble with schoolwork to take a reduced load. At the present time many schools are urging their better students to take more courses during the regular academic year and to take courses in summer school, thus getting much more out of secondary education faster.

Acceleration

Educators vary in their opinions concerning acceleration of superior students in secondary schools. Nevertheless, this is one way to provide special educational opportunities for the gifted, and several types of accelerated plans are being used.

Some schools are allowing certain students with fine achievement records and superior intelligence to take extra subjects and, in some cases, to finish secondary school a year ahead of their fellow students who possess only average or below-average ability. This usually involves some summer schoolwork in addition to the extra subjects taken. Administrators of these schools believe that many gifted students can complete the secondary school program in three years and should be allowed to do so in order that they might begin the long period of preparation for a profession.

Many schools are urging brighter students to take more subjects, not to enable them to be graduated more quickly, but to provide the student with a broader educational program. While this is another method of accelerating secondary students, it does not permit them to graduate any sooner. Many educators argue that this is not a good procedure; others say it is the best approach because these students can profit from a broader program and thus

[13]Alexander and Saylor, *op. cit.,* p. 507.

should not be rushed through high school. Some schools are finding the answer to their dilemma by providing advanced placement programs for college-bound students. These programs make it possible for students to remain in high school, but instead of taking more secondary schoolwork of a traditional type, they take courses for which they will receive college credit or courses that will enable them to take special tests qualifying them for advanced standing in college.

A third method of acceleration is to allow gifted students to complete a course in less time than is required by other students and then to spend the remainder of the class time working on some other type of activity. Not many secondary schools have tried this plan.

Guidance

If a secondary school does not have an adequate guidance program, much that has been presented in this discussion of special education will be impossible. Some educators take the position that guidance services, when rendered by a competent staff in a well-organized program, constitute the most important provision the school can make in the area of specialized education. They feel that only through a well-planned system of guidance can special needs be determined and appropriate educational programs planned. Guidance thus brings together specialized needs on the part of a heterogeneous student body and specialized opportunities provided by the school. Guidance services in the modern secondary school are offered by specialized guidance personnel and classroom teachers working together. Guidance and counseling will be discussed at greater length in Chapter 10.

Specialized high schools

Though specialized secondary schools are commonplace in most European countries, they are mainly restricted to large cities in this country. Even in large cities, with the exception of New York City, only one or two specialized high schools can be found. The multipurpose high school has generally been considered best, although many people who favor the European system see this as a weakness in the American educational system. Most American educators would agree with the stand taken by Dr. James B. Conant:

I am convinced that a satisfactory course of study for the bright boy or girl (the academically talented) can be offered in the public high school which is of a general or comprehensive type; and I believe that, with proper organization and a good guidance system, a very large percentage of the able youth will elect a course of study which challenges their intellectual capacity, provides precise formulation of ideas, and develops habits of hard work. I am further convinced that the students in the comprehensive school derive certain advantages from their school year which are denied to their contemporaries in special schools. . . .

I have just spoken of my conviction about what can be accomplished by the American public high school in regard to the development of the academic talents of certain kinds of boys and girls. I have equally strong convictions as to what can be accomplished in the comprehensive high school for all types of youth. Indeed, I might say what must be accomplished, if our democratic society is to remain cohesive.[14]

It should be pointed out that most specialized high schools require of their students, either before or after entrance, a certain amount of general education. In fact, in the United States the term *specialized high school* is a relative term.

In some cities high schools have been classified as *technical, general,* and *college-preparatory,* although most specialized secondary schools have been developed for vocational education. There are several hundred vocational high schools in this country.

Some states—North Carolina, for example—have developed vocational centers for students who have been graduated from the secondary school and for those who have dropped out of secondary education prior to graduation. Wisconsin has a great network of locally operated, autonomous schools of vocational, technical, and adult education. In Milwaukee, for example, there are two separate school systems, each with an autonomous board and its own taxing power. One is the regular public school system; the other offers vocational and technical training to people of all ages and stations in life, ranging from slow-learning high school drop-outs to future chefs, diesel technicians, and grandmothers seeking to qualify for office jobs.

The overall result of Milwaukee's dual arrangement is a vast complex of educational opportunity with hundreds of free courses. The vocational system embraces five divisions under a single

[14]James B. Conant, "The Public High School and the National Interest," *Bulletin of the National Association of Secondary-School Principals,* XLII (April 1958), 346.

administration. These divisions, centered in two massive down-town buildings, are as follows:

1. A continuation school for sixteen- and seventeen-year-old drop-outs from the regular school system.

2. An adult high school which offers students eighteen and over a second chance to gain a diploma.

3. An adult school offering a wide variety of noncredit courses in business education, home economics, graphic arts, personal services, industrial, and academic subjects.

4. An apprentice school that graduates several hundred jour-neymen annually in fifty trades ranging from machinist to stone cutter.

5. The Milwaukee Institute of Technology which offers two-year programs in five broad categories:
   a. Technical (structural, mechanical, chemical and metal-lurgical, diesel, nursing, and restaurant and hotel cook-ery).
   b. Business.
   c. Graphic and applied arts.
   d. Television.
   e. General education (called the junior college).

In the 1962–1963 school year, this abundance of educational programs served more than 19,400 full- and part-time students enrolled in Milwaukee's day and evening sessions.

The city's regular school system has a large boys' trade and technical high school. This school is not a "dumping ground" for inferior students enrolled in the regular system; it is, rather, a specialized school where, in addition to full-strength academic courses, students receive concentrated vocational and technical training. After graduation from this school, many enroll in the Milwaukee Institute of Technology or as engineering students in four-year colleges and universities. Students who do not go to college often become tradesmen's helpers or enter technical occu-pations while developing their capacities in evening courses of the adult school; many others become apprentices.

There still remains the question of whether specialized educa-tion can best be provided in specialized schools or in multiple-pur-pose schools. Some educators believe that the secondary school dedicated to one purpose can offer a better program more econom-ically. Further, they contend that since such a school has a more homogeneous student body, better instruction can be provided. Other educators, however, favor the comprehensive secondary school, arguing that it is more in keeping with the democratic philosophy and the American belief in equality of opportunity. Many believe that specialized schools foster class consciousness and that specialization in single purpose schools is unwise because general education is neglected, a serious matter particularly when the student may not be sure of his future plans.[15]

Special education for the handicapped

It is beyond the scope of this discussion to present an adequate description of the many approaches to the problem of educating the handicapped; however, an attempt will be made to identify briefly some of the major provisions for the handicapped in secondary schools. In a later chapter the problems of slow learners will be discussed; therefore, this group will not be considered at the present time.

Until very recently the secondary schools of the United States have not done very much for the handicapped. Some school systems have had excellent programs for the handicapped in elementary education, but many of these same systems have done little for such students at the secondary level. The picture is changing. however; and today a greater number of systems are providing special programs for the handicapped at the secondary level. Provisions for these students involve the construction of special facilities.

There is a difference of opinion as to whether pupils with physical handicaps — speech defectives, the crippled, the hard-of-hearing, the partially seeing, and those with other special health problems — should be placed in regular school classes or segregated from other students. Some take the latter view on the grounds that it is best for the handicapped and for the normal student; others take the stand that handicapped individuals are a part of everyday life and should be placed with normal students unless the handicap is so pronounced that it would be impossible for the individual involved to benefit to any appreciable extent from the regular classroom. Many feel that when normal and handicapped individuals are placed together, a mutual feeling of understanding and appreciation can be better developed.

There is a general agreement that when a handicap is severe enough to require special treatment, it is best to provide special schools or classes. This will enable specially trained teachers to do much more than could be done by regular teachers in a regular

---

[15]Alexander and Saylor, *op. cit.,* p. 474.

classroom. Recently some states have created state-wide programs to deal with the handicapped. The United States Office of Education described as phenomenal the increase in provisions for the handicapped and the enrollment in special courses designed to fit their needs during the school year 1952–1953.[16] More recent studies show that the trend is continuing.

Speech defects

Some specialists estimate that over 10 per cent of all students of secondary school age have some sort of speech defect. Most are not serious and therefore go undetected. Among the leading speech defects are stuttering, poor articulation, stammering, and lisping.

Secondary schools often employ speech correctionists who are able to give special help and instruction. Many school systems do not provide a specialist for each high school but do provide such a person on a visiting basis. In most instances such a specialist works with extreme cases only. Large secondary schools find it best to have a full-time specialist, working in a specially equipped room. With such a program some students will see the specialists only once or twice a week; others, one class period a day; and still others may spend most of the school day with the specialists. Some schools have even found it necessary to have one room for extreme cases and another room for minor ones.

Crippled students

Severely crippled students are usually cared for in special classes; however, most schools attempt to give these students as many opportunities as possible to be a part of the total school life. The less severely handicapped can often fit into most school activities with the exception of regular physical education classes and the sports program. However, excellent experiences in physical education can be provided for the crippled student on an individual basis. Many school systems have special schools for the crippled, whereas others make no provisions for such individuals.

Hard-of-hearing

Programs developed for students with hearing difficulties attempt to place them in the regular classes and program of student activities as much as possible. Hearing aids have proved a great help to many of these students; others have mastered the technique

---

[16]"Statistics of Special Education for Exceptional Children, 1952–53," Chapter 5 in *Biennial Survey of Education in the United States, 1952–54,* U.S. Office of Education (Washington, D.C.: Government Printing Office, 1954), p. 19.

of lip reading and are able to profit from a regular classroom situation. Most programs designed to help the hard-of-hearing in secondary schools are built around the use of amplified instruction, hearing aids, and lip reading.

Partially seeing

What has been said concerning provisions for crippled students, the hard-of-hearing, and students with speech defects applies to the partially seeing. The school tries to make as many adjustments as possible in normal situations. Many schools provide specially equipped classrooms where students with visual problems can do all the work that involves close eyework. In the case of blind children, as in the case of deaf students, the schools feel that it is best to provide special classes or schools whenever possible.

Other health problems

The above discussion makes no mention of many students having such health problems as epilepsy, heart trouble, glandular trouble, or tuberculosis. Many are, of course, in special hospitals; some are home-bound cases, while others are able to engage in some of the normal school activities and are segregated only for special treatment. Of necessity, those with contagious diseases, such as tuberculosis, must be separated from the regular students.

Special education for the socially maladjusted

There are some students who because of social and emotional problems cannot adjust to the typical classroom situation, and many times they create grave problems. Those who are seriously maladjusted usually drop out of school, but before they do, they can do much harm to the regular learning situation while profiting very little from normal instruction. Extreme cases are often referred to juvenile courts or welfare organizations, and many are placed in private schools or public custodial institutions.

Some school systems, such as that in New York City, have developed special schools to care for the most difficult cases. While these schools seem to be achieving some success, they cannot in themselves remove the causes of maladjustment. Most educators feel that the best the average secondary school can do is to attempt to prevent maladjustment by providing an appropriate curriculum supplemented by guidance services and by trying to diagnose maladjustment in its early stages. This is not to say that the secondary school can do very little; instead it is an attempt to be realistic. The school can help many students overcome or adjust to emotional, mental, and physical handicaps, but many of these problems are beyond the control of the regular teacher in the typical classroom. Here is a problem that society in general will have to attack. It may be that more special schools such as the ones in New York will be the answer.

Selected references

Adapting the Secondary-School Program to the Needs of Youth. Fifty-second Yearbook. National Society for the Study of Education. Chicago: University of Chicago Press, 1953.

"Advanced Placement Programs in Secondary Schools," *Bulletin of the National Association of Secondary-School Principals,* XLII (December 1958), 1–171.

ALEXANDER, WILLIAM M. AND J. GALEN SAYLOR. *Modern Secondary Education.* New York: Holt, Rinehart & Winston, Inc., 1959.

BENT, RUDYARD K. AND HENRY H. KRONENBERG. *Principles of Secondary Education,* 4th ed. New York: McGraw-Hill Book Company, Inc., 1961.

CONANT, JAMES B. *The American High School Today.* New York: McGraw-Hill Book Company, Inc., 1959.

——. "The Public High School and the National Interest," *Bulletin of the National Association of Secondary-School Principals,* XLII (April 1958), 343–356.

CRUICKSHANK, WILLIAM M. AND G. ORVILLE JOHNSON, EDS. *Education of Exceptional Children and Youth.* Englewood Cliffs, N.J.: Prentice-Hall, Inc., 1958.

CUTTS, NORMA E. AND NICHOLAS MOSELEY. *Teaching the Bright and Gifted.* Englewood Cliffs, N.J.: Prentice Hall, Inc., 1957.

DOUGLASS, HARL R., ED. *The High School Curriculum,* 3rd ed. New York: The Ronald Press Company, 1964.

FEHR, HOWARD F. "High-School Mathematics for the Second Half of the 20th Century," *Bulletin of the National Association of Secondary-School Principals,* XLII (April 1958), 318–324.

FRASER, DOROTHY M. *Current Curriculum Studies in Academic Subjects.* Washington, D.C.: National Education Association, 1962.

HOVET, KENNETH. "What Are the High Schools Teaching?" *What Shall the High Schools Teach?* 1956 Yearbook. Association for Supervision and Curriculum Development, National Education Association. Washington, D.C.: NEA, 1956.

KRUG, EDWARD A. *The Secondary School Curriculum*. New York: Harper & Row, Publishers, Inc., 1960.

WILES, KIMBALL. *The Changing Curriculum of the American High School*. Englewood Cliffs, N.J.: Prentice-Hall, Inc., 1963.

Crucial issues in curriculum planning

Since the establishment of high schools and junior high schools, educators have been concerned with providing a curriculum to meet the differing interests, abilities, and needs of students. For decades people in the field of education have written and spoken of this critical matter, but no easy solution has been advanced.

There are several varying points of view as to how the secondary school can provide an appropriate curriculum for a heterogeneous student population. Efficient learning cannot take place unless the learning activities and the instructional materials are geared to the abilities of the students. Furthermore, unless the activities and materials have meaning and are related to the students' lives, little, if any, permanent learning will take place. Attempts to provide more effectively for the individual differences among students have led to many curriculum adaptations such as the establishment of the junior high school, homogeneous grouping, special evaluation practices, various promotion practices, special classes for slow and rapid learners, and special elective courses.

It must be realized from the outset that more has been attempted through administrative practices than by teachers within the classroom. But regardless of administrative arrangements, the degree of success reached by secondary schools in meeting the individual differences of their students in the 1960's is to a tremendous extent dependent upon the work of the individual teacher in his classroom. Teachers must work with individuals in their classes whether the classes are grouped homogeneously or not. The following discussion will identify some of the major issues in providing for individual differences in the curriculum.

Individual differences must be identified if they are to be dealt with effectively. The school personnel—administrator, teachers, and counselors—must know as much as possible about students. It is especially important that classroom teachers know their students well—their home and family backgrounds, previous achievements, special interests, psychological backgrounds, health and physical backgrounds, and their general mental abilities.[1]

The school needs to know the socioeconomic status of the student's family, the occupation of the father, the number of children in the home, the language spoken in the home, and the general cultural background of the family. Teachers and counselors should know the pupil's intelligence quotient, general aptitude for the various subjects offered, mental and emotional adjustment, and the way he relates himself to his peers. Information concerning the student's sight, hearing, and health history is often important to teachers, as is awareness of such disorders as heart ailments, epilepsy, and nervous difficulties. The school staff can work more effectively when they know the individual's previous grades, his scores on standard achievement tests, his performance on diagnostic tests, and the activities in which he has participated.

A pupil's teacher and counselor can work with him in a much better way when they have information about his educational goals and vocational interests. Often a knowledge of the individual's social activities, special interests in such areas as reading or sports, or any special talents in fields such as music, speech, or art can help the adults who work with students in the secondary school. At times information concerning a pupil's participation in community organizations, his citizenship record, efforts in school service clubs, out-of-school employment, friendships, ability to work with others, travel, or vacation experiences is helpful.

Determining individual differences

Among the many ways of securing information about secondary school students are formal or informal conferences with the students' previous teachers. Core teachers, teachers in general education classes involving extended or double class periods, or home-

---

[1]William T. Gruhn and Harl R. Douglass, *The Modern Junior High School* (New York: The Ronald Press Company, 1957), pp. 202–203.

room teachers can often provide much valuable information. However, a teacher should be very cautious in his evaluation of information furnished by those who have previously worked with his students, especially when extreme criticism or praise is offered. In no case should such information—whether obtained from former teachers or from other sources—result in prejudice on the part of the present teacher toward his students.

Another excellent source of information is the records kept in the principal's office and by guidance personnel. This information is so important that many schools have regular provisions for making it available to teachers. The teacher should familiarize himself with this information as quickly as possible at the beginning of a new school year or semester.

The student's home can often provide necessary information for the teacher. Many teachers, particularly homeroom teachers, make it a practice to visit the homes of as many of their students as possible. In most cases, it is impossible for the teacher to visit all of his students, but the conscientious teacher will do some visiting and, when possible, will have conferences with parents at school.

Studying the student is still another way of gaining vital information that can furnish important guidelines for teachers. Teachers can learn much by observing students as they work and by evaluating the quality of their finished work. Other means of securing information about students are conferences, questionnaires, autobiographies, sociometric tests, case studies, interest inventories, standardized achievement tests, tests of mental ability, aptitude tests, and diagnostic tests.

Information about students is, of course, worth little or nothing unless it results in proper adaptations and modifications in teaching. For example, information obtained from diagnostic and achievement tests should lead to appropriate action on the part of the school staff. Do the results show that students have not mastered certain elements in skill subjects such as English, mathematics, or foreign languages? If so, these areas of deficiency must be attacked. If, on the other hand, the test results show that the students have mastered basic skills or specific areas of knowledge, then the teacher must plan his teaching so that needless duplication and boredom will be avoided.

Information about students' ability often makes it necessary for the teacher to do some grouping within his class. Teachers who know that certain students need special remedial work can provide such help in special groups. Similarly, a knowledge of students' interests may suggest ways to individualize instruction. By relating class instruction and required out-of-class projects to student interests, the teacher can often get pupils to work harder in the course.

A teacher's knowledge of a student's home background, health records, and psychological background can often help in avoiding embarrassing situations in class. This knowledge may lead to special arrangements in grouping, seating arrangements, and special adaptations in learning activities. Such information can also be used for a positive approach that will enable the teacher to promote interest, provide opportunities for mastering skills, help establish purposes when home and social life have failed to stimulate a student, and thereby help him avoid discouragement and a spirit of defeatism. Teachers who have information about their students can anticipate difficulties and make adaptations in their teaching to overcome them.

Identifying students' needs

It is easy to say that the school's program should be based on the educational needs and goals of its students. Doing so is a difficult and involved task, however, because there are many differing opinions as to what student needs can be met by the school and what type of educational experiences should be provided to fulfill them. Creating a curriculum is so time-consuming that a school's staff usually only attempts to adapt the curriculum organization of other schools to its own situation.[2] Thus, curriculum planning becomes a process of making modifications as demands for new activities and materials become apparent and the necessity for existing experiences can no longer be justified.

Despite the fact that schools generally have simply adapted their curriculums to particular situations, most educators believe it is possible to identify the educational needs of youth and to plan to meet them. These educators identify an educational need as a social or personal need that the school can help meet. But attitudes vary considerably. At one extreme are those who hold that educational needs consist only of so-called "felt" needs; they believe, in other words, that only as individuals feel a need for a skill or area of knowledge can there be any such thing as efficient teaching or learning. Therefore, the subscribers to this school of thought would plan the curriculum "on the spot" for individual students and would make little effort to identify and meet the common needs.

[2]William M. Alexander and J. Galen Saylor, *Modern Secondary Education* (New York: Holt, Rinehart & Winston, Inc., 1959), pp. 345–346.

Another point of view is that all adolescents have basic common needs as a result of common life problems, that these needs can be anticipated, and that a prescribed curriculum can be planned to meet them. Advocates of this viewpoint consider the matter of individual educational differences of secondary importance and think of the best curriculum as one which is planned in much the same way for all.

Other educators take the position that while there are common life problems and therefore common needs, there are also special needs on the part of all individuals. They agree that there should be prescribed subjects and activities in the curriculum, but they insist that the school can and must attempt to identify the special interests and requirements of its students and must provide a framework for specialized education in which specific individual needs can be satisfied. For example, these theorists believe that all students should be able to communicate effectively with others and that the curriculum should offer opportunities to develop communication skills. Yet they realize that students planning to enter professions require communication skills which differ from those needed by pupils going into skilled trades. This same line of reasoning they would apply to science, mathematics, and other areas. This point of view—that common and special needs can be anticipated—is accepted by most educators.

It must be acknowledged that it is difficult and often impossible to draw a line between general education and specialized education. For example, the need to make a living is a common one; yet to meet this one need, the school must provide opportunities in general as well as specialized education. Both the vocational and the general education curriculum involve much content that is academic in nature—English, mathematics, science, and social studies. No doubt almost any academic subject can be closely related to preparation for higher education, general education, or a vocation and thus can increase a student's chances to succeed; however, the student must see "clearly what outcomes selected from the academic subjects can give help."[3]

There are two major methods of identifying the educational needs of youth. One method, already discussed in this chapter, is to study adolescents and their individual differences. This study should include present students, those who left school before graduation, and those who graduated. These studies can furnish information on students' success in business, college, skilled

[3]L. O. Taylor and others, *The American Secondary School* (New York: Appleton-Century-Crofts, 1960), p. 183.

trades, and other areas. This data can then be used in the modification of the school's curriculum if such seems warranted. Follow-up studies can also often furnish information on leisure-time interests, family life, difficulties in social adjustment, and communication skills that may have meaning for the school.

Another method of identifying the educational needs of adolescents is to study available research on the subject and the work of commissions and committees devoted to this problem. Many teachers have benefited from the study done by such groups as the following:

1. Commission on the Reorganization of Secondary Education, 1918.

2. Various regional associations and the United States Office of Education and their work in the National Study of Secondary Education, 1929–1930.

3. American Youth Commission, 1935.

4. Commission on Secondary-School Curriculum, 1942.

5. Educational Policies Commission, 1944, 1946.

6. National Association of Secondary School Principals, 1947.

7. Commission on Life Adjustment Education for Youth, 1945.

8. The studies of Dr. James Conant and his staff, 1958–1959.

9. The School Mathematics Study Group, 1955–1964, and similar groups in mathematics and other subject areas.

Outstanding educators such as James B. Conant and Robert J. Havighurst have furnished much information that has great implications for any school faculty concerned with meeting the needs of youth in the secondary school curriculum. In his *Human Development and Education* Havighurst lists what he terms the developmental tasks of adolescence.[4] Conant's *Slums and Suburbs,* a study of schools and student needs in metropolitan areas, presents a discussion of schools and youth in city slums and wealthy suburbs. *Schools for the Sixties,* a study by the Project on Instruction, deals in depth with the crucial problem of good education for today's students.

Other critical issues

Thus far two very important questions have been advanced: how individual student differences can be known and how the educational needs of students can be identified. While these ques-

[4]Robert J. Havighurst, *Human Development and Education* (New York: Longmans, Green and Company, Inc., 1953).

tions spotlight several issues in secondary education, there are other critical issues to be considered.

Why universal education

Many individuals challenge the concept of universal secondary education. Some argue against compulsory attendance in secondary schools; others would lower the compulsory attendance age and remove from the secondary schools students who do not have good academic records. In short, they would adopt a policy similar to that sponsored in France or Germany. This would ensure, they feel, that students with academic ability would work harder and those without it would be prevented from wasting time and taxpayers' money. Students without the ability to do well in academic areas could drop out of school and go to work or be placed in some type of trade education.

Vast numbers of other individuals in the United States would prefer no public education at all. They believe that education, especially secondary, should be the responsibility of the home and private and parochial schools. This feeling on the part of many is one reason why, as James B. Conant reported in 1961, parochial schools in some cities in the United States enrolled more than one third of the school population.[5]

Most educators in this country, however, believe that secondary education with a worth-while curriculum must be provided for all youth. Such a curriculum would include courses in languages, English, mathematics, science, and the traditional social studies, plus many other opportunities such as vocational education. Individuals who favor secondary education for all are calling for major changes in the curriculum patterns found in the secondary school today.[6] They realize, too, that better guidance services must be made available to students.

Determining the major responsibility of the secondary school

In addition to academic instruction and a host of activities, the secondary school has assumed responsibility for many special services such as health services, safety education, transportation services, food services, guidance services, and library services. Although these special services could be provided by agencies other than the school, society has either delegated them specifically

[5]James B. Conant, *Slums and Suburbs* (New York: McGraw-Hill Book Company, Inc., 1961), p. 3.
[6]*Planning and Organizing for Teaching,* Project on Instruction, National Education Association (Washington, D.C.: NEA, 1963).

to the schools or has failed to make any provision for them; consequently, educators have felt compelled to attempt to meet needs in these areas.

Many people wonder whether the secondary schools, in attempting to do so much, may neglect their major role which, they believe, is the intellectual development of the student. Some educators, believing that schools should concern themselves with only the intellectual development of the student, say schools are often anti-intellectual. They would de-emphasize vocational courses, physical education, sports, social activities, and guidance. They feel that the home and other agencies must take care of the non-intellectual needs. There is no suggestion as to what existing agencies might meet these needs, nor is there any recommendation on how the home would be made a more influential institution in the lives of adolescents. Such critics also ignore the fact that intellectual development does not take place in a vacuum; emotional and social growth are vital factors that influence intellectual development.

Other educators recognize the great importance of the emotional and social development of young people and acknowledge that adolescents must often have help in making vocational, educational, and social plans. They realize that many of the responsibilities heaped upon the school could be assumed by the home, religious institutions, and community agencies, but they are also aware that in most communities these institutions have no plans for assuming more responsibilities. Nevertheless, these educators maintain that some changes must be made — that the home and the community must be responsible for desirable recreation for students and the schools must give less time to athletics and marching bands and more time to academic work.

What is the answer? The following elements are worth considering. The secondary school cannot meet all needs of students, and intellectual development is certainly of primary importance. The student, however, must be considered as an individual with important social and emotional needs which cannot be divorced from his intellectual development.

Learning by its very nature demands that teachers be concerned with the emotional and social development of the student.[7] This does not mean that such interest is placed above the school's efforts to provide for intellectual development. Some schools have asked teachers to assume too many responsibilities which relate to

[7] Gail M. Inlow, *Maturity in High School Teaching* (Englewood Cliffs, N.J.: Prentice-Hall, Inc., 1963), pp. 23–31.

student activities of a social or recreational nature, often draining the teacher of energy that should be used in the educational program. Many interscholastic sports, social activities, recreational activities, and money-raising activities that were introduced years ago are not so easily justified in the 1960's as they were in the past.

Furnishing effective universal education

Providing for the educational differences found among students is no easy task. During the last quarter of the nineteenth century the vast majority of students graduated from high schools went on to higher education. Secondary school pupils today are a much less homogeneous group. While a large number of students plan to go to college, an even larger number have other plans after graduation, and many will not even graduate. The school must take all these young people with every shade of mental ability, with every conceivable type of background, with every type of interest and expectation, and somehow give them meaningful educational experiences.

Harold Hand stated the problem well in 1958 when he declared that "no uniform approach to the problems of learning, no single pedagogical technique, and no single course of instruction can serve all the students of a given grade equally well."[8] The answer to the problem evidently is that the individual schools must modify and adapt their teaching procedures and curriculums to the needs of their own students. An idea of the changes needed in order to adjust instruction and curriculum content to individual abilities is suggested by Hand as he declares that "competent scholars"[9] believe "that about half the school population is incapable of learning algebra as it has been taught in the past."[10] When schools insist that students take subjects which they cannot master or subjects in which they have no interest, the schools are not only frustrating both students and teachers and forcing them to waste time but are also wasting the taxpayers' money.

Providing the proper type of experiences in the curriculum is perhaps the most important problem in secondary education today. Schools cannot plan just for the average student; they must also provide for the rapid learner and the slow learner. The gifted student often is not challenged, and the slow learner may be neglected and frustrated because his abilities do not enable him to perform

[8]Harold C. Hand, *Principles of Public Secondary Education* (New York: Harcourt, Brace, & World, Inc., 1958), p. 62.

[9]By "competent scholars" Hand is referring to the authors of the Harvard Report on *General Education in a Free Society.*

[10]*Ibid.,* p. 60.

successfully the educational tasks in most academic areas as they are taught.

What is the answer? It surely does not lie in a European plan of selectivity, nor does it lie in a "watered-down" curriculum geared for the average range of intellectual ability. The answer probably lies in a flexible approach to the curriculum—flexible enough to provide special courses, sections of courses, and grouping within sections for all students. In other words, it is necessary to have variety in methods of teaching, in school organization, and in curriculum materials and experiences.

Many secondary schools are already offering educational opportunities that are making it possible for adolescents to receive a challenging and meaningful education even though these students differ greatly. The secondary school is providing opportunities for them to learn of their cultural heritage, to master communication skills, to become self-supporting and informed adults, and to prepare for citizenship in a democratic country.[11]

Teachers who believe in secondary education for all and who are willing to spend time and effort in planning their instruction to challenge and provide meaning for their students can offer excellent educational programs in difficult situations. They will find ways to adapt their instruction to the wide range of student abilities.

Providing a balanced curriculum

One of the most frequent criticisms of secondary education is that much of the work is lacking in sound scholarship. Some critics go so far as to say the secondary schools often foster an attitude of anti-intellectualism. Others criticize the evaluation and promotion standards which they feel are too low. These critics look to European schools or to the days in this country when secondary education was very select.

At the same time, there are others who would prefer that the secondary school go in the opposite direction toward more vocational education and work experiences and a de-emphasis on the number of required academic subjects. These critics point to the high percentage of failures and drop-outs in high schools and suggest that the solution lies in a more functional curriculum and a more flexible approach in teaching methods.

Most educators take a broader view of the school and its students than do any of these critics. The answer does not seem to lie

[11]*Schools for the Sixties,* Project on Instruction, National Education Association (New York: McGraw-Hill Book Company, Inc., 1963), Chapter 4.

either in a strict academic program or in an anti-intellectual approach. Rather, most educators believe, an excellent elective program should be provided with required academic work and many types of elective courses—of an academic and vocational nature. They also believe, as has been stated before, that teaching methods must be adapted to individual differences. Students of superior ability should be given opportunities to do work involving more difficult concepts and requiring greater intellectual effort, not just more of the same type of work done by average or below-average students. At the same time, all students should be taught in such a way that they can progress as far as their abilities will permit. The vocational subjects must not become a "dumping ground" for students of limited ability; nor should such students be deprived of challenging opportunities in general education subjects such as English, mathematics, science, and social studies.

Determining proper grouping

The question of grouping involves grouping not only by and within classes but also by schools. Among secondary education personnel there has been much speculation on whether grades seven and eight should be placed in secondary or elementary education, but there has been little objection to the policy of grouping by grades. However, educators and many laymen feel that the system of grades often handicaps students who could progress through elementary and secondary education much faster.

The issue of grouping by types of schools brings forth varying viewpoints. Many educators today argue for the establishment of more specialized schools for the gifted and for those desiring vocational education. Still others see in such a form of grouping grave threats to the educational systems in the United States and to the American way of life.[12] Most educators and laymen seem to favor the comprehensive American high school; however, it is doubtful that any responsible person would abolish the specialized high schools now in existence or would be so dogmatic as to oppose the establishment of local, specialized high schools when a particular community feels a need for such a school.

Grouping also involves what is known as homogeneous and heterogeneous grouping, a system of classifying students on the basis of their achievement and ability. Some critics argue that such a process is undemocratic and detrimental to the mental health of students, while others feel that this is an excellent way to promote

[12]James B. Conant, *The American High School Today* (New York: McGraw-Hill Book Company, Inc., 1959), Section II.

more efficient instruction on the part of the teacher and better learning on the part of the student. In many small high schools the issue is of little significance since there is only one class section in most courses, but larger secondary schools may have a number of sections in certain classes. Some educators believe that the students' interests are best served when they are grouped homogeneously subject-by-subject in grades seven through twelve in such areas as social studies, mathematics, science, and English.[13] This approach in large schools would result in three groups—a large middle or average group, a small group of superior ability, and a small group of below-average or limited ability.[14]

Although many educators believe that homogeneous grouping should be extended to most class sections, they prefer that students be grouped heterogeneously in some student activities and in some general education classes. A blanket policy of homogeneous grouping based on a single criterion usually is not favored; rather the preferred policy is subject-by-subject grouping based on ability and achievement. In other words, a student would be grouped in each subject according to his aptitude and past achievement in that subject.

Homogeneous grouping was very popular in the early junior high schools, especially in the 1920's. In the 1930's it lost some of its popularity, however, because many parents, principals, and teachers felt that the practice was working against the emotional and mental health of students. Although this plan seems to be regaining favor, especially in the comprehensive high school, few educators want an extreme form of homogeneous grouping, and most of them insist that students should be grouped heterogeneously at some point in their educational experiences.

There is also the feeling among educators that the elective system—although not an exact type of homogeneous grouping—provides the best answer, since students usually elect college-preparatory or vocational courses in which they are interested and able to do the work. Most teachers would be quick to reply to this argument that many times students make grave mistakes in their choices and waste much time in areas for which they do not have the ability.[15]

Perhaps one of the most important methods of grouping pupils is the practice of subgrouping within classes. Elementary teachers have long used this method very effectively. It is used in

[13]Conant, *Slums and Suburbs,* p. 64.
[14]*Ibid.,* pp. 64–65.
[15]Alexander and Saylor, *op. cit.,* pp. 376–377.

secondary schools on a much smaller scale, and many teachers make no attempt to utilize this approach. Even when students are grouped homogeneously, the teacher will frequently employ subgrouping within a class in order to relate the curriculum to the students' needs. Discerning teachers will find many opportunities to group those students who have special interests and needs as a result of individual achievement and differences.

Evaluating students

The question, how should students in secondary schools be evaluated, like Banquo's ghost, "will not down." Certainly, no ironclad rules can be set forth on this subject, for if teaching is to assume an individual as well as a group approach, it would appear that evaluation must take into consideration individual differences as well as group achievement. This should not be interpreted to mean that no concern should be shown for high standards of achievement. On the contrary, teachers of academic subjects and vocational subjects must at all times strive to have their students perform on a high level.

Although individual excellence should be the goal in general education courses, how can a teacher apply a rigid marking system in courses that all students must take? It is impossible unless the teacher is willing to drive a high percentage of students out of secondary education, which is already losing about one third of its students before graduation. Therefore, in this matter of evaluation and promotion, it would seem necessary to consider carefully individual abilities and talents. In other words, in the junior high school and in those subjects required of all high school students, grading, evaluation, and promotion policies must not lose sight of the individual. When evaluation focuses on the individual student and his individual performance in light of his abilities; when it is based on teacher-made tests, student projects, group participation, and in some cases even conferences between student and teacher; most students should not be failed. It may be best to have certain students repeat general education courses; for example, a student who is far behind in reading ability or other communication skills will doubtless be unable to perform satisfactorily at a more advanced level. The teacher should ask himself, "What can we do for this student as he repeats this course? Will the school provide opportunities suitable for him as he goes through this course again? Can the school provide special remedial work that might enable the student to go on successfully? Will remedial work be provided in this course if he appears to be failing again?"

Evaluating students in academic courses leading to higher education presents quite a different problem. In the first place, high schools should not encourage students to enroll in these courses when their achievement and their mental capacity indicate that they cannot handle advanced academic material. This will enable teachers of these courses to require a high level of performance and would allow them to fail without hesitation those students who have not done or cannot accomplish the work required.

Determining the teacher's responsibility in meeting student needs

Teachers must know their students well. They should study cumulative records and carefully observe students in the present learning situation. They should constantly ask themselves such questions as: "Why is this student doing well in my course? Could he do better? Why is he failing to achieve? What can I do to help?"

Teachers should study and help plan the school curriculum. They must evaluate what they are doing in their own courses, look into the work of others in similar fields and courses, and serve on committees in their particular school and in the school system. Such efforts give the teacher an opportunity to view his responsibilities more objectively, to make intelligent and informed comparisons, and to make revisions in his own work when necessary. It will also enable him to serve on committees that are responsible for making recommendations for system-wide curriculum changes.

Teachers must be willing to experiment and study, and they must always be looking for better ways to present materials, develop activities, and stimulate students to do more. In other words, teachers must be informed, flexible, and eager to learn.

Teachers must realize that they themselves are ultimately going to determine within their own classes how well students progress. The success of all administrative arrangements designed to provide for individual differences and all attempts at grouping students for the same purpose depend on the work of the individual teacher. This is the place where the final, vital steps must be taken in relating the curriculum to student needs.

Selected references

ALEXANDER, WILLIAM M. AND J. GALEN SAYLOR. *Modern Secondary Education.* New York: Holt, Rinehart & Winston, Inc., 1959.

BRACKENBURG, ROBERT L. *Getting Down to Cases.* New York: G. P. Putnam's Sons, 1959.

CONANT, JAMES B. *The American High School Today.* New York: McGraw-Hill Book Company, Inc., 1959.

————. *Slums and Suburbs.* New York: McGraw-Hill Book Company, Inc., 1961.

Education for All American Youth: A Further Look. Educational Policies Commission, National Education Association. Washington, D.C.: NEA, 1952.

The High School in a Changing World. American Association of School Administrators, National Education Association. Washington, D.C.: NEA, 1958.

INLOW, GAIL M. *Maturity in High School Teaching.* Englewood Cliffs, N.J.: Prentice-Hall, Inc., 1963.

Planning and Organizing for Teaching. Project on Instruction, National Education Association. Washington, D.C.: NEA, 1963.

The Pursuit of Excellence: Education and the Future of America. Special Studies Report V. Rockefeller Brothers Fund. Garden City, N.Y.: Doubleday & Company, Inc., 1958.

Schools for the Sixties. Project on Instruction, National Education Association. New York: McGraw-Hill Book Company, Inc., 1963.

SCOTT, C. WINFIELD, CLYDE M. HILL, AND ROBERT W. BURNS, EDS. *The Great Debate: Our Schools in Crisis.* Englewood Cliffs, N.J.: Prentice-Hall, Inc., 1959.

WOODRING, PAUL. *A Fourth of a Nation.* New York: McGraw-Hill Book Company, Inc., 1957.

Current trends
in the secondary school curriculum

chapter **8**

This chapter will attempt to pinpoint major trends in the secondary school curriculum that transcend subject lines. It must be realized, however, that the curriculum is subject to societal influences which can result in many diverse changes. For example, the depression of the 1930's and World War II in the 1940's exerted strong influences that brought about curriculum modification, and at the present time international tensions and the cold war are definitely affecting the content and organization of the curriculum. Despite these considerations students of secondary education must attempt to anticipate emerging patterns; professional people must constantly strive for improvement in the institutions in which they work. Improving on present practices and anticipating future developments can best be done by using existing data, studying frontier practices, and engaging in research and experimentation.

In recent years the most helpful information on experimentation and realistic trends in the curriculum has come from the following sources: the Ford Foundation; the Fund for the Advancement of Education, which is under the auspices of the Ford Foundation; the National Association of Secondary-School Principals; the National Education Association; the School Mathematics Study Group; the Physical Science Study Committee; the Chemical Education Materials Study; the Chemical Bond Approach Committee; and similar groups.[1]

Content changes in the curriculum

Current trends in the curriculum employed by the secondary school can be classified into two major areas: those related to curricular materials and experiences and those related to organizational approaches. The major trends that affect the content of the curriculum are discussed below.

Greater emphasis on guidance

Secondary schools today are placing growing emphasis on guidance in the curriculums of both the junior and senior high school. Although guidance is not new at either level, the amount of attention being devoted to it and the number of professional personnel involved are greatly increasing. Schools are seriously attempting to utilize guidance in personal, social, educational, and vocational areas through organized programs involving counseling the individual, relating guidance and the curriculum to individual needs, and carefully planning group guidance and activities. Attempts are also being made to acquire adequate information about students so that counselors can advise them intelligently.

Better programs for exceptional students

Secondary educators are now attempting to offer more for the exceptional student, that student who deviates from the so-called average. The term *exceptional student* is used here in referring both to those who are physically and mentally handicapped and to those who have outstanding mental ability.

More provisions are being made for those students with physical handicaps such as severe loss of hearing and speech defects, which usually require the help of specialists. When the handicap is not severe, pupils merely need special help and consideration from the regular classroom teacher.

Slow learners and the mentally retarded are no longer being "dumped" into vocational or practical arts courses; instead, secondary schools are accepting the fact that these students can be

---

[1]Examples of the important information these sources have made available are Alexander J. Stoddard, *Schools for Tomorrow: An Educator's Blueprint* (New York: Fund for the Advancement of Education, 1957); J. Lloyd Trump and Dorsey Baynham, *Guide to Better Schools* (New York: Fund for the Advancement of Education, 1961); and *Schools for the Sixties,* Project on Instruction, National Education Association (New York: McGraw-Hill Book Company, Inc., 1963). Others are listed at the end of this chapter.

taught general education material when they are grouped in special classes with sympathetic and well-trained teachers. It has been found that these students, when shunted into practical arts courses, often present problems just as difficult to solve as the ones they create in academic courses; therefore, programs developed especially for them seem to be the answer.

Special classes and programs are also being created for the gifted and talented learners, a necessity if these students are to develop their abilities fully. Schools are not only encouraging them to do more work and a higher level of work in the required courses, but the better school systems are also offering special sections of these courses, providing for flexible assignments in heterogeneously grouped classes, developing accelerated classes, and offering independent study and advanced placement courses that often qualify students for college credit.

In some secondary schools gifted students are permitted to spend ten or twelve hours a week in independent study. The student does not spend this time in a study hall; rather, special facilities, such as study alcoves and study desks, are provided. To be really effective, the independent study assignments must encourage students to work on their own initiative. The school can make available a variety of activities, such as reading, writing, and observing, and materials, such as books and audio-visual aids.

Educators recognize that when students, through their own efforts, obtain, analyze, and evaluate information and then use it to solve problems which are of interest and importance to them, learning at its very best is taking place. However, the traditional secondary school has not had enough materials available to ensure success in independent study. According to Trump and Baynham, not only should a great diversity of equipment and materials be available to students doing independent study, but these should be placed in special rooms, individual booths, and laboratories.[2] In addition, they insist, the school library must provide reference books and other materials on an open-stack basis for individuals doing independent study. These authors would make resources available for students, with adult supervision, to do independent work in mathematics, social studies, the sciences, English language arts, foreign languages, the fine arts, practical arts, and physical education.

During the late 1950's and early 1960's the National Association of Secondary-School Principals, working through its Commis-

---

[2]Trump and Baynham, *op. cit.*, p. 28.

sion on the Experimental Study of the Utilization of the Staff in the Secondary School, made experiments in independent study one of its research projects. Under the auspices of this commission, the University of Illinois High School in 1958–59 began five projects directed toward increasing students' responsibility for their own learning.[3] The projects were devoted to biology, advanced French, advanced problems in science, chemistry, and school-college articulation.

Some insight into these experiments and how they were conducted can be gained by looking at the project in science. At the beginning of the fall semester each pupil was required to have an interview with the instructor in charge to identify and select problems in science appropriate for self-study. Each student was assigned a desk and a bookshelf in a special room used only for this particular science course. The teacher met with the class only at biweekly seminars where the pupils discussed their work. Three or more conferences with the instructor per year were also required. Results of the project indicated that those students of above-average ability could learn science very well under such conditions and that, in addition to the content mastered, they were able to make excellent progress in independent study skills.[4] All five of the projects in the University of Illinois High School are being continued because they have proved so successful.

Better college preparation for more students
Although the development of better college-preparatory programs by secondary schools is not a new concern, the growing percentage of high school graduates seeking a college degree makes it increasingly important. Today over 40 per cent are furthering their education in institutions of higher learning, whereas twenty years ago only 20 to 25 per cent of high school graduates attempted to go to college. Our complicated and complex society, the demand for specialization, the emphasis on science and technology, and the continued rise in standards of living will probably cause the percentage to maintain its upward trend.

As the number of students seeking admission to colleges and universities swells, these institutions are forced to set up more rigid systems of selection and performance; therefore, secondary schools must develop improved guidance systems and more chal-

[3]David M. Jackson, W. L. Shoemaker, and Paul Westmeyer, "University of Illinois High School, Urbana, Illinois, Experiments Further with Independent Study," *Bulletin of the National Association of Secondary-School Principals*, XLV (January 1961), 199–208.
[4]Trump and Baynham, *op. cit.*, p. 87.

lenging programs to prepare students for advanced educational opportunities. While schools must be concerned with developing better curriculums for all pupils, there is definitely a trend in the secondary schools to provide a more suitable academic program for students planning college attendance.

Reorganization in subject areas

As was indicated earlier, many schools are organizing some of their general education courses through correlation, fusion, and core programs. This departure from the practice of merely requiring certain subjects is an attempt to be more specific and functional in providing opportunities and experiences considered necessary for all students. As was pointed out previously, many of these new approaches, as well as the traditional courses, are being reorganized around central themes or units of instruction.

Development of marketable skills

An increasing number of secondary schools are more concerned than they have been in the past with programs in which students can learn marketable skills. High schools are trying to provide programs for girls who are interested in becoming proficient in typing, stenography, and the use of clerical machines. Programs are being offered to prepare boys for various trades and different areas of industry, such as auto mechanics, tool and die making, building trades, electrical work, printing, metal trades, welding, and agriculture.

Many vocational programs, particularly those in distributive education, are planned so that students attend classes part of the school day and receive supervised on-the-job training during the rest of the day. Students receive credit for this school-supervised work, and they are also paid a salary by their employers. Excellent programs along these lines relate the classroom work to the work students are doing in their supervised jobs.

The communication arts approach

Another recent trend is the emphasis being placed on communication arts, those subjects that serve as tools or instruments for further learning and study in other fields. For example, pupils in English courses should become competent in oral and written communication, acquire reading skills, develop refined tastes and appreciation for leisure-time reading, and become intelligent readers of magazines and newspapers and discriminating viewers of television and motion pictures. Other examples can be found in the field of mathematics, which some educators say is "a necessary tool to be mastered and used in science, music, maps, charts, graphs, history, geography, consumer education, and homemaking."[5]

Emphasis on experience in the curriculum

Another trend that has been and is influencing the secondary school curriculum is the emphasis being placed on the value of organizing activities in harmony with the realization that learning is experiencing. Psychological research has proved to educators that individuals learn from the interaction of the entire nervous system with the environment. To learn, a person must really experience; he cannot remain passive but must enter into the opportunities provided. With this realization in mind, the people who are responsible for curriculum development are attempting to focus attention upon the type of experiences the learner should have, instead of placing emphasis upon the mastery of subject per se. This does not by any means rule out the importance of subject matter; instead, it shows concern for more effective learning of subject matter, skills, and understandings through a process of careful selection of content, attempts to utilize student interest and motivation, and lesson planning designed to make classroom instruction more meaningful to students.

Organizational changes in the curriculum

Organizational changes are modifying the curriculum in many ways. Some of the major ones are discussed below.

Use of large and small groups

Some secondary schools, trying to get away from the standard arrangement under which twenty-five to thirty-five students meet five days a week in the same class, are organizing classes of ten, thirty, and even seventy or more students in which several teachers work together to plan instruction and present materials. Those who are specially qualified present materials to large groups, while others conduct small-group discussions. Since some classes are smaller and some larger, the student generally must assume greater individual responsibility for his own learning. When this plan is used, at least a part of the school, and in some cases all of the school, is organized around three types of experiences and activities: large-group instruction, small-group discussion, and individual study.

[5]J. Minor Gwynn, *Curriculum Principles and Social Trends*, 3rd ed. (New York: The Macmillan Company, 1960), p. 414.

The large-group instruction, which occupies about 40 per cent of the students' time, often involves one hundred or more individuals. The group is conducted by very able teachers who are given adequate time for class preparation and who are capable of using the very best instructional aids. Listed below are some of the activities that can be conducted as effectively in large groups as in a traditional class:

1. Lectures designed to introduce new topics, explain new concepts, develop motivation, stimulate interest, identify problems to be solved, and clarify methods of study to be used.

2. "Buzz sessions" and panels that allow students to share information not readily available to all pupils and to analyze varying points of view.

3. Reviews, drills, and summaries.

4. Some demonstrations.

5. Viewing of filmstrips and instructional films.

6. Use of resource people from outside the school.

7. Development of understandings and concepts.

8. Summarization of understandings, principles, and concepts that can be transferred to other situations.

9. Guidance of pupils into self-analysis of knowledge.

10. Question and answer period by students and teachers.

In the small-group discussion, which takes up about 20 per cent of the time, students examine terms, concepts, and solutions of problems; discuss various topics that were presented in large-group meetings or discovered in individual study; and make attempts to reach areas of agreement and disagreement.

During the remaining 40 per cent of the allocated time, pupils engage in study activities independently or in groups of two or three, with some supervision by school personnel acting primarily as consultants. The students are free to read, see films, listen to records and tapes, formulate questions, run experiments, write, and do research. This time is also used for conferences between students and instructors, which help clarify goals, content, and personal problems.

The large-group instruction is conducted in auditoriums, little theaters, cafeterias, study halls, classrooms joined by closed-circuit television, and classrooms that have been enlarged. Large-group instruction on an extensive scale necessitates a school building with two or more teaching rooms or auditoriums large enough to seat 100–150 students and designed for instructing large groups. Although some secondary schools have used the regular auditorium and the cafeteria for this purpose, these facilities tend to limit the effectiveness of this type of instruction. To ensure the greatest effectiveness, the large classroom or teaching auditorium should be so designed that each student can easily see and hear the instructor and should be equipped with overhead, opaque, filmstrip, and motion picture projectors; a screen; chalkboards; and a built-in public address system. While it is expensive to equip such a room, this can be done more economically than providing four or five classrooms with only part of the necessary equipment.

Practically all schools which have experimented with the large-group approach are continuing and even expanding its use. Many new schools are being constructed to implement large-group instruction along with small-group discussion and independent study.[6]

It must be emphasized here that secondary schools using the large-group approach also employ small-group discussions. These smaller groups are usually composed of from twelve to twenty students and are normally scheduled to permit follow-up work dealing with the material introduced in the large-group meetings. Some schools refer to their small groups as seminars, and indeed, in many cases, they are similar to their college-level counterparts.

Most of the work in the seminars is designed to clarify, analyze, and develop the subject matter presented in the large-group sessions. More specifically, the seminars are used to examine concepts, to correct errors and misunderstandings, to probe deeply into understandings and generalizations requiring analysis beyond that received in the large-group meetings, to discuss written assignments, and to coordinate reading and other out-of-class work of the students.

Despite the fact that there are definite advantages to large- and small-group instruction, these approaches present some problems. To be effective, they require special facilities, as has already been indicated, and they demand very careful planning and preparation on the part of teachers. It seems, however, that they provide greater incentive for the teachers to make better preparation, perhaps because they realize the greater opportunity and responsibility which is theirs.

Another problem associated with large-group instruction is the impracticality of permitting students to ask very many questions during the actual presentations. This disadvantage is offset to some extent by the better presentation of material and the opportunities

[6]J. Lloyd Trump, *Images of the Future*, Commission on the Experimental Study of the Utilization of the Staff in the Secondary School, National Association of Secondary-School Principals (Washington, D.C., 1959), pp. 7–8.

given students to ask questions in the small-group sessions. Since greater preparation is demanded of teachers instructing large groups of students, it becomes very important for administrators to give the teachers involved a schedule that allows them the time needed for polishing their presentation and securing necessary materials. Teachers of large groups should not be required to conduct as many classes as the teacher of normal classes.

Still another problem which can arise when certain teachers are designated to teach large groups is that of teacher morale. In some cases, teachers have become very discouraged because they have not been selected to work with any of the large groups; in others, teachers have become resentful because they were asked to participate in such work when they did not want to be a part of it. Poor morale on the part of faculty members tends to stifle initiative and curtail creativity in teaching. This danger can be avoided, however, through wise leadership by the principal in developing a plan whereby the teachers of large groups are alternated and those who do not want to be involved are not compelled to.

Team teaching

Team teaching, another major trend manifesting itself in secondary education, must be used in the large- and small-group approaches, but it is also utilized in situations that involve little or no variation from the traditional class size. In team teaching, two or more teachers share responsibilities for instructing certain classes or groups. This means that teachers working as a team must have classes assigned to them during the same periods and that they must share common planning periods. Team teaching enables two or more teachers to pool their knowledge and talents in teaching a larger number of students than is usually possible in the conventionally organized school. It also facilitates individual help and small-group instruction when needed.

The composition, organization, and size of teaching teams vary greatly. Most teams are composed of professional teachers only, but in others are found both certified and noncertified personnel. In general, team teaching is organized to make optimum use of each teacher's professional talents. Traditionally, much of a teacher's time and energy are devoted to such duties as making reports, keeping records, administering tests, and grading papers. Many of these activities can be done by a clerical assistant working with a teacher team, thus permitting the teacher to spend more time in instructional preparation and student-teacher conferences. A good curriculum and expert instruction require careful planning and preparation by teachers, and these efforts require time — an element which is often limited for staff members in the typical school. More information on the procedures used in team teaching is given in Chapter 9.

Modified schedules

Team teaching, large- and small-group instruction, and emphasis on independent study require a schedule that is very different from the traditional one. The typical secondary school schedules pupils so that they proceed from one class or study hall to another, six or seven periods a day, with the same periods repeated five days a week.[7] Students are generally expected to spend six to seven hours a week on each of five subjects: this usually means attending a daily fifty- to fifty-five-minute class session plus approximately twenty minutes of study daily in school or at home. In schools that use forty-minute class periods, pupils are expected to spend from thirty-five to forty minutes in outside work for each class. In other words, students spend about thirty hours a week in school, not including the time allowed for extraclass activities and homerooms.

Today there is a trend in many secondary schools to schedule pupils in classes for an average of only eighteen hours a week, rather than thirty. Twelve of the eighteen hours are spent in large-group instruction and six in small-group discussions. The average student is scheduled for an additional twelve or more hours in individual study. Most students continue to devote about thirty hours a week to their school subjects, but many spend more than this amount of time on work in school.

Some of the more important schools that have experimented with modified schedules, large- and small-group instruction, and independent study and have obtained good results are listed below:

Newton High School, Newtonville, Massachusetts
Snyder Public Schools, Snyder, Texas
Secondary schools of Jefferson County, Colorado
South Bend Public Schools, South Bend, Indiana
Urbana High School, Urbana, Illinois
Syosset High School, Syosset, New York
Beecher High School, Beecher, Illinois
Fairfield Community High School, Fairfield, Illinois
Schools in the Catskill, New York, area
Chicago University Laboratory High School, Chicago, Illinois
Schools in Arlington Heights, Illinois

[7]*Ibid.,* pp. 13–14.

Evanston Township High School, Evanston, Illinois

Wilmington Secondary Schools, Wilmington, Illinois

Alexander Ramsey High School, Roseville, Minnesota

Hinton High, Sandstone High, and Summersville High, Summersville, West Virginia

Junior high schools of Weber County, Utah

Westside Community Schools, Omaha, Nebraska

These schools and many others have been engaged in modification of their programs since 1956, when these approaches were considered nothing more than widespread experiments. Today they are well-established practices in many schools.

But what have been the results received by schools employing such approaches? Schedule modifications and team teaching have produced results in student achievement which are just as good as — and, in many cases, better than — those of traditional approaches. Schools have also found that many of these innovations can be employed with little or no increased expense to the schools. Some of the other encouraging results are as follows:

1. Student morale is better, and most of the students favor the changes.

2. Pupils feel that they are accomplishing more and that the new approaches make school more interesting.

3. Teachers spend more time in preparation for class work.

4. Teachers are freed from many nonprofessional jobs such as clerical duties.

5. More teaching aids are used.

6. Specialists and teachers with special abilities are used to better advantage.

Of course, there have been difficulties, as was indicated earlier. In some cases, a team spirit has been slow in developing among certain teachers. Problems have arisen in scheduling, and many schools have found that some of their facilities were not adequate for such experiments. Some teachers preferred not to participate in the new approaches, and at times the new approaches do cost more.

Teaching aids

There is a strong trend in secondary schools to use more teaching aids, especially mechanical and electronic aids. Many visual and auditory experiences are being brought to students through the use of excellent instructional films, television, language laboratories, records, tapes, and programed materials. Although records, tapes, and films have been used on a large scale for many years, they are now being employed more for individual and group study, especially in English, speech, music, and foreign languages. Through the use of closed-circuit television and educational television stations, many schools are making it possible for more of their students to be taught by "master teachers."

Programed instruction. One of the fastest growing movements in the secondary school curriculum is the use of programed instruction, with or without the help of teaching machines. In 1954 B. F. Skinner, director of the Psychological Laboratories at Harvard University and a leading authority on learning, introduced a teaching machine utilizing the linear method of programing. Although teaching machines of several types had been invented in the early 1920's by Sidney L. Pressey of Ohio State University, Skinner's experiments attracted wide attention and gave great impetus to programed teaching.

Programed instruction is a self-teaching approach which breaks the subject matter to be studied into small, discrete, logical steps, or frames. Each frame consists of three parts known as the stimulus, the response, and the confirmation. The stimulus consists of a small bit of information, followed by a question to be answered or a blank to be filled. The last part of the frame contains the correct answer, against which the student checks his own response. Research has proved that the more immediate the confirmation, or reinforcement, the better an individual learns. This is also true if the student's response is wrong, because the error is immediately corrected.

When well written, the programed material will present the material to be learned in such a way that the pupil will give a correct response most of the time. Another characteristic of an excellent program is that the individual learns more than just the right answer for each frame, because the reinforcement of his response actually confirms the learning of all that is presented in the stimulus and relates it to that which was given in the previous frames. The pupil's knowledge is constructed in a step-by-step manner as he proceeds through the programed material; the answers he gives are based on what he has mastered in earlier frames. In this way he progresses from relatively simple to more complicated material.

Linear programing and *branch* programing are terms referring to the two major methods used in writing frames. The linear method uses constructed-response frames, which generally require the pupil to formulate his own answer to each stimulus by filling in a missing phrase or word. It relies on a very careful arrangement of small steps which lead the student through the program with a minimum of errors. The maximum probability of the learner's supplying the right answer is ensured by extensive testing and prior analysis of the errors that could be made. Requiring the student to recall the correct response, rather than to recognize it among several alternatives, results in more efficient learning, according to Skinner.

In the branch method of programing, often called selected-response or multiple-choice programing, the learner reads a part of the material and is then given a multiple-choice test item. The next step is determined by his answer. If it is correct, he goes on to more advanced frames; if it is incorrect, the next frame corrects his response and sends him along a branch of remedial frames to ensure his understanding before he returns to the main line.

Some educators advocate the selected-response type of frame, while others feel that learning is more efficient when constructed-response frames are employed. Margulies insists that "to maintain student interest through variety and to increase efficiency, both approaches should be used in the same program, each mode in its own place."[8]

The question arises as to how programed instruction should be used in the classroom. Should it be the primary means of instruction, or should it be used to supplement other methods? Programed materials have been utilized to enrich or accelerate the learning of gifted students and to provide remedial instruction for retarded learners, and in some situations they have become the basic core of the course. The trend, however, is to use programed instruction to supplement the classroom presentation of the teacher. Some teachers have developed their own programed materials rather than relying on commercially prepared ones.

Several proved advantages seem to justify the use of programed instructional materials:

1. The student can proceed to learn the subject matter at a rate commensurate with his own ability; thus programed instruction is an excellent means of providing for independent study.

2. It can free the teacher from the presentation of certain parts of the subject matter and permit him to devote more time to pupils' individual needs.

3. Self-instruction programs can make a valuable contribution to the attainment of all types of teaching objectives—knowledge, understandings, skills, attitudes, and appreciations.

[8]Stuart Margulies, "The Multiple-Choice Frame," *Programed Instruction* (February 1962), p. 4.

4. Students can master certain types of complex materials in much less time through the use of programed materials than through conventional methods.

As more research studies on programed materials are completed, the list of advantages may be expanded.

Teaching machines. The use of teaching machines with programed instructional materials is not a major trend in secondary education, but certain schools have experimented with the machines and have reported them helpful.[9] Many different types of teaching machines — ranging from simple, manually operated devices to complex, electromechanical machines — are available, and more than one hundred companies are presently manufacturing them. Regardless of the degree of complexity of the teaching machine used, it performs three main functions:

1. It makes it difficult for the pupil to look ahead to the correct answer before he supplies his own.

2. It records the learner's response to each item, thus permitting later analysis of his performance and the quality of the program.

3. It provides immediate feedback to confirm or correct the pupil's response.

Research evidence at the present time shows that there is no significant difference between machine and programed textbook presentations in the effectiveness of student learning. Several studies show that the use of programed textbooks requires less of the students' time — for learning and manipulating — than do teaching machines. Time, of course, is an important consideration in planning a good curriculum.

While research evidence does not indicate the superiority of teaching machines over the use of programed textbooks, the value of the machines in the curriculum has been adequately demonstrated.[10] The question which must be answered through more experimentation and research is: "How should teaching machines be employed to make an optimum contribution to the teacher-learning situation?"

Television and the curriculum. Since the early 1950's, when the great potential value of television as a medium of instruction was

[9]Lawrence M. Stolurow, *Teaching by Machine* (Washington, D.C.: Government Printing Office, 1961), p. 103.
[10]William Clark Trow, *Teacher and Technology* (New York: Appleton-Century-Crofts, 1963), Chapters IV and V.

recognized, educational television has expanded rapidly throughout the United States. The Federal Communications Commission originally reserved 264 channels for educational purposes, but this number has been increased in recent years. These channels are allocated to educational stations in communities which demonstrate the capability to finance and manage a station devoted to educational programs. In contrast to programed instruction, which places emphasis upon individualizing instruction, television has its great potential in mass teaching.

During the past decade many experiments, a large portion financed by the Fund for the Advancement of Education, have been conducted with both open- and closed-circuit television. The research evidence on teaching by television indicates that it is an effective means of instruction at all grade levels and that live television, kinescopes, and televised conventional films are equally effective. When the usual tests of achievement are used to measure student learning, there is no significant difference between teaching by television and by conventional methods. From a survey of the research material on teaching by television, Schramm derived the following conclusion:

There can no longer be any doubt that students learn efficiently from instructional television. The fact has been demonstrated in hundreds of schools, by thousands of students, in every part of the United States, and in several other countries. Schools and colleges have been able to teach virtually every subject effectively by television. The conclusion is that the average student is likely to learn about as much from a TV class as from ordinary classroom methods; in some cases he will learn more and in some less, but the overall verdict has been, "no significant difference."[11]

One of the largest experiments conducted with television teaching was begun in 1956 in the Washington County, Maryland, school system, where approximately 90 per cent of the students receive at least one period of television instruction daily. In 1957 the National Program in Use of Television in Public Schools, another large-scale project involving public school systems of three states and a dozen cities scattered across the United States, was begun. This project now includes more than 1000 schools and over 300,000 pupils. According to a report by the Fund for the Advancement of Education, the project has achieved two objectives:

[11]Wilbur Schramm, "Learning from Instructional Television," *Review of Educational Research* (April 1962), p. 156.

. . . First, it showed that TV could be used to teach very large classes, with resultant savings in teaching time and classroom space; second, it gave preliminary confirmation to the belief that the use of TV could improve the quality of teaching without an increase in cost.[12]

Both these studies have shown that the use of television in teaching large classes enables many teachers to concentrate on students' individual needs through both individual and small-group instruction.

In 1961 the Midwest Council on Airborne Television Instruction started telecasting educational material to thousands of students by means of a video-tape-equipped airplane circling at an altitude of 23,000 feet over northern Indiana. This means of telecasting makes possible a potential listening audience of 5 million students in 13,000 grade schools, high schools, and colleges in six states.

Although some educators have been reluctant to accept educational television for fear it will eventually displace teachers, results of pertinent research do not substantiate this fear. Television should be recognized and accepted as a tool for teaching, much the same as the motion picture projector or tape recorder. It may prove to be the most expedient way of providing instruction in some situations. For example, in small school districts it might be the only means of giving breadth to the curriculum. Most small high schools are unable to offer two or three foreign languages along with physics, chemistry, and biology because they cannot afford to hire the qualified teachers needed; participation in a program like the Midwest Program of Airborne Television Instruction might be a solution to their problem.

Television is an invaluable asset in bringing to a large group of students such things as a science demonstration by a superior teacher or a presentation by an outstanding guest lecturer. In team teaching, which attempts to capitalize on the strengths of the teachers comprising the team, television can play a vital role.

Where student response and teacher-pupil interaction are essential, there are obvious limitations to the medium, although with closed-circuit television it is possible to get delayed feedback. It should also be kept in mind that students can become just as bored and disinterested with televised instruction as with conventional teaching.

[12]*Decade of Experiment,* Fund for the Advancement of Education (New York: The Georgian Press, Inc., 1961), p. 58.

One of the major problems connected with television as a medium of teaching is that of the initial cost of equipment. In some projects it has been found that the cost of televised instruction became comparable to conventional methods when two hundred or more pupils were taught simultaneously in a given course; as the number of pupils increases, of course, the per pupil cost decreases. The practice of having several school systems share the cost of television teaching appears to be one feasible way of overcoming the problem of finance.

Another problem in the use of televised instruction is that of keeping the pupils' progress abreast of the televised course. In the conventional classroom a teacher can adjust his teaching pace to meet the needs of the learners, but in teaching by television this is not possible; the students must adjust to the pace of the course. Scheduling can also present a problem when it is necessary to have class time conform to the programing of televised instruction.

For these reasons some educators contend that television as a medium of instruction is of questionable value, not because it is an ineffective teaching device, but because of its inflexibility, which forces the school's instructional program into a strait jacket. These same educators point out that neither pacing nor scheduling presents a problem when instructional films are used in the class-room; therefore, they favor the use of films over that of television. Even so, it is evident that the use of television in secondary schools is one of the major trends in secondary education today. As stated by Schramm:

. . . The pertinent question is no longer whether a teacher can teach effectively on television, but rather how, when, for what subjects, and with what articulation into classroom activities instructional TV can most effectively be used.[13]

The cooperative approach in curriculum planning

In the past, curriculums were made by subject-matter specialists and administrators who very often were concerned with mastery of subject matter alone. They decided what would and would not be taught. As the school enrollments grew and as the range and complexity of subject matter increased, it became apparent that there must be more careful decisions about what would be taught. As a result, a new method of curriculum planning evolved, representing

[13]Schramm, *op. cit.,* p. 165.

the cooperative efforts of subject-matter specialists, experienced teachers, curriculum coordinators, educational psychologists, administrators, and, in some cases, parents.

In recent years faculty members of colleges and universities have been active in secondary school planning. Their efforts have been very influential, and several examples of their contributions will be briefly discussed here.

Bruner's report

One of the best known examples of cooperation among historians, linguists, mathematicians, scientists, educationists, and psychologists is summarized by Jerome S. Bruner.[14] He takes the position that the various subjects have separate structures that distinguish each one from the other. He contends that it is this important structure, or framework, which the secondary school pupils must grasp if they are to be able to apply the knowledge, understanding, and skills of the various disciplines to their daily experiences; enjoy their study of various subjects; and, of great importance, continue to learn throughout life. Bruner's report and its implications should be studied carefully by students of education.

Project English

Project English has raised interesting possibilities for the language arts in secondary schools. The project, sponsored and supervised by the United States Office of Education, has established in cooperating universities curriculum centers which are producing materials to be used in curriculum planning and in the classroom in the areas of speaking, reading, writing, and listening.

The National Council of Teachers of English is also working with the Office of Education and with other organizations on curriculum materials for English. In October 1962, for example, representatives of over twenty organizations interested in English teaching attended a conference dealing with the coordination of efforts to upgrade the curriculum.

The Physical Science Study Committee

The Physical Science Study Committee (PSSC), composed of scholars and secondary school teachers, has developed a program in physics which gives rational cohesion to sound, heat, light, molecular physics, electricity, nucleonics, and an agglutination of

[14]Jerome S. Bruner, *The Process of Education* (Cambridge, Mass.: Harvard University Press, 1960).

mechanics. The authors have drawn upon other areas of science to complete the structure of their course and to make it more interesting.

The Chemical Bond Approach Committee

The Chemical Bond Approach Committee[15] (CBAC) has produced instructional materials that deduce, from theories of molecular and atomic structure, generalizations that are of great importance for high school students. To improve and centralize science laboratory work, college professors working with high school teachers developed materials that give students a minimum of directions and help them discover for themselves important generalizations of chemistry.[16]

The American Institute of Biological Sciences

The National Science Foundation has stimulated both rationalization and modernization of secondary school science courses by establishing many summer and yearlong institutes. The American Institute of Biological Sciences has developed three sets of instructional materials for secondary school biology, the most difficult of which emphasizes modern genetics and the chemistry of hereditary transmission.[17]

The School Mathematics Study Group

New mathematics courses employing the commutative law, statistics, probability, set theory, and other fundamental generalizations have been developed in detail. The new courses attempt to make the language of mathematics more precise; they give old ideas new uses; and they renew the emphasis on understanding "why" and "how" without undue dependence on rules. Courses planned by the School Mathematics Study Group[18] (SMSG) are the most popular today.

The National Defense Education Act and foreign languages

The federal government, through the National Defense Education Act (NDEA), has furnished necessary funds for schools and scholars to develop new materials and approaches to the teaching

[15]*Chemistry: Trial Edition,* Chemical Bond Approach Committee (Portland, Ore.: The Reed Institute, 1960).

[16]*Chemistry: An Experimental Science,* Chemical Education Materials Study (Berkeley, Calif.: The Regents of the University of California, 1960).

[17]*High School Biology,* American Institute of Biological Sciences, Biological Sciences Curriculum Study (Boulder, Colo.: University of Colorado, 1960).

[18]*Mathematics for High School,* School Mathematics Study Group (New Haven, Conn.: Yale University Press, 1960).

of foreign languages; the emphasis is now on the students' achieving fluency in speaking a language rather than on the grammatical, critical, and historical approaches.

Efforts in the social studies

In the early 1960's the American Council of Learned Societies and the National Council for the Social Studies entered into a joint project concerned with improving the social studies curriculum. The results of this project were published in a book, *The Social Studies and the Social Sciences,* published in 1962. In this publication scholars set forth concepts and information about the social studies that students in high school should know. The book deals with the teaching of geography, history, economics, political science, sociology, anthropology, Russia, elements of communism, Eastern Europe, and Asia.

Importance of the cooperative approach

Subject-matter specialists are thus making important contributions to the school curriculum. At the same time, better educated and better prepared teachers who have studied psychology and taken courses in curriculum development are working in the classroom with students; certainly their role is crucial in deciding what is taught. School administrators today are required to have a good liberal education, professional training, and successful teaching experience before assuming their administrative positions; thus experience and education qualify them to make valuable contributions to curriculum planning. Parents are, in many cases, well educated and usually desire the best educational advantages for their children; many school systems have found it helpful to give them an opportunity to share in planning curriculums. Cooperative approaches, which draw on contributions from all these sources, do not minimize the role of the curriculum specialist who can help teachers discover successful techniques and materials to be included in the school's program.[19]

Traditionally, curriculum resources consisted of the teacher and the textbook. Other materials were used at times but were not given much consideration by curriculum planners. As the objectives of education and the conception of curriculum broadened, however, the necessity for many types of resource materials also developed, so that today educators who plan the curriculum attempt to provide resources pertinent to the problems with which

[19]Harl R. Douglass, ed., *The High School Curriculum,* 3rd ed. (New York: The Ronald Press Company, 1964), pp. 116–120.

learners may need help. Materials should be designed to promote good work habits and skills, scientific attitudes, open-mindedness toward controversial issues, appreciation of the arts, and better understanding of subject matter.

Curriculum planning is continuing to change, and if present trends are an indication of the future, it will lead toward greater flexibility in school programs. Planning is now being done in terms of the needs and abilities of the pupils against a background of demands made on individuals by society, the usefulness of different types of knowledges and skills, and the psychological and logical nature of learning.

Scope and sequence

In some schools the textbook had always been the course of study, supplemented, of course, by materials the teacher offered. In many secondary schools today the scope or coverage of the curriculum is limited only by the ability and readiness of the pupils, the creativity of the instructor, and the availability of reference books, instructional films, programed material, community resources, laboratory facilities, and electronic aids. The goal at present is to provide a broad-scope curriculum, rich and varied in resource materials and teaching methods designed for a heterogeneous student body in a complex society.

In most schools sequence has been primarily concerned with what must be taught in the different grade levels in order to prepare students for the next grade. While there is still a great deal of emphasis on this conventional type of sequence, educators today believe that curriculum sequence must be designed with the learner in mind as well as with the logical arrangement of subject matter. Since pupils differ in their experimental backgrounds and abilities and respond differently to the same stimulus, much discretion must be left to the individual teacher as he plans a continuum of learning experiences for his classes. This does not mean that a school system should not have curriculum guides and courses of study which attempt to develop what teachers, administrators, and curriculum specialists believe is a good sequence. Such written plans are needed. But educators realize that no planned educational experience can be precisely designed at the same time and place for all students.

Units of subject matter and meaningful educational activities and experiences can be properly offered by grades and within classes only when certain principles and factors are considered.

Some of these are the maturity of students, the necessity of continuity in fundamental skills and subject-matter areas, carefully evaluated sequential arrangements, the probability of students withdrawing from school, and the probability of students attending college. Knowledge must be acquired according to a planned, orderly organization; instruction should not be offered on a hit-or-miss basis. Time must be given for students to study, to experience, and to assimilate; opportunities must be planned so that students can use what they have learned and can build on past experiences.

Related materials must be presented in such a manner that understandings and skills basic to further learning will be presented first. Examples of this can be found in European history, which furnishes a background for a better understanding of American history, and in mathematics, where a knowledge of multiplication and subtraction must precede that of long division.[20]

If students are to profit from opportunities offered in the curriculum, they must be mature enough physically and psychologically to understand and grasp different elements. Some materials must be offered early in secondary education; others should be postponed until later. General education should be offered to all students in junior high school and should occupy most of their time. In the senior high school, students should be required to take some courses in general education, but they should be required to take progressively fewer subjects that are constants and given more opportunities to elect those in keeping with their interests, abilities, and needs.

Guidelines for curriculum planning

Certain principles should guide the individuals who teach in secondary schools and who engage in curriculum planning. Most of these have been implied or stated previously, but for the sake of clarity and emphasis, they will be restated here.

Curriculum planning should provide for good articulation between the elementary school and the secondary school and between the secondary school and college. The junior high school curriculum should be planned with consideration for the curriculum of the higher elementary grades, thereby reducing duplication of effort and material, preventing omissions, and ensuring a well-integrated, continuous program. The work of the senior high school

[20]Rudyard K. Bent and Henry H. Kronenberg, *Principles of Secondary Education,* 4th ed. (New York: McGraw-Hill Book Company, Inc., 1961), p. 236.

must be planned so that the transition from junior high school will not be difficult and good articulation will be possible; it should also prepare students for life, and for college if they have the interest and ability to profit from higher education.

Flexible secondary curriculums should be provided. If the curriculum is going to reflect the rapid changes in society and provide the necessary educational experiences for young people, the curriculum must be very flexible. Another reason supporting this point of view is that secondary school students are immature — they change their minds about their goals or have experiences that change their plans, and as a result, they often transfer from one program of curriculum to another.

Appropriate student activities should be provided. Many schools require participation in some form of extraclass activities; others have no special regulations in this area. The desirable situation is one in which such a variety of activities is offered that all students will engage in them voluntarily.

Extraclass activities, which should be organized only if the students want them, must be just as carefully planned as other areas of the curriculum in order to ensure a well-balanced program. Schools should not overemphasize interschool contests for the few to the exclusion of intramural programs for the many. Most interschool teams place too much emphasis on winning and not enough on sportsmanship and participation on the part of more students.

A well-planned program of student activities will help adolescents develop sportsmanship, character, and worth-while leisure-time interests. The school should offer student activities appropriate for each individual and should sponsor those activities which will have the greatest carry-over value in life.

Reading should be taught by secondary school teachers at every level. Every high school teacher should set a good example in the use of English, and every one should teach reading. This position is taken for three reasons:

1. Correct English is mastered in a functional setting. Thus each teacher should set a good example and should help his students overcome errors.

2. Reading is a skill that cannot be mastered in either the elementary or the secondary school alone. It is a developmental process that requires time and special effort from teachers at every level.

3. Different subjects require special reading skills. Thus the various teachers must help their students acquire the skills needed for the different subject areas.

The curriculum should be planned for effective adaptation to the varying abilities and interests of the students. Youth are required to attend school. This costs the general public money; it will cost society even more if these individuals are not educated. Therefore, learning experiences that will challenge the ability of the most gifted student, the average student, and the slow learner are essential. The curriculum must be planned in such a way that the slow learner will not be left behind or overlooked, the so-called average student will make continuous progress, and neither the gifted student nor the others will be bored. This will involve the grouping of students according to ability and interests, availability of special materials, and, in some cases, provision of special teachers.

There should be sound reasons for the selection of activities and materials that are going to be used in the curriculum. Development of a school curriculum around vested interests, tradition, the theory of mental discipline, or the influence of pressure groups is no longer an acceptable procedure.

What are some elements that would compose sound criteria for curriculum selection? The common needs of all youth dictate that general education must be offered. The varying interests and abilities of a heterogeneous student body require flexible materials and many areas of special education. Preparation for life, college entrance requirements, and local and state regulations that are carefully formulated serve as sound reasons for including or omitting elements from the curriculum.

The curriculum should help the school fulfill its philosophy of education and achieve the goals drawn up by administrators, teachers, and parents. Such important lists of goals as the Seven Cardinal Principles of Education and the Ten Imperative Needs of Youth have an important place in the selection of curricular activities and materials.

Schools should not attempt to teach subjects or offer activities that require personnel, facilities, and equipment which the schools do not have.

The curriculum should offer experiences that enrich the lives of young people in the present as well as opportunities that will equip them to function effectively in the future. Indeed, the best preparation for the future is to meet and solve challenging problems in the present. The school can and should provide interesting activities that will enable all students to know success, thus following a sound curriculum principle which is also conducive to good mental health.

Curriculum planning should be a cooperative effort. As was indicated earlier, the curriculum can no longer be the product of the administrators or the subject-matter specialists only. Curriculum planning calls for the cooperative and continuous efforts of educators and parents, to create a curriculum that teachers can accept as worthy of their best efforts.

Selected references

BRUNER, JEROME S. *The Process of Education.* Cambridge, Mass.: Harvard University Press, 1960.

Chemistry: An Experimental Science. Chemical Education Materials Study. Berkeley, Calif.: The Regents of the University of California, 1960.

Chemistry: Trial Edition. Chemical Bond Approach Committee. Portland, Ore.: The Reed Institute, 1960.

Decade of Experiment. The Fund for the Advancement of Education. New York: The Georgian Press, Inc., 1961.

FRASER, DOROTHY M. *Current Curriculum Studies in Academic Subjects.* Washington, D.C.: National Education Association, 1962.

GWYNN, J. MINOR. *Curriculum Principles and Social Trends.* 3rd ed. New York: The Macmillan Company, 1960.

High School Biology. American Institute of Biological Sciences, Biological Sciences Curriculum Study. Boulder, Colo.: University of Colorado, 1960.

MARGULIES, STUART. "The Multiple-Choice Frame," *Programed Instruction* (February 1962), p. 4.

Mathematics for High School. School Mathematics Study Group. New Haven, Conn.: Yale University Press, 1960.

Physics. Physical Science Study Committee. Boston: D.C. Heath & Company, 1960.

STODDARD, ALEXANDER J. *Schools for Tomorrow: An Educator's Blueprint.* New York: Fund for the Advancement of Education, 1957.

STOLUROW, LAWRENCE M. *Teaching by Machine.* Washington, D.C.: Government Printing Office, 1961.

TROW, WILLIAM CLARK. *Teacher and Technology.* New York: Appleton-Century-Crofts, 1963.

TRUMP, J. LLOYD. *Images of the Future.* Commission on the Experimental Study of the Utilization of the Staff in the Secondary

School, National Association of Secondary-School Principals. Washington, D.C., 1959.

TRUMP, J. LLOYD, AND DORSEY BAYNHAM. *Guide to Better Schools*. New York: The Fund for the Advancement of Education, 1961.

Extraclass activities
in the secondary school

Several terms have been used to classify and describe the many extraclass activities available to students in the American secondary school. Earlier in this century these activities were referred to as *extracurricular activities,* which denoted how most educators felt about them. They were considered "extra" because they were separate and apart from the school's regular subjects. Many people rejected *extracurricular* because they felt it failed to convey the fact that the activities did have value for the curriculum, and the term *extraclass* came into usage. This classification still carried the implication that the activities were not closely related to the formal school subjects; therefore, a new term, *cocurricular activities,* was invented to express the important idea that the activities sponsored by the school were closely related to the curriculum itself and that they involved important educative experiences needed by all students. Other terms that have been used are *out-of-class activities* and *allied activities.*

In the present discussion these so-called *student activities, extracurricular activities,* and *allied activities* will be referred to as *extraclass activities.* This term is used not with the idea that these activities should be set apart from the rest of the curriculum, but rather to distinguish them from the experiences which are usually part of the subject areas. The distinction is an arbitrary one, however, because in many secondary schools it is very difficult to separate regular class activities from extraclass activities. For example, orchestra, band, choir, and glee clubs are often scheduled in a school's program just as any other course. Many schools give students credit toward graduation for serving on the newspaper and yearbook staff. Intramural sports are often included in the physical education program, and the student council is sometimes allocated a place in the regular daily schedule.[1]

Although the matter of terminology and classification has been a problem in this particular area of secondary education, there is the realization that these activities have educative value and are a legitimate part of education. Young people find them interesting, satisfying, and worth while, as is indicated in Pogue's study of over six thousand students in selected Illinois high schools.[2]

History of student activities

Originally, extraclass activities were started by students and adults apart from the school itself. Secondary schools in general confined their work to the teaching of conventional subjects. The young people, seeking outlets for their creative impulses and finding few or no avenues of self-expression in the regular class work, organized debating societies, literary societies, school magazines, yearbooks, singing groups, and athletic teams with little or no assistance or supervision by school officials. Their objectives were to have fun, to let off steam, to have social relations with other young people, and perhaps to acquire knowledge, skills, and experiences not generally offered in the formal instructional program.

The beginnings of extraclass activities were usually spontaneous. A group of students would decide they wanted a debating team or club, would organize one, and would debate various topics of current or philosophical interest. Or a group of boys would organize a ball team just for the joy of playing and then schedule games with similar teams from other schools. Clubs in history, science, literature, and other areas were organized in a similar way.[3] From such beginnings as these have come the present-day interscholastic sports programs, spelling contests, debating tournaments, speaking contests, band contests, music festivals, and essay

[1]Vernon E. Anderson and William T. Gruhn, *Principles and Practices of Secondary Education.* Copyright © 1962, The Ronald Press Company, p. 279.

[2]J. Lloyd Trump, "Extracurricular Activities: Some Principles of Management," in *The American Secondary School*, ed. Paul B. Jacobson (Engelwood Cliffs, N. J.: Prentice-Hall, Inc., 1952), pp. 212–213.

[3]William Marshall French, *American Secondary Education* (New York: The Odyssey Press, 1957), pp. 397–398.

contests. Although such activities usually had no school sponsorship, sometimes school facilities were used or a member of the school staff acted as sponsor.

Some educators in the academies and early high schools resented extraclass activities; many others ignored them. Between 1900 and 1920, secondary school educators began to take more interest in extraclass activities, and by the end of the 1920's the activities were considered a legitimate part of secondary education. Two major factors led to the shift in attitude: (1) pressure exerted by parents, students, and a few educators who wanted the extracurricular activities sponsored and supervised by the schools; and (2) a great and rapid shift in educational philosophy which held that the school should develop personal and social competencies and that student activities could serve as one of the best vehicles for reaching these goals.[4]

During the 1920's and 1930's, student activities, while accepted by the schools, were classified as extracurricular. Civic leaders, parent-teacher associations, colleges of education, and school administrators urged the schools to develop these activities and to provide time for them during the school day, but they were still considered separate programs that could merely parallel the regular curriculum. In general, student activities during this period were not given much, if any, time in the school day, and there were few attempts to make them an integral part of the curriculum.

Today there is general agreement that extraclass activities are worth while and should be sponsored by the secondary school; however, actual practices vary from school to school. Although some of the more traditional schools schedule the activity program after school hours,[5] most present-day schools provide a regular time during school hours for extraclass activities. Serious attempts are made to merge these activities with the program of studies and to plan them so that the greatest possible educational results can be realized. Some extraclass programs, such as dramatics, music, speech, and physical education, have become a part of the school's curriculum and carry units of credit toward graduation.

Values of extraclass activities

What are the values that can be realized from an excellent program of extraclass activities? Most parents, students, and

[4]Nelson L. Bossing, *Principles of Secondary Education* (Englewood Cliffs, N.J.: Prentice-Hall, Inc., 1955), p. 430.
[5]Harl R. Douglass, *Secondary Education in the United States,* 2nd ed. (New York: The Ronald Press Company, 1964), p. 348.

teachers feel that such activities help build school spirit, train for future citizenship, increase interest in school, and provide important opportunities for leadership. A survey of the literature dealing with extraclass activities reveals that educators in general feel that the major values of these activities are as follows:

1. Education for citizenship.
2. Education in social relations.
3. Education in leadership.
4. Development of school spirit.
5. Increased motivation for learning.
6. Experiences necessary for recreational choices.
7. Valuable esthetic experiences.
8. Valuable health experiences.
9. Valuable opportunities to develop special interests and abilities.
10. Opportunities to discover new interests.
11. Opportunities to improve intellectual development and scholarship.
12. Opportunities for better school-community relations.
13. Aid in retaining students in school.
14. Opportunities for valuable experiences in vocational training.
15. Services rendered to the school and the student body.
16. Opportunities for better student-teacher relationships.
17. Additional opportunities to practice much that is taught in the subject areas.
18. Contribution to the total school program.

Extraclass activities are meaningful and educative if they are well planned and are a means of student expression. Students should play a large part in initiating such activities and, under school supervision, should be primarily responsible for conducting them. Extraclass activities have value only if students are interested in them and are willing to put forth time and effort to make them a dynamic part of the school. They should feel that the extraclass activities are theirs. When faculty members control activities, students are reluctant to participate in them, or they participate in a superficial way. This is not to say that guidance and direction should not be furnished by the teachers. It is, rather, to emphasize that much of the value of extraclass activities is lost when they are dominated by school personnel.

Extraclass activities are also educational because they help achieve widely accepted goals of education. As was previously mentioned, educational theory has shifted its emphasis from strict mastery of encyclopedic information to the development of desirable social and personal competencies along with growth in knowledge, understandings, skills, attitudes, and appreciations. The modern school has not only accepted student activities; but, in many areas, it has emphasized their importance as a medium of learning.[6]

In 1960 Hamilton conducted a study of extraclass activities in high schools in Texas. He found that the students felt extraclass activities were especially helpful to them in the following ways:

1. Developing new appreciations in science, music, athletics, etc.

2. Developing greater interest in school.

3. Learning sportsmanship and skill in working with others.

4. Developing greater loyalty to their schools.

5. Developing new and worth-while leisure-time interests.

6. Developing better relations with teachers and administrators.

7. Learning how to conduct and participate in group meetings.

8. Gaining valuable information that would not have been received in a regular course.[7]

Types of extraclass activities

No attempt will be made here to list and discuss in detail all of the extraclass activities available in secondary schools. But since most activities can be classified into well-established categories, some of the major types of activities will be discussed briefly.

Student council

One of the most important extraclass activities is the student government organization. Secondary schools are concerned with preparing students for citizenship in the larger society, and the student government organization provides an excellent opportunity for all students to acquire valuable citizenship training and to put into practice the knowledge, desirable attitudes, and good habits they acquire. Most student councils consist of members selected by the various classes or homerooms; the process by which these representatives are elected offers the adolescent lessons in democracy that are valuable both for his present activities and for his

[6]Bossing, *op. cit.*, p. 437.

[7]Homer H. Hamilton, "The Educational Values of Pupil Activities," *Texas Study of Secondary Education,* Research Bulletin No. 29 (Austin, Tex.: University of Texas Press, 1960).

future adult role as a citizen. Not only do the students elect their own representatives and, in some cases, serve as officers and members of the council itself, but they also learn to abide by the guidelines established by their representatives.

The student council is perhaps the most crucial form of extraclass activity. It can be a vital organ in the coordination of all such activities and may determine to a great extent whether other student activities succeed or fail. Members of the council keep the lines of communication open between the students they represent and the faculty and administration. They can sound out the student body on important matters, and the students can, in turn, let their feelings be known. A good council can become the cornerstone of an excellent extraclass activity program.

Listed below are some of the major objectives of a good student council:

1. Providing opportunities for students to learn democratic processes.

2. Providing opportunities to develop leadership abilities.

3. Providing opportunities for students to participate in the management of the school.

4. Providing opportunities for better relationships between students and school personnel.

5. Providing opportunities for better coordination of all student activities.

6. Providing a better atmosphere for learning.

7. Providing opportunities for the students to help sponsor worth-while projects.

8. Providing ways for new students to become better oriented to the school.

9. Providing ways for needed organizations to come into being in the school.

10. Assisting the student body in its evaluation of the extraclass program.

The student council is not an organization through which immature adolescents attempt to run the school but rather a way of enabling students to participate in the government of their school under the leadership of school personnel. It is undesirable from a legal, practical, and educational standpoint for those who have the legal responsibilities of operating the schools to turn their duties over to students. As has been acknowledged earlier, one of the greatest values of student activities is the development of student leadership in a gradual way under the concerned guidance of school officials with well-distinguished limitations as guidelines.

This is in keeping with the point of view in learning and group dynamics which emphasizes that there must be gradual increases in responsibility and freedom if students are to grow in self-direction and judgment.

School officials should not expect the student council to run the schools for them; but neither should they treat the council as a rubber stamp. Student government works best when student representatives work with the faculty and the administration in establishing and enforcing rules and policies that will govern the school.

There are times and situations in which the student council may legislate, but such legislation should, in reality, be recommendations rather than laws or mandates. Much controversy would be avoided if the council's functions and its true relationship to the overall administration and operation of the school are clearly explained to all concerned at the beginning of the school year. The school principal or his representative should attend every council meeting to remind council members and the student body that the public in general, the state, the board of education, parents, teachers, and taxpayers have an equity in the schools.

Council members should be encouraged to set forth the students' point of view, and the school administrators should treat these viewpoints with respect and give them honest consideration. This is, after all, one form of practical experience which gives not only the council members but the entire student body experience in citizenship and democracy. Student government can be an opportunity for pupils to learn that cooperation is a two-way street.[8]

In other words, if the administration expects real support and acceptance on the part of the student body, it must give the council proper authority to assist in the management of the school. When students are aware of the ground rules or the framework within which their council can function, little frustration and confusion will result. If, for example, recommending changes in the subjects taught in the school is not its responsibility, the student council should know this. If it is to help set standards and develop policies for behavior in the school, the council should be aware of this.

Clubs

Clubs are a second major type of extraclass activity in secondary schools. They serve many student interests and are capable of helping achieve many educational goals. Such groups as the service clubs, hobby clubs, social clubs, and honor clubs help develop

[8]Harl R. Douglass, ed., *The High School Curriculum*, 3rd ed. (New York: The Ronald Press Company, 1964), pp. 519–520.

personal and social skills, basic understandings, new interests, and many other worth-while educational objectives.

Most writers classify school clubs according to the purpose they are designed to fulfill. Some of the well-recognized ones are discussed below.

1. *Service clubs* exist primarily to serve the school and the student body. Some examples are Audio-Visual Aids Club, Library Club, American Junior Red Cross, Pep Club, and Usher Club.

2. *Curriculum clubs* are organized in relation to the subject areas in the school's instructional program and provide opportunities for more learning in these areas in an informal manner as well as opportunities for social and recreational activities. Some examples are French Club, German Club, Spanish Club, and Science Club.

3. *Clubs affiliated with national organizations* are generally concerned with building character and vocational preparation. Some examples are HiY Club, 4-H Club, Boy Scouts of America, Girl Scouts of America, Future Farmers of America, and Future Teachers of America.

4. *Hobby clubs* are educationally worth while in that they provide opportunities for gaining more knowledge, and they are also very helpful in the development of excellent leisure-time interests. Some examples are Photography Club, Rocket Club, Collectors' Club, Book Club, Chess Club, and Music Club.

5. *Honor societies* exist for the promotion of scholarship, service to the school, and citizenship. They elect their own officers and conduct their own projects. Some examples are the National Honor Society, National Forensic League, Pen and Sable, Quill and Scroll, Spanish National Honor Society, and the National Athletic Scholarship Society.

In many schools almost all extraclass activities are organized as clubs, each with its own sponsor. Club programs cut across grade lines and provide opportunities for making new friends by bringing together students who are not enrolled in the same courses or sections.

The school officials should provide time within the school day for club activities and meetings. If clubs meet after school, many students will be denied membership because they work or ride a school bus. Most schools now provide for an activity period during which clubs can meet, or there is a special schedule on certain days when club meetings and assemblies can be held. At least thirty minutes is needed for these meetings, and most schools find that from forty-five to sixty minutes is better.

Some of the advantages of scheduling student activities during regular school hours are as follows:

1. Teachers are more willing to serve as sponsors when they do not have to add extraclass activities to a full day of work.

2. Students can participate in the activities without missing classroom instruction.

3. Students who are transported to school will have the same opportunities as pupils who live near the school.

4. Students may participate in activities without encountering conflicts with after-school duties.

5. It is easier for the school to control the number of student activities in which a student participates.[9]

Dramatics

Large schools offer special courses in dramatics in addition to sponsoring a club. Smaller schools, as a rule, do not offer special electives but do sponsor dramatic activities.

Young people respond enthusiastically to pageants and plays in which other adolescents take part. Because a dramatic production involves many different activities, students with varying interests and abilities can find worth-while things to do. For example, advertising, selling of tickets, costuming, make-up, and ushering provide valuable experiences in human relations and in practical experience. Planning, practicing, and presenting plays can provide rich intellectual experiences for pupils.[10]

Publications

Publications, whether produced by an elected or volunteer staff or by the journalism class, serve many worth-while purposes in the secondary school. They offer students fine educational experiences in journalism, advertising, retail sales, and English usage, and they help build school spirit and thus unite the student body.

The following publications are frequently found in the secondary schools:

1. Student newspaper.

2. The school annual or yearbook.

3. Literary magazines, published several times during the school year in larger schools.

4. Student handbooks.

5. Special publications such as programs of special events, student directories, and bulletins sponsored by the student council.

[9]L. O. Taylor and others, *The American Secondary School* (New York: Appleton-Century Crofts, 1960), p. 239.

[10]Douglass, ed., *op. cit.*, p. 531.

The school newspaper—probably the most important student publication—serves as a medium of communication in the school by presenting information regarding problems or areas of general concern to students, and it helps unify school activities and interests. The newspaper and other school publications provide adolescents with the opportunity to develop special interests and abilities in editing, writing, and other operations related to publishing. School magazines and annuals can help develop school morale and furnish an outlet for creative pupils. In many schools students help develop and publish handbooks and directories which are very useful in orienting new students.[11]

Assemblies

If carefully planned, assembly programs can offer real educational values for secondary school students. They are also an excellent way to build school spirit since school traditions and loyalties are often perpetuated through the assembly.

Students usually play a large part in selecting and conducting the programs. Sometimes the student council and representatives of the various clubs help the administrators plan the assembly programs for the entire school year. Often the president of the student body presides at an assembly program or the speakers are introduced by students.

Although it is occasionally desirable to bring in outside speakers or entertainers, most assembly programs should consist of student presentations. Some excellent assembly programs are the results of class activities and may even consist of the culminating activity of a unit of work or a class project. Programs often give recognition to various groups within the school, thus furthering the objectives of the entire school.

Many school systems have developed special guides to assist teachers, students, and administrators in the planning and selection of programs for the assemblies. Well-planned student assemblies can help achieve the following objectives:

1. Education
   a. To reveal new vocational and educational interests.
   b. To present classroom activities.
   c. To involve maximum pupil- and minimum teacher-participation.
   d. To widen and deepen the interests of the students.

[11]William M. Alexander and J. Galen Saylor, *Modern Secondary Education* (New York: Holt, Rinehart, & Winston, Inc., 1959), p. 606.

   e.   To develop creative abilities.
   f.   To cultivate good manners and good taste.
2. Citizenship and Character
   a.   To cultivate school spirit.
   b.   To train high-minded, capable leaders.
   c.   To train for democratic citizenship.
   d.   To establish high ideals for the school.
   e.   To train the student to adapt himself to the needs of the community.
   f.   To contribute toward the solution of a school problem.
   g.   To inculcate ethical ideals.
   h.   To bring to the school the resources of the community.
3. Communication
   a.   To provide an opportunity for each pupil to share with the school his choicest experiences.
   b.   To provide an opportunity for growth and ease in expression.
   c.   To serve as an example of the best voice and speech as used by students and adults.[12]

Athletics

Athletics were one of the first types of student activities to gain acceptance in the secondary schools. Today athletic activities — football and basketball being the leading ones — are very popular and do much to build school loyalty among students and the alumni.

Competitive athletics also cause a great deal of concern for parents and the public in general. They are often criticized because of the danger of injuries to students and because of the amount of time required for practice and participation — time often taken at the expense of regular school work. Fortunately, competitive sports are now closely regulated by the school and by state and regional athletic associations. But there is still room for improvement in this area, because the demands placed on team members do jeopardize the scholastic opportunities of some students.

Another criticism leveled at competitive athletics is that often too few students are able to participate in such sports. Good secondary schools are developing intramural programs in softball, golf, swimming, tennis, and volleyball so that more students have the opportunity to become involved in athletic activities. For example, Peter J. Collodi, writing in the *Public School Digest* about his school, the Sharon (Pennsylvania) High School says:

[12]*Assembly Guide for Secondary Schools*, Board of Education of the City of New York, Curriculum Bulletin, 1954–1955 Series, No. 11 (New York: The Board, 1956.) pp. 5–6.

We . . . hold to the belief that every boy in our public school system, regardless of his ability, has the right to experience the thrill of competition. If inter-school athletics are good for the few that qualify, it logically follows that an intra-school program will benefit all who desire to participate regardless of their ability.[13]

Homerooms

Because of the increased size and complexity of the American secondary school, most educators today consider a homeroom organization an absolute necessity. Homerooms are used to handle such routine school business as official attendance records, collections of various fees and student donations, distribution of report cards, and group guidance (discussed in Chapter 10). In the junior high school a homeroom helps the student who has recently left the self-contained classroom adjust to the departmentalized secondary school by giving him a home base and a teacher who knows him well.

A carefully planned homeroom program with a reasonable time allotment allows teachers to assist girls and boys in planning their educational program, solving their personal problems, and developing better personal relations. In some schools the homeroom serves as a democratic unit in the school's government where students can propose or criticize the actions or policies of their student council. The homeroom periods can also be used for discussion on topics which are of great interest and importance to the students.

There is no set pattern of organization for secondary school homerooms. Although homerooms are usually organized heterogeneously, some schools group by ability, some on the basis of sex, and others use such methods as grouping by feeder schools or by selecting a certain number of students from two or three grade levels.

The amount of time set aside for homerooms, the number of meetings, and the nature of the meetings also vary from school to school. In some secondary schools the homeroom meets every day for about ten or fifteen minutes and is little more than an administrative device for making announcements and checking attendance. In other schools it meets weekly for thirty minutes or more and is used for guidance, for activities related to student government, or for social activities.

[13]Peter J. Collodi, "Every Boy at Sharon High School an Athlete," *Public School Digest*, VII (January 1955), 6–7.

Practices to avoid

Every activity in the secondary school should have a clear educational value that can justify its existence. In many schools extraclass activities have not been planned but, like Topsy, have just grown. Unless the school evaluates what is being done, some activities will continue to exist after they have ceased to serve a useful purpose, and others, though still valuable, will be allowed to degenerate into uselessness because of a lack of concern on the part of students, teachers, and administrators.

In 1952 Johnston[14] summarized some of the weaknesses or malpractices in extraclass activities:

1. Many schools accept activities without much thought or understanding on the part of students and teachers as to what these activities are supposed to accomplish.

2. Many schools refuse to let students have very much responsibility in the management of student activities. School personnel are afraid of democracy; they have no confidence in the students' ability to help plan, to make intelligent decisions, and to accept responsibility.

3. Participation in extraclass activities is limited to too few students. In some cases students cannot participate because of school regulations such as scholastic averages; in other cases they are not offered a reasonable selection of activities.

4. Competitive aspects of student activities are overemphasized. The emphasis on winning or on giving a perfect performance often overshadows more important educational values.

5. In some schools national organizations are sponsored as ends in themselves without a proper program providing for valuable objectives and results.

6. Special interest groups in some communities promote activities to further their own selfish interests.

7. At times the extraclass activities are not vitally related to the school curriculum.

8. Too often there is little or no effort to evaluate activities in terms of educational objectives.

9. Many teachers are not trained or prepared to sponsor student activities.

10. Too often extraclass activities are not recognized as a part of the teacher's workload.

[14]Edgar G. Johnston, "Critical Problems in the Administration of Student Activities," *Bulletin of the National Association of Secondary-School Principals*, XXXVI (February 1952), 1–12.

Principles for extraclass activities

The better secondary schools find that the following principles serve as important guideposts in developing and maintaining a worth-while program of extraclass activities:

1. Extraclass activities should be closely related to the school curriculum and should help the school achieve its objectives.

2. The goals of the extraclass program should be understood by students and teachers.

3. Administrators, teachers, and students should constantly evaluate the extraclass program.

4. Sufficient time for the extraclass program should be provided within the school day.

5. Extraclass activities should be scheduled as far ahead as possible.

6. Every student should be encouraged—but not forced—to participate in some extraclass activity.

7. Participation in most activities should not be limited by scholastic averages.

8. The financial status of the student should not eliminate him from participation in any activity.

9. Students should not be denied participation in any extraclass activity because of race, creed, or national background.

10. Secret organizations should not be allowed.

11. Students should plan their participation in the extraclass programs just as carefully as they plan their courses.

12. Sponsors of student activities should be members of the school's staff.

13. Sponsors should guide students in extraclass activities, but they should not exert too much control.

14. The sponsorship of extraclass activities should be considered an integral part of the teacher's load.

15. The board of education should provide the necessary finances through the school budget for most activities.

16. Activities should be held on the school grounds except for special occasions.

Administration and planning

Administrators cannot neglect their responsibilities for extraclass activities any more than they can neglect other school functions. If extraclass activities are to be educationally worth while, they must be carefully planned and periodically reviewed by competent educators. The organization and administration of these activities demand centralization of authority and supervision, which is the responsibility of the principal or assistant principal and others to whom authority has been delegated. Good administration requires that the time and place of all meetings be scheduled as far in advance as possible, and it requires audits and adequate control of all extraclass activity funds.

Extraclass activities should be accepted and planned as an integral part of the instructional program. Since these activities are designed to help students develop their interests and abilities, they are not merely supplemental to the major objectives of the school. They are, instead, an inseparable part of the total educational process which is planned to help students develop mentally, physically, and spiritually to their greatest potential.

The development of the extraclass program shows that new additions have been brought about because of pressing demands for modification and enrichment of the existing curriculum. Each new addition affects the school program, and often it becomes a part of the curriculum itself. Many educators feel that extraclass activities have had a profound effect upon the total school curriculum because the students have had so much interest in these activities and have been willing to work hard to make them succeed.

Student participation

Educators differ in their opinions as to whether students should be required to take part in extraclass activities. Of course, all students are enrolled in homerooms, if the school has them; and all usually participate in student government either directly or indirectly. When it comes to other extraclass activities, some educators contend that all pupils should be required to engage in at least one because they believe participation results in desirable growth and development on the part of the student. Others argue that there is much value in permitting students to decide for themselves whether to participate. They further claim that forced participation destroys much of the students' interest and spirit, which are so necessary for a successful activity program. It is true that, if allowed to decide for themselves, some students will not become involved in the activity program, but many educators feel that this disadvantage is offset by the fact that those who do participate are then served by a superior program. In 1955 Hovis reported that only 4 per cent of the fifty-one schools he studied required students to take part in some extraclass activity.[15]

[15]James E. Hovis, "A Survey of Certain Extra-Curricular Practices in Some Secondary Schools of the Tri-State Area," *Public School Digest,* VII (January 1955), 12–14.

Balance in the student's educational program must also be considered when discussing this problem. More ambitious students may attempt to take part in too many extraclass activities. Most teachers are aware that certain students get involved in so many activities that they are overburdened with work in their subjects and student activities. Many schools, in trying to prevent students from having unbalanced programs, have devised a point system whereby a certain number of points are assigned for holding office or membership in an activity. Pupils are allowed a maximum number of points that they must not exceed. Other schools specify the number of offices a student can hold and the number of activities in which he can participate. Scheduling most activities during an activity period is one way to limit participation automatically. Many educators feel that the best way to have a balanced program for the student is to provide an excellent counseling program whereby parents, teachers, and guidance personnel help students make wise choices concerning the activities in which they will participate.

Sponsorship

The extraclass program can be responsible for overloading the teachers. While some activities require relatively little of the teachers' time, others are very time consuming. Teachers often find it difficult to do a good job teaching their subjects while acting as sponsors of activities. Many principals try to avoid assigning sponsorship of any activity to beginning teachers or asking any teacher to accept too many extraclass responsibilities.

Since teachers are concerned with providing the best types of learning experiences which will result in desirable growth on the part of boys and girls, extraclass activities are of great concern to them. Most schools ask teachers to sponsor at least one activity in addition to their regular classroom teaching responsibilities, and the prospective teacher should assume that he will be called upon to act as a sponsor. Indeed, he should look forward to this further opportunity to contribute to the students' development.

Teachers are not really prepared to assume a teaching position unless they have had some experience and preparation in leading student activities. Teachers should be aware of the problems associated with sponsoring such activities, and they should also be acquainted with the many educational possibilities inherent in these activities. The intelligent and alert prospective teacher will examine the various types of student activities and will prepare himself for efficient leadership in several of these extraclass activities.

Selected references

ANDERSON, VERNON E. AND WILLIAM T. GRUHN. *Principles and Practices of Secondary Education.* New York: The Ronald Press Company, 1962.

COLLODI, PETER J. "Every Boy at Sharon High School an Athlete," *Public School Digest,* VII (January 1955), 6–7.

"Creativity," *Educational Leadership, XVIII.* Association for Supervision and Curriculum Development (October 1961), 3–42.

DEYOUNG, CHRIS A. AND RICHARD WYNN. *American Education.* New York: McGraw-Hill Book Company, Inc., 1964.

DOUGLASS, HARL R. *Secondary Education in the United States,* 2nd ed. New York: The Ronald Press Company, 1964.

———, ed. *The High School Curriculum,* 3rd ed. New York: The Ronald Press Company, 1964.

FREDERICK, ROBERT. *The Third Curriculum.* New York: Appleton-Century-Crofts, 1959.

MCKEAN, ROBERT C. *Principles and Methods in Secondary Education.* Columbus, Ohio: Charles E. Merrill, Inc., 1962.

TOMPKINS, ELLSWORTH AND VIRGINIA RAL. "A Survey of Inter-Scholastic Athletics Programs in Separately Organized Junior High Schools," *Bulletin of the National Association of Secondary-School Principals,* XLII (November 1958), 1–47.

WILES, KIMBALL. *The Changing Curriculum of the American High School.* Englewood Cliffs, N.J.: Prentice-Hall, Inc., 1963.

The role of the teacher
in the secondary school

PART III

The guidance program and the teacher

chapter **10**

Never before has the guidance program in the secondary school been more important than it is at the present time. This is true for a number of reasons.

First, there is a higher percentage of youth of secondary school age attending school today. These students represent a wide range of intellectual ability.

Second, though the percentage of drop-outs has been reduced, there are still about one million students quitting school each year. The problems that manifest themselves to these individuals and to society are great. The drop-out is often unable to obtain employment; in many cases he becomes at best a ward of society and at worst a criminal. Recent trends in employment indicate that fewer and fewer unskilled workers will be able to find jobs in the years ahead and that professional and white-collar workers will be in great demand. Thus high school drop-outs, who now constitute a major problem in large city slums, will be even more of a problem in the future than they are today unless action is taken to remedy the situation. The one area that seems to offer great hope for these students is the service occupations.[1]

Third, today's world has become exceedingly complex. This makes it necessary for youth to have more and better education

[1]James B. Conant, *Slums and Suburbs* (New York: McGraw-Hill Book Company, Inc., 1961), p. 51

if they are to avoid maladjustment and if they are to become constructive contributors to their country.

Fourth, in attempting to meet the needs of all students, the educational program of the school has, of necessity, become much more complex than it was twenty-five years ago. Guidance programs must help teachers identify students' needs, and the schools must provide ways whereby the student can select and avail himself of the best educational experiences.

Fifth, psychology has produced a tremendous amount of information on the nature of learning, individual differences, and adolescents themselves. This valuable information not only emphasizes the absolute necessity of a good guidance program for the secondary school student, but it also provides school personnel with a foundation for more effective guidance.

Sixth, the demand for better quality in secondary education and the increased difficulty of gaining admission to the more select colleges and universities underline the importance of improved guidance in the home and in the school.

Seventh, studies and reports by distinguished educators emphasize the need for guidance. For example, in 1959 Conant wrote the following as his first recommendation for school board members and school administrators:

In a satisfactory school system the counseling should start in the elementary school, and there should be good articulation between the counseling in the junior and senior high schools if the pattern is 6 – 3 – 3 or between the counseling in the elementary school and the high school if the system is organized on an 8 – 4 basis. There should be one full-time counselor [or guidance officer] for every two hundred fifty to three hundred pupils in the high school[2]. . . .

Eighth, the world situation is such that the people of the United States cannot afford to waste their valuable human resources. Guidance programs in secondary schools can make great contributions toward a better utilization of this nation's human and educational resources. In 1958 the Rockefeller Brothers Fund, Inc., published *The Pursuit of Excellence: Education and the Future of America,* which expressed special concern for providing guidance for all students as well as for offering superior programs for gifted students.

[2]James B. Conant, *The American High School Today* (McGraw-Hill Book Company, Inc., 1959), p. 44.

Recognizing the importance of guidance, Congress in 1958 passed the National Defense Education Act, which authorized the expenditure of millions to develop guidance in secondary schools through two types of programs. Program A allocates matching grants to the states for use in developing counseling programs to encourage able students to enroll in colleges and universities. This program also provides funds for testing programs designed to identify gifted and talented students. Program B gives federal support to institutes and workshops in the field of guidance.

Guidance in the secondary schools is a practical way of showing this country's interest and concern for the dignity and value of the individual, and excellent guidance programs must be provided for the welfare of society and for the development and benefit of the individual. As the following quotation points out, many times in the past and even in the present, society and the schools have failed to provide for individual guidance of the student:

The failure to provide guidance programs is a failure of national vision—for we have tended to see human beings as statistics, children as weapons, talents as materials capable of being mined, assayed, and fabricated for profit and defense. We have the cart before the horse if we think that we can order up units of talent for the national defense. The only sure defense of democracy will be its inner growth, and the first essential of this growth is something far less grandiose but far more difficult of realization than a National Defense Education Act, or a crash program under any other title—namely, a true recognition that each child in each classroom in our schools is a unique human being, who one day must make choices and give consents that will help to perfect us all.[3]

While it is true that there has been increased emphasis on guidance in recent years, it should be noted that some teachers and principals have always attempted to render such service. However, the great changes in society during the last thirty years have made it mandatory that all secondary school personnel be concerned with guidance and be informed of guidance services in the school and community.

Guidance is not a separate service that can be divorced from the curriculum of the secondary school; rather, it is an integral part of the school's total program. Guidance is not making decisions for young people. It is a process of helping students analyze, deter-

[3]John Hersey, *Intelligence, Choice, and Consent* (New York: Woodrow Wilson Foundation, 1959), pp. 27–28.

mine, and understand their abilities, limitations, interests, opportunities, needs, and problems; and, in light of this information, assisting them in making sound decisions and plans of actions that will help them adjust to school and life and prepare for their place in society.

The secondary school staff and guidance

The guidance program cannot be developed by administrators and guidance specialists alone. All staff members — teachers, guidance specialists, and administrators — must believe in the value of the guidance services and be willing to work together to achieve the objectives of the program. This program cannot be imposed upon teachers; they should have a part in developing the entire program. Only when the value of guidance is realized by all staff members can it serve students in the best possible way.

Guidance specialists

Guidance specialists are necessary, especially in the larger secondary schools which usually employ a director of guidance who, under the principal's supervision, is responsible for the guidance program. In most schools the director's duties are as follows:

1. To name the counselors with the principal's approval.

2. To conduct an in-service program for the faculty on guidance and counseling.

3. To establish testing programs and to supervise all testing except that which is carried on in the regular instructional program.

4. To interpret the results of tests to students, teachers, and parents.

5. To handle the more difficult counseling cases.

6. To refer to psychologists or psychiatrists those students who, because of mental or emotional maladjustment, need the help of such specialists.

7. To develop an efficient system of gathering needed information about students.

8. To maintain an adequate system of records and to make sure teachers and counselors have access to them when needed.

9. To work with community agencies and to use the resources of the community in meeting the needs of students or staff members.

10. To conduct follow-up studies of students.

11. To provide information concerning colleges, universities, and various occupations.

In small schools the principal or a person named by him usually serves as part-time director or coordinator of guidance, and in very small schools he may be the *only* person charged with guidance services. Some schools make no provision for guidance so far as assigning specific responsibilities to individuals is concerned.

Counselors

Although counselors are usually appointed by directors of guidance with the approval of the principal, in small schools where there is no director, the principal will appoint the counselor or counselors. In a few school systems the superintendent of schools not only appoints the directors of guidance but also names the counselors.

In most cases counselors are teachers who have performed on a superior level and who have had special course work in guidance. They are, or should be, persons who are interested in students as individuals and who have found it easy to establish rapport with students. The teachers who are selected to serve as counselors are generally given a reduced teaching load so that they may have time for counseling.

What are the responsibilities of counselors? Each counselor is assigned a certain number of students, whom he assists with the selection of courses that seem most appropriate to their individual needs. In order to determine their interests, aptitudes, and potentialities, the counselor must study the cumulative records of his counselees. In the better guidance programs counselors hold from two to four interviews each semester with the students assigned to them.

Many well-trained counselors are unable to provide effective guidance programs because they have too much to do in too little time. Some school boards and administrators, untrained in guidance, do not understand the amount of time necessary for satisfactory student personnel work and assign counselors more pupils than they can serve well. Some writers, although supposedly well trained in guidance and presumably aware of the time-consuming nature of student personnel work, have helped foster this policy by advocating too many students per counselor. They defend on paper a number that in practice proves definitely unsound. For example, some state that a counselor can serve 100 pupils or more for each class period during which he is engaged in guidance work rather than teaching. These writers evidently do not consider teaching and guidance of equal importance, for no one thus far has recommended that a classroom teacher should have 100 students or more per class period.[4] Many educators believe there should be one full-time counselor for every 250 to 300 students in the secondary school.

Classroom teachers

What is the role of the classroom teacher in guidance and counseling? There is a tendency to think of him as the key person in the entire guidance program, for he is in closer contact with students than is the counselor and thus in a better position to know them as individuals, to sense their needs, and to offer help. He is constantly on the scene to answer students' questions concerning educational, personal, or vocational problems. The teacher who is friendly, well liked, and trusted will often be sought out by students who would otherwise be slow to ask for an appointment with a counselor.

When the teacher knows that he does not have all of the essential facts or that the student needs special help, he should arrange an interview for the student with a counselor. This should always be done when the student has a complex emotional or mental problem or a very difficult vocational problem. In other words, classroom teachers can handle some counseling problems, but others should be referred to specialists.

The teacher, a specialist in one or more subjects, can point out to students how a particular field can help them adjust to society and reach their life goals. If the teacher is to do these things, however, he must be interested in the students he teaches as well as in the subject matter being taught. It is common knowledge that many teachers make little effort to understand their students or to know them well; others are more interested in their subject matter than they are in the students. Such teachers will not be interested in providing guidance for students.

In addition to advising students what to do in academic areas, teachers should also have the essential insights or skills for helping pupils arrive at decisions concerning personal problems. Good teachers will be able to help a student change an emotionally charged situation into a concisely stated problem, which is a necessary step toward achieving a reasonable decision or solution.[5]

Either as student adviser or simply as classroom instructor, every teacher should assist students in planning their programs. To do so, the teacher must have an understanding of the total school

[4]Jane Warters, *Techniques of Counseling* (New York: McGraw-Hill Book Company, Inc., 1954), p. 5.
[5]L. O. Taylor and others, *The American Secondary School* (New York: Appleton-Century-Crofts, 1960), p. 333.

program so that he can answer students' questions, suggest alternatives, and thus help each student select a course of action that will meet his needs.

Teachers should also keep up-to-date on guidance matters pertaining to their particular field of study. For example, the English teacher should be informed about college requirements in English; the commercial teacher should be acquainted with the employment opportunities and on-the-job problems his students will face when they enter the labor market; and the art teacher should know about the art schools and types of training available to his students. While this information is appropriately available in the counselor's office, it must be placed in the teachers' hands so that they may use it in their daily contacts with students.

Guidance-minded teachers will find many opportunities to do incidental counseling before and after school as students stop to talk, as they help students plan their extraclass programs, and as student and teacher meet at social functions or in the lunchroom. There is almost no limit to the influence teachers can have on the growth and adjustment of their students provided they understand child development — what to expect at a specific age level — and have a broad interpretation of the entire school curriculum, particularly as it relates to their subject area.[6]

Organization of the guidance program

The variations in secondary school guidance programs are due to two major factors — the size of the school and the amount of money available for guidance services. Nevertheless, if guidance is to be provided effectively, the school must have some organized system through which these services are rendered.

Most large schools no longer dump responsibility for the administration of guidance services on one person, such as the secondary school principal or a guidance director; all staff members share the responsibility for guidance. Most schools, however, have made the principal and the guidance director responsible for coordinating the program. These two individuals then appoint the counselors and structure the counselors' workload so that most of their time can be devoted to guidance work.

The director of guidance often leads the faculty in an in-service training program on the "what" and "how" of effective guidance.

[6]*Guidance in the Curriculum.* 1955 Yearbook. Association for Supervision and Curriculum Development, National Education Association (Washington, D.C.: NEA, 1955), pp. 122–123.

He must establish efficient ways of acquiring information about pupils, including the development of a satisfactory testing program, and he is responsible for maintaining an adequate system of records and reports. The guidance director must provide for the referral of students to counselors and, in the case of special problems, to proper individuals and agencies outside of the school. Recognizing that teachers play a vital role in the guidance program, the director is constantly concerned with providing worth-while information and working with them on curriculum problems.

Principles of organization

A good plan of organization for guidance (just like a satisfactory plan of organization for anything else) must be based on sound principles:

1. The school principal should be in charge of the program in his school, but in large schools he will, of necessity, delegate responsibilities to a guidance director and other staff members.

2. The guidance director and the counselors should have special training in guidance, counseling, and testing.

3. The importance of guidance services must be understood and accepted by the entire faculty.

4. The provision of guidance services must be a cooperative effort on the part of specialists and the staff as a whole.

5. An adequate system of records and testing must be maintained.

6. Adequate space, materials, and equipment must be supplied by the school.

7. The guidance program and the educational program should be closely coordinated.

8. The guidance program should allow for close cooperation between elementary schools and junior high schools, between junior high schools and senior high schools, and between senior high schools and colleges.

9. The guidance program should include the placement of students in business and labor and follow-up studies of drop-outs and graduates.

10. The program should be subject to constant evaluation.

Many schools have faculty committees that work with the principal and the guidance director in studying a school's guidance needs and in planning better guidance services. Sometimes the plan of organization will provide for guidance committees that are responsible for special areas such as student activities, group guidance, occupational information, educational guidance, follow-up studies, community agencies, and guidance and the curriculum. As noted previously, however, in many small schools the principal must assume responsibility for records, testing programs, college and vocational placement of students, and most of the counseling. He may or may not have teachers to whom some of these duties can be delegated.

Guidance services

The recent increased interest in guidance has resulted in programs of a very diverse nature. Most of the well-planned programs include attempts to offer the services discussed below.

Counseling. Most educators consider counseling the core of the guidance program. While most staff members are at one time or another involved in some form of counseling, many schools have special staff members who devote a major portion of the school day to counseling services. Counseling is not telling students what they can and cannot do; it is a service of an intimate and confidential nature aimed at helping students solve their own personal-social problems and make wise decisions based on a careful study of alternatives and end results.

Group guidance. Since it is not always necessary or desirable to provide guidance and counseling on an individual basis, group guidance programs can be used, particularly by teachers in the regular classroom.

One important type of group guidance is the *orientation* activity which is aimed at helping students make a good transition from elementary to junior high schools, from junior high to senior high schools, or from senior high schools to colleges or jobs. Sometimes this is done through assemblies and special handbooks in special freshman and senior classes. Sometimes it involves tours of the institution the student expects to enter or visits to businesses, trade schools, and job situations, thus providing students with first-hand information. Schools provide career days, send students to college conferences, and invite special assembly speakers so that students may obtain needed information.

Many schools still use *homerooms* to provide group guidance. If carefully planned and given sufficient time, the homeroom can be used to provide students with answers to many of their questions and to offer information on topics that interest them, ranging from boy-girl relations to effective study habits.

Testing. Testing services are fundamental to effective guidance and counseling. Tests are used by the school staff and by the school in general for the following purposes:

1. Tests aid in screening for entrance and in placement of students into grades, curricula, and classes. Through tests, schools identify the exceptional pupil, discover unusual abilities, and determine class or school achievement.

2. Tests are used in diagnosing student problems, in predicting individual success, and in establishing opportunities for counseling.

3. They can be used for diagnosing educational difficulties; for grouping students within the classroom; in discovering group interests, attitudes, and problems; and in assigning a grade or mark referent point.

4. They can be used to determine students' interpersonal strengths and weaknesses by comparing their psychological organization with that of others. Tests may also provide insight into intrapersonal strengths and weaknesses by analysis of attitudes and reactions.[7]

The most common tests given to all students in most secondary schools are academic aptitude tests, interest tests, achievement tests, and diagnostic tests.

Records. The better secondary schools try to obtain as much information as possible about their students from year to year, thus developing some type of cumulative record for each student. This information may be kept on a card, in a large envelope, or in a folder; or a combination of these methods may be used.

The cumulative record usually includes personal information such as the student's name, date of birth, place of birth, nationality, sex, and place of residence and academic information in the form of grades, subjects completed, and honors received. Scores made on standardized tests, the student's attendance record, and important information concerning his health and physical condition are also included. Information concerning the student's home and community environment, teachers' comments and observations, the student's participation in extraclass activities, and his employment record may also be a part of the cumulative record.

Printed guidance materials. The modern secondary school provides a large collection of college bulletins and catalogs for students planning to do further study after completing high school. In

---

[7] H. B. McDaniel and others, *Readings in Guidance* (New York: Holt, Rinehart & Winston, Inc., 1959), p. 57.

addition, information on many occupations and industries is provided. Ideally, this information should point out some of the advantages and disadvantages of each vocation, the nature of the work in a particular occupation, salaries that could be expected, the amount of education or training demanded, age limitations if any, the amount of time required for preparation, the supply and demand for people, and major trends within the occupation.

Pamphlets or books which help the adolescent understand and handle his personal and social problems are generally available in the school library or in the counselors' offices. At times this information is distributed directly to the students.

Placement.   Secondary schools have come to the realization that their responsibility does not cease when students quit school or graduate. Some schools now try to help drop-outs find employment, and in continuing to work with these students, the schools are often successful in convincing them to continue their education on a part- or full-time basis. Schools also feel they should help the graduate — sometimes by making him see the need for more education while on the job and sometimes by finding him a better position as he receives more training and experience.

While all staff members may be involved in student placement, most large schools have one person in charge of vocational placement services. This person will work with business and labor leaders who are looking to the secondary schools for new employees. Efforts are made to place the right student in the right position. Such a service is beneficial to the student, to the employer, and to society in general.

Follow-up services.   Many secondary schools conduct follow-up studies on their students' success in college and on the job. The results of such studies, which should include drop-outs as well as graduates, often have serious implications for the schools' curriculum and guidance programs.

Many methods are used in such studies. Counselors or teachers may interview former students or ask them to fill out questionnaires. Employers may be queried, or the academic records of former students who have gone on to higher education may be studied carefully in order to pinpoint the graduates' successes and failures. The results of these studies help the secondary school determine how it should prepare students for college and the labor market.

Other guidance services found in secondary schools are listed below:

1. Preparing case studies.

2. Setting up parent-teacher conferences.

3. Placing students in remedial reading, English, or similar classes when a need for such work is indicated.

4. Building school morale.

5. Helping students plan their courses and their participation in student activities.

6. Placing students in part-time jobs.

7. Preparing special guidance materials for both students and teachers.

Selected references

BERNARD, H. W. *Mental Hygiene for Classroom Teachers,* 2nd ed. New York: McGraw-Hill Book Company, Inc., 1961.

CONANT, JAMES B. *The American High School Today.* New York: McGraw-Hill Book Company, Inc., 1959.

——*Slums and Suburbs.* New York: McGraw-Hill Book Company, Inc., 1961.

CROW, LESTER D. AND A. CROW. *Introduction to Guidance,* 2nd ed. New York: American Book Company, 1960.

FOSTER, C. R. *Guidance for Today's Schools.* Boston: Ginn and Company, 1957.

FROEHLICH, C. P. *Guidance Services in Schools.* New York: McGraw-Hill Book Company, Inc., 1958.

Guidance in the Curriculum. 1955 Yearbook. Association for Supervision and Curriculum, National Education Association. Washington, D.C.: NEA, 1955.

HERSEY, JOHN. *Intelligence, Choice, and Consent.* New York: Woodrow Wilson Foundation, 1959.

JOHNSON, W. F., B. STEFFLRE, AND R. EDELFELT. *Pupil Personnel and Guidance Services.* New York: McGraw-Hill Book Company, Inc., 1961.

Planning and directing classroom learning experiences

chapter **11**

Teaching in the modern secondary school is a subtle, complex responsibility as well as a rewarding opportunity. Teachers today are expected not only to impart knowledge and understanding but also to help develop individual personality. The goal of teaching is the mental, social, emotional, ethical, and physical growth of young people. In keeping with this objective, it is mandatory that the school offer a broad curriculum and well-planned instructional activities and that the person guiding the classroom experiences of adolescents be a well-adjusted individual, possessing a good general education and extra training in his areas of specialization.

The typical instructor in a modern school must, in the course of a week, plan lessons, grade papers, construct and give tests, counsel students, and talk with parents. In addition to these professional tasks, he must perform such clerical duties as filling out reports and records, collecting money for school and nonschool activities, and, in many schools, helping supervise the halls and lunchroom.

The teacher's most important function, however, is that of providing academic leadership. He must plan and conduct his classes in such a way that pupils acquire important knowledge of the past and present, and he must encourage them to develop fundamental skills, to evaluate concepts and events, and to formulate a basic value system. This means that he should be familiar with many curriculum resources and methods and that he must carefully plan his daily activities, his units of instruction, and, indeed, his entire courses. To do this type of planning, the teacher must have not only a fine general education but also a thorough knowledge of his special subject areas, professional skill in planning, organizing, and presenting subject matter, and skill in communication.

This chapter is primarily concerned with the second prerequisite—skill in planning, organizing, then presenting instructional activities. Fulfilling this prerequisite successfully involves the careful formulation of objectives for instruction, careful selection of subject content, detailed selection of methods and procedures, well-organized classroom presentations, and thoughtful, comprehensive evaluation of student progress.

Identification of educational objectives

The general objectives of secondary education discussed in Chapter 2 should serve as valuable guides in planning the curriculum, but they are too broad to serve as guidelines in specific courses. The teacher must therefore formulate goals for each course he teaches. These objectives should be based on a careful analysis of the subject, and they should be the focal point for planning and organizing classroom activities. Carefully conceived and well-expressed teaching objectives help establish clear purposes and meaningful direction for learning. Of course, the objectives for specific subjects should be in harmony with the school's philosophy and with the broad, general goals of secondary education.

Experienced teachers find it helpful to plan their objectives according to the different types of learning they want their students to achieve.[1] These objectives are often grouped into three broad categories: (1) knowledge and understandings, (2) skills, and (3) attitudes and appreciations. Some subjects are more pertinent to one particular type of learning, while certain courses may be directly related to all three types. For example, a course in shorthand is concerned primarily with the development of speed and accuracy in a skill, while a high school American history course is concerned with the acquisition of historical knowledge, understandings related to the past and present, appreciation of the American way of life and American government, and skills in research, writing, reading, and discussion—objectives under all

---

[1]Hubert H. Mills and Harl R. Douglass, *Teaching in High School,* 2nd ed. (New York: The Ronald Press Company, 1957), pp. 103–121.

three major categories. Most secondary school courses are directly related to one or two of the major classifications of learning outcomes, but any course will have some objectives under all three categories.

The "knowledge and understandings" goal has traditionally received great emphasis in secondary schools. During the past twenty-five years educators have been focusing more attention on vocational skills and communication skills. Because of the intangible nature of attitudes and appreciations and because of the widespread belief that these objectives were the responsibilities of the home and religious organizations, teachers were slow in devoting time and effort to this realm of learning. Some of their reluctance was also due to the belief that such changes of behavior were "caught rather than taught." Most teachers today do not accept this point of view, and increased effort is being directed toward these learning outcomes. The change is fortunate, since attitudes and appreciations are very powerful determiners of human behavior. Indeed, many educators would say that they are basic in education for citizenship.[2]

Principles for planning teaching objectives
Some teachers do not consciously establish teaching objectives at all but merely set their major goal in "covering the textbook" and having pupils absorb as much of its content as possible. Although some learning results from this practice, a higher level of achievement would probably be reached if the instructor and students were guided by clearly defined goals. Without objectives, a teacher's work may well be compared to a ship without a rudder. Teachers should know what they are trying to teach, why they are teaching it, how it can best be taught, and how students can be evaluated to determine how well learning has taken place.

Objectives should be compatible with the ability and readiness level of the students. Teachers must know about their pupils' mental ability and past educational achievement before they plan course objectives. What can instructors reasonably expect of learners in light of their intelligence level and their past educational experiences? How much background and what depth of understanding do they have for a course? What are their strengths and weaknesses? What are their educational goals, interests, and vocational aspirations? Are the students who compose a class relatively

[2]Benjamin S. Bloom, ed., *Taxonomy of Educational Objectives* (London: Longmans, Green and Co., 1956), pp. 7–8.

homogeneous or heterogeneous with respect to the aforementioned factors? The answers to such questions provide valuable information for the formulation of realistic objectives for the teacher and his pupils.

In general, objectives for required courses in secondary schools should not be formulated as very rigid standards of achievement which must be met if students are not to be failed. Instead, course objectives and course work must be commensurate with the varying abilities of the students. Only in elective courses, especially advanced academic electives, should rigid objectives and standards be established.

Objectives should be pertinent for the particular course. This criterion may seem unnecessary, but secondary school students are often victims of irrelevant teaching. For example, the French teacher in one school spent the first four weeks of a second-year French course lecturing on French plays she had studied in college. Although this topic was related to the life and literature of France, the class time could have been used more effectively in teaching the French language.

Each course should have specific goals which are more appropriate for it than for any other course. If a course does not have these specific and unique objectives and values, its inclusion in the program of studies can hardly be justified.

Objectives should contribute to the development of good citizenship on the part of students.   Being born and reared in the United States is not an adequate guarantee that a person will understand, appreciate, and defend the American way of life. When teachers remember the problems, privileges, and responsibilities which life in American society places upon young citizens, they will probably make a far greater contribution toward helping their students become informed, capable, contributing citizens.

Objectives should contribute to the liberal education of students. Teachers can become so immersed in their own academic areas that they are unconcerned with or forget about other subjects. A much better learning environment exists when they attempt to relate their teaching to other subject areas. For example, history teachers should realize the value of English and communication skills for the student of history.

Objectives should be commensurate with the proved psychological foundations of learning. Learning is an interactive process between the learner and his social environment. What a student learns depends on his ability, motivation, efforts, and past experiences. Education should help him become a self-directive person; therefore, teaching objectives should be realistic in terms of his abilities and opportunities. Teachers must establish objectives that are feasible in light of the available time, the learning situation, and the available instructional materials. To formulate learning objectives and to discover the best conditions under which the realization of these objectives is possible, the teacher needs a thorough understanding of the basic psychological principles of learning.

Objectives should be stated as behavioral outcomes on the part of pupils. Education is primarily concerned with the modification of pupils' behavior—overt behavior as well as the way they think and feel. When teachers state their goals in terms of specific behavioral outcomes, they have a keener perception of what the end product of their instruction should be and, consequently, a better basis for selecting course content, methods to be used, and procedures for evaluation.

Teaching objectives may be expressed in terms of the teacher or the student. The form of expression is not so important as the scholarly thought which has gone into their development. Many teachers prefer to express their objectives in the form of statements. Some examples are as follows:

1. The pupil understands the use of modifiers in oral and written communication.

2. The student understands and is able to apply the Pythagorean Theorem to mathematical problems.

3. The learner is familiar with, and has an appreciation for, the amendments to the Constitution, and he realizes their value in the protection and preservation of freedom for the individual.

These objectives are stated in terms of the pupil, but they could be expressed in terms of the teacher. The first goal might be: "The instructor presents the use of modifiers in oral and written communication." Formulating teaching goals in terms of the student has the advantage of bringing learning activities into proper focus, of making the work of the teacher and pupil more specific. For a teacher to say he is going to present or cover a topic is one thing; it is quite another matter to say that he is going to help the student *understand, use,* or *appreciate* subject matter or a specific skill. If learning is to take place, objectives must eventually be translated and interpreted in terms of the pupil; therefore, it seems expedient to state them in that manner from the beginning. Many teachers find it helpful to formulate a list of goals for themselves and a separate list for their students.

Regardless of the form in which they are stated, objectives must be specific if they are to be functional. Objectives stated in general terms such as "to develop good citizenship," "to acquire esthetic appreciation," or "to put leisure to worthy use" may be acceptable for long-range goals at the institutional level; but they are too abstract and general to be helpful as teaching objectives for a particular course.

Teachers can go to the other extreme; that is, they can state objectives in too much detail to be of optimum use. For example, instead of having as an objective, "the student understands and applies the rules of capitalization," a teacher might develop a long cumbersome list such as "to learn to capitalize the first letter of proper names, to learn to capitalize the first letter of cities, etc." It is important that teachers become skilled in formulating and stating their objectives with a proper degree of specificity if goals are to be of optimum use in instruction.

Examples of teaching objectives

Some examples of teaching objectives for each of the three major classifications of learning outcomes are listed below:

1. Knowledge and understandings

Mathematics:	Pupils understand the nature of sets.
Science:	Pupils know and understand the difference between physical and chemical changes.
Social Studies:	Pupils understand the effects of mechanization on production and the worker.
English:	Pupils understand the importance of good outlines and their use in writing themes.

2. Skills

Mathematics:	Pupils become proficient in mathematical computation involving bases other than ten.
Science:	Pupils develop skill in using the metric system of measurement.
Social Studies:	Pupils develop the ability to obtain information from maps, charts, and graphs.
English:	Pupils become proficient in diagraming the various types of sentences.

3. Attitudes and appreciations

Mathematics: Pupils acquire an appreciation for the order and exactness of mathematics and the importance of mathematics in today's world.

Science: When conducting scientific experiments, pupils appreciate the need for withholding judgment until all available evidence has been analyzed and evaluated.

Social Studies: Pupils realize that all people regardless of race, color, national origin, or religious creed are entitled to equal rights of life, liberty, and the pursuit of happiness.

English: Pupils acquire an appreciation for various types of literature.

A study of these objectives and similar lists will show the interrelationship of the three classifications of teaching goals. To become competent in a specific skill usually requires the acquisition of certain knowledge and understandings related to the skill, and the degree of proficiency often depends on the appreciation the learner has for the skill. For example, a pupil cannot become very competent as a typist without knowing the principles of writing business letters and the rules of punctuation. Even with this knowledge, he will probably not become an excellent typist unless he appreciates the personal and vocational value of typing skill.

Teachers and curriculum specialists should work together in planning the curriculum and its goals so that learning experiences will not be duplicated or important areas omitted. A lack of cooperative planning, for example, often explains why some high school graduates know and understand little English grammar but have a good background in literature. Such situations probably arise because some English teachers prefer to teach literature and that is what they do at the expense of grammar. To avoid omissions and duplications in all subject fields, school systems should have curriculum committees to study the goals and content of each major subject area.

In addition, if the class is composed of reasonably mature young people, the teacher may use a responsible democratic approach to instruction which allows pupils to establish some of the pertinent objectives. If pupils have a voice in formulating the goals of their learning, their motivation is usually much greater. The competent teacher, however, will exercise his prerogative and tactfully delete objectives that are not appropriate for the course of study and curriculum organization of the school.

Alert teachers are not only concerned with the pupil's attainment of the objectives unique to a specific course; they are also aware of valuable concomitant objectives — those understandings, skills, attitudes, and appreciations which the student should possess for his own well-being and successful participation in a democratic society. For example, the science teacher as well as the English teacher should be concerned with helping students develop their written and oral communication skills. To the science teacher, however, this is a concomitant objective rather than a subject-content objective as it is in the case of the teacher of English. The attainment of competency in the use of the school library and reference materials is another example of a goal which might be an important content objective for an English course but would be considered a concomitant objective for a course in science.

Concomitant objectives are often neglected, but their realization can be of greater importance to the student than the attainment of content objectives. To use science as an example, such concomitant values as a desire to know more about science, skill in describing experiment results, and the ability to do necessary research in scientific literature are just as important as are objectives directed at specific content. Other concomitant objectives with which all teachers should be concerned are developing such character traits as honesty, punctuality, self-reliance, and industriousness.

Selection of subject content

Once clearly defined teaching objectives have been formulated, the task of selecting course content has been largely accomplished. Using these objectives as guides, the instructor can determine which topics to emphasize and which to treat lightly or to delete. Curriculum guides and courses of study will also help the teacher determine the scope of the subject content, how thoroughly it should be presented, and where it should be injected into the overall sequence of the course.

While a certain amount of factual knowledge is basic to achievement in any academic field, the more important objectives are concerned with the application of what is learned. Learning is of little value unless it will transfer to situations where it is usable. This statement should not be narrowly interpreted. For example, knowledge of literature and appreciation of music are usable, as are communication skills and factual knowledge in mathematics. Of course, they are useful in different ways: literature and music help enrich life, while communication skills and factual knowledge may do this as well as help an individual solve problems in daily living. Teachers should, therefore, use good judgment in selecting subject content that is functional. It is the excellent teacher's desire to have what is taught today retained and utilized by the learner in his immediate future and throughout his life. If this goal is to be achieved, a course must not be cluttered with irrelevant content, and the content must not be verbalized in isolation from use and meaning.

Because subject fields are changing rapidly and the accumulation of knowledge is at present so rapid, the teacher must exert a conscientious effort to keep up with his major teaching field or fields. Change in the curriculum is not only necessary but inevitable, and the curriculum must be kept closely correlated with the change. Therefore, it is inexcusable for a teacher to teach the same course year after year without revising the subject content and activities.

Selection of teaching methods

The term *method,* as used in relation to teaching, generally refers to the composite or combination of efforts whereby learning is initiated or sustained.[3] The teacher's methods are the various individual approaches and efforts used to create and sustain a learning situation; they run the gamut from the informal homework assignment to the formal lecture, and from group work to drill by the teacher. In educational nomenclature *method* is sometimes confused with the term *technique*. Method is an orderly procedure in instruction, whereas a technique is a specific part or element of the method. For example, drill is a method, while the specific ways in which the teacher leads the class in drill are techniques. Small-group discussion is a method, while the specific way of dividing the class into discussion groups, such as alphabetical grouping, interest grouping, or ability grouping, is a technique. Method refers to the pattern of instruction employed to bring about the realization of learning outcomes or goals. It is what the instructor and the students do in the classroom to attain specific teaching objectives.

The major factors that should determine the type of methods a teacher uses are his teaching objectives; school policy; the abilities, backgrounds, and past achievement of his students; the subject

[3]Gail M. Inlow, *Maturity in High School Teaching* (Englewood Cliffs, N.J.: Prentice-Hall, Inc., 1963), p. 49.

matter; the materials and school facilities available; the teacher's personality and abilities; and, in some cases, legal provisions. The teacher's objectives are the most important factor in selecting the teaching method or methods. Methods should vary as do the objectives, and the attainment of some goals requires the use of several methods. For example, an efficient teacher would not rely solely on the lecture method to teach theme writing, nor would he use memorization of facts about the Constitution of the United States as the only approach to bring about an appreciation of America's democratic form of government.

The superiority of any one method of teaching for all learning situations has not been established by research, but there is much evidence to show that the use of a variety of methods and procedures improves the teaching-learning situation in most classrooms. Since this is true, the teacher needs to have at his command skill in the use of a variety of teaching methods. Certain procedures have proved superior for the realization of clearly defined objectives under a given set of conditions. The nature of teaching is such that a method which proves very helpful for a teacher on one occasion may prove to be relatively ineffective when employed by the same instructor with a different group of pupils. The conventional assign-study-recite approach to teaching may produce good results in one situation and prove to be dull and ineffective in others.

Conventional methods frequently employed

Conventional methods are those which are, in general, dominated by the teacher and in which much emphasis is placed upon mastery of subject matter, often with little concern for the interests, abilities, or needs of the student. This emphasis on subject matter is traditionally followed by a rigorous oral interrogation of students or a written test. With this approach, the memorizing of much factual information is often the pupil's key to good grades.

Lecture. A lecture may be formal or informal. A formal lecture is a verbal presentation by the teacher which is highly organized and may or may not be supported by other learning media. Generally, such a lecture in the secondary school lasts at least fifteen or twenty minutes. It can be used to present an overview of a new topic or unit, to summarize important information not readily available to students in reference books, to clarify materials being studied, to explain a process, to express varying points of view, or to summarize ideas or information at certain stages of instruction. Teachers can use this method when all students need a common core of information and when time is limited. It serves very well in some of the new approaches to teaching such as large-group instruction and teaching by television. To be used effectively, however, certain factors must be present in the learning situation; the more important ones are high verbal ability on the part of pupils and teacher, excellent planning and good pacing by the teacher, and skill in note taking on the part of students.

When using the formal lecture, teachers should watch for the following dangers and guard against them:

1. Talking "down to" or "over the heads of" pupils.
2. Lack of concern for individual abilities.
3. One-way communication; neglecting pupil participation.
4. Concern for subject-matter mastery only.
5. Placing too much emphasis on memorization.

The informal lecture, which usually involves visual material and student participation, is better suited to most classroom situations in the secondary school. A good example is the lecture-demonstration used in science, English, social studies, and other subject areas. The use of the speak-hear approach is necessary in teaching, but it should be adapted to the specific learning situation. The informal lecture, supplemented with printed or written materials, maps, filmstrips, and pupil participation, provides an excellent way to accomplish this.

Teachers can improve their lectures by considering the instructional objectives they have set for their students, presenting the material from the pupil's point of view, using good illustrations and demonstrations, outlining important parts of the lecture on the chalkboard, and talking fluently with little reference to notes or actual reading of materials. Since adolescents are often restless and generally have short attention spans, teachers should make reasonable efforts to gain and hold the students' attention, possibly by some of the following means:

1. Arranging the pupils in a circle or semicircle so that all can see the teacher.
2. Urging students to ask questions if they do not understand any part of the lesson.
3. Encouraging students to give pertinent comments or points of view.
4. Encouraging students to take notes and holding them responsible for the information presented.

When the lecture method becomes the predominant procedure and emphasizes a vast amount of strictly factual information in an uninteresting manner, it is an ineffective approach to teaching.

Evidence indicates that the worth of this method depends upon the objectives sought.[4] If the teaching goal is to transmit information or develop a topic or subject, the lecture can be an efficient method. Research on the value of the lecture method of teaching indicates the following:

1. More mature pupils profit most from this method.

2. Students who have highly developed verbal abilities are the most likely to respond to the lecture method.

3. Existing rapport within the classroom group and between the teacher and individual pupils has a direct bearing upon the method's effectiveness.

4. The relationship between the lecture and the pupil's problems and needs significantly affects the method's usefulness.

5. The ability of the teacher to lead students to share and assimilate his material contributes directly to the values of the lecture method.[5]

Question and answer method. Traditionally, the question and answer method has been referred to as the assign-study-recite method, and the title is indeed descriptive of the overall process. As it is conventionally employed, the teacher assigns material in the textbook which the students are expected to learn in order that they can answer questions during a recitation period. In some cases the teacher follows a set order in his questioning, calling on students in alphabetical order or in seating order. If communication is limited to the teacher and the individuals to whom he addresses the questions — a practice which generally should be avoided — there is no opportunity for pupils to discuss topics among themselves. The use of questions requiring application of knowledge, the drawing of generalizations, and the relating of ideas greatly improves the effectiveness of this method and, in most cases, allows for some discussion.

Although the question and answer method, in the narrow sense of the term, has been severely criticized for many years, research indicates that it is still widely used in secondary schools. There are several reasons for its survival: it is a very simple approach requiring little preparation by the teacher, some teachers feel it is the most expedient way to cover material, and many teachers seem unable to utilize other approaches. Too often it is used by the

[4]Benjamin S. Bloom, "Thought Processes in Lectures and Discussions," *Journal of General Education*, VII (April 1953), 169.
[5]William H. Burton, *The Guidance of Learning Activities*, 3rd ed. (New York: Appleton-Century-Crofts, 1962), pp. 286–287.

teacher to fire rapid questions covering factual information in order that he may check on students to see if they have memorized the materials. This practice can result in an unfavorable relationship between teacher and students, and it can also create aggressive reactions among the students themselves when a highly competitive atmosphere is allowed to develop in the classroom.

Teachers should plan the use of this method well so that they will not be guilty of overusing it and so that they can build interaction skills involving oral discussion and develop skill in attentive listening on the part of their pupils. (When used well, the question and answer method can help students learn from the person answering the question; and it may cause some pupils to study more because they expect to be called on in class. The following procedures are suggested when a teacher employs this method:

1. Ask questions in a pleasant, conversational manner.

2. In most cases ask the question and then call on a student.

3. Do not repeat questions continually for the benefit of students who are not paying attention.

4. Spread the questions throughout the class.

5. Try to ask questions that will demand thought and discussion by students.

There is an art to asking good questions. Questions that will stimulate thought and discussion must be well planned. They usually involve one or more of the following elements:

Comparison or contrast—This type of question involves the enumeration of likenesses or differences arrived at through reflective thinking. Example: What is the difference between weather and climate?

Decision for or against—Questions of this type require a weighing of the factors or conditions involved. Example: Should we trade with Communist countries? If the answer can be arrived at without such weighing of factors or use of judgment, the question is simply one of recall.

Application in a new situation—Example: Suggest ways of correcting a bad case of reverberation in an auditorium or church.

Classification—This type of question involves comparison of two or more things in order to (1) place them in a predetermined group based on similarity, differences, or other relationships or (2) define a group. Example: What kind of change occurred in each of the following: ice melted, sugar dissolved in water, milk soured, warm pop foamed out of the bottle, and zinc dissolved in acid?

Relationships including cause and effect—This type of question requires the student to perceive the interdependence or connection between phenomena, conditions, or other data. Example: What is the relation between friction and the efficiency of a machine?

Example or illustration—This type of question, usually the converse of classification, asks the learner to give an example of a principle. Example: Describe a case that you have actually witnessed where inertia was a disadvantage.

Statement of aim or purpose—Questions involving the author's purpose in the selection or arrangement of materials would fit into this category. Example: Why is the author interested in the history of elements?

Practice and drill methods. Drill or student practice is one of the most controversial teaching methods. Some educators say it is used too much; others say it should be used more often. While avoiding excessive use, a teacher can employ drill effectively by interweaving it with meaning and relevance.

The student and the teacher should clearly understand the importance of drill or practice. Under good guidance, a person learns to type by typing, to write by writing, and to swim by swimming; in most instances he does not learn as well by merely hearing about an operation or seeing it performed. Therefore, it is necessary in many courses to have direct participation by the student in the form of drill. Pupil performance is one of the oldest teaching methods, but, as with other teaching procedures, its use should be determined by instructional objectives. While the drill method is best suited to teaching a skill, it can also be used to achieve an appreciation or an understanding.

Because students are performing a certain act, however, does not mean that they will learn well or that they will learn at all. Some biology students cut up earthworms but learn little except to dislike science. If pupils are not interested in the subject or do not practice with purpose, they will learn little by experimentation or by drill. Student motivation is just as crucial in practice or drill as in any other method. An effective motivating device for drill is competition, and the best type of competition is with one's own past record. Whether students compete with themselves, with each other, or with other classes, however, competition should be properly controlled; and care should be taken to see that it is not carried to the point of creating ill will.

Because drill or practice is the heart of many learning activities, the factors that cause learning when drill is used should be carefully examined. The major factors are motivation, explanation, demonstration, student performance and teacher supervision, and evaluation. Pupils can be motivated to learn a skill or to master materials if they understand its importance in terms of their present and their future, if they know how the content or skill will be useful. Students need good explanations of what they are supposed to do or learn, and considerable discussion of theory may be necessary before they achieve this understanding. Teachers should demonstrate a skill or procedure in order that the pupils will achieve the desired lesson outcomes and that they will become interested in learning by doing. Then the student should practice under instructor supervision. If the skill is a simple one, it may be practiced in its entirety immediately after the demonstration; if it is complicated, it should be divided into steps or parts.

The evaluation of drill or practice is the final and most important factor in learning since it is here that the teacher determines how well his students have learned. Unless they can perform and apply the skill or knowledge without assistance from the instructor, they should be required to do remedial work.

Teachers should remember that drill and memorization are not always the same thing. Skills that are learned will have meaning, because a skill is an act or response, motor or mental, that is performed relatively identically and automatically in similar situations. Some examples are counting, using an index, using correct punctuation, and typing. Definitions, principles, relationships, and other types of understandings that do not operate identically and automatically because of the variables they involve are not skills. Teachers must make sure that the student understands and can apply such elements, for he can sometimes verbalize them without being able to apply them.

Making assignments.   Assignments may be work the student is to do in class or in a study hall, such as drill or reading, or work he is to do at home. But whether the work is to be done in school under supervision or at home independently, all assignments should be purposeful. No one likes to do busy work. Students will usually not resent worth-while assignments, particularly if teachers make them clear and suggest ways and materials to be used. The value of assignments is determined by how well they are planned by the teacher and the students.

Reviewing.   Reviews often avoid half-mastery of skills and subject matter by helping students grasp relationships, evaluate the important elements in a lesson or unit, see the different parts of a course in proper perspective, acquire greater permanence of learning, recognize their need for more learning, and provide a better basis for future learning. Sometimes it is desirable to spend time reviewing at the beginning of a class period; other times it is better to review at the end of a class. Frequently teachers review at the beginning or end of a week's, month's, or semester's work, and usually reviewing is done just before large tests or final exams. Many techniques may be used — summarization by students and teacher at the end of units of work, question and answer sessions, discussions, problem solving, or a study guide to lead students in independent study and review.

The laboratory method. In the laboratory method pupils are given the needed materials and equipment to solve an assigned problem or to perform a given task; they may work individually or in small groups. The term *laboratory method* has different meanings, and the procedures employed differ considerably. Generally, the term brings to mind the science laboratory and the techniques utilized therein; however, the laboratory method is applicable to other fields, ranging from vocational subjects to the social studies and foreign languages. Many secondary schools, for example, have installed language laboratories which are used by the pupils to develop oral-aural facility in a foreign language. In fact, some schools now have laboratories for mathematics. Although use of the laboratory does not require special rooms, it is necessary to set up special problems or projects and to provide the students with the time, materials, and equipment needed to solve the problems or complete the projects.

Project and activity methods. The terms *project method* and *activity method* have frequently been used interchangeably. Because so many procedures and practices have been employed under these labels, no universally accepted definitions of the terms have ever been developed. Usually *project method* denotes a long-term undertaking of a rather complex task involving the solution of several related problems. The project should consist of a task through which the student can realize some definite goal of value to him. Ideally, the pupil should plan, execute, and evaluate the entire project himself under teacher supervision. Teachers should guide the learner in his selection of an appropriate project, help him select suitable materials, and provide suggestions for carrying out and evaluating the project.

The most frequent criticism of the project and activity methods has been that students often become so involved with projects that they neglect the attainment of other important knowledge and understandings. Another criticism is that teachers have difficulty in rendering the needed assistance and supervision for pupils. Many teachers have found, however, that focusing the students' efforts on projects has resulted in a high level of motivation, and there is some research evidence to substantiate the value of this approach.[6]

Discussion method. The sharing of information and ideas resulting from the experiences and study efforts of pupils and the teacher in an informal classroom discussion is generally referred to as the discussion method or socialized recitation method. The teacher may serve as discussion leader, particularly with immature groups, but the discussion is often conducted with a student serving as chairman and leader and the teacher assisting as consultant or resource person. Other class members listen attentively with complete freedom to express themselves at any point.

The discussion method is subject to certain weaknesses which the teacher must strive to avoid. The more extroverted pupils may attempt to dominate the discussion; the discussion may wander far from the intended topic; or it may become shallow and fail to explore the more profound aspects of the subject. These pitfalls can be avoided by tactful injection of a well-timed question or comment.

Panel discussions and symposiums are often used along with the discussion method. All three methods can be very helpful in enhancing the pupils' powers of self-expression, increasing their ability to participate effectively in groups, developing greater tolerance of the views of others, gaining wider knowledge through the shared efforts of the group, and acquiring a stronger inclination to consider the pros and cons of an issue before arriving at a decision. As with other approaches, the success and value of these methods largely depend upon the skill of the teacher and the nature of the objectives.

Small-group methods. Small-group methods involve dividing the class into groups for the purpose of attaining specific objectives. The small group or committee, under the guidance of the teacher, selects a topic for study and eventual presentation to the whole class.

Small-group methods strengthen motivation because the student has an opportunity to select an area of study in which he is inter-

[6]Ralph K. Watkins, *Techniques of Secondary School Teaching* (New York: The Ronald Press Company, 1958), pp. 258–259.

ested; he is involved in finding, assimilating, organizing, and presenting part of the course content; and he and his associates achieve better coverage of the subject than would be possible for an individual. The disadvantages combine those of the discussion method and the project and activity methods—the outgoing students tend to dominate the group and do most of the work, the pupils sometimes deal with only peripheral information rather than the heart of the subject, and the teacher often finds it difficult to give each group the needed amount of supervision.

A brief description of some small-group methods follows.

Panel discussion—Four or five students assume responsibility for studying a problem or one phase of a topic. With one member of the group acting as chairman, the panel presents a discussion of the topic before the class. Members of the class are generally permitted to raise questions for the panel to discuss.

Small-group discussion—The teacher divides the class into groups, very often on the basis of ability or interests, thus permitting the assignment of remedial or enrichment work as may be needed by the individual members. When group members are sufficiently mature, a student may serve as chairman with the teacher assisting as a consultant or resource person whose main job is to guide and stimulate the students' thinking along lines appropriate for the subject, to help the students overcome obstacles, and to direct them to needed resource materials. With a rotating chairmanship, each student is given the opportunity to develop leadership skills—a most important concomitant objective of virtually all courses in the curriculum.

It should be realized that small-group instruction will not produce the desired objectives if the teacher conducts the sessions in the same manner that he conducts a class of twenty-five to thirty-five pupils. Attention and effort must be devoted to involving the students in discussion if this method is to yield optimum results.

British-style debate—Two teams of students are organized with one team taking the affirmative position on an issue and the other the negative. The affirmative and negative positions are presented alternately, and after the last speaker has made his presentation, other class members may speak or ask questions of a debater.

Dramatization—When carefully planned, written, and rehearsed by a committee of students and the teacher, the dramatic presentation of an event related to a topic of study can be a potent learning experience in some courses.

Sociodrama—A sociodrama is an unrehearsed dramatization of a problem, presented by students who, without scripts, extemporaneously play the roles assigned to them. It is usually based upon situations involving social problems and can be used effectively in social studies and English classes.

New approaches to instruction

Just as the body of knowledge in many subject fields has expanded and changed, so have instructional practices. Some of these changes have come about through a slow evolutionary process, while others have occurred rather suddenly. Many more innovations and changes in teaching will undoubtedly occur as educators seek ways of improving the teaching-learning process. Some of the new instructional practices can be expected to survive the test of time and others to fade into oblivion. Several of the more prominent present-day trends in instructional practices are described below.

Large- and small-group instruction. Large-group instruction requires careful planning and preparation on the part of the teacher if it is to be effective. Using a variety of carefully chosen visual materials and supplying study guides such as an outline of the presentation or a list of study questions are effective ways of improving large-group instruction.

Small-group discussion, recommended as a supplement to large-group instruction, enables each pupil to ask questions, to present his point of view, and to develop the necessary skills for being a contributing member of a working group. Another special value of the small-group sessions is that desirable attitudes and appreciations can more readily be developed and re-enforced through the normal give-and-take among the participants than is possible with large-group instruction alone.

Team teaching. Team teaching can be started quite easily in a limited way in secondary schools large enough to require two or more sections of a course during the same class period. Any secondary school with two hundred or more pupils at a given grade level usually fits this category. The teachers of the two sections work together in planning and organizing the instruction so that each will prepare and present the portions of the subject for which he is best qualified. On the basis of pretests and other techniques of appraisal, the pupils can be divided according to their special needs. For example, some students may report to one teacher for instruction in the mechanics of English while the rest of the group reports to the other teacher for instruction in composition. On certain occasions the two groups may be combined for viewing a film, observing a demonstration, or listening to a lecture or panel discussion. In schools having more than two sections of a given course meeting at the same time, the possibilities of team teaching are enhanced.

There is a growing trend in secondary schools to organize teaching teams which include noncertified personnel as well as qualified teachers. The composition of these teams varies greatly from one school to another. A very competent teacher, strong in scholarship, instructional know-how, and leadership, is usually responsible for coordinating team efforts. The rest of the team may be made up of one or more of the following types of personnel: certified teachers, intern teachers, clerks, lay readers, and technicians. The noncertified personnel, usually referred to as teacher assistants or teacher aides, are given a variety of tasks to perform, thus relieving the teacher from many nonteaching tasks and permitting him to devote his time to the genuine professional task of the school—instruction.

In most schools where certified and noncertified personnel have been utilized, the team is responsible for instructing one hundred to two hundred pupils. Part of the instructional time is devoted to large-group instruction, part to independent study, and part to small-group discussion. The Commission on the Experimental Study of the Utilization of the Staff of the Secondary School suggests that 20 per cent of the time be devoted to small-group discussion and 40 per cent to each of the other two methods.[7] Under this plan the team leader or master teacher is usually responsible for making the large-group presentations, sometimes with the aid of closed-circuit television, while the teacher aides and intern teachers supervise the discussion groups and independent study.

Independent study. Independent study involves a variety of activities, such as reading, writing, using automated learning devices, making recordings, listening, and observing. It occupies about 40 per cent of a student's in-school time.

When supervising independent study, the successful teacher not only helps the students to identify areas of study but also keeps informed of each student's progress and evaluates the end product. This necessitates close observation and supervision, individual conferences, administering tests, and the keeping of records. One of the teacher's primary functions is to provide or help the student find needed references and other instructional materials.

[7]Lloyd Trump, *Images of the Future*, Commission on the Experimental Study of the Utilization of the Staff in the Secondary School, National Association of Secondary-School Principals (Washington, D.C., 1959), p. 9.

Independent study appears to be a very effective way of providing for individual differences and will undoubtedly be employed to a much greater extent in the secondary schools of the future. Because of the greater sophistication and maturity of the students, it holds greater promise for the senior high school than for the junior high school.

Problem solving. The problem-solving approach to teaching has become increasingly widespread as a result of the concern for educating boys and girls to become self-reliant and contributing members of a democratic society. Many educators believe that developing the student's problem-solving ability is one of the most important objectives of secondary education, since it is directly applicable to the problems of everyday living.

The teacher's first task in this approach is to lay the foundation or background so that the student will understand the problem, realize its importance, and develop a desire to undertake its solution. The learning which results from the problem-solving approach will be very superficial unless it relates to or has some bearing on the student's background of experience. The problems may range from the purely hypothetical to the genuine or real life. Although the more realistic problem tends to generate greater motivation on the part of both the learners and the teacher, some teachers are very successful in utilizing hypothetical problems. The most effective learning occurs when the problem originates with the pupil himself as an outgrowth of his work in the class.

The problem-solving approach to teaching involves several distinct steps, two or more of which may be undertaken simultaneously. The first step is the identification and statement of the problem. Limiting and refining the problem through the use of precise language is most essential if the learner is to know where and how to begin working toward its solution. One means of getting the problem-solving approach under way is for the teacher to state a problem and then ask the students to undertake its solution, but a more meaningful method is to let the problem evolve out of a discussion.

The second step in the problem-solving process involves formulating a hypothesis or tentative conclusion. A carefully formulated hypothesis serves as a guide to the students in gathering and analyzing data for the solution of the problem. The student's ability to formulate a hypothesis depends, to a large extent, upon his experiential background. Students with little experience related to the problem will have difficulty in deriving a feasible or workable hypothesis and will, therefore, have to study the problem before this step in the process is completed.

Collecting information to prove the hypothesis tenable or untenable is the next step in the problem-solving process. In addition to studying the textbook, students employ numerous references and various types of library materials and community resources. In some cases, experiments are conducted. The teacher's major responsibility in this phase of the problem-solving approach is to give the learners guidance as to what information is needed and where it may be obtained.

The fourth step in the problem-solving approach, often performed in conjunction with the data-gathering process, is the analysis and synthesis of data. Charts and graphs are often made, questions answered, reports prepared, and demonstrations performed. The teacher serves as a consultant in helping the students organize their material and prepare their reports.

The next step in this method of teaching is the drawing of conclusions by evaluating the hypothesis in terms of the information gathered and the knowledge and understandings gained. If the hypothesis cannot be proved false, it is accepted as being true. The teacher assists the students in evaluating the hypothesis and in formulating the conclusions in terms of what has been learned.

After the conclusion has been formulated, it is often tested to confirm its correctness and to reinforce the learning of the students. This task usually provides students with an opportunity to apply their new skills, knowledge, and understandings.

As a final step in the problem-solving approach, the class should be led to evaluate the overall process which it has just experienced. Such questions as the following should be considered: How did the problem arise? How was the hypothesis formulated, and what purpose did it serve? From what sources was the pertinent information obtained, and how was it organized for testing the hypothesis? If the problem were to be repeated, how could the overall procedures be improved? A discussion of these and similar questions will enable the students to develop greater competence in the problem-solving process.

The problem-solving approach lends itself to most subject fields within the secondary school curriculum — not just science and mathematics as some teachers think. The teaching of social studies, literature, and vocational subjects can be enhanced through this approach.

Although a teaching unit of several weeks' duration may be focused upon the solving of a problem, all problems need not be that lengthy. The solution of some problems may require no longer than the class period or perhaps only a part of it. A problem such as "What are the functions of the white corpuscles in the blood?" may be satisfactorily solved in one day's lesson, whereas the problem, "Should the United States government increase or decrease foreign aid?" may require two or three weeks for adequate study and still not be solved.

One of the advantages of the problem-solving process is that it makes pupil involvement a necessity, requiring active rather than passive participation on the part of the learner, which in turn results in better learning. Another value is that problem solving relates to everyday living, and the learner is thus better prepared to face life's problems.

There are, however, several disadvantages that can manifest themselves when the problem-solving approach is used in teaching. Many teachers are not trained to use this method, and many schools cannot or will not provide necessary materials for its use. Another disadvantage is the fact that students very often have had little or no experience with problem solving. These disadvantages can be overcome, of course, but teachers should be aware of them and take the proper steps to prevent them from creating a poor learning situation.

Use of multiple instructional resources.   A notable characteristic of secondary education in the United States is the availability and widespread use of many different types of high quality instructional materials. Each year a greater quantity of these materials is made available, a fact which undoubtedly has contributed to the widespread utilization of multiple instructional resources by teachers.

Another factor which has contributed to the rapid development and expanding use of multiple resources, particularly audio-visual materials and equipment, is the realization that learning proceeds better through a multisensory approach than when a single sense is involved. For example, sound moving pictures involving two senses are more effective in bringing about the development of concepts and understandings than are silent movies which involve only the sense of sight. In the science laboratory the student is provided the opportunity to acquire perceptions through smelling, tasting, and touching various substances as well as through the more frequently used senses of sight and hearing. Although it is not always possible or desirable to provide students with first-hand experiences involving all the senses, the involvement of more than sight or hearing contributes to the quality of learning.

The student of high intelligence and well-developed verbal abilities can learn efficiently and expediently from a good textbook, but every experienced teacher knows that a sizable portion of many secondary school classes finds the textbook incomprehensible. This may be due to poor reading comprehension, or it may be attributable to the fact that the student has not had the needed background of experiences to make the verbal presentation meaningful. In the absence of this needed experiential background, he must be provided with actual or vicarious experiences to help overcome his deficiency. If the teacher has a variety of types of instructional materials and resources at his command, learning situations providing appropriate experiences which will motivate and meet the needs of all the learners can be structured.

Perhaps the most important of the printed instructional materials available to the teacher is the adopted textbook. The standard practice is to select and adopt a textbook as the basic source of study material for the student. In virtually all subject fields the school system may choose its adopted textbooks for each course from a number of attractive and well-written books. Some schools utilize a multiple textbook adoption for certain courses, adopting from two to as many as five different textbooks. Each pupil may be issued two or more textbooks, but the more common practice is to issue a portion of the students textbook A, another portion textbook B, etc. The students usually exchange books periodically, thus broadening their perspective of the course by becoming familiar with more than one author's point of view.

In addition to textbooks, the typical teacher utilizes many other types of printed materials, ranging from encyclopedias down to free or inexpensive pamphlets. Among printed materials frequently used in the secondary school are newspapers, magazines and other types of periodicals, specially prepared curricular materials, and a wide assortment of reference books. The alert teacher has little difficulty in procuring an adequate supply of instructional materials to increase his effectiveness in working with students of varying interests and different ability levels.

Audio-visual materials and devices, such as maps, charts, pictures, slides, filmstrips, films, exhibits, mock-ups, television sets, projectors, and tape recorders, have become common teaching aids at the secondary school level. Many of these materials are commercially produced and sold, but teachers often prepare their own audio-visual aids.

Community resources are being utilized more than ever before in conjunction with the instructional program of the secondary school. Surveys and studies of community problems provide first-hand experiences which reinforce and give meaning to the vicarious experiences provided for students in the classroom. In addition to making community surveys and studies, pupils can profit from visits to business establishments, industrial plants, governmental agencies, museums, libraries, and many other places of educational value. The use of resource people should not be overlooked as a valuable way of enriching the instructional program; practically every community large enough to support a secondary school will contain people who can make a significant contribution to the instructional program. Work experience programs, camping, field trips, and school excursions are all means of utilizing community resources in supplementing the instructional program with real experiences.

Many free and inexpensive materials are employed by teachers to enrich the classroom instructional program. Printed materials, flat pictures, graphic materials of many types, films, and filmstrips are often made available free or for a very nominal cost by industries, governmental agencies, and other organizations. The teacher should, of course, use only those free or inexpensive materials which will contribute significantly to the attainment of the teaching objectives, making sure that the ones chosen are not biased in their presentations and that they do not contain excessive advertising.

To provide the learning experiences needed in today's secondary schools, teachers must have ready access to all the types of instructional materials. While some are contained in the school's library, the varied types of audio-visual aids are often housed elsewhere. Many modern school systems have established materials centers for the purpose of preparing, securing, maintaining, housing, and distributing instructional materials. In some school systems the center also contains a professional library for teachers and serves as a curriculum laboratory. In addition to textbooks and reference books, courses of study, curriculum guides, resource units, and other types of curriculum materials prepared by other school systems are often contained in the professional library. With this type of arrangement, in which the center serves as a curriculum laboratory, teachers can obtain adequate materials and the necessary professional help to develop instructional resources for classroom use.

Television. Secondary schools are using television in three different forms—programs on commercial stations, programs on educational stations, and closed-circuit television. The last two forms hold the greatest promise for improving instruction in the school. Chapter 8 presented a discussion of the use of television in the school's curriculum, but a few comments on utilizing television as a method of teaching seem pertinent here. Teachers who teach by television should be excellent instructors who are given special time to make good presentations. They must have teacher monitors or proctors to help them in the receiving rooms by keeping order, answering questions, collecting and distributing materials, evaluating student progress, and keeping records.

The entire process begins with the planning by one or more teachers of a design for subsequent projection. This is followed by the programing phase, in which the master teacher presents instruction either live or on tape. The viewing sessions are usually followed by smaller class sessions in which the material presented on television is discussed, interpreted, and reviewed.

Programed learning. Teaching machines and programed learning, also discussed in Chapter 8, are being used in most cases to supplement other classroom methods. Sometimes the material is presented by a machine operated by the student; in other situations books prepared on a commercial basis or study guides prepared by the teachers themselves are used. In either case the content is arranged sequentially and presented to students frame by frame or step by step. The frame stimulates student thought and response. If his response is correct, he is told immediately that he has the right answer; if the response is not correct, he is informed of his error, and he may be presented with review frames before being allowed to continue.

Language laboratory. The language laboratory is a classroom furnished with individual booths, each containing a set of earphones, a microphone, and a circuit control. All booths are connected to an electronic monitoring console controlled by the instructor. The console has a switchboard and tapes or disks by means of which one program or a combination of programs can be sent to any one or all of the students. The teacher can use the system to listen to or converse with any pupil. In this way he can monitor student performance and give assistance when needed without disturbing others.

The two types of language laboratories being used in secondary schools are the broadcast and the library. The library type differs from the broadcast type in that it is somewhat more sophisticated. As the name implies, it has a greater variety of tapes and disks. The student may also record his own voice as he attempts to use a foreign language and then play back the recording. Although the broadcast type is better suited to large-group instruction, it can be adapted to small-group teaching by using several different tapes simultaneously. When used in this way, it serves the same function as ability grouping and costs less than the library type. The library type, however, is more flexible and better suited for individualizing instruction for a greater number of students.

The language laboratory is very useful to teachers who employ the oral-aural method of teaching. Pupils emulate native speakers and then listen to a recording of their own performances, a practice which most foreign language teachers believe is conducive to learning a new language. The laboratory enables a teacher to work more closely and effectively with individual students and allows all students to be more active than they ordinarily can be in a conventional classroom setting. In addition to these advantages, students in the laboratory can hear well regardless of their seating arrangement; and because of earphone reception and closer contact with the teacher, they experience fewer distractions.

On the other hand, there are some disadvantages associated with the language laboratory. It is a costly teaching device, which not all secondary schools can afford. The teacher must prepare very carefully, must exercise keen judgment in selecting recorded materials, and should have some mechanical knowledge in order to cope with the electronic equipment.

Classroom presentation

The fourth step in the teaching process, making the presentation to the students, consists of actually putting into operation the three preceding steps. If appropriate objectives, content, and methods have been selected and careful planning and preparation have been carried out, the presentation should prove effective.

A written plan or guide to follow in presenting each day's lesson to the class will prove to be very useful. The lesson plan should include the day's objectives, the assignment, information needed to present the lesson, information concerning the activities in which the students are to engage, suggestions for evaluating the lesson, and any other information needed by the teacher to ensure a successful presentation.

The instructor's presentation may be conceived as falling into the following phases: (1) the initiating stage, (2) the developmental stage, and (3) the culminating stage.

The initiating stage, or introduction, is comprised of the procedures and activities used by the teacher to focus the pupils' attention on the goals or objectives and to stimulate their individual interests and desires to attain these goals. Effective teaching results when the learner perceives the importance of the objectives and the relationship of the instructional activities to the attainment of these desired outcomes. The student who does not understand the objectives or who sees little value in them will probably not profit from the instructional activity. Purpose is essential to learning and, for optimum results, must be acquired in the early stages of the presentation.

During the initiating stage the work to be done in the developmental and culminating stages is outlined and made clear to students. The teacher's role in this connection is to assist the students in analyzing their tasks and to give them guidance in working out plans for successfully completing the work. In some cases it is a matter of helping the pupils determine what information is needed, where it can be obtained, and how it is to be assimilated. It is at this point in the teaching process that the teacher can differentiate the tasks to be accomplished on the basis of abilities, interests, or needs; thus, a skilled teacher will be successful in establishing an environment conducive to study and learning.

The study and work phase of a method is often referred to as the developmental stage. What is done in this stage depends primarily on the nature of the objectives which have been established. If the objectives are skills, then meaningful practice constitutes the chief task of the learner; but if the goals of learning have to do with the development of understandings, perhaps a problem-solving approach would be more appropriate. In the latter case the problem is defined, a hypothesis or tentative conclusion is formulated, various types of information bearing on the solution of the problem are gathered, the data are synthesized and analyzed to test the hypothesis, and the conclusions are drawn. Other types of objectives may require different approaches, but regardless of the approach or method, it is in the developmental stage that most of the work and study is done and the major portion of the learning occurs.

The culminating stage of teaching is devoted to relating the new learnings to previous learnings and to the future objectives of the course. If feasible, the students should be provided the opportunity of applying their new skills, understandings, or appreciations. The application of certain types of learning to out-of-school situations is obvious and natural, but the learner may need to be shown how transfer of other types of learning takes place. For example, in order for ninth-grade civics students to gain a better understanding of the operation of the civil courts system, a trip to the courthouse to witness a trial and to have a prearranged conference with a judge might well serve as the culminating stage of a unit of work on civil courts. In other situations the culminating stage could be accomplished through skits, demonstrations, or discussions — any activities which give the teacher an opportunity to observe the degree to which the new learnings have become functional.

With experience, the alert instructor will learn a great deal about the selection and use of various teaching techniques and methods for various types of educational outcomes. These guidelines should prove helpful:

1. From the first day of instruction, establish a classroom environment conducive to learning.

2. Employ a variety of teaching techniques and methods.

3. Utilize methods commensurate with the group's level of ability.

4. Make provision for the individual differences in interests, abilities, and needs of the learners.

5. Know your own strengths and weaknesses in employing the various methods of teaching.

6. Make optimum use of class time.

7. Conduct a continuous appraisal of the effectiveness of teaching procedures and the learning taking place.

Evaluation of pupil progress

Evaluation of pupil progress was listed earlier in this chapter as the last step in the overall teaching process. It should not be regarded, however, as a task which the teacher performs after the other steps are completed. In fact, the competent teacher is constantly appraising the effectiveness of the teaching-learning process from the time he begins formulating the objectives. In this way he is able to make the modifications in his teaching that are necessary to assure the realization of the objectives.

Unless there is a systematic and comprehensive plan for evaluating pupil progress, determining the effectiveness of teaching is left largely to chance. In a modern secondary school where instructional leaders are concerned with the quality of the school's program, a well-planned evaluation program will have these characteristics:

1. Evaluation procedures related to the objectives and designed to determine the degree to which both the tangible and intangible types of learning outcomes have been attained.

2. A variety of appraisal procedures, including self-evaluation techniques and devices.

3. Continuous evaluation, as an important function in all stages of the teaching-learning process.

4. Students individually aware of their overall progress and informed as to individual strengths and weaknesses.

In conclusion, it must be emphasized that the major responsibility of the teacher in planning and directing classroom learning experiences is the establishment of a climate wherein young people are helped to learn. This means that the teacher must be more than an imparter of knowledge. He must, in reality, be an engineer of learning situations and experiences. The methods he uses do not and cannot exist as a discrete entity. On the contrary, the teacher's methods are a direct function of such factors as educational objectives, school policy, the characteristics and needs of students, and the nature of the subject being studied.

Selected references

BLOOM, BENJAMIN S., ED. *Taxonomy of Educational Objectives.* London: Longmans, Green and Co., 1956.

BURTON, WILLIAM H. *The Guidance of Learning Activities,* 3rd ed. New York: Appleton-Century-Crofts, 1962.

CRAM, DAVID. *Explaining Teaching Machines and Programming.* San Francisco: Fearon Publishers, 1961.

Decade of Experiment. Fund for the Advancement of Education. New York: The Georgian Press, Inc., 1961.

INLOW, GAIL M. *Maturity in High School Teaching.* Englewood Cliffs, N.J.: Prentice-Hall, Inc., 1963.

LUMSDAINE, ARTHUR A. AND ROBERT GLASER. *Teaching Machines and Programmed Learning: A Source Book.* Washington, D.C.: Department of Audio-Visual Instruction, National Education Association, 1960.

NORDBERG, H. ORVILLE, JAMES M. BRADFIELD, AND WILLIAM C. ODELL. *Secondary School Teaching.* New York: The Macmillan Company, 1962.

Planning and Organizing for Teaching. Project on Instruction, National Education Association. Washington, D.C.: NEA, 1963.

Programs '62. The Center for Programed Instruction, Inc. Washington, D.C.: Government Printing Office, 1962.

STILES, LINDLEY J., LLOYD E. MCCLEARY, AND ROY C. TURNBAUGH. *Secondary Education in the United States*. New York: Harcourt, Brace & World, Inc., 1962.

STOLUROW, LAWRENCE M. *Teaching by Machine*. Washington, D.C.: Government Printing Office, 1961.

TRUMP, J. LLOYD AND DORSEY BAYNHAM. *Guide to Better Schools*. Chicago: Rand McNally Company, 1961.

The secondary school teacher

chapter **12**

The secondary school teacher has two basic responsibilities — to guide and direct students in their educational experiences and to stimulate each student to apply himself in getting an education. A good teacher will plan and adapt instructional materials and activities to the needs of his students; he will adjust teaching methods and procedures to specific individuals, classes, and situations; he will manage and control his classroom in a democratic, efficient manner; he will attempt to avoid dead spots in classroom work; he will attempt to make instruction meaningful to students; he will work well with students, parents, and the community.

The teacher must work with all types of students. He must strive to challenge the gifted students, for if they are to be the major source of future leadership, their abilities must be developed. At the same time, the good secondary school teacher is equally concerned about average and slow students, making sure that they have excellent programs in general education and specialized opportunities in keeping with their abilities and interests.

The teacher's role

Teaching is a complex activity; it is not a profession for the incompetent or lazy. However, it offers much in the form of personal satisfaction and can be a rewarding profession.

Teachers, constantly engaged in work that is creative in nature, must utilize their knowledge, skill, and insight in planning both classroom and out-of-class learning experiences that will enable adolescents to perform at their best. Teachers use many resources each day to assure student interest and growth. If teachers are to be professionally competent, they must keep abreast of their sub-ject-matter fields, be sensitive to the needs of their students and of society, and be mentally alert at all times.[1]

Because a great portion of a young person's life is spent in the classroom, teachers at all educational levels are a significant in-fluence on the development of his emotional behavior and mental attitudes. Professional teachers consciously assist pupils in the acquisition of favorable attitudes toward learning and schoolwork as well as toward life in general.

The teacher working with boys and girls in the secondary school has the privilege of making a significant contribution toward shaping society and social structures toward desirable ends. His opportunity in these areas is perhaps second only to that of par-ents. Most educators are aware that with a good teacher learning comes easily and students make progress, while with a poor teach-er the educational process seems to be hampered or even blocked. Studies have been made which indicate clearly that well-adjusted teachers with stable personalities are likely to develop acceptable and efficient classroom situations, while neurotic teachers are likely to create an atmosphere of tension and friction in their classrooms.[2]

Positions available

In the fall of 1964 there were more than 700,000 classroom teachers in public secondary schools.[3] As school enrollments con-tinue to swell, the problem of filling positions in the secondary schools with qualified teachers grows more and more severe. In the 1964–1965 school year 2.1 million students were expected to receive high school diplomas.[4] Further complicating the problem is the fact that available teachers are unevenly distributed in sub-ject-matter areas. For example, the supply of mathematics, science, and foreign language teachers has become so critical in recent

[1]Harl R. Douglass, ed. *The High School Curriculum*, 3rd ed. (New York: The Ronald Press Company, 1964), pp. 127–130.
[2]Gordon C. Lee, *Introduction to Education in Modern America* (New York: Holt, Rine-hart & Winston, Inc., 1957), p. 316. Copyright © 1953, 1957.
[3]*NEA Reporter*, III (October 30, 1964), 21.
[4]*Ibid*. p. 2.

years that the federal government has offered loans and scholarships to encourage students interested in teaching these subjects.

In addition to teachers, secondary school administrators are more and more in demand. Hundreds of new principals, vice-principals, and supervisors are being employed in secondary schools each year, and openings for such administrators, as well as for deans of boys, deans of girls, guidance directors, counselors, directors of secondary education, and librarians, are bound to become more numerous as the increase in enrollments continues.

Teachers' salaries

Unless adequate salaries are provided, most of the young people who train to become teachers will never enter the teaching profession, and many who begin teaching will leave. It is true that people are attracted to teaching because of the nature of the work and the chance to serve youth and society; however, these people also want to marry, have homes, and earn an income sufficient to provide them with a decent living standard.

Teachers' salaries change so rapidly in today's society that it is difficult to determine just what the exact salaries are from year to year. In 1962–1963 the average salary of classroom teachers was $5735.[5] In the 1964–1965 school year the mean salary for public classroom teachers in the United States was $6222.[6]

Although salaries have increased substantially during the past twenty years, in some areas they are still very low when compared to salaries paid in business and in other professions.

A careful study of teachers' salaries during the past twenty years reveals the following:

1. *Single-salary schedules, based solely on training and experience, have almost completely replaced other types of schedules.* This type of schedule has its weaknesses, but it seems to be preferred by most teachers today.

2. *Differentials in salaries based on race or sex have almost disappeared.* This has been one of the significant developments in salaries during the past twenty years. As late as 1941 almost half of the school systems in the United States provided for salary differentials based on sex or race.

3. *Almost all school systems now have salary schedules.* Most states have laws requiring salary schedules. All states with mini-

[5]See *Rankings of the States, 1963* (Washington, D.C.: National Education Association Research Division, January 1963), p. 29.

[6]Gertrude N. Stieber, "Teacher Salary Trends," *NEA Journal,* LIV (September 1965), 20.

mum salary scales allow local school systems to add to the minimums.[7]

4. *Gaps between median salaries of classroom teachers in the various educational levels have been greatly reduced.* Salaries paid to elementary teachers are based, in most cases, on the same criteria that determine the salaries of high school teachers; that is to say, salaries for both groups in most school systems are based on degrees earned and the number of years of teaching experience.[8]

5. *The amount of salary dollars paid to teachers during the past twenty years has been substantially increased.* However, the cost of living has also had a substantial increase.

6. *Teachers' salaries, however, have not kept pace with increased salaries of other employed groups.* Before 1941 the average salary paid to teachers was greater than the general salary level, but by 1945 the relationship had been reversed—though not in all states and, of course, not in all local school systems.

Only in recent years has continuing salary information become available on professional workers other than teachers. A recently established annual survey by the U.S. Bureau of Labor Statistics includes five professional groups, the salaries of which have been summarized by the NEA Research Division in a single average for the five groups—salaried accountants, auditors, attorneys, chemists, and engineers. These are neither the highest nor the lowest paid professional workers, but they are a substantial segment of the national total of persons employed in a professional capacity.[9]

The average salary of the five professional groups in 1960, the first year the study was made, was about $4200 above the average paid classroom teachers. In 1964 the gap had widened to $4784, or 80 per cent above the average for classroom teachers.[10]

Recent revisions in salary schedules throughout the country have meant not only the more usual annual salary increments but also additional across-the-board raises, or a general improvement in the entire salary scale. While it is not possible to predict future trends in salaries, all evidence points to an improvement in the economic position of teachers in relation to employees in business and other professions. Many school systems now have salary schedules providing maximum salaries of $9500 to $10,000 for experienced teachers with graduate degrees.

[7]Marvin D. Alcorn and others, *Better Teaching in Secondary Schools*, rev. ed. (New York: Holt, Rinehart & Winston, Inc., 1964), p. 577.

[8]Chris A. DeYoung and Richard Wynn, *American Education* (New York: McGraw-Hill Book Company, Inc., 1964), pp. 302–304.

[9]Stieber, *op. cit.* p. 20.

[10]*Ibid.*

Teachers have a professional obligation not only to render the high quality of service that deserves adequate salaries but also to furnish the leadership that helps improve the professional status of their work. To do this and to work for salary improvement, they must be well informed on fiscal policy and salary trends and have a knowledge of the factors which determine salary levels.

The single-salary schedule

The single-salary schedule is based on the theory that all teachers should be compensated equally, regardless of the grade level at which they teach, for their college or university preparation and their years of teaching experience. Educators who favor the single-salary schedule feel that it ensures better teaching at every level since it encourages teachers to take advantage of in-service educational programs with greater motivation because higher salaries are paid for advanced degrees and training. On the other hand, increasing numbers of educators are joining many laymen in pointing out that the single-salary schedule does not reward the better teachers as it should. This is discussed further in the following section.

Merit-salary schedule

Despite the fact that most systems in the United States use the single-salary schedule, there is growing opposition to the practice of determining teachers' salaries by training and experience only. Many teachers, school board members, and interested laymen are demanding a plan for salaries that will evaluate the quality of the teacher's work and reward him accordingly. There is general agreement that some type of merit rating is desirable, but there is great disagreement about how to define good quality in teaching, how quality can be measured, and just how the merit-salary schedules should be implemented. There are those who say such a schedule could never be worked out satisfactorily. This is a rationalization that needs to be evaluated carefully by teachers and school administrators. In business and industry and in civil service, merit-pay schedules are commonplace, and it therefore seems reasonable that a system could be devised for rewarding teachers who perform on a high professional level.

The systems that are now using merit rating are placing great emphasis on the following criteria as a basis for such rating:

1. Competence in subject matter taught.
2. Skill in explaining well.
3. Skill in evaluation of students.

4. Skill in providing for individual differences on the part of students.

5. Skill in working with students in extraclass activities.

6. Skill in guidance and counseling of students.

7. Advanced degrees earned.

Advantages in teaching

Several practical advantages make teaching attractive. Some of them are discussed below.

Tenure

There is general awareness of the importance to teachers of security in their positions, and by 1965 thirty-nine states had some type of tenure law. When a teacher is given permanent tenure, he cannot be fired except for specific causes stated by law, and even then only on the basis of proof presented at a hearing he attends.

Retirement provisions

All states now have some type of retirement plan for teachers. In 1954 the federal social security program was opened to teachers. The teachers in a state can participate in the program if their legislature authorizes participation and if, as a group, they vote to join. Most states have accepted the plan. Retirement allowances and pension plans, along with social security, have done much to improve teacher morale and the type of individuals attracted to teaching.

Vacation periods

Teachers have from twelve to sixteen weeks of vacation during the calendar year. While it is true that most teachers are not paid for vacation periods, their salaries are on an annual basis. Recently an increasing number of schools have started summer programs. While eliminating much of the summer vacation period for students and teachers, it is, nevertheless, a practice approved by many teachers. Teachers who teach in summer school are given extra pay for this work.

Leaves of absence

Some school systems will grant leaves of absence to teachers who desire to do advanced study, travel, or act as exchange teachers in foreign countries. Many grant leaves of absence for married women who drop out of teaching temporarily because of pregnancy. Today school teachers are generally given a certain number of days of sick leave each year.

Desirable working conditions
In times past very little attention was devoted to teachers' working conditions. Today things are greatly improved, and most secondary teachers enjoy pleasant working conditions. Many teach in new, or relatively new, buildings. Most teachers have at least one class period during the day for planning and relaxation. An increasing number of school administrators are freeing their teachers from such extra duties as lunchroom supervision and hall duty, and many are providing clerical help for teachers.

Most secondary school teachers are well educated and make congenial associates with whom to work. The secondary school faculty is usually closely knit and works well together.

Education of secondary school teachers

The first officially recognized and publicly supported teacher education programs in the United States were begun in the 1830's, at the time of the great movement for universal education. According to some historians, society realized that if it was to assume responsibility for providing education for the masses, it had to assume responsibility for ensuring that the teachers be properly prepared. Teacher certification was another outgrowth of society's acceptance of responsibility for mass education. Today all states set forth specific requirements to be met by individuals desiring to teach in their respective public schools.[11]

The requirements established in recent years and the teacher training programs developed by universities and colleges indicate a belief that academic subject specialization and professional education courses should be integral and interdependent elements in the preparation of teachers. There is growing recognition that, in addition, all teachers should have a good general or liberal education and that their education courses should be the type that will help them understand young people—their interests, desires, capacities, and needs—and learn the methods and procedures of teaching them most effectively.[12]

---

[11]Lee, *op. cit.*, pp. 344–345.
[12]Carol Joy Hobson and Samuel Schloss, *Fall 1962 Statistics, Teachers, and School-housing in Full-Time Public Elementary and Secondary Schools*, U.S. Department of Health, Education, and Welfare (Washington, D.C., 1963), p. 1.

Certification of secondary school teachers

State governments attempt to safeguard the rights and welfare of its citizens by establishing minimum certification requirements for teachers. The various types of teachers' certificates, their requirements, and the qualifications needed for renewal are regulated by law or by a state educational authority.

Since they regulate the qualifications of members of the profession, certification regulations and practices promote or retard the realization of desirable standards within the profession. Bright and able young people who may be prospective teachers are attracted to the profession when it has high standards of admission. Through reasonable renewal provisions, certification regulations can also encourage professional growth and development on the part of teachers already in service.

Purpose of certification

The most important purpose of teacher certification is to provide better educational instruction for all children. This important purpose should be foremost in the minds of members of the teaching profession, state legislatures, and state departments of education whenever certification is discussed.

A second purpose of certification is to protect the properly qualified members of the teaching profession from ill-prepared, or incompetent would-be teachers. The policies and practices of certification should operate in such ways that malpractices within the profession are curtailed or prevented, thereby enhancing the quality of education and upgrading the teaching profession.

Certification requirements

Although laws and policies on teacher certification change constantly, a knowledge of the present situation is important if the teaching profession is to play a responsible role in certification now and in the future. Periodical publications and statements by authorities in state departments of education, national professional educational organizations, and regional educational accrediting associations are the primary sources of information on current policies and regulations.[13]

Most states now require a four-year college course and a bachelor's degree before a person is permitted to teach in the secondary

[13]During recent years one of the best sources on certification practices has been W. Earl Armstrong and T. M. Stinnett's *A Manual on Certification Requirements for School Personnel in the United States* (Washington, D.C.: The National Education Association). Published bienially in the odd-numbered years.

school. Several states and the District of Columbia require graduate study of individuals seeking positions in their schools above the junior high school level. Twenty-four to thirty hours of subject specialization in a first teaching field, eighteen to twenty-four hours of special subject work in a second teaching field, and eighteen to twenty-four hours, including student teaching, in professional education are usually needed for certification. An example of one state's certification requirements for secondary school teachers is given below:

1. *For a Secondary School Certificate (Grades 7–12)*
    A. Academic Foundations (approximately 2 years)
    The Academic Foundation's portion of the preparation program shall consist of approximately 50 per cent of the total four-year program and shall be composed of (1) foundation courses in arts and sciences involving the first two years of college work and applying equally to junior colleges and senior colleges and (2) the additional courses, introductory or advanced, required by each senior college for satisfying degree programs including electives.
    B. Academic Specialization (48 semester hours)
    (1) Plan I. Preparation to teach two fields—24 semester hours in each area, including 12 semester hours of advanced work in each. These may include courses in academic foundations.
    (2) Plan II. Preparation to teach related fields—48 semester hours in a composite field with at least 18 semester hours of advanced work. These may include courses in academic foundations.
    C. Professional Development (18 semester hours of junior standing or above)
    The student shall be required to complete 18 semester hours of junior standing or above, of which at least 6 semester hours shall be in student teaching.
    D. Study of History and Government
    Each student preparing to teach in the State of Texas shall be required to complete a three-hour government course that deals with the Federal Constitution and with State Government, and the course must be taken in an institution of higher learning in Texas. Furthermore, a student must complete six hours of American History or three hours of American History and three hours of Texas History, but this work in history does not have to be in a Texas school.[14]

---

[14]Summarized from *Changes in Certification in the State of Texas,* a special bulletin published by the State of Texas, Fall of 1961.

Teachers and professional organizations

The most important basis of a profession is service to others. As educators have become more aware of the teacher's responsibility for the student's welfare, the public has begun to recognize teaching as a true profession. The teacher's attitude toward his work, as well as his qualifications, is an important factor in winning the respect of the public and his fellow teachers. A well-balanced education, conscientious service, high ideals, and serious efforts at self-improvement add to the professional status of the teacher.

Most teachers look upon their professional organizations as agencies that can help them in two major ways—first, in attempts to improve the quality of educational service, and second, in efforts to improve the teaching profession and conditions of teacher welfare. By belonging to one or more professional organizations, teachers can contribute to the betterment of the profession as well as benefit from the close association with fellow teachers and educators.

Functions of professional organizations

In general, professional organizations for teachers offer dynamic leadership in public relations. They are constantly striving to increase the public's understanding and appreciation of the value and needs of education. Most organizations strive to build solid support for education and to raise professional standards by working for adequate salaries, reasonable tenure practices, retirement benefits, and better working conditions. They sponsor meetings, conferences, and programs designed to contribute to the in-service growth of teachers. Professional organizations render services through research and publications. They offer the profession an opportunity to pool its strength and move toward greater quality in education.

Types of professional organizations

Professional organizations are of many different types. Some are classified by area as national, state, or local associations. Examples of these would be the National Education Association, the North Carolina Education Association, and the St. Louis County (Missouri) Teachers' Association. Professional organizations can also be grouped according to their membership or the specialized groups whose interest they primarily promote, such as the Department of Higher Education or the Junior High School Teachers' Association. Sometimes organizations of specialized memberships are classified not by school level but by areas of instruction. Two examples are the National Teachers of Science and the National Council of Teachers of English. Still another way to classify professional educational organizations is according to the duties performed by the specialized membership. Examples are the Department of Classroom Teachers, the Department of Audio-Visual Instruction, and the National Association of Secondary-School Principals.

While it is impossible to list here all the activities, programs, and purposes of the many professional education organizations, a brief description of two major national organizations can be included.

National Education Association (NEA). Oldest and largest of the professional organizations for teachers, the National Education Association was founded in 1857. In the spring of 1965 it enrolled over 800,000 members. Many of the leading educators of the past have been members of this organization, and many of the more responsible educators of our day are members. The association has exerted tremendous influence on public education in the United States through its members and by the use of major committees and commissions that have studied various aspects of public education and made recommendations on the basis of their studies. Its publications constantly deal with the major areas of education and strive to keep the membership informed.

In efforts to advance teacher welfare, the NEA has worked with state committees and groups to gain enactment of laws that would raise the educational level within individual states and improve the salaries and working conditions of teachers. At the national level the organization presents information to congressional committees and works with individual members of Congress in an attempt to get them to use their votes and their influence to improve education in the nation. In 1935 the NEA created the Educational Policies Commission, which is charged with the responsibility of studying the various phases of education and formulating policies for the organization and for American education in general.

Among the many departments within the NEA that are vitally concerned with secondary education are the National Science Teachers Association, the National Council of Teachers of Mathematics, the National Council for the Social Studies, the Department of Home Economics, the Association for Supervision and Curriculum Development, and the Speech Association of America. Each of these groups has its own budget and organization, but it is closely affiliated with the NEA in matters of general concern to education and teacher welfare. At the same time, each works for sound educational programs and procedures in its own particular area and has its own publication. Many issue yearbooks.

The NEA is not a governmental organization; it is a private, voluntary organization controlled by its members. Except through voluntary affiliation, it is entirely independent of state and local associations, and the same is true of local and state associations affiliated with the NEA.

American Federation of Teachers (AFT). The American Federation of Teachers, affiliated with the American Federation of Labor since 1916, consists of state federations of teachers' unions. From its headquarters in Chicago, the AFT seeks to bring about better employee-management relations for members of the teaching profession just as other unions have done for various labor groups. Working through the Education Department of the AFL-CIO, it tries to influence Congress to give greater attention to education. In many of the larger cities of the United States the AFT has been moderately successful in recruiting members and in achieving its goals, but teachers generally have been reluctant to join the organization, and in many communities school administrators and school board members have opposed it.

Should teachers affiliate with unions or join independent associations such as the various state associations or the NEA? This is a controversial question, and there are good arguments for both a positive and a negative response.[15]

The teacher's relationship with professional organizations

Secondary school teachers should work with an appropriate professional organization to advance their interests, as do members of other professions. In fact, all teachers have a responsibility to their fellow teachers and to education in general to do what they can through cooperative and individual endeavors in their various professional organizations.

Beginning teachers especially will find the organization-sponsored publications and conferences of great help. Of course, what a teacher gets out of his professional organization depends to a great extent on the teacher himself; he should be willing to accept offices, serve on committees, submit articles for publication, attend conferences, and serve in other ways to further the work of his professional organization.

[15]For a good summary of the opposing viewpoints on this problem, see DeYoung and Wynn, *op. cit.*, pp. 305–308.

Characteristics of professional teachers

A study of the traits considered desirable in teachers as seen by educators, parents, and students shows that responsible people expect to find the following characteristics:

1. Good health and physical fitness
2. A high level of intelligence and scholarship
3. Emotional stability and good social adjustment
4. Good cultural background and a variety of interests
5. Interest and identification with the community
6. An attitude of concern and responsibility toward young people, education, and major social institutions
7. High morale and enthusiasm
8. Attractive personality
9. Skill in teaching
10. Adaptability
11. Resourcefulness
12. Patience

Secondary school teachers are not fully prepared for teaching when they assume their responsibilities in the classroom; even experienced teachers must continue to grow in professional competency. An excellent teacher is, among other things, one who is constantly doing something to improve himself.

What are some of the opportunities available to help teachers become better teachers? Some of the more important ones are summer schools, correspondence courses, extension courses, professional reading, travel, research, and work on curriculum projects or problems related to other aspects of education.

Selected references

CONANT, JAMES B. *The Education of American Teachers.* New York: McGraw-Hill Book Company, Inc., 1963.

CYPHERT, FREDERICK R., EARL W. HARMER, JR., AND ANTHONY C. RICCIO, EDS. *Teaching in the American Secondary School.* New York: McGraw-Hill Book Company, Inc., 1964.

DEYOUNG, CHRIS A. AND RICHARD WYNN. *American Education.* New York: McGraw-Hill Book Company, Inc., 1964.

MCGRATH, EARL J. AND CHARLES H. RUSSELL. *Are School Teachers Illiberally Educated?* New York: Bureau of Publications, Columbia University, 1961.

Professional Organizations in American Education. Educational Policies Commission, National Education Association. Washington, D.C.: NEA, 1957.

VON SCHLICHTEN, ERWIN W. "The Idea and Practice of Teacher Certification in the United States," *Teachers College Record*, LIXC (April 1958), 411–426; and "Idea and Practice of a Fifth-Year Requirement for Teacher Certification," *Teachers College Record* LX (October 1958), 41–53.

Organizational and administrative framework of secondary education

13

In the fall of 1965 there were over 12.5 million students in grades nine through twelve, more than 11.1 million in the public schools and 1.5 million in nonpublic schools. Millions of others were enrolled in grades seven and eight in junior high schools and in the elementary schools. The cumulative enrollment in elementary and secondary schools in the spring of 1965 was 43.1 million, an increase of 3.3 per cent over the 1964 enrollment and 39 per cent over ten years ago. This was the twelfth consecutive year of annual increases of 1 million or more pupils. To offer education for this many young people, society must provide schools that are well organized and administered. The plan of organization employed by a school system has a direct and significant influence on the character and quality of its educational program.

Historical development

Local responsibility for the organization and administration of schools has a long tradition in America. The geographic and political conditions existing in the eighteenth century were such that a pattern of small units of administration developed. Difficulties in transportation and communication seemed to demand independent, decentralized, local units of school organization. Each community established its own schools, and local units of educational administration multiplied. As settlers moved westward, they carried this small school district plan with them, and today it blankets most of the nation. Despite the fact that the patterns of school organization of the Mid-Atlantic states and the South were somewhat different from those in New England, there was similarity in the practice of local control of education. The idea and principle of local control of schools became firmly entrenched during the eighteenth century.

The Revolutionary and Constitutional periods were featured by repeated and vigorous assertions of the integral role of education in a democratic state. The late eighteenth century was replete with proposals and plans for increased governmental responsibility for and provision of schools and colleges, even to the serious consideration in high circles of the establishment of a national university. By the early nineteenth century there developed a growing realization that democracy's needs were not being adequately served by a heterogeneous collection of completely autonomous educational jurisdictions. Increasingly, there was recognition of the fact that local school districts if left to themselves would not necessarily or automatically produce genuinely adequate schools. Neither was there any assurance, and this became vitally important to the American citizen as the nineteenth century progressed, that the independent school districts would concern themselves with providing acceptable schools for all children. This is a reference to the problem, still critical, of providing equality of educational opportunity.[1]

Because the federal Constitution did not mention education, provisions for the organization and administration of public education were considered the legal responsibility of the states. Most states, while slow in assuming this responsibility, finally began to establish schools in response to demands by the people and the realization by most leaders that a democratic government is dependent upon educated citizens. When necessary, state constitutions were amended to permit passage of laws placing education under state control.

State governments have largely contented themselves with laws and regulations designed to ensure all individuals a free public education and, within properly defined limits, have depended on local boards of education to formulate policies for the public schools. Local school districts generally assume authority and responsibility for maintaining the minimum program prescribed by

[1]Gordon C. Lee, *Introduction to Education in Modern America* (New York: Holt, Rinehart & Winston, Inc., 1957), p. 229. Copyright © 1953, 1957.

the state. They can exceed this program as their financial abilities and the desires of the local residents dictate, however, and the better local school systems are never content with limiting their educational offerings to the minimum state requirements.

The decentralized systems of public schools which developed in most states during the nineteenth century did not provide for secondary schools. In general, the state pattern of organization called for elementary schools only, and most school districts were too small to operate both elementary and secondary schools. In fact, as late as the 1954-1955 school year, 39,061 of the 59,270 school districts in the United States maintained only one-teacher elementary schools.[2] On the other hand, the urban areas usually had enough wealth and people to organize and support public secondary schools. As high schools increased in popularity, they spread to the small towns and many rural areas, though in such localities most schools were and have remained very small. In the fall of 1964 about half of the secondary schools in the United States enrolled more than 265 students and the proportion with under 100 students was less than one in five.

Despite the many problems involved in abolishing local districts and consolidating them into larger administrative units, much progress in school district reorganization has been made in recent years. In 1931–1932 there were 127,244 local districts; in 1964 the number had been reduced to approximately 39,100.[3] Since many of the present districts do not operate secondary schools, reorganization is still an urgent problem if enrollments are to be large enough to support an excellent secondary school educational program. To achieve this reorganization and to ensure adequate financial support for schools, many states are passing laws aimed at eliminating inefficient local units and providing state funds to supplement local revenue and reduce inequalities existing among school districts.

Present patterns of organization

Present patterns of organization in American secondary education are in a process of transition. Provisions for organization differ both among and within states; nevertheless, it is possible to identify common patterns found throughout the country. The unitary (or ladder) system of organization is the form almost always followed; that is to say, there is a continuous plan or program offered

[2]*The High School in a Changing World*, American Association of School Administrators, National Education Association (Washington, D.C.: NEA, 1958), p. 383.
[3]*NEA Reporter*, III (October 30, 1964), 2.

from the first grade of the elementary school through graduate education in the universities. Students who complete one level move on to the next without such restrictions as the special qualifying examinations often used in European schools.

Vertical organization

Until the mid-twentieth century the generally accepted plan was a seven- or eight-year elementary school followed by a four-year high school. This graded system originated in Germany and was introduced in the Boston school system in 1847. Until that time there were levels of reading and writing, but schools were not organized by grades. With the use of the graded system, teachers were able to work with groups of students who supposedly had reached the same level of achievement. The arrangement was conducive to specialization in subject matter and grade level on the part of the teacher.

Prior to the Civil War the number of years of schooling offered by high schools varied, but with the development of state school systems in the last half of the nineteenth century, the four-year high school became general. The reader will recall, however, that the 8–4 plan was criticized by the Committee of Ten in 1893 and by the Commission on Reorganization of Secondary Education in 1918. These national committees and other groups recommended a six-year elementary school followed by a six-year high school.

When reorganization came, it was not in the form of the 6–6 plan recommended, although some smaller school systems have used this plan during recent years because they have felt it made more efficient use of staff and facilities. Most systems preferred that the students attend a six-year elementary school, a three-year junior high school, and a three-year senior high school. A few districts adopted a plan providing for a six-year elementary school, a two-year junior high school, and a four-year senior high.

The 8–4 plan, still found in many communities, leaves much to be desired. It devotes too much time to elementary education, is not as effective in keeping adolescents in school, and, in general, does not offer an educational program as well suited to the needs of students as is provided in schools organized along other lines. In 1920 over 94 per cent of all secondary schools in the United States employed the 8–4 plan of organization; by 1959 only 24 per cent were using this plan, and they enrolled only 18 per cent of secondary school students.[4]

[4]Edmund A. Ford, "Organizational Pattern of the Nation's Public Secondary Schools," *School Life* (May 1960), p. 11.

By the fall of 1963 only one in four school systems in the United States was still using the 8 – 4 plan of organization. Over 40 per cent were organized on the 6 – 6 plan and more than 30 per cent on the 6 – 3 – 3 plan. Approximately one half of the students enrolled in school beyond the sixth grade were enrolled in junior or senior high schools, 20 per cent were in six-year secondary schools, and only 30 per cent in traditional four-year high schools.

Often reorganization of schools within states is brought about by laws governing the establishment of school districts. Nearly all states have legislation providing for the reorganization of secondary schools when the people desire it. In some states, however, the existence of a large number of small, independent school districts serves as a barrier to reorganization. Unfortunately, reorganization seems to depend more often on the wealth and size of the school districts than upon anything else. The need for additional space in old school buildings and for the construction of new buildings is more often the determining factor than the educational needs of a community.

There has been some interest in a 6 – 4 – 4 plan of organization, but comparatively few school systems have employed it. As far back as 1915 the North Central Association of Colleges and Secondary Schools recommended an organizational plan that would include six years of elementary education, four years of secondary education, and four years of what was termed upper secondary education, extending through grades eleven to fourteen. Two years of college work would be included in grades thirteen and fourteen.

Another plan, recently adopted by Virginia and officially recommended to school districts in that state, is the 7 – 5 plan. Those responsible for education in Virginia believe that the 7 – 5 plan will reduce the number of adjustments students must make in school.

A movement currently under way in a few secondary schools involves the nongraded program, an innovation already used in many elementary schools, especially in the Midwest and East. The Melbourne High School, near Cape Kennedy, Florida, has been experimenting with the nongraded high school since 1958 and has received wide publicity in popular magazines and educational publications. It is termed the first high school in the United States in which the "lockstep" of grade levels has been entirely eliminated. Melbourne has not only abandoned all grade levels as a basis for organization but has also closed all study halls and put students to work in independent study. Ability grouping is used as an alternative to conventional grade grouping, and students are allowed to advance when they have demonstrated, on standardized achievement tests, that they are intellectually ready. Courses are composed of five regular phases, or tracks, plus two special phases. Since a student is allowed "phase mobility" as well as continuing progress within each phase, he can move as fast and as far as his abilities permit.

The effect of this nongraded plan is that a pupil is accelerated through subject matter on a continuing rather than a yearly basis. Those in charge of the school claim the following advantages for their approach:

1. The abolition of grades makes a school ideally structured for problem-oriented education and the development of critical thinking.

2. Educational activity is more meaningful and realistic because advancement is based on the student's level of achievement.

3. The percentage of students dropping out of school has fallen to a phenomenal low of 4 per cent, as compared with the national average of 33 per cent.

4. College enrollment of Melbourne graduates has jumped from 40 to 70 per cent.

5. Melbourne had a Third Place Westinghouse Talent Search winner in 1961 and a First Place winner in 1962.

6. Courses such as electronic engineering, Chinese, Asian philosophy, and Russian have been successfully introduced.[5]

Many of the people who have moved into the Cape Kennedy area are far from typical of the general population. Great numbers of them are highly educated scientists and mathematicians who might be expected to encourage their children's academic achievement in every way. Also, the intellectual stimulation of the work being done there undoubtedly affects the students and teachers in the school. Nevertheless, the intelligence quotient of the student body is reported to be the same as the national average for schools of the same size, and Melbourne High School is being run on a budget that is well below the national average.

Many of the procedures discussed in Chapter 8, such as large- and small-group instruction, independent study, and supervised research on the part of students, are being employed in this school. It will be interesting to watch the future of the nongraded approach.

Internal organization

Internal organization refers to regulations governing administration, supervision, and instruction within the school. It largely

[5]B. Frank Brown, *The Nongraded High School* (Englewood Cliffs, N. J.: Prentice-Hall, Inc., 1963), Chapters 2–8.

dictates the arrangement of teachers' and students' programs, the size of classes, procedures for testing and reporting, and provisions for guidance and counseling services.

Patterns of internal organization vary from school to school. Small schools require only very simple plans. If the superintendent does not assign the teachers' duties, that job is handled by the principal. In most cases there is no assistant principal. The principal is also responsible for supervision; special supervisors are often provided for certain subject areas such as science. In many schools the staff is so small that some of the teachers must provide instruction in subjects outside their special fields. The small school usually has only one secretary for the entire school, and it may not provide guidance services and lunchroom facilities.

In general, large secondary schools have one or more assistant principals, guidance and counseling specialists, and several clerks and secretaries. The assistant principal provides administrative aid in whatever ways the principal and the school superintendent specify. A study of more than one hundred schools in Texas revealed that the assistant principal's usual duties were in the areas of discipline, attendance, and supervision.

Large staffs enable teachers to work exclusively in their special fields. In most large schools major subject areas such as mathematics, English, and the social studies are given departmental status with an experienced teacher serving as department chairman. This plan makes study and improvement of the curriculum easier and facilitates handling of routine problems peculiar to specific areas. Many schools release department heads from some instructional duties so that they may help with supervision and work on curriculum problems in their specific areas.

In schools of over 1000 students it is not unusual to find other subordinate officers such as deans of girls and boys, guidance directors, and directors of student activities. Research seems to indicate that in schools where more teachers are thus drawn into the formulation of school policies and curriculum planning staff morale benefits.[6]

Internal organization determines the type of schedule which regulates the work of students and teachers during the school day. The traditional schedule provides for six class periods of about fifty-five minutes each. Large schools usually allow one such period to teachers for class preparation and require them to teach during the other five. Teachers in small schools often have to teach

[6]Francis S. Chase, "Factors for Satisfaction in Teaching," *Phi Delta Kappan*, XXXIII (1951), 127–132.

during six class periods. As has been pointed out, however, an increasing number of schools are beginning to use schedules that modify the traditional one.

A pertinent example is the John F. Kennedy High School in the Edgewood School District of San Antonio, Texas, where a "laboratory" program has been adopted. Instead of six fifty-minute periods, the program provides for only three periods, each of which lasts two hours. A pupil registers for three courses, which he is required to complete in four and one-half months. For each course he receives one unit of credit. He then enrolls for three more courses for four and one-half months, so that by the end of the school year he has gained six units of credit.

This program provides more time for pupils to take an active part in courses in which previously they were silent listeners. For example, in language arts classes, emphasis can be placed on the development of oral and written expression. The two-hour period also gives teachers an opportunity to provide systematic individual attention to students who need special help and to encourage gifted and talented students to achieve their greatest potential. Teachers at the John F. Kennedy High School feel that they have a more reasonable work load in the new plan of organization.[7] They also indicate that in matters of class preparation, testing, and grading of papers, their work is more meaningful. Without reducing the amount of work connected with a given course, this program makes possible an approach which the educators in this school believe brings better results.

There are some other interesting features in the internal organization of this school. Each day the 3000-seat cafeteria with its formal dining area and informal sitting areas is open to the pupils at 7:30 A.M. It serves as a gathering, visiting, and study center. Classes begin at 8:30 A.M., and there is a twenty-minute break between the two morning periods. At 12:30 P.M. a thirty-minute lunch period begins. Following the afternoon period, which extends from 1 to 3 P.M., a thirty-minute period is reserved for special group activities such as assemblies in the 1500-seat auditorium, band and other music activities, club meetings, and teacher counseling with students. The library is open to students until eight o'clock each evening.

Many teachers whose requests for transfer into this new type of organization have been granted have planned their programs in detail. A typical class period will begin with a discussion of the

[7]Bennie F. Steinhauser, "A Modern Approach to Education," *The Texas Outlook* (January 1964), p. 23.

scope of the activities for that period and the establishment of aims and objectives, followed by preparation for the more formal period of discussion and lecture; then comes a brief evaluation and, perhaps, testing of the information considered. The latter part of the period is usually devoted to preparation for the next day, supervised study, individual projects, and the usual homework type of assignment. This allows the teacher who made an assignment to supervise study and homework.

Those responsible for developing this plan of organization recognize that it presents problems but feel that the advantages outweigh the disadvantages. Some advantages they give are as follows:

1. Each teacher has only three groups of pupils rather than the traditional five and should be able to work more closely and effectively with individuals.

2. Teachers are able to plan more thoroughly when they have only three groups of students.

3. Pupils can concentrate on only three areas of instruction, thus learning more than they can in a situation which rushes them through five or six courses.

4. Homework assignments are more meaningful and instructional and less burdensome.

5. Many of the high school students in the conventional organizational plan have a work day of from twelve to fifteen hours. The better organized and more meaningful instructional efforts being put forth during the school day under the new plan have reduced the need for stereotyped homework assignments, thereby reducing drudgery for the pupils.

6. Teachers can encourage more and better pupil participation and involvement and thus increase the students' ability to work independently.

7. In the longer class period audio-visual devices, filmstrips, tape recorders, and records may be used to greater advantage in connection with classwork.[8]

Some possible disadvantages to be guarded against in this system are the following:

1. A natural reaction on the part of students and parents against the idea of a longer class period.

2. Problems of continuity in courses such as music and physical education.

[8]*Ibid.*, p. 22.

3. Transfers to or from a school using a conventional plan of organization.[9]

This plan has worked so well in the John F. Kennedy High School that after consultation with members of the Texas Educational Agency, the state's department of education, the new type of organization went into effect during the 1964-1965 term at another school in the district, the Edgewood High School.

Guidelines for school organization

A school system needs to develop its own sound and workable plan of organization in light of its financial ability and local community setting. Nevertheless, there are principles of organization that should guide educators in all secondary schools. Some of the more important ones relating to the educational program are as follows:

1. The educational program provided at all levels should be planned to avoid overlapping and duplication and to provide good articulation.

2. Carefully formulated goals should be carried out through the instructional program, which should be broad enough to provide for the maximum development of all adolescents in the community.

3. No artificial barriers should exist to hinder a student's progress from one level to another.

4. The program should be planned so that no serious gaps occur in a student's education, and the types of learning activities offered in each grade should be the ones most appropriate for the students at that level.

5. The program should be so organized that staff members, especially teachers, can use their knowledge and abilities to make maximum contributions to the education of young people.

6. The program should be so organized that there will be an efficient division of teaching duties and other responsibilities. (It is especially important that teachers' not be asked to teach outside their special fields.)

7. Clerical duties and other nonprofessional responsibilities should not prevent teachers from having enough time to teach effectively.

8. Interruptions in the daily instructional activities should be kept to a minimum.

9. The organizational plan for the education program should be evaluated constantly.

[9]*Ibid.*, p. 22.

The plan of organization used to govern the working relationships and duties of staff members is known as *line-and-staff*. In a small school clarification of duties is a simple matter; in large schools it can become very complex. The larger schools usually provide all employees with a handbook explaining areas of responsibilities and authority. In general, principals are in charge of the schools, subject to the policies of the superintendent, the board of education, and the state. Assistant principals, department heads, guidance specialists, and noncertified personnel are subject to the authority of principals. Pupils are under the authority of principals and teachers but are often given some responsibilities through their student government; their authority in such instances is controlled by the school principals.

The following principles have proved to be helpful as guidelines for the organization of school staffs:

1. The organizational plan should provide teachers and other staff members with a voice in school administration. (This is done in most cases through discussions at staff meetings and through committees composed of teachers and administrators who study and plan the work that must be done.)

2. The responsibilities and authority of all staff members should be clearly defined.

3. Policies governing staff relationships should be carefully formulated and made available to all school employees.

4. Staff members should be given responsibilities only to the extent that they have been given authority to fulfill such duties.

5. Staff members who willingly accept authority should be responsible for its use.

6. All staff members should carry out their responsibilities willingly, adequately, and punctually.

7. The services of all school employees should be cooperatively evaluated; that is to say, staff members should know how and on what basis they are being evaluated, and they should personally, or through committee representation, have a hand in developing the policies that govern their evaluation.

The teacher's role in school administration

While it does not seem appropriate to deal with the broad topic of secondary school administration here, it is important that prospective teachers be aware of the very important part teachers play in a school's administration. There is a trend toward more democratic administration of schools. Among other things this means more free discussion by the school staff concerning the work to be done and how it can best be accomplished. It also means the delegation of proper authority to staff members and their acceptance of responsibility for their decisions and actions and the use of committees to help develop policies.

Democratic administration does not mean that the school is to be administrated by committees. It does mean that the principal must evaluate the ability of teachers, students, and noncertified staff members for participation in the administration of the school under his supervision. Research indicates that schools which involve the staff in administration can do a better job in the areas of curriculum reorganization and development, modified schedules, guidance problems, and other school services than can those organized along authoritarian administrative lines.[11] It should be understood, however, that the principal must always exercise his authority to see that necessary policies are developed and carried out efficiently; otherwise, chaos will result. Some of the major ways in which teachers share in the administration of schools are as follows:

1. Knowing and carrying out school policies.

2. Helping conduct faculty meetings and participating in discussion of school policies at such meetings.

3. Serving on committees that help formulate and carry out policies.

4. Becoming familiar with and working within proper lines of authority.

5. Making reports and keeping records as required by school policy.

6. Submitting requests to proper authorities for school supplies and equipment needed.

7. Promoting cooperation among staff members.

8. Helping administer student activities.

9. Helping conduct in-service education programs.

10. Participating in self-studies sponsored by the school to gain or maintain membership in an accrediting association.

Organization for special school services

Most secondary school districts today accept the necessity for providing certain special services for pupils. Some of these are

[11]Woodrow B. Sugg, "A Study of the Relationship between Program Development and the Working Patterns of School Principals" (Unpublished University of Florida doctoral dissertation, 1955).

available to all students; others are intended for those who have particular problems.

Special services involve bringing into the school personnel who are capable of providing special help for students. New services and larger staffs demand better organization so that responsibilities may be properly delegated and services effectively utilized. Examples of specialized personnel are guidance specialists, counselors, social workers, and teacher aides.

Some of the more important special services offered in secondary schools today are listed here:

1. Library services and service centers providing special audio-visual aids.
2. Evening classes for adults.
3. Summer schools.
4. Guidance and counseling.
5. Transportation to and from school.
6. School lunch programs.
7. Work-experience programs.
8. Special classes for the physically handicapped.
9. Visiting teachers for students confined to their homes because of extended illness or handicaps.
10. Special provisions for the mentally handicapped.

Selected references

ANDERSON, VERNON E. AND WILLIAM T. GRUHN. *Principles and Practices of Secondary Education.* New York: The Ronald Press Company, 1962.

BROWN, B. FRANK. *The Nongraded High School.* Englewood Cliffs, N.J.: Prentice-Hall, Inc., 1963.

CROW, LESTER D., HARRY E. RITCHIE, AND ALICE CROW. *Education in the Secondary School.* New York: American Book Company, 1961.

SIMPSON, RICHARD L. "Vertical and Horizontal Communication in Organizations," *Administrative Science Quarterly*, September 1959.

STEINHAUSER, BENNIE F. "A Modern Approach to Education," *The Texas Outlook,* January 1964.

STILES, LINDLEY J., LLOYD E. McCLEARY, AND ROY C. TURNBAUGH. *Secondary Education in the United States.* New York: Harcourt, Brace & World, Inc., 1962.

Comparative secondary education

PART IV

Private and parochial secondary schools

Private and parochial schools, under various agencies of control, have existed in the United States since colonial days. During the nineteenth century, when public secondary schools were struggling for acceptance and when religious prejudices were prevalent, nonpublic schools flourished. Today they enroll about 12 per cent of the secondary school students of the nation.

Twelve per cent of the secondary school population cannot be ignored if one is to have a comprehensive view of American education. Since students often transfer from private to public schools, and vice versa, it is important for teachers to know as much as possible about the nonpublic institutions. And since such schools employ thousands of teachers and administrators, all those who are planning careers in education should be especially concerned with the problems, opportunities, philosophies, and procedures associated with private and parochial institutions. [1]

Although the free, publicly supported high school with its doors open to all has been the ideal of secondary education in the minds of most Americans for over a century, private schools have persisted for many reasons. The greatest factor is the religious one. Supporters of parochial schools have felt that the public schools could not give the proper attention to religious instruction; there-

[1] William Marshall French, *American Secondary Education* (New York: The Odyssey Press, 1957), pp. 247–248.

fore, they have felt it necessary to establish schools at their own expense to provide this additional instruction. Another large group supporting nonpublic schools is made up of those who desire a better education for their children than they believe the typical public school can provide. Finally there are parents who send their children to private schools for reasons of social prestige.

Private secular schools

Private secondary school means one that subsists without the support of public funds. *Parochial* secondary school means a private school closely tied to a particular religious group—so closely tied that individuals of other communions or faiths ordinarily do not attend. There is still another group of schools which does not fall clearly into either classification. Schools in this group maintain a relationship with a church organization; but many times the relationship is hardly more than historical, and the particular school would definitely not be considered a parochial school. In the discussion that follows, the term *independent* school will sometimes be used interchangeably with the term *private* school.

Types of private secular schools

The private secular secondary school should not be spoken of as if it were one type of institution. All private schools are not alike; they are of many types and have various qualities. Some are endowed, and some are not; some are coeducational, and some are devoted to the education of only one sex; some are classified as military schools, and many others have no military characteristics whatsoever; some are boarding schools, others are day schools; some are of moderate cost, others are expensive; some are located in urban areas, others in rural areas; some have long-established traditions, others are new; some operate to make a profit, others are nonprofit; some offer superior programs, others offer very weak programs. In other words, just as there is a lack of uniformity among public schools, there is also no uniformity among private secular secondary schools.

The first private secondary schools in the United States were the so-called private-venture schools conducted by teachers as a business enterprise.

These schools, if such they should be called, sprang up in many of the large towns of the colonies, especially Philadelphia, Boston, and New York. They arose to meet the need of the people for a practical education to enable them to carry on their growing commercial and shipping activities.

In the larger cities, especially during the first part of the eighteenth century a person seeking an education could locate private teachers who offered instruction in practically any subject. The most common offerings were in the fields of modern languages, mathematics, surveying, bookkeeping, astronomy, English and navigation; but work in logic, philosophy, drawing and the like was also available.[2]

Private secondary education was dominant until the rise of the free academies in some states and the public high schools after the Civil War. Many educators in the private secondary schools fought to prevent the development of public secondary schools for fear they would force private ones out of existence. These fears were, in most cases, false ones, because private schools have continued to grow and flourish.

Endowed and unendowed private schools. When a school is forced to operate on the basis of tuition and fees, it finds itself in a hazardous situation, for the number of families who can afford to pay the high costs is limited. Yet many schools are operated in this way, relying on income from students to meet all their expenses.

Other private secondary schools are more fortunate in that they receive financial support from alumni and other benefactors. These supporters may give funds to be used directly in meeting current expenses or for special projects such as new buildings, or they may contribute to a permanent endowment, of which only the interest can be spent. The better private schools usually have large endowments which produce money for current expenses and thus reduce the tuition and fees students must pay. [3] Many give full and part scholarships to worthy students from the money earned by the endowments. For example, the Francis W. Parker School of Chicago has given more than two million dollars in scholarships during its fifty-plus years of existence.

Endowments can greatly increase the quality and stability of a school. Since its existence will not be jeopardized by failure to enroll a maximum number of paying pupils, a well-endowed school can afford to be more selective in its admission of students. Some of the older private secondary schools have endowments that were established in colonial days and have been steadily growing ever

---

[2]Chester W. Harris, ed., *Encyclopedia of Educational Research,* 3rd ed. (New York: The Macmillan Company, 1960), p. 1233.
[3]French, *op. cit.,* p. 251.

since. Private schools are now putting increased emphasis upon "living endowments"—that is, annual gifts by alumni, friends, and others who are interested in the work of these schools—because the tax situation today makes the huge bequests of earlier times virtually impossible. These schools also appeal to corporations for tax-deductible gifts, often on the emotional basis that independent schools, like businesses, are part of the American free enterprise system. Sometimes the officials of private schools stress their conservative philosophy as they seek money from business leaders. At other times corporations are urged to offer support on the grounds that they will be making a good investment in the education of future leaders and stockholders.

Private secondary schools that do not have endowments are, in most cases, less stable than the endowed schools. Because they must have a certain number of students each year in order to survive, the unendowed schools often cannot afford to be selective in admissions, nor can they ordinarily attract and hold good teachers. This does not mean that all unendowed schools are inferior in quality. What it does mean is that the unendowed school is handicapped and, in general, cannot afford to offer its students the type of instruction or facilities that endowed schools can.

Military private schools. Many private secondary schools are modeled after West Point and Annapolis, offering a program similar to those of other private schools but adding military training. A military spirit of obedience and precision dominates these schools. Many of the students who attend them are preparing for the service academies; others have been difficult behavior problems in public schools or at home, and their parents hope that the stern discipline will enable them to adjust to group life. Other parents send their sons to military academies because they believe these schools provide the best opportunity for a boy to develop leadership abilities. In many families, especially in the South, education received in a military school carries a high degree of prestige.

Coeducational and non-coeducational private schools. Most private schools are not coeducational; those that are coeducational are generally private day schools rather than boarding institutions. Non-coeducational institutions stress in their literature the values of separating the sexes during adolescent years, while the coeducational schools insist with equal vigor that there are more values in having the sexes together during adolescence.

The major reasons set forth for the separation of boys and girls are these:

1. Boys and girls mature at different rates and present different types of learning needs; therefore, they should be taught separately.

2. Coeducation presents too many distracting influences.

3. It is best for boys to be taught by men.

4. Traditionally, private schools are not coeducational. Many of the older ones were founded before coeducation was considered acceptable, and they see no reason to change.

Coeducational schools claim that their policy is superior for the following reasons:

1. Schools for only one sex provide unnatural environments and create unlifelike situations.

2. Segregation of the sexes leads to excessive daydreaming about the opposite sex, which can result in unnatural emotional development that may become pathological.

3. It is unnatural to separate girls and boys in school because in ordinary life males and females associate regularly. Unnatural separation can deprive the individual of opportunities to develop needed social skills, can handicap him in associating with members of the opposite sex, and can hinder him in making an intelligent choice of a mate.

It cannot be proved that young people who have been educated in non-coeducational institutions display civic and social characteristics superior to those of individuals educated in coeducational schools.[4] Neither can the contention that coeducational products are superior be demonstrated.

Private boarding schools. Earlier in the history of this country when transportation was crude and most of the people were living in rural areas, the majority of private schools were, of necessity, boarding schools. Today some of the more famous private secondary schools attract students from all over the nation and from abroad. Some educators feel that the boarding school can provide a better education for its students, and they give the following reasons for taking this position:

1. The boarding school can better influence the student's total development since it can control his complete environment.

2. The boarding school can keep the student from many of the distractions of modern life.

[4]Harl R. Douglass, ed., *The High School Curriculum*, 3rd ed. (New York: The Ronald Press Company, 1964), p. 669.

3. The boarding school can help the student learn to live and work with his peers more effectively because of their round-the-clock association.

4. The boarding school that draws students from all over the United States and abroad can promote among its pupils better understanding of individuals from a variety of environments.

Private day schools.   During the past twenty years there has been a rapid growth of private day schools in most urban areas, particularly in suburban areas of metropolitan centers. They are like other private schools except that their pupils live at home. The curriculum is usually based on college-preparatory programs.

Several reasons probably account for the recent rapid growth of these private secondary day schools. First, money has been more plentiful during this time, making private schooling economically feasible for many more students. Second, many parents concerned about providing their children with the best preparation for college have turned to private schools, particularly when the public schools in their communities have not developed programs of good quality, are overcrowded, or lack good teachers or facilities. Third, the day school offers the advantages of private education without costing as much as the boarding school and without requiring the student to live away from home.

Cost of private secondary education
The cost of attending a private secondary school varies greatly. The better boarding and day schools are usually so expensive that attendance is restricted to students from the upper economic levels of society, although some students from less well-to-do families receive scholarships that enable them to attend.

The range in rates for tuition, room, and board during the 1964–1965 school year in the United States was from $910 to $2600 plus. The median cost was between $1550 and $2150, depending on the location and type of school. In 1964–1965 tuition rates in private day schools that offered instruction in grades nine through twelve ranged from $300 to $1575 per year. The median cost of private secondary day schools was about $985 in most parts of the country.

Curriculum and methodology
A few private secondary schools antedate the American Revolution; for example, the Hopkins Grammar School, Phillips Academy, Governor Dummer Academy, and others. Since the primary

goal of private schools is the preparation of their pupils for college work, most are conservative in curriculum offerings and in methods of teaching. At times some have adopted the most up-to-date practices. The early use of language laboratories by certain private schools is a good example. One reason why many have followed traditional methods and curriculum is that their teachers are college graduates who have never had any training in methods of teaching or educational psychology; consequently, they use the conventional college-lecture approach with many outside assignments.

In some private schools the situation is changing, however. It is no longer unusual to find teachers who have had and are taking courses in professional education. Committees on teacher preparation of the National Council of Independent Schools have urged that psychology and certain education courses be included in the training of teachers planning to teach in private schools.

Although many private schools provide an excellent curriculum, studies at leading universities have shown that on the average public school graduates do as well or better than private school graduates. For example, David and Frederiksen studied the performance of freshmen and sophomores at Princeton and found that the graduates of public schools made superior grades. After studying all members of the 1955 class who were candidates for the A.B. degree—there were more than two hundred public school graduates and almost four hundred private school graduates—they reported:

> This study investigated differences in academic performance of public and private school graduates at Princeton University when ability, as measured by preadmissions data and by first-term performance, is held constant. It was found that on the average the public school graduates made a higher academic average for the freshman year, in relation to ability as measured by the Scholastic Aptitude Test—Verbal Section, than did private school graduates. The same was true for the sophomore year average when ability was measured by the average grade for the first term of the freshman year, by the College Board Aptitude Test, or by a measure on secondary school rank in class.[5]

Further study by Davis and Frederiksen revealed that the reason why graduates of public schools did better was that they seemed to possess greater motivation. They usually came from

[5]Junius A. Davis and Norman Frederiksen, "Public and Private School Graduates in College," *The Journal of Teacher Education*, VI (March 1955) 18–22.

families of lower socioeconomic status and evidently had greater determination to succeed than did the graduates of private secondary schools. The study contradicts a belief of many people that the products of private schools do better in college. It should be acknowledged, however, that this study was concerned with only one major university, Princeton. Although a study made at Harvard in 1943 and 1944 showed similar results, more studies should be made before conclusions are drawn concerning the graduates of public and private schools.

The quality of private as well as public secondary school curriculums varies greatly. Some private institutions do outstanding work and provide excellent opportunities for the moral, social, and intellectual development of their students; others have very poor programs, inadequate facilities, and poor teachers.

. . . Nationally speaking, it is true beyond question that there are many more second- and third-rate schools than there are first-class ones; and this fact further colors the public reputation of them all. . . .

Were nothing more important involved, it would be merely a matter of curiosity and of mild entertainment to discover what it is such schools think they must offer in order to "sell" themselves competitively speaking, to prospective patrons. Too often it is the trivia: buildings and equipment, beauty of setting; or an appeal to privilege and to exclusiveness based on material superiority. And it is common and painful knowledge to any private school head that, to many parents, these are precisely the things that do count. In part, they constitute the snob appeal, an ill to which all private schools are heir, but from which the inferior school protests its immunity through the simple expedient of calling the disease by some less ignominious name. It is these run-of-the-mill institutions which are responsible for the opinion, widely held in America, that the private school is typically a place for the problem child, the delinquent, or the snob, rather than a place where the pursuit of excellence and high standards may be found; that only those who don't get along, who need special this and that, whose homes are not what they should be, go to private schools.[6]

Snobbery and private secondary schools

Although headmasters of private schools deplore snobbery and blame that which does exist on the social climbers and the nouveaux riches, most will admit that the private school does have a special

[6]Allan V. Heely, *Why the Private School?* (New York: Harper & Row, Publishers, Inc., 1951), pp. 60–62. Copyright, 1951, by Harper & Brothers. Reprinted by permission of Harper & Row, Publishers.

appeal to social snobs. This seems to be especially true of the better private secondary schools, whose students come from the leading families in society and the business world. Headmasters are often pressured to admit children from families seeking the prestige associated with these schools.

In 1951 Heely of the Lawrenceville School wrote:

As for the widely held opinion that the private school is socially exclusive, there is damaging evidence in support of it. I do not mean the sort of exclusiveness that favors the well-to-do. That emphasis is unfortunate and regrettable, but it springs, as I have shown, from the necessity of private schools to meet their costs. I mean the sort of exclusiveness that has prompted the private schools, by and large, to discriminate among their applicants on grounds of race, color, religion, or social or economic background. The motivating force is sometimes snobbery—the conviction held by many Americans, some of them unfortunately in school work, that the only "nice" people are their own kind of people; and they themselves write the definition. This attitude, however, is never snobbery pure and simple. It is perhaps one part snobbery and two parts timidity and fright. For there are a few schools which are apparently free from any impulse to discriminate; and their experience has been entirely reassuring. There is no evidence to support the apprehension that a non-discriminatory admissions policy frightens away from private schools other desirable customers, or does damage to a school's general reputation, or militates against its usefulness. Such limited evidence as there is points in exactly the opposite direction. The misgivings of the fearful would seem to be unjustified. Yet the majority of private schools do follow an admissions policy which may not unfairly be described as a "Let's be as inclusive as we can, but let's be careful" policy.

This is a matter whose implications transcend the preferences or the prejudices of a single school. It is a question of whether the private schools mean or do not mean to put themselves, utterly and unreservedly, at the disposal of the public interest. It is not a question of whether a policy of discrimination can be legally practiced; it is a question of whether it can by any means be justified.[7]

The fact is that snobbery exists in many forms and in all levels of society. Perhaps more of it exists in some private schools than in most public schools, but this would be most difficult, if not impossible, to prove. If snobbery is greater in the private schools, it

[7]Heely, *op. cit.*, pp. 65–66. Copyright, 1951, by Harper & Brothers. Reprinted by permission of Harper & Row, Publishers.

should be remembered that were it not for the existence of the private schools, there would surely be more snobs in the public schools. In 1950 Dr. John F. Gummere, headmaster of the William Penn Charter School, wrote the following on the subject of snobbery and the private school:

First let us define the snob. He is seen everywhere; he is prolific and despicable and can be heard sneering at the rich just because they are rich, or at the poor just because they are poor. He is by no means a creature of any particular kind of school, but only of a mean mentality and a nasty nature. It is idle to attempt to define his habitat, for he is everywhere.

Many people of many organizations are afflicted with the false charge of snobbery because the difference between snobbery and decent standards is often not apparent to some people.

Some will call you a snob if you shave every day, or shine your shoes. To others you are a snob if, as part of the audience at a radio show, you do not applaud the miserable inanities of a performer or the failure of some contestant to say anything. The crowd applauds as directed; any standard which differs from the mediocre is suspect.

And so generalized objection to the independent school sometimes arises from the mistaking of standards for exclusiveness. More often, it springs from ignorance of facts.[8]

Private schools often strive hard to create a democratic atmosphere in which their students may learn to judge others on their own merits rather than on the financial resources or social standing of their parents or other relatives. Many private schools give scholarships to worthy students who otherwise could not attend an independent school. Some maintain a very simple environment, and others require all students to engage in some type of manual labor. Certain private schools require all students to wear a uniform. In many there are fewer apparent differences among students than are found in the typical public school.

Justification for private schools

Some people do not feel that private and parochial schools should be allowed to exist. The state of Oregon in 1922 passed a compulsory education act that, had it been carried out, would have destroyed all private and parochial schools in that state. This particular act provided that, with very few exceptions, children

---

[8]John F. Gummere, "The Case for Private Schools," *Changing Times, The Kiplinger Magazine* (July 1950) p. 14.

between the ages of eight and sixteen had to enroll in and attend a public school. While aimed primarily at Catholic parochial schools, it would have affected other private schools as well. The Supreme Court of the United States declared the act unconstitutional.

Charges leveled at the private schools at various times are listed below:

1. They weaken public institutions because, by educating the offspring of the economically and socially privileged, they deprive the public schools of the interest and support of these influential citizens.[9]

2. Since their tax-exempt facilities are available to only the small number of citizens who can afford to pay a high tuition, they are undemocratic.[10]

3. They create and encourage social cleavage.[11]

4. They impair the quality of the public schools by depriving them of gifted students and imbue their own students with an attitude of arrogant superiority.

5. Their programs are too traditional and do not fully meet the needs of youth.

6. They perpetuate outmoded methods and procedures and neglect modern philosophies of education and new methods.

On the other hand, there are some sound arguments which can be advanced for private schools:

1. Many excellent students receive a superior education in the better private schools. This is a valuable contribution to society because the individual with educated ability is always needed.

2. The best independent institutions can do a superior job of teaching because they are relatively immune to undesirable outside pressures such as textbook purges and local pressures of many kinds.[12]

3. Independent schools provide a means whereby any responsible, interested individual or group can engage in educational research and experimentation from which all other institutions can profit.

4. For students from broken or unhappy homes, private boarding schools offer acceptable replacements for home environments.

5. Private schools are free to teach religion, whereas public schools are not. This is an element of great importance to many

[9]Heely, *op. cit.*, p. 25.

[10]French, *op. cit.*, p. 264.

[11]James Bryant Conant, "Unity and Diversity in Secondary Education," *Harvard Alumni Bulletin* (April 19, 1952). Copyright Harvard Bulletin, Inc., 1952.

[12]James L. Mursell, *Principles of Democratic Education* (New York: W. W. Norton & Company, Inc., 1955), pp. 203–206.

people who look upon religious instruction as being fundamental in education.[13]

6. Independent secondary schools are part of America's political, economic, and social heritage. They are protected by the Dartmouth College decision and the Oregon case and are constant reminders that education can be a private privilege as well as a public responsibility.[14]

Certainly some private schools are open to criticisms, but so are many public schools. At the same time, many private schools are serving society well; they give scholarships to worthy students, maintain high moral standards, and provide a challenging intellectual environment. Certainly society must protect the parents' right to send their children to private schools if they so desire. No doubt some parents will be motivated to send their offspring to private schools because of snobbery, but many others will do so because they feel that private schools can do a better job of educating their children.

Granted that private schools have the right to exist in American society and do serve important functions, there is persuasive logic in the position taken by Dr. James B. Conant in 1952:

I do believe, however, that there is some reason to fear lest a dual system of secondary education may in some states, at least, come to threaten the democratic unity provided by our public schools. I refer to the desire of some people to increase the scope and number of private schools. At present the proponents of such a movement are often not outspoken in their demands, but a dual system of schools with tax money flowing in some form to private schools seems to be a possibility in some people's minds.

What is the basic objection to a dual system of education, you may ask. Or put it the other way round, what are the advantages of free schools for all? To ask these questions is almost to give the answers. If one accepts the ideal of a democratic, fluid society with a minimum of class distinction, the maximum of fluidity, the maximum of understanding between different vocational groups, then the ideal secondary school is a comprehensive public high school.

If one has doubts about the ability of secular schools to promote the growth of moral and spiritual values, then these doubts must be weighed against the democratic objectives I have just listed. Similarly,

[13]Russell Lynes, "Can the Private Schools Survive?" *Harper's Magazine* (January 1948) pp. 11–14.
[14]Fred M. Hechinger and Grace Hechinger, "The Key Role of the Private School," *The New York Times Magazine* (May 10, 1959) pp. 12–14.

if a family questions the ability of a high school to prepare a gifted boy adequately for university work, the family will have to balance these misgivings against the advantages to the boy of mixing with all sorts of people when he is young.

Of this much there can be no doubt. A society which wishes generation after generation to perpetuate class distinction based on hereditary status would certainly demand a dual system of schools; so too would a society like that in the Province of Quebec which wishes to perpetuate two different cultural groups. A dual system serves and helps to maintain cleavages, and the absence of a dual system does the reverse. This is particularly true of the secondary schools. Indeed, I would plead with those who insist on sending their children to denominational schools that they might limit their insistence on this type of education to the elementary years.[15]

Parochial secondary schools

As was mentioned earlier, a parochial school is one closely identified with a particular religious group, usually so closely linked that persons of other denominations do not enroll in appreciable numbers.

From the seventeenth through the mid-nineteenth century the churches led the way for the growth of education in this country, and parochial schools were the dominant type of secondary school. Many academies of the early nineteenth century were established by churches.[16] Immigrant groups as a rule made provision for schools under the leadership of their denomination, a practice that was accelerated after the 1840's when for the first time large numbers of Catholics came to the United States. During this period religious groups such as Methodists, Episcopalians, Presbyterians, and Congregationalists maintained secondary parochial schools. Today, however, these groups have almost no parochial schools as such in operation; their secondary institutions would more properly be classified as private schools, since religion or denominationalism is not stressed to any great extent. This is also true of the schools sponsored by the Society of Friends.

At the present time four religious groups sponsor most parochial secondary schools: the Roman Catholic Church, with the greatest number, approximately 2500 secondary schools; the Missouri Synod of the Lutheran Church; the Seventh Day Adventist Church; and the Jews.

[15]Conant, *op. cit.*, pp. 12–14. Copyright Harvard Bulletin, Inc., 1952.
[16]Gordon C. Lee, *Introduction to Education in Modern America* (New York: Holt, Rinehart and Winston, Inc., 1957), p. 479. Copyright © 1953, 1957.

Financing parochial schools

The separation of church and state prevents the use of public money for parochial schools at the present time; however, there are those who feel that these schools should share in the use of tax funds, and they are working toward that end.

Many Roman Catholics take the position that their schools should receive state aid. Pope Pius XI in 1929 stated his views as follows:

> And let no one say that in a nation where there are different religious beliefs, it is impossible to provide for public instruction otherwise than by neutral or mixed schools. In such a case it becomes the duty of the State, indeed it is the easier and more reasonable method of procedure, to leave free scope to the initiative of the church and the family, while giving them such assistance as justice demands. That this can be done to the full satisfaction of families, and to the advantage of education and of public peace and tranquillity, is clear from the actual experience of some countries comprising different religious denominations. There the school legislation respects the rights of the family, and Catholics are free to follow their own system of teaching in schools that are entirely Catholic. Nor is distributive justice lost sight of, as is evidenced by the financial aid granted by the State to the several schools demanded by the families.[17]

Many Americans, including members of religious groups engaged in education, are not ready to accept this position, for they do not feel that religion should be supported by the state. In fact, many educators cannot fully agree with the following position taken by the Missouri Synod of the Lutheran Church:

> [The] Synod is strictly against the use of public funds for its schools, but believes that parents and children, as citizens, are entitled to various social services, such as bus transportation, library service, medical inspection, all of which are not an essential of the school proper.[18]

It is argued by opponents of this position that when the state pays for transportation, books, lunches, library, or other services, it is definitely aiding a particular religious group. Individuals who

---

[17]Pius XI, "The Encyclical on Christian Education of Youth, 1929," *The Catholic Mind* (February 22, 1930) p. 15.

[18]A. C. Stellhorn, *Lutheran Schools: A Manual of Information on the Schools of the Lutheran Church* (St. Louis, Mo.: Missouri Synod of the Lutheran Church, 1956) p. 15.

rejoice over the fact that their religious schools are now being thus subsidized by tax money might well look at the schools of England that were once private and independent but are now controlled by the state.

Often the parish as a whole is held responsible for educating the children within the parish, and in most cases parents who can afford it are asked to pay tuition for their children. Generally, parochial school students who are not affiliated with the faith sponsoring the school are charged tuition.

Curriculum in parochial schools

The curriculum of the parochial school is, in general, about the same as that of the public school, the big difference being that religion is taught as a separate subject. The curriculums of some parochial schools are more traditional than are those of the average public secondary school; for instance, the Catholic schools place much more emphasis upon Latin than do most public secondary schools. The typical parochial school places less emphasis upon shop courses and vocational subjects.[19] This does not necessarily mean that parochial schools are anti-vocational; rather, it usually means that they cannot afford the required facilities.

When and where it seems appropriate to them, parochial schools educators do not hesitate to place doctrinal emphasis on subject matter, although there is, of course, no such thing as Catholic language study or Lutheran mathematics.[20] Teachers in denominational schools make great efforts to strengthen the faith of students in the dogma of their particular church and to weed out or de-emphasize areas that are hostile to or conflict with the teachings of that institution.

Most teachers in Roman Catholic secondary schools are members of religious orders devoted to teaching. Recently, because of the great increases in enrollments, many lay teachers have been hired by these schools, a practice which will probably increase in the years ahead.

In the Missouri Synod schools most teachers are men. The Lutheran Church sponsors special synodical teachers' colleges to prepare men and women for teaching in its parochial schools. Male graduates are given the status of ministers, but this is not true of the female graduates, who generally teach only the smaller children. Despite the fact that they maintain two colleges to pre-

---

[19]Douglass, *op. cit.*, p. 659.
[20]*Ibid.*, pp. 659–666.

pare teachers, the Lutheran Church also finds it necessary to hire teachers trained in other schools.

Justification for parochial secondary schools

Catholic schools exist because many Catholics feel that religion should be taught along with other subjects in schools and that all education should be conducted in a religious atmosphere. The purpose of Catholic schools can best be understood by reference to the following quotation:

The purpose and immediate end of Christian education is to cooperate with divine grace in forming the true and perfect Christian. . . .

For precisely this reason Christian education takes the whole aggregate of human life, physical and spiritual, intellectual and moral, individual, domestic, and social, not with a view of reducing it in any way, but in order to elevate, regulate and perfect it, in accordance with the example and teachings of Christ.

Hence the true Christian, product of Christian education, is the supernatural man who thinks, judges, and acts constantly and consistently in accordance with right reason illuminated by the supernatural light of the example and teachings of Christ; in other words, to use the current term, the true and finished man of character.[21]

Additional insight into the Catholic position can be gained from the following:

Education is essentially a social and not a mere individual activity. Now there are three necessary societies, distinct from one another and yet harmoniously combined by God, into which man is born: two, namely the family and civil society, belong to the natural order; the third, the church, to the supernatural order. . . .

Since, however, the young generation must be trained in the arts and sciences for the advantage and prosperity of civil society, and since the family of itself is unequal to this task, it was necessary to create that social institution, the school. But let it be borne in mind that this institution owes its existence to the initiative of the family and of the church, long before it was undertaken by the State. Hence, considered in its historical origin, the school is by its very nature an institution subsidiary and complementary to the family and to the church. It follows logically and necessarily that it must not be in opposition to, but in positive accord with those other two elements, and form with

[21]Pius XI, "Christian Education of Youth," *Five Great Encyclicals* (New York: The Paulist Press, 1941), p. 8.

them a perfect moral union, constituting one sanctuary of education, as it were, with the family and the church. Otherwise it is doomed to fail of its purpose, and to become instead an agent of destruction.[22]

Further explanation of Catholic thought is given by the following:

If the question arises as to the need for the Catholic system of schools, rising side by side with the great public school system and with many other high schools under private control, it is not necessary to look far for the answer. Fundamentally the motivation has come from the spirit of the church, fulfilling its commission to go and teach. When the councils urged the establishment of schools connected with every church, bishops, priests, parents, and teachers responded, surmounting difficulties and persevering at times against open hostility in establishing and maintaining schools of high standards so that Catholic boys and girls should have in them all the opportunities for education which they would find in other schools. . . . And guiding the entire project has been the religion in the school, where it appears not only as a formally taught subject, but also as the leading inspiration of everything that is done. . . . Because man has a spiritual and immortal soul and a free will, he looks forward, after a life that accords with God's designs, to an eternal life in heaven with his creator.

If the process of education, then, is to fulfill its function of developing the whole person, a principle which has universal approval, the Catholic educator considers the task incompletely performed unless knowledge of God and our duties to Him are included in the educational program. Schools consider it their duty to aid parents in every other phase of the development of children—in matters of health, of home life, of leisure pursuits, as well as in intellectual skills and habits; the duty of the school also includes, therefore, the development of the spiritual life, which cannot be accomplished without religion, which is its source.

Adhering to these fundamental truths in American life, Catholic leaders have promoted education which includes religion on elementary, secondary, and college and university levels. And their task will continue so long as the world exists.[23]

From the above it is evident that the principal argument of the Roman Catholic Church for its parochial schools is that education

[22]Pius XI, "The Encyclical on Christian Education of Youth, 1929," p. 12.
[23]Sister Mary Janet, S.C., *Catholic Secondary Education: A National Survey* (Washington, D.C.: Catholic University of America Press, 1949), pp. 8–10.

without religion is incomplete. Essentially, this is the major argument of all groups supporting parochial schools. Consider the position of the Missouri Lutheran Synod:

The Lutheran Church—Missouri Synod, like some other church bodies, is committed to the school, elementary, secondary, or higher, as the only agency of the church which, like the Christian home, offers a complete Christian education in its sphere. The Christian home, which is an educational agency established not by the church, but by God Himself, is both God's and the church's ideal and pattern for an undivided Christian training of the youth; and the Christian school is regarded as coming closest to this ideal and pattern in formal education. The difference between a school and the church's part-time agencies, which combine their religious course with the secular curriculum of the public schools in the formal education of the child, is so pronounced that it places the school and part-time agencies in classes by themselves. It is this difference that induces congregations to shoulder the very considerable expense of maintaining a school, in addition to supporting the public schools, morally as well as financially, in the interest of public welfare. This extra expense amounts to about ten million dollars per year.

The principle is correct, and accepted by many outside of the church, that man should have an education in religious as well as in non-religious matters. His nature demands it, and in it lies and is sought his moral stability. But it is not correct to divide his education into a religious and a non-religious category, to separate the one from the other, and to set up a dual education offered by institutions which differ in their nature and philosophy. A unitary training does not so divide education; instead, the agencies of education involved have the same philosophy and thus do not work at cross purposes. There is thus achieved an integration of the educational influences affecting the child.

What is more, it is impossible not to teach a religion. A non-religious school is non-religious in theory only, or in the sense that it is "non-sectarian," which means that it does not profess and teach any one of the recognized denominational religions. But it is nonetheless religious, because man is by nature religious. Call it his philosophy of life, his perspective, his world view, it is his religion.[24]

This position rules out the argument advanced by many that religious instruction can be given in Sunday schools or in weekday

[24]Stellhorn, *op. cit.*, pp. 11–12.

religion classes attended by students on a released-time basis. Supporters of parochial schools maintain that religion should permeate all instruction. Other reasons for parochial schools are that they ensure that a larger number of young people will become full-time religious workers and that they prevent many from falling away from the particular religious faith.

To summarize, the position of most parochial school educators would involve some or all of the following as reasons for parochial secondary schools:

1. Very thorough indoctrination and exercise in the Scriptures.

2. Instruction and training by teachers who are well prepared for this work.

3. Daily contact with teachers and students of the same faith.

4. Preparation for membership in a congregation and the church in general.

5. Absence of any educational influence that is inimical to the positive religious education of the individual.

6. Provision of a fruitful recruiting ground for the ministry of the church.

7. Study of man's best interests and the undergirding of society with righteous, Christian citizenship.[25]

Selected references

CARR, WILLIAM G. "The Partnership of the Independent and Public Schools in the Future of America," *Education Digest* (September 1956).

CONANT, JAMES BRYANT. "Unity and Diversity in Secondary Education," *Harvard Alumni Bulletin* (April 19, 1952).

DAVIS, JUNIUS A. AND NORMAN FREDERIKSEN. "Public and Private School Graduates in College," *The Journal of Teacher Education*, VI (March 1955), 18–22.

DEYOUNG, CHRIS A. AND RICHARD WYNN. *American Education.* New York: McGraw-Hill Book Company, Inc., 1964.

DOUGLASS, HARL R., ED. *The High School Curriculum,* 3rd ed. New York: The Ronald Press Company, 1964.

FRENCH, WILLIAM MARSHALL. *American Secondary Education.* New York: The Odyssey Press, 1957.

FUESS, CLAUDE M. "Golden Days for Independent Schools," XLV *Saturday Review of Literature* (August 18, 1962), 46–48.

[25]*Ibid.*, p. 14.

HARRIS, CHESTER W., ED. *Encyclopedia of Educational Research,* 3rd ed. New York: The Macmillan Company, 1960, p. 1233.

HEELY, ALLAN V. *Why the Private School?* New York: Harper & Row, Publishers, Inc., 1951.

MURSELL, JAMES L. *Principles of Democratic Education.* New York: W. W. Norton & Company, Inc., 1955.

Secondary education
in England and France

Some readers may object to the inclusion of this chapter and the next on the grounds that it is enough to inform oneself about the American system of secondary education. They may ask: "Why should Americans concern themselves with secondary education in other countries?"

The United States has an excellent system of education. Few if any Americans would exchange it for any system in Europe. Yet it is presumptuous to assume that this country has all the answers and cannot learn from the rest of the world. One should recall that the United States was one of the last major countries to learn that elementary education could and should be provided in a six-year system, thus giving more time for secondary and higher education. This was a case where Americans learned from the rest of the world. Many other sound educational theories have originated outside the United States — grouping by grades, mass instruction, and the use of graded textbooks — and it is essential that we keep in touch with educational developments in other lands.

A second reason for studying the secondary schools of other countries is to acquire a basis for informed comparisons. In recent years a number of prominent Americans have made recommendations that, if carried out, would convert part of the public secondary system into schools similar to those in Europe. Would this be proper? Just how would some of the European practices improve

American education? Are there dangers in some of the recommendations? A study of the major European systems should provide a factual basis for answering these questions and should help the individual understand why other peoples feel as they do on certain issues and why they follow certain practices.

While this discussion is not comprehensive, it does outline the more important factors and characteristics of European secondary education. It should be remembered, however, that what is true today may not be so tomorrow, for the educational systems of these countries are also in a state of constant change. An attempt will be made here to describe the more important aspects of secondary education in England and France. The secondary schools of Russia and West Germany will be discussed in the next chapter.

European education
before the nineteenth century

Education in Europe before the nineteenth century cannot be separated from the class structure. The schools of any society are a reflection of the society itself, and in Europe they reflected the social classes. This is a fact that some Americans do not fully understand. Until the present century secondary education in Europe was reserved, in the main, for the elite.

Before the nineteenth century secondary education in Europe was for boys. Young ladies, with very few exceptions, were fortunate to receive even an elementary education. Secondary education was not offered to girls, because society in those days felt that since women in general were not fitted for positions in the church, business, trade, or government, it was not necessary to provide them with opportunities in secondary schools.

From the sixteenth through the eighteenth centuries secondary schools existed primarily to prepare individuals for the universities, and the curriculums of the various schools placed great emphasis on classical subjects. (The Latin grammar school of Colonial America, which had been transplanted from England, followed the classical tradition.) Even today, secondary education in the better European schools is planned along strict academic lines.

Secondary education in England

Before the nineteenth century secondary education in England was sponsored by national societies, secular philanthropic bodies, and religious groups. There were in existence the Great Public

Schools, which were really private institutions supposedly endowed for the good of the public, and many Latin grammar schools. It has been estimated that there were approximately five hundred grammar schools by the eighteenth century, most of them controlled by religious societies. To ensure the church's authority over secondary education, the Act of Uniformity, which required every school teacher to affirm his loyalty to the Established Church, was passed in 1662. A later law forbade dissenters to fill positions in the schools and forbade children of nonconformists and dissenters to attend the secondary schools. As a result, the excluded groups established their own secondary schools, referred to as academies. John Milton was one of the outstanding individuals who advocated this new form of secondary education, new in the sense that the academies offered subjects along practical as well as traditional lines.

In England, by law and tradition, secondary education was considered to be a private responsibility, and it was not until the latter half of the nineteenth century that some progress was made in popularizing secondary education. There were, however, some political reforms that paved the way for changes in education —passage of certain child labor laws in 1802, the Political Reform Act of 1832, and other measures passed in 1884.

Important government measures

The first important action by the English government was taken in 1833, when it set aside 20,000 pounds as an annual grant to support certain segments of education, namely, the Anglican National Society and the Nonconformist British and Foreign School Society. Six years later this amount was increased to 30,000 pounds, and for the first time other religious groups and some nonreligious societies received some of the money. By 1860 the annual appropriation had increased to 800,000 pounds. During the following ten-year period a policy was followed whereby the amount of money allocated to a school was based on the performance of its students on yearly examinations administered by the state, a practice known in England as the policy of "payment by results." Naturally enough, much of the teaching concentrated on preparation for the state examinations.

In 1862 the Department of Science and Art, created by the government, began to promote the establishment of secondary schools by providing a limited amount of financial help from the government. Within ten years about one thousand of these schools, designed to place special emphasis upon the practical aspects of science for industry, had been created. An act known as the Technical Instruction Act of 1889 gave county and town councils the authority to raise taxes for the support of these schools.[1]

The Education Act of 1902. The Education Act of 1902 was very important in the development of education in England, because it increased the influence of the national government in education and resulted in the unification of the control of elementary and secondary education, which prior to this time had been subject to separate authorities. This act was the result of demands by "voluntary," or church, schools, which sought a share of the tax money in order to expand their elementary schools and set up secondary schools. The Education Act of 1902 gave them this right; however, it also placed them under the supervision of county or borough councils called Local Educational Authorities (L.E.A.).

The L.E.A.'s controlled secondary as well as elementary schools. They had the power to establish county technical schools at the secondary level, to provide financial assistance to the grammar schools operated by private societies and church groups, to create colleges for teacher training, to coordinate elementary, secondary, and higher education, and to offer scholarships in secondary education for needy children. In fact, one of their responsibilities was to make secondary education available to more young people because, as the reader will remember, secondary education was not free. Even in the mid-1920's only about 35 per cent of the pupils in secondary education were receiving their education free. Until 1930 scholarships were given only to students who had successfully taken qualifying examinations. In many cases these were really competitive examinations, because there were not enough secondary schools for all students who passed. In 1919 about 20,000 pupils who had passed qualifying examinations or had the necessary tuition money were turned away for lack of secondary school facilities.[2]

Despite the fact that the Education Act of 1902 gave the L.E.A.'s power to inspect private secondary schools and to make them conform to certain governmental regulations, no attempt was made to alter the type of curriculum or activities.

The Fisher Act of 1918. In 1918 another important education act, the Fisher Act, was passed "to secure that children and young

---

[1]Nelson L. Bossing, *Principles of Secondary Education* (Englewood Cliffs, N.J.: Prentice-Hall, Inc., 1955), p. 90.

[2]H. C. Dent, *Secondary Education for All* (London: Routledge and Kegan Paul, Ltd., 1949), pp. 43–44.

persons shall not be debarred from receiving the benefits of any form of education by which they are capable of profiting, through inability to pay fees." It was an attempt to make education available to all from the elementary school through the university level. It called for an adequate tax levy to provide this education under government control. But passage of this act did not ensure free secondary education for all; it was still based upon the idea of offering free tuition and scholarships with the hope that these would meet the needs of all individuals who aspired to receive secondary and higher education.

Until 1918 children were required to stay in school only until the age of twelve. The Fisher Act required two additional years of secondary education of all students, but the government was not able to enforce this provision.

Major secondary schools existing before 1940

Until the early 1940's secondary education was being furnished by six different types of secondary schools. The English themselves would probably say five different types, because, until recently, the practical education offered in their technical and trade schools was not considered a legitimate part of their secondary educational system. By tradition, secondary education in England and, indeed, throughout Europe has been academic education. The major types of secondary schools were trade and "central" schools, the "Great Public Schools," endowed and unendowed grammar schools, private secondary schools, council schools, and secondary schools for girls.

Trade and "central" schools. Trade and "central" schools offered many English adolescents an education in various trades and other practical areas. The "central" schools, called higher elementary schools, concentrated on vocational preparation for early adolescents. The Department of Science and Art, which established schools concerned with practical education, had been created in 1852, and by 1872 there were 948 such institutions in England. Just before the end of the nineteenth century additional taxes were levied by the local councils to provide greater support for these schools and for technical classes in other schools. After 1902 junior technical schools were organized, but since the mid-forties a type of school known as a secondary technical school has been replacing them.

Great Public Schools. The Great Public Schools such as Eton, Harrow, and Rugby were and are the most highly respected in

England. These schools are aristocratic and very selective. Despite the fact that secondary education has been changing in England, they have retained their esteemed position, and they continue to flourish. (Their curriculum will be discussed briefly later in this chapter.)

Endowed and unendowed grammar schools. Before the 1940's the many endowed and unendowed grammar schools in England followed a strict academic curriculum and were similar to the Great Public Schools. In fact, they are often referred to as "public schools." Because their students were preparing for the universities, they concentrated on high scholarship and·catered to a select social class. These schools did receive tax money, however, and were required to accept some tuition-free students.

Private secondary schools. Before 1940 one could find many private secondary schools in England which did not enjoy the prestige of the schools mentioned above. Those which met government requirements, such as accepting tuition-free students and accepting supervision by the Board of Education, received annual national grants. Those schools which wished to be free of government control did not accept government grants.

Council schools. After 1902 a system of secondary schools free of denominational influence, called council secondary schools, was established by the Local Educational Authorities. Although they were operated by governmental agencies, these schools did charge some tuition. A few of the council schools were coeducational.

Schools for girls. Many private secondary schools for girls were established in England during the nineteenth century. After the passage of the Educational Act of 1902, girls were given an opportunity to have equal educational privileges, since the council schools could be coeducational if the local authorities wanted them to be. Before 1930 about one third of the secondary schools receiving government grants were coeducational; the other two thirds were about evenly divided between separate schools for boys and separate schools for girls.

Major developments between World War I and II
As was mentioned previously, the Fisher Act of 1918 required all students to remain in school until the age of fourteen. In 1921 the L.E.A.'s were given permission to set the compulsory attendance age at sixteen if they desired, and in 1936 the law was revised

to provide that children who were not "beneficially employed" must remain in school until they were fifteen. Once again, however, the law was not fully carried out.

The higher age limit made it necessary to consider reorganizing the educational system to provide for students compelled to remain in school two years longer. This reorganization was supposed to take the form of a new institution, a nonselect school called the senior school, which would provide a suitable curriculum for advanced elementary students who were unable to qualify for admission to a secondary school. Unfortunately, for financial reasons, most of the reforms that might have been possible under provisions of the Fisher Act were never accomplished. Thus, little progress was made. However, some so-called senior schools were established.

In 1939 the Spens Report, officially titled *Secondary Education with Special Reference to Grammar Schools and Technical High Schools*, was published. This report recommended that all senior, central, secondary, and technical high schools attempt to achieve greater uniformity in their administration and operation; it also called for the abolition of fees as soon as financial conditions would permit. The committee responsible for the report rejected the American idea of a comprehensive secondary school. This report led to the publication by the English government of a document known as *Educational Reconstruction*, a new plan for secondary education which became the law known as the Butler Education Act, passed in 1944.

The Butler Education Act

The main objectives of the Butler Education Act are as follows:

1. To provide greater central direction of education while maintaining local initiative.

2. To make all administrative districts large enough to ensure many kinds of educational services.

3. To raise the leaving age by one or more years in secondary education.

4. To provide secondary education as a continuation of elementary education, and to furnish appropriate kinds of education free to all youth, specifying three types of secondary schools — secondary grammar schools, secondary modern schools, and secondary technical schools.

5. To offer working youth further education.

6. To preserve efficient parochial and independent schools.[3]

[3]H. G. Good, *A History of Western Education*, 2nd ed. (New York: The Macmillan Company, 1960), p. 539.

The law also provides for a complete system of education – primary, secondary, and further education. The primary, or elementary, schools are supposed to offer educational opportunities from which all can profit. The secondary system offers several different types of schools that will provide for individual interests and abilities. Most elementary students, at the age of eleven, take examinations which determine what type of secondary school they will attend. Education beyond secondary school can take several forms. Unless an individual between the ages of fifteen and eighteen is attending a university or a technical college, he is required to continue his schooling part time. Thus, the law again attempted to extend the compulsory age to fifteen years, and this time England was financially able to enforce the act.

Selective examinations, intelligence tests, and the students' elementary school records are used to classify them for secondary education; the best students are selected for the academic schools. Those who do not show literary ability but indicate that they might do well in mechanical and scientific fields are placed in technical schools. The remaining students, about 70 per cent of the total, are placed in what is known as the secondary modern school.

There are many objections to this system of classification in England. Some educators acknowledge that the selective examinations have resulted in cramming by students and coaching and distorted teaching for the examinations by teachers. Others emphasize that such a system promotes anxieties and tensions in children and parents.

This matter of classification has become a political issue, with the Conservatives generally favoring the existing classification system and the Labour party denouncing it. The Labour party prefers the establishment of comprehensive high schools as opposed to the traditional schools, which, it claims, tend to preserve the class structure of society.[4] Labour party members maintain that the prestige of the Great Public Schools and grammar schools is not warranted, that this prestige is artificial and should be "exploded." They believe graduates of Eton and other such schools have gained important positions not because of superior education but because they come from influential families.

The Act of 1944 also established special schools for handicapped students, provided that all government-sponsored primary schools, secondary schools, and county colleges be free, and set up scholarships for students attending schools that charged tuition. In

4*Ibid.*, p. 542.

addition, the act provided money for students who were financially unable to participate in student activities; for physical examinations, medical treatment, and free lunches and milk; and for the establishment of recreation, social, and physical training facilities. Scholarships to a university or a technical school were created for students who demonstrated ability but could not afford higher education.

Thus, England established a complete system of free education for all children from five to nineteen years of age. Most private schools now receive government subsidies, but they are subject to greater control and supervision than they have ever been. This control is to ensure that all children receive a good education. Some of the public schools continue to exist without the subsidies, but they are supervised to some extent by the government.[5]

Secondary education after 1944

Since England was engaged in a struggle for her very existence in 1944, it was not until after the Second World War that she was able to do anything about implementing the Act of 1944. After the war she found that her educational facilities were inadequate, her supply of teachers was very short, and the number of students had greatly increased. As a result, reform became a necessity, but in some cases it was not possible to achieve the established objectives immediately. For example, it was only in 1947 that England could really attempt to keep all students in school until age fifteen. The Act of 1944 had stated that schools in sufficient numbers and types were to be provided so that all pupils could receive a suitable education. This goal presented a staggering task for a country that had never made such opportunities available to all its citizens and particularly for a country whose resources were depleted as a result of a great war. Despite these facts, since World War II England has been able to accomplish many provisions of the Act.

Although the school laws did not specify the type of schools that were to be established, the government did publish several pamphlets on the subject. At this point it seems appropriate to discuss the types of secondary schools found in England since 1944. Some coeducation exists, but only in the modern schools. Most of the schools are still designed for students of one sex only; this means that under each type of school, there are separate establishments for girls and boys.[6]

[5]William M. Alexander and J. Galen Saylor, *Modern Secondary Education* (New York: Holt, Rinehart & Winston, Inc., 1959), p. 239.
[6]*Ibid.*, p. 24.

Secondary modern schools. The secondary modern school is nonselective and enrolls most of the students in secondary education. In many ways it is similar to the American high school, for it provides a wide selection of courses aimed at preparing students for life rather than for higher education. Many of its students leave school at the age of fifteen and continue their education on a part-time basis in a vocational school.

The first years in a secondary modern school are devoted to a study of English, geography, history, science, mathematics, religion, and foreign languages. Music and art are also taught, and instruction in such subjects as handicrafts, needlecraft, and cooking is offered. Special provisions are made for students needing remedial work in mathematics, reading, and English.

During the last two years of work in this school the student can study agriculture, distributive trades, commerce, printing, nursing, motor engineering, and home economics. Of the almost four thousand modern schools existing in 1965 about one half were coeducational; however, in most of these schools separate classes were maintained for girls and boys.

Technical secondary schools. Some of the technical secondary schools have been in existence since the beginning of the present century; yet they have been slow to develop. The reasons for this are as follows:

1. There is a lack of buildings and teachers.
2. Some of these schools are still part of local technical colleges.
3. Many have higher age requirements than other secondary schools.
4. Many people do not regard them as secondary schools because their predecessors were not so regarded. [7]

Admission to a technical secondary school is selective, and very often qualified students are not accepted because of the lack of facilities. In the technical schools students are prepared for such fields as carpentry, electricity, agriculture, stenography, interior decorating, engineering, and mechanics. Students also devote part of their time to general education just as they do in many of the so-called specialized high schools in the United States. Recently, the English have become concerned with providing more technical training at the secondary and college levels, perhaps as a result of the emphasis on technology in today's world. These technical

[7] *Ibid.*, p. 243.

schools are now offering more courses in science and advanced mathematics, and students may prepare themselves not only for better jobs in society but also, in some cases, for university work. Originally, this type of college preparation was offered only in the grammar schools.

Grammar schools. As stated previously, the grammar schools are concerned primarily with preparing students for the universities. In most cases students remain in the grammar schools until the age of eighteen. The chief studies offered are ancient and modern languages and literature, mathematics, science, geography, history, music, and art. The last two years of work at the grammar schools are a period of specialization which is supposed to prepare the students for the highest form of the general certificate examination given at the completion of academic secondary education. There are three levels of this examination—ordinary, advanced, and university scholarship. The grammar school program generally is similar to that of the famous Great Public Schools. A grammar school diploma is considered a symbol of social distinction and honor, and grammar school graduates fill the better positions in government, business, and the armed forces. In general, there seems to be a conviction on the part of many educators in England that a student with an intelligence quotient of less than 120 should not be assigned to a grammar school. [8]

Great Public Schools. The Great Public Schools include such well-known institutions as Rugby, Winchester, Harrow, Eton, and St. Paul, some of which date back to the fourteenth century. These schools offer many scholarships, but the enrollments continue to be dominated by boys from families with wealth and social prestige.

The curriculum of these schools is designed for college preparation. Through the years the schools have been known for their physical education programs and their athletic teams, which are still important aspects of their academic environments. Most of the Great Public Schools also stress religious training and are affiliated with the Anglican Church.

Comprehensive secondary schools. Because there are individuals in England who desire a school that will offer a broad educational program similar to that offered by the American comprehensive

[8]James Mulhern, *A History of Education,* 2nd ed. (New York: The Ronald Press Company, 1959), pp. 690–691.

high school, several schools of this type have been established in the London area as experiments. However, they are not yet popular with most Englishmen. The comprehensive school is one into which all types of students, regardless of abilities, goals, or social background, are admitted.

In 1950 the Labour party made the comprehensive secondary school an important issue and requested the government to assist the L.E.A.'s in promoting it. The London County Council, elected on that platform in 1953, has since adopted the comprehensive school plan.[9] While the Conservative party has continually opposed this plan, ministers of education who were Conservatives have approved it as an experiment.

Preparatory schools. In England today there are about five hundred expensive boarding schools concerned with preparing students between the ages of eight and fourteen for work in the Great Public Schools. Most of these are proprietary schools which enforce strict discipline and pride themselves on the development of character.

County colleges. The county colleges are another type of secondary school, in some ways much like community colleges in the United States. Designed to accommodate students who are in school on a part-time basis before reaching the age of eighteen, they offer a wide selection of courses in vocational fields and in general education. They also offer courses in adult education. The development of these schools was slow at first, but in recent years enrollments have grown rapidly. They are supported by the Local Educational Authorities, workers' associations, and other voluntary groups.[10]

Since 1944 England has made great progress in secondary education. The Butler Act, which has received the moral support of the English people, has been moderately successful. This has perhaps been true because the people were well informed of educational needs by official studies and reports, the press, radio, and television.[11]

In England in 1964 about 78 per cent of a total school population of over seven million students were in publicly controlled schools, 10 per cent in Anglican schools, 9 per cent in Roman Catholic schools, and 2 per cent in other denominational schools.

[9]*Ibid.*, pp. 691–692.
[10]*Ibid.*, pp. 694–695.
[11]Good, *op. cit.*, p. 539.

There is no tuition in the state-controlled schools, which are administered by local authorities. A minister of education occupies a cabinet post in the English government, and he and his staff supervise allocation and expenditure of government money by the schools. He also performs other supervisory activities such as the administration of the selective eleven-plus exams. The national government is not, however, oppressive in its relationship to the local schools.

The teacher shortage is a serious problem in England. Only one out of every four girls who graduate from teacher training colleges can be counted as an additional teacher; the others merely replace those who leave the profession. In schools controlled by the state a teacher must have a license to teach. This is not true of schools not controlled by the state, but the better independent schools do require their teachers to have a university education.

Comparison and contrast

In the United States local control of education is stressed. The fifty states are free to manage their own educational systems so long as they do not violate the provisions of the Federal Constitution. The states, to a great degree, achieve their responsibility in education through the local districts, and most of the American people do not favor a federal system or federal control of education. The United States has a free, unitary public system of education that generally extends from the first grade through the twelfth grade. Some states include kindergarten and junior, or community, college in their requirements.

England did not provide a system of free public education for all students until the middle of the 1940's; in fact, there are still barriers that keep some students out of secondary education. In England students are assigned to the various secondary schools on the basis of their performances on selective examinations, whereas students in the United States have the privilege of attending the secondary school in their district and are free to select and pursue the program of studies they desire.

Education in England is under strict government control. In the United States, on the other hand, the federal government exerts control over vocational education and other special programs only insofar as the expenditure of federal funds is involved, and the local school system has a choice of whether or not to participate in these special federal programs.

In the United States coeducation is the rule, except in certain private schools; in England coeducation is only just beginning to be accepted widely. Young people in England are required to continue in education, at least on a part-time basis, until the age of eighteen. In this country most states have an age limit of sixteen.

Secondary education in France

During the Middle Ages education in France was sponsored by the church. Cathedral, monastic, and other church schools were the principal types of educational institutions, and the state was content to leave education in the hands of the church. After the thirteenth century some municipal, guild, and private schools began to appear, and during the Renaissance and Reformation the state and the church developed joint policies for the provision of church schools and semi-public secondary schools.

The French Revolution, which eliminated the autocratic monarchy and most class privileges, produced demands for reforms in secondary education. Universal free education was delayed for almost a century, however, because of the disorder that followed the Revolution, a lack of financial resources, an ineffective tax system, the absence of a tradition of free public education, and the great shortage of professional teachers. Nevertheless, some progress was made in secondary education as a direct result of the Revolution. This progress took the form of the establishment of a system of secondary, or central, schools designed especially for students from the middle-class homes. The schools were few in number, however; and although they attempted to develop a modern, practical curriculum, they were never able to compete with the *lycées*—the strong, state-supported, traditional, classical schools —established in the larger cities of France. The *lycées* were designed for students preparing for the universities.

The *Ecole Normale Superieure*, created in 1795 for the purpose of having an advanced school of science to prepare teachers to teach in the *lycées*, was reopened by Napoleon, who was particularly interested in secondary and technical education. One of his first moves was the establishment of four military schools. He also started a system of *collèges* and *lycées*, and in a few years, more than four hundred such schools were opened. They offered about fifteen subjects, including Latin, French, mathematics, and science. These were boarding schools; and while the law defined their curriculum, the state gave little help except in the form of buildings.[12] The money necessary to run the schools at this time came mainly from tuition of the students.

[12]*Ibid.*, p. 296

This system of *collèges* and *lycées* was the beginning of modern secondary education in France. Napoleon felt that the first objective of education should be political indoctrination of the people by the state. In 1808 he set up a strict system of education control called the Imperial University, a national ministry which controlled education from the primary schools through the universities. The main functions of the Imperial University were to govern the schools, disburse funds, appoint teachers, and set school examinations. The decree establishing this system of control declared that "no school, no establishment of instruction whatsoever may be set up outside the Imperial University and without the authorization of its head."[13]

The *lycées* and *collèges* were firmly supported but remained unpopular with parents, who continued to patronize private and parochial schools.[14]

With only minor changes, the administrative system which Napoleon established has survived in France to the present. In 1877 French education was organized into a single national system with a strong, central system of administration and supervision. The centralized plan gave the Minister of Public Instruction great authority over the schools. A check and balance between the national government and local interests was supposed to be provided by the Central Superior Council and the Academy and departmental councils, but these agencies received little public support and played a very minor role in the administration and control of the schools.

The French educational system established in the 1870's was opposed by the Catholic Church, and as a result drastic regulations were imposed on religious teaching orders. The controversy between those who favored church control of education and those who favored free, public education under lay professional teachers was a bitter one, and it still persists to this day.

Secondary education after 1870
Secondary education in France since 1870 has been offered in *lycées*, *collèges*, *cours complémentaires*, vocational and technical schools, parochial schools, and special schools for girls.

Lycées and collèges. The *lycées* and *collèges* were the major types of secondary schools during the nineteenth century. They provided an education in the classics and prepared students for the

---

[13]*Ibid.*, p. 297.
[14]Mulhern, *op. cit.*, p. 541.

universities. The prerequisite for entrance was graduation from a special primary school, often operated in connection with the *lycées* or *collèges*. Students entered these secondary schools at the age of eleven and took a seven-year course, at the completion of which they were graduated as *baccalauréats*. (This degree is not the same as the bachelor's degree conferred by American liberal arts colleges.)

There were many expressions of dissatisfaction with these schools and their classical, literary, and traditional approaches to education; but those who called for a more democratic and practical system were ignored. The goal of secondary education was viewed as the development of intellectual power, and it was felt that the classics provided the surest means of attaining it. It was the firm belief of many that, since French culture was rooted in that of classical antiquity, the nation must hold to the classics or experience a moral and spiritual decline.[15] The first major reform was made in 1902 when a single *baccalauréat* was created for all secondary schools and was declared open to all students. Until this time two different *baccalauréats* had been awarded: one was given to students following a classical curriculum, and a second was awarded to students following a course of study that placed less emphasis on classical subjects and required more work in mathematics and science. (It should be pointed out here that applied science was not emphasized in either program.)

Since 1945 some modern secondary courses have been added to the curriculum of the *lycées* and *collèges*; that is to say, there have been more science and mathematics courses added. Technical and vocational courses are still not taught in the *lycées* and *collèges*. Throughout France technical education continues to exist side by side with the *lycées* and *collèges*, and there are almost insurmountable barriers confronting the student who would like to transfer from an inferior secondary school or from a technical school to one of the academic schools.[16]

Until 1930 the secondary schools of France required students to pay tuition. Prior to this time there were very few scholarships for the poor, and most students from the poorer classes could not accept these scholarships anyway because they did not have the money to pay for the many hidden costs in secondary education or for further professional preparation after the completion of secondary education.

[15]*Ibid.*, p. 547.
[16]Roger Gal, "The Development of Education in France—1945 to 1960," *Phi Delta Kappan*, XLIII (November 1961), 60–61.

The situation was made even more hopeless because of the lack of coordination between primary and secondary schools. Before 1902 the primary and secondary schools were considered to be separate systems. The studies in the primary schools were so organized that transfer from the primary to the secondary school was almost impossible. After 1902 the law required the curriculum of the first class in secondary school to follow a plan coordinated with the fourth class in the primary school. While this move theoretically improved articulation between the two educational levels, in actual practice there was little change. Individuals who had attended the primary schools, instead of the special elementary-preparatory schools, still found it difficult to enter the secondary schools.

Cours complémentaires. Another type of secondary school, not as famous as the *lycée* or the *collège* but worthy of mention, is the *cours complémentaires*. Organized to follow the primary school, it offers four classes corresponding to the first four classes in the *lycée*. These schools, generally located in county seats and larger towns, offer industrial and commercial courses and work in general education, agriculture, and homemaking. Students entering the *cours complémentaires* must take an entrance examination and must be at least eleven years old.

Vocational and technical schools. During the early 1950's, 14 per cent of the students who were of secondary school age were in public and private secondary schools. About 4 per cent of the adolescents between eleven and eighteen years of age were in the *cours complémentaires*, and another 5 per cent were in technical schools. What about the remaining 77 per cent? After attending the primary schools and perhaps the *cours complémentaires*, these students engaged in apprenticeship training for a trade in a technical or vocational school, on the job, or in both ways. The schools offering apprenticeship training, first established in 1939, were called apprenticeship centers. There was no tuition in these special centers, and some of the graduates received scholarships and government grants to do further study in a technical school. Although the apprenticeship centers concentrated on subjects of a practical nature carried on under shop conditions, general education courses such as history, geography, French, science, mathematics, and physical training were taught.[17]

[17]Carl G. F. Franzen, *Foundations of Secondary Education* (New York: Harper & Row, Publishers, 1955), p. 146.

The second type of apprenticeship training was offered in factories and businesses which established special schools or centers to offer instruction in their various vocational fields. In the late 1940's and early 1950's these schools were considered private vocational schools despite the fact that the government did give them some financial aid and also some supervision. They are, however, administered separately from other secondary schools. Students are urged, but not required, to take some general education classes such as general mathematics, science, and literature.

While the current type of apprenticeship center is less than thirty years old, apprenticeship schools were recognized as part of the primary education system in 1886, and as early as 1897 vocationalized higher primary schools, named by law as "practical schools of commerce or industry," were placed under the control of the Minister of Commerce and Industry.[18] In most cases these schools have been more concerned with pre-vocational education than vocational training and have left much of the technical knowledge to be acquired on the job.

In addition to apprenticeship training and primary pre-vocational education, state and many local authorities have created a great variety of vocational schools devoted to arts and crafts, mining, navigation, agriculture, and the fine arts as they relate to industry. Through the years the vocational and technical schools have been established to serve primary school graduates who do not plan to attend a secondary school; yet many students do not take advantage of the opportunities.

In 1920 all vocational and technical education was placed under the supervision of the Minister of Public Instruction, thus making it an integral part of the national system. Until this time these areas of education had been controlled by such agencies as the Ministry of Commerce, of Agriculture, or of Public Works.

Since the Second World War vocational and technical education has been supervised by secondary school authorities, and a new school called the *collège technique* has been established. This technical secondary school awards a *baccalauréat* to its graduates. Some of these *collège technique* schools offer a three-year course for students who want to enter occupations requiring only lower levels of occupational skills; others offer a seven-year course that prepares the student for occupations requiring more advanced skills. They also offer courses in general education. Technical courses have been added to the curriculum of some higher elemen-

[18]Mulhern, *op. cit.*, p. 547.

tary schools, now called *collèges modernes*, some of which are specialized.[19]

Schools for girls.   Except at the university level, coeducation has been rare in France. This is perhaps due to the strong Jesuit tradition that dominated secondary education for such a long period. Wherever possible, the French have insisted on separate local schools for boys and girls. Secondary schools for girls were created by official provision in 1880, but they were not equal to the secondary schools for boys. The girls were to have a course of only five or six years rather than seven, and their school program did not lead to the *baccalauréat*. To attain this degree, it was necessary for girls to obtain special permission to transfer to a boys' school.

A seven-year degree course was finally established for girls in 1924. By this time special *lycées* and *collèges* for girls had developed in most of the major cities and large towns of France. Before 1930, females were not admitted to a school for boys unless there was no school for girls available, and even when admitted, girls were not allowed to constitute more than one fourth of the enrollment in any one school, and the total number in any one school could not be over fifty. The course of study for girls was similar to that for boys except that the girls also studied home economics, music, needlework, and translations of certain types of foreign literature.

An interesting development in France has been the increased university enrollment of women; in 1949 they comprised almost half of the entire student body. In fact, nearly one third of those students studying law and medicine were women.[20] These facts point up the increase in educational opportunities which have been made available to women in France within the past twenty-five years.

Church schools.   Most of the parochial schools in France are Catholic, although there are a few Jewish and Protestant schools. About 1,157,000 students were enrolled in secondary education in 1956, and about 40 per cent of these were attending Catholic schools. In most cases, teachers in parochial secondary schools have the same education as teachers in the public schools, but the church schools are much more conservative than the public schools. Since 1951 these schools have been receiving financial support from

---

[19]*Ibid.*, p. 548.

[20]*World Handbook of Educational Organization and Statistics,* (United Nations Education, Scientific, and Cultural Organization, 1951), p. 174.

the government, which in recent years seems to have been anti-clerical but not anti-religious. Even public secondary schools are closed on Thursdays throughout France so that students may be instructed in religion, but they are in session again on Fridays and Saturdays.

Teacher education

French secondary school teachers are educated in universities and the higher normal schools. Those who aspire to teach in the *lycées* must meet the highest standards. They study for three years in a university or other type of school to receive a special degree for teachers (*licence d'enseignement*). Then, if they desire appointments in *lycées*, they must take a competitive examination called the *agrégation*. Only about 10 per cent of the candidates who take this examination receive the title of *agrégé* at the completion of the university course. The surest path to this honor is by way of one of the four *Grandes Écoles Normales*, two for men and two for women. Students must pass a competitive examination before they are granted admission to these special schools. Some of the larger *lycées* provide special post-*baccalauréat* preparation for the *Grandes Écoles Normales*. The standards for teaching in the *collèges* are not quite so high as they are for the *lycées*. Special higher normal schools have been established in recent years to train teachers of vocational and technical subjects.[21]

Recent attempts at reform

In France the *lycées* and *collèges* have dominated secondary education for the academically talented student since the Renaissance; however, it should be remembered that most secondary students in France are not in these schools. Secondary education in the classical schools was and still is concerned with training a small percentage of the upper classes to be intellectual leaders. On the other hand, there have been advances in technical and vocational secondary education in recent years aimed at the larger portion of the student population.

In January of 1944 a group known as the Algiers Commission, whose aim was the democratization of the educational system of the nation, made some specific recommendations for reforms in secondary education. Although the recommendations were refused, a new commission headed by Paul Langevin and Henri Wallon was created by the French government. In 1947 this commission,

[21]Mulhern, *op. cit.*, p. 550.

composed of many outstanding scholars, published its report and recommendations. The plan proposed raising the leaving age to eighteen and dividing the educational system into three cycles: basic cycle, ages six to eleven; orientation cycle, eleven to fifteen; and determination cycle, fifteen to eighteen. In the United States the third cycle would probably be called the period of specialization.

The plan, commonly referred to as the Langevin Plan, set forth new proposals for the preparation of teachers and urged teachers to employ "more active teaching methods."[22] It also implied that too many students had been excluded for too long from proper educational opportunity. In the opinion of the authors of these proposals, the various forms of education, such as technological courses, were as worth while for their own purposes as were the classics and were just as necessary in the modern world. The plan was not adopted, probably because it threatened the prestige of the classicists, who constitute a very large portion of the educated of France and who did not want to erase the line that separates the scholar who reads Euripides from the student who will help build steel bridges and concrete runways.

Although the plan was not adopted, it was influential. Outstanding scholars had supported a progressive, democratic plan for education. No doubt the plan was partly responsible for some of the increased secondary educational opportunities in France and for the introduction of some of the recent vocational programs on the secondary level.[23]

There have been some reforms in the internal administration and the teaching methods of the secondary schools, but much remains to be done. Teachers in the secondary schools bear the official title of professor, and most of their teaching is in the form of lectures. Most secondary school teachers of France have not had any courses in child growth and development or educational psychology.[24] Much pressure is put on secondary school students, many of whom are in school nine hours a day and are also required to do a large amount of homework. Examinations are very difficult, and failures are numerous.

The French do have plans for reforms and are at present seeking alternatives to what has been a narrow path to advancement. There seems to be a greater meeting of minds between individuals employed in scientific, industrial, and technological work and those

---

[22]Good, *op. cit.*, pp. 535–536.
[23]*Ibid.*, pp. 536–537.
[24]Gal, *op. cit.*, p. 62.

engaged in literary skills. It is obvious that this process of change will take considerable time in France.[25]

Comparison and contrast

The French, like the English, have a national system of education, but the French system has a much more conservative tradition of academic education. The French have maintained a more highly centralized system with little emphasis on local administration and supervision such as the local educational authorities of England render within their national framework. Teachers in England have much more freedom and are not controlled by as many regulations and prescriptions as are teachers in France. National inspectors do not control teaching methods and the curriculum in English schools as they do in France.

In the United States secondary school teachers are required to meet standards established by the various states, but regulations are few when compared with the many prescriptions and regulations placed upon secondary school teachers in France by the national government. In American secondary schools, teachers are relatively free to develop their own courses of study and to experiment with new methods and techniques; this is not true in France.

French secondary school students do not receive instruction on Thursdays but do attend school on Saturdays. On Thursdays they are freed to receive religious instruction. The parochial schools receive tax money and are subject to inspection by the central ministry of education. Their students must take and pass state examinations, as must all other secondary school students before they are graduated.

French secondary pupils do not study civics or participate in any student activities especially designed to prepare a person for citizenship. By contrast, secondary education in the United States emphasizes the education of the adolescent for citizenship.

Selected references

ALEXANDER, WILLIAM M. AND J. GALEN SAYLOR. *Modern Secondary Education.* New York: Holt, Rinehart and Winston, Inc., 1959.

BENT, RUDYARD K. AND HENRY H. KRONENBERG. *Principles of Secondary Education*, 4th ed. New York: McGraw-Hill Book Company, Inc., 1961.

[25]M. A. Eckstein, "Present Trends in Public Secondary Education in Western Europe," *The High School Journal,* XLIV (October 1960), 17–18.

CONANT, JAMES B. "An American Looks at European Education," in *The High School in a New Era*, eds. Francis S. Chase and Harold A. Anderson. Chicago: The University of Chicago Press, 1958.

DENT, H. C. *Growth in English Education, 1946–1952*. London: Routledge and Kegan Paul, Ltd., 1954.

DOBINSON, C. H. "English and Russian Education Contrasted," *Educational Forum*, XXII (May 1958), 401–411.

Education in France. Editions France Actuelle. Washington, D. C.: France Actuelle, 1956.

"The French Educational Reform," *Education in France*. New York: French Cultural Services, October-December 1957.

The French System of Education. French Cultural Services. New York: The Services, 1958.

GOOD, H. G. *A History of Western Education*, 2nd ed. New York: The Macmillan Company, 1960.

HALE, GIFFORD G. "Contrasting the European and American Plans of Education," *Phi Delta Kappan*, XXXIX (October 1957), 8–11.

HUNT, HAROLD C. "Is European Education Better?" in *American Education: An Introduction Through Readings*, ed. Tyrus Hillway. Boston: Houghton Mifflin Company, 1964.

International Yearbook of Education. Paris: UNESCO. Annually.

KING, EDMUND J. *Other Schools and Ours*. New York: Holt, Rinehart & Winston, Inc., 1958.

Secondary education
in the Soviet Union
and West Germany

chapter **16**

Because the Soviet Union is a major world power, its educational system is of great interest to millions of Americans. In light of the cold war and the determination of the Soviets to extend their system of government, it is also of great strategic importance. Secondary education in West Germany is also worthy of consideration, because Germany has always been an important European country and is now one of America's major allies.

Secondary education in the Soviet Union

Since 1917 when the Bolshevik Revolution took place in Russia, sweeping educational developments have occurred in that country. The political tyranny under the Tsarist regime limited the available educational opportunities to the upper classes, the aristocrats. The Communists were determined to create a new political system in which universal education would play a key role.

In October 1917 the Communist leaders set forth the following goals for education:
1. The complete liquidation of illiteracy.
2. Secular, free, universal, compulsory education.
3. Equal educational opportunity for all citizens.
4. Well-trained teachers.
5. Adequate financial support.[1]

[1]Nelson L. Bossing, *Principles of Secondary Education* (Englewood Cliffs, N.J.: Prentice-Hall, Inc., 1955), p. 99.

From available evidence it appears the Russians have been successful in reaching these objectives. When the Communists took over, less than 30 per cent of the population was literate. By 1940 the Russians were claiming that their people were almost 100 per cent literate. Although this claim is subject to question, they have done well in their attempts to realize their other goals. This is true despite the fact that they had very few teachers to start with and that an educational system had to be organized, teachers trained, and books written in many different languages.

Gradually the educational reform was accomplished. It was this educational revolution that secured the political and social revolution and made possible the industrialization of the once backward Russia. It has trained the party leaders; produced the trained, skilled workers; educated the scientists; and helped place the Soviet Union among the leading nations of the world.

Russia under the Tsars had provided very few state schools. These schools had been developed along the lines of the German secondary schools, which will be discussed later in this chapter, and were even more selective. They existed to educate a small group of leaders chosen from the elite for public service and for the professions. The Communist regime set about making education available to all.

What principles govern secondary education in Russia? The outstanding ones are service to the state, equality of all citizens (including equality of the sexes), and the importance and dignity of physical work. Education is viewed as a lifelong process integrating the ideals, needs, and practices of the Communist state. The objectives of the educational system and the government are always to be identical. Teachers are to inculcate in youth the secular political morality that has been approved by the state, and the school must promote the entire system of state-approved social, political, economic, ethical, and philosophical ideology.[2]

The Communists continue to stress technical education for a technological, industrial society. They feel that technical and vocational education should be given the same dignity and respect as academic education.

Soviet educators in the 1920's accepted many of the theories set forth by progressive educators in America. As a matter of fact, while many American educators were talking about new theories, the Russians were actually applying them. Problems of the home and the community were closely associated with activities of the

[2]James Mulhern, *A History of Education*, 2nd ed. (New York: The Ronald Press Company, 1959), pp. 690–691.

school. The project method was used widely as Russian educators attempted to show how education could improve Communist life and the state. Student government was not only permitted but encouraged, and students were given opportunities to participate in planning class activities in the management of the school. To give the students a more realistic knowledge of the world about them, field trips were used extensively.[3]

Most of the Russian teachers, however, were not ready to use such methods; and it became very evident to the Communists that, by stimulating independent, critical thinking, these methods and practices could be very dangerous to their own plans. This realization resulted in a decree in 1931, followed by others, that started a movement toward a more authoritative, traditional form of education and away from the progressive, democratic approaches which had prevailed.

General organization

Education below the university level in Russia has been provided in an organized 4 – 3 – 3 system, with the different levels known as primary, incomplete secondary, and complete secondary. The use of identical courses of study and methods of instruction throughout the Soviet Union has been attempted, but some compromises have been necessary to meet local conditions. Students moving from the incomplete secondary school to the complete secondary school must pass a difficult examination. As in the case of the examination English children take at age eleven, a student's performance on this test usually determines the future course of his life.

Very little use is made of psychological tests by Russian educators. They feel that these are devices used by capitalists to verify predetermined decisions and objectives and thus should not be used in the Communist educational system.

Until 1959 the ten-year schoool organization provided the basic plan for general education in the Soviet Union. (A slightly different plan, initiated in 1959, will be discussed later in this chapter.) Differences could be found, however, in the quality of the educational program offered in the rural and urban schools. Despite the fact that the Communist party was working for uniformity, the rural schools could not offer the same opportunities as were offered in the urban schools. In fact, many young people still do not attend full-time schools after they have reached the age of fourteen; as a result, part-time schools are provided in the towns and cities and

[3]Bossing, *op. cit.*, pp. 100 – 101.

part-time evening schools in the country. Such schools were established during World War II (1943) and became a permanent part of the school system in 1958.

Except for being excluded from certain trade schools and railway schools, girls were given equal educational opportunities in Russia until 1943, when coeducation was limited in some ways. In 1954 it was restored to its prewar status, and the principle of equality of the sexes is still strictly adhered to.

Administrative hierarchy. While there is no single federal ministry of education, the educational system of the U.S.S.R is highly centralized and control is retained by the party and the state. Operational responsibility for the education and training of millions of students has, of necessity, been delegated in ever widening concentric circles until it rests on local communities and groups.

The nature of the Soviet regime might lead a person to imagine that the identical subject is taught at the same time, in the same way, in the same grade, in the same type of school throughout the land, and that teachers lecture only on prescribed subjects in a prescribed manner. Such is not the case.

One of the main reasons this is not true is the diversified population of the country. The U.S.S.R. is a vast country with people living in widely separated areas, many of them isolated for months each year. In the Far North, pupils with cultural traditions akin to those of the Eskimos are going to school and enjoying experiences that are very different from those of children in Moscow schools. Throughout Central Asiatic Russia many pupils are from Moslem cultures and speak entirely different languages. Then there are the Georgians, the Armenians, the Baltic peoples, the Ukrainians, and others with differing needs, traditions, environments, and languages. Thus, while some Soviet children live in tents and are accustomed to using camels as beasts of burden, others live in areas where the reindeer is the main source of milk, meat, and hides for clothing. In a country of so many contrasts, effecting absolute centralization of education would seem to be impractical as well as extremely difficult.

Because the Soviet leaders attach such great importance to "correct" education for all Soviet citizens—education that is all-embracing and over which the party and the state can retain control—it is interesting to see how they allow for local differences, stimulate local initiative, and encourage local support while, at the same time, demanding from their citizens a uniform Communist outlook on life.

Guiding directives on education are discussed at Communist party congresses and in meetings of the party's Central Executive Committee. Laws and resolutions having significance for the general educational development of the whole country are promulgated by the Supreme Soviet of the U.S.S.R. and the Council of Ministers. Sometimes they are cosigned by the party. Such decrees specify types of schools to be established, basic organization, academic programs to be followed, and general provisions concerning compulsory education. Levels of government involved in the educational organization are the national government, union and autonomous republics, local administrative units within republics, and administrative bodies responsible for different types of educational facilities.

At each level and for each type of training, a branch, or organ, of the party exists to ensure that state and party policy is carried out. Party organs are charged with carrying out political indoctrination, maintaining discipline, influencing the school programs through the Communist youth organizations which function in schools, and popularizing training programs.

Of great importance in the administration of Soviet education is the surveillance maintained by the secret police on the political reliability of administrative personnel, teachers, students, and all others from the highest ranking official to the lowest. The secret police operate through the "special department" (*spetsotdel*), an integral part of every educational administrative unit. In the files of the secret police are dossiers on persons within the jurisdiction of each "special department." The chain of command of the secret police runs parallel to that of the party and state administrative machinery, with little if any crossover up to the highest echelons.[4]

The major governmental organs concerned with schools include (1) the Union-Republic Ministry of Higher Education, (2) the ministries of education in the Soviet Republics, (3) the Chief Directorate of Labor Reserves under the U.S.S.R. Council of Ministers, with local branches subordinate to the republics' councils of ministers, and (4) the Union-Republic Ministry of Culture, with subordinate ministries of culture in each of the republics. In addition, a number of other ministries and governmental agencies, through their directorates of education, administer funds appropriated for their schools and training courses and are responsible for maintenance and business management.

[4]*Education in the USSR,* Division of International Education, International Educational Relations Branch Bulletin, 1960. No. 14 (Washington, D.C.: U.S. Government Printing Office, 1960), p. 21.

General, or nonspecialized, education, most of the teacher training for the kindergartens and primary-secondary schools, and most of the extraclass activities are administered by a ministry of education in each of the Soviet republics. The ministry has the responsibility for the educational attainments of the republic and exercises control and direction over the education ministries of autonomous republics within its boundaries.

The Russian (RSFSR) Union Republic, which seems to predominate in comparison with the others, has a ministry of education which provides facilities for educational research in its Academy of Pedagogical Sciences. This ministry also takes the lead in formulating standard study programs, working out new procedures, setting up academic attainment criteria, transmitting results of educational experiments, and similar activities. All union republics exercise autonomy in translating approved textbooks and getting them published and distributed, in preparing grammars and books devoted to local history and literature, in expanding school curriculum and examination schedules to provide additional hours for non-Russian-speaking children, and in deciding various other matters peculiar to a given republic.

Some union republics have one or more autonomous republics within their borders. Since an autonomous republic is a large administrative unit generally composed of people with a cultural background and language different from that of the union republic itself, there is a subordinate ministry of education in each autonomous republic. The autonomous republics are further subdivided into regions and smaller units called *raions*. The subdividing continues down to small administrative units within a city or, in the case of rural districts, to territorial education administration. The head of each sub-administration is appointed by the Soviet of Workers' Deputies at the corresponding administrative levels; each Soviet of Workers' Deputies has a standing committee for education whose members are generally selected from among persons with experience in education.

At the local level there is close cooperation among the responsible education authority or committee, the Soviet of Workers' Deputies, the branch of the teachers' trade unions organized at the school, and the local party unit. It is the education authority at the local level that is charged with appointing school heads and approving the appointment of teachers recommended by the head of each school. Together with branches of the teachers' trade unions, the education authority provides refresher courses for teachers, enlists teachers in advanced study and in-service training programs, and arranges for local teachers' conferences. A considerable amount of responsibility for school construction and primary responsibility for repair and maintenance of classrooms rest at the local level. Local groups concerned with education are expected to work together to provide supervised, systematic programs of extraclass activities for children and various types of educational-cultural pursuits for parents.

Each ministry of education maintains a staff of inspectors who visit schools in their assigned areas. Inspectors, who are generally appointed from among those considered better teachers, work with the school head and share in some measure the responsibility for the school's reputation. The primary function of the inspector is to ensure approved teaching standards in the schools. He sits in on lessons and examinations, surveys party youth organizational work, checks on school discipline, and reviews teaching problems with the staff.

Opinion on the position of the inspector varies. Some teachers feel that since the inspectors are former teachers who had achieved success in their profession, they are able to help solve local school problems through direct contact with the ministry; others, particularly from the Baltic Republics, say inspectors are political informers. In any event, inspectors represent the party and state in seeing that official policy and procedure are carried out in the schools.

Educational finance. Presented below are some pertinent facts relating to the financing of Soviet education. No attempt is made to draw direct comparisons between financial data for the U.S.S.R. and the United States since the statistics are not similar.

1. The meaning of the term *education* differs in the two countries. Funds for education in Russia come under the division of the planned budget which is for "health and educational-cultural activities and social services," regardless of the national, republic, or other governmental channel through which the money is to be distributed. Allocations to the individual union republics are announced, and since many government functions do not fall within the jurisdiction of union republics, the percentage of their budgets devoted to "health and educational-cultural activities and social services" is relatively high. For example, in 1965 the percentage appears as 54.6 in the Ukrainian SSR, 66.2 in the Russian Union Republic, 62.6 in the Latvian SSR, 68.1 in the Byelorussian SSR, and 68.9 in the Georgian SSR.

Within the broad division for "health and educational-cultural activities and social services," the portion which appears to have been designated for educational-cultural activities amounted to about 13 per cent of the total planned budget, as compared with about a third of that amount classified under housing. These educational-cultural activities include, for example, subsidies to finance (a) deficits of state-controlled political rallies and rural clubs; (b) deficits of radio, press, and television systems of the country; (c) state-owned theaters and national symphony orchestras; (d) public libraries, orphanages, lecture series to popularize scientific and engineering knowledge, and research establishments, including many which directly support military development programs; and (e) schools and institutions of higher learning.

In contrast to the Soviet data, education expenditures compiled biennially by the United States Office of Education include only expenditures relating to schools and institutions of higher learning. To illustrate more detailed differences, funds planned for physical education in the U.S.S.R. are provided under the "health" section—not under "educational-cultural activities." The training of teachers of Soviet history according to the philosophy of Marx, Lenin, and the party is not an educational item; its cost is borne by the Communist party. In the United States the cost of physical education is a part of educational expenditures, and the financing of the training of American history teachers does not differ in any way from that of teacher training in other subject areas.

2. Financial data presented for the U.S.S.R. relate to the planned budget; those for the United States relate to expenditures unless otherwise noted.

3. Under the centrally controlled, planned economy of the U.S.S.R., the planned budget relates to *public* funds from the general revenue of the state. Taxes are not levied specifically for educational purposes, and there is no privately financed educational system. Planned budget figures for education in the union republics appear again in the total planned budget for the U.S.S.R.

Under the decentralized capitalistic economy of the United States, powers not specifically mentioned in the federal Constitution are reserved to the states. Powers relating to education are thus vested in the states—not in the federal government. Publicly controlled and privately controlled education programs exist, often side by side. Type of control over an educational institution in the United States is not necessarily synonymous with its type of financial support. A private educational institution may be entirely supported by private funds, or it may receive most of its funds from private sources and some from public sources, or it may receive public funds in excess of its private funds. The source of funds for a public educational institution may be public, or it may be public and private. The totals for state and local public expenditures, for federal expenditures, and for private expenditures are discrete totals which, when added together, give the total expenditure for education throughout the nation.

The director of each educational institution in Russia sends his budget estimates for the coming year to the authority having jurisdiction over his school. For a Bashkir ten-year school the budget would be proposed by the Bashkir Autonomous Republic Ministry of Education; for an agricultural vocational school in Frunze, the Kirghiz Ministry of Agriculture; for the University of Leningrad, the Union Republic Ministry of Higher Education. These budgets are then submitted through channels to the national level.

The state budget, a consolidation of all the others, is presented annually by the Ministry of Finance to the Supreme Soviet for its approval. The budget is for the calendar year, and in the past it frequently has been presented in the early spring of the year it covers. Available data on planned budgets are more detailed and specific than data on expenditures and tend to show changes in emphasis.

After the budget has been approved, money is supposed to be disbursed by the director of each educational establishment and training program. He enjoys some leeway in determining how the funds are to be spent, but he is held personally responsible for their use and for detailed accounts of all expenditures.

Out of the funds allotted to the director comes money for the following, depending upon the type of school:

1. Salaries of the teaching and auxiliary staffs and staff traveling expenses for attending meetings, conventions, and the like.

2. Laboratory materials, audio-visual aids, and equipment including desks and maps.

3. Reimbursement for students' practical training periods in industrial, agricultural, and other economic enterprises.

4. Library facilities.

5. Stipends and other subsidies for students.

6. Building construction and upkeep, furniture purchase and repair, plant maintenance (water, electricity, heating, cleaning).

7. Equipment for dormitories.

Local support exists for various types of educational facilities and programs in the Soviet Union, but these expenditures do not appear in the state budget. For example, parents or other community groups may bear the expense for repairs in a local school, or a farm management in a rural area may allot land to the schools for experimental agricultural projects. Collective farms are required to provide their teachers with housing and an adjacent plot for a garden, to supply schools with fuel, and to help with janitorial service. Most urban schools have neighboring industrial plants or factories which act as sponsors or patrons, making equipment available for a workshop or providing other facilities; a trade union may bear the expense of an improvement or addition to the school.

Curriculum. To separate the curriculum of the elementary school from that of the secondary school is almost impossible, because both levels are concerned with general education and are united into one unbroken organization. The major subjects being taught in recent years are Russian language and literature, history, mathematics, physics, biology, chemistry, astronomy, foreign languages, logic, psychology, geography, the constitution of the U.S.S.R., physical education, drafting, drawing, shop work, and singing. Thirteen of these subjects are offered in grades one to seven; nine of them were required subjects throughout the old ten-grade system.[5] The leading foreign languages are English, German, and French.

State textbooks and a uniform grading system are used throughout the Soviet Union. Great emphasis is placed upon laboratory work and audio-visual instruction, and examinations are used at every grade level as the basis for promotion.

Students in eighth through tenth grades attend classes six days a week, thirty-three weeks a year. Students in grades five through seven go one extra week to provide time for field trips. Most classes last forty-five minutes, and the school day consists of six class periods. Students in the incomplete secondary school and the complete secondary school study ten or twelve subjects each year; classes in most subjects meet two or three times per week.

Children in all Russian schools furnish their own textbooks, the school uniforms they are required to wear, instructional supplies such as paper and pencils, and lunches. No tuition has been charged in the secondary schools since 1956.

Extraclass activities. A well-planned program of extraclass activities is carried on after school hours.These activities are often coordinated with classroom instruction, and a serious attempt is made to provide experiences to suit individual areas of interest and ability. Special clubs exist for students with special interest in

[5]Mulhern, *op. cit.*, p. 705.

science and technology. These clubs plan experiences that help the students develop and acquire greater skills and more knowledge in these areas, and they give the students opportunities to apply that knowledge. There are special television programs and many children's theaters, and emphasis is placed on sports and athletics.

Youth organizations—the Pioneers, the Octobrists, and the Komsomols—are a vital part of this system of extraclass activities. Soviet officials want to produce citizens who will be active in the affairs of their society while accepting unquestioningly the policies laid down by the rulers. Under very close supervision of the Communist party, these youth organizations are used for recruiting and training young people for membership in and loyalty to the party.[6] For example, the charter for the Komsomol organization lists the obligations of a member—ranging from one's being a selfless patriot for the Soviet Motherland, ready, if necessary, to give one's life for it, to one's duty to continue his education both in Marxism-Leninism and in academic subjects.

State boarding schools. In 1956 the Twentieth Party Congress set forth a plan whereby boarding schools for the masses would be established, and within the same year some of these schools were opened. By the following year the Soviet Union reported that they had already organized over one thousand such schools, the purpose of which was to bring the entire life of the child under a more complete Communist influence.

The Soviets believe that boarding schools, called "children's collectives" at times in Russia, are better suited than is the home for inculcating the best social patterns. Stanislav G. Strumilin, an outstanding Soviet writer, in his book *The Problems of Socialism and Communism in the USSR*, published in 1961, sets forth the theory that the advantages of public boarding schools over family living are so great that they justify whatever public expense may be necessary. This philosophy is resulting in a large-scale attempt to make over the institutions of Soviet society and the minds of the Russian citizens. The principal agent chosen to change the society is the school, and the boarding schools are being called upon to play a leading role in this movement.[7]

In 1962 there were over 600,000 elementary and secondary school children in the state boarding schools, and by 1965 the

---

[6]Ira Schlesinger, "Moral Education in the Soviet Union," *Phi Delta Kappan*, XLVI (October 1964), 74. ·

[7]Albert L. Weeks, Jr., "Brain Surgery on Soviet Society," *Phi Delta Kappan*, XLIII (February 1962), 206.

enrollment had increased to over two million. These schools stress general education and polytechnical training; that is to say, the students study mathematics, science, history, the Russian language, some foreign languages, music, and art. But polytechnical labor is also stressed, and students are required to work and study in technical areas. Sometimes the labor opportunities are offered in the school or on the school grounds; occasionally students spend part of their time in nearby towns or cities getting practical, on-the-job training.

Higher education

Although this discussion is primarily concerned with secondary education in Russia, it is important to consider higher education because the secondary schools and the more advanced schools are so closely related. Upon completion of the complete secondary school, and occasionally before graduation, students have the opportunity to attend a variety of institutions offering additional training. Among these are the State Labor Reserve, technicums, and universities and technical institutes of higher learning.

The State Labor Reserve. In 1940 a system of manual and vocational training, called the State Labor Reserve, was organized for boys and girls from fourteen to nineteen years of age. The course of study, which always provides on-the-job training, may take from six months to two years, the longest course consisting of science, mathematics, Russian, Communist doctrines, and physical education. As the name "State Labor Reserve" indicates, the young people who participate make up a reserve labor force that can be called into service anywhere labor is needed in the Soviet Union. These schools are designed to produce skilled workers and were created chiefly for nonacademic youth. Mathematics, physics, the Russian language, physical education, and political doctrines are taught in addition to job training.

Technicums. The technicum represents a type of semi-secondary, semi-higher education existing outside the regular system in Russia. The technicum curriculum overlaps that of the complete secondary schools. Considered preprofessional secondary schools, most technicums offer a four-year program following graduation from the incomplete secondary school. Some authorities, however, estimate that about half of the students in technicums are graduates of the complete secondary school and have already had ten years of education.

Each technicum specializes in only one area. In 1962 there were over twenty major specialized areas offered, including physical culture, engineering, public health, art, and teacher education. Admission to technicums is very selective, and the demands for workers in a particular phase of industry determine to a great extent the number selected for any particular school.

In 1962 the enrollment in all technicums totaled over 1,335,-000, and by 1963 the technicum was considered the most important type of technical school in Russia.[8] There is a great network of these schools under the control of the Ministry of Higher Education, which regulates admission requirements, standards, and curriculums.

Technicum students attend school from forty to fifty hours per week, about thirty-two weeks each year, usually for four years. A final examination and a thesis are required, and upon successful completion of all requirements the student is placed at once in a position in his chosen field. During the past few years a system of part-time technicums offering evening courses has enabled employed individuals to gain more advanced training and to rise faster in their chosen fields.

Universities and institutes of higher learning. Because the number of secondary school graduates far exceeds the opportunities for higher education in the Soviet Union, a strict system of selection exists. Selective examinations test students in mathematics, science, foreign languages, and Russian language and literature. Some students, however, such as superior secondary school graduates, World War II veterans, and children of officials in industry, have been admitted to the universities without taking the examinations.

In 1957 there were thirty-four universities and over seven hundred institutes of higher learning in the Soviet Union. By 1960 the enrollment in these schools had reached 2,500,000. The university programs consist chiefly of academic subjects, while the institutes stress applied science.

Students employed in industry while enrolled in higher education receive many privileges in Russia. They are granted regular leaves of absence from their jobs, ranging from ten to forty days, to do research and prepare for examinations. While on leave, they continue to draw their full salaries from industry. Students approaching graduation are given an absence of four months with full pay to prepare for their final thesis.

[8]*Ibid.*, p. 75.

Teacher education

In most cases teachers, highly respected as professionals in the Soviet Union, are appointed to their positions for life. They are paid relatively well, with salaries varying for the different types of positions, and they can retire with a government pension after twenty-five years of successful service. Although three fourths of all teachers are women, most secondary school teachers are men.

Most teachers' colleges offer five-year education programs for secondary school teachers. These colleges are organized into departments and faculties, the term *faculty* referring to what Americans designate a *school*, such as a School of Business Administration. Teachers' colleges have faculties in literature and language, geography and natural science, mathematics and physics, foreign languages, and history. Students in these schools are required to take courses in Marxism and in education.

Russian secondary teachers usually have more preparation in professional education courses than American secondary teachers are now receiving. They also have more extensive specialization in the subjects which they teach. The Russian high school teacher specializes in only one teaching field, whereas the American teacher is usually required to qualify in two or three subject areas.

Russian high school teachers are expected to engage in research and to keep abreast of their subject field; they are expected to be specialists with scholarly obligations similar to those assumed by a college teacher in the United States. To help teachers maintain a high level of scholarship, the work load in the secondary school consists of only eighteen hours of teaching per week. This compares with thirty or more class hours of teaching required of secondary school teachers in the United States.[9]

Recent developments

In September of 1958 Premier Khrushchev set forth some of his ideas on secondary and higher education in *Pravda*. His proposals, which were approved by the Presidium of the Central Committee of the Party, were adopted by the Supreme Soviet of the U.S.S.R. in December 1958. Khrushchev proposed that the existing system be reorganized to stress manual training in the earlier grades. Under the new organization most children who had completed the seven-year school would go to work in agriculture or industry, continuing their education on a part-time basis at night if

[9]Lindley J. Stiles and others, *Secondary Education in the United States* (New York: Harcourt, Brace and World, Inc., 1962), p. 509.

they so desired; but children who showed high intellectual ability would continue in school.

Khrushchev's plan provided for two stages of general education — the first stage a compulsory eight-year program for all children. During these eight years

. . . attention must be concentrated on instruction in the fundamentals of knowledge, on polytechnical training and the teaching of work habits, and on the education in communist ethics, the physical development of the children and their "innoculation" with good aesthetic taste. But, withal, we cannot have the school children overburdened to the extent that their health would be impaired.[10]

The second stage of general education, in most cases, would be vocational training on the job and in special part-time schools. The universal compulsory eight-year course was to replace the universal compulsory seven-year program and was to provide pupils with fundamentals of general education and polytechnical knowledge. This school would also be charged with the responsibility of inculcating in students a love for work, a readiness for socially useful activity, and a "pursuit of a moral, physical and aesthetic education."

The Soviets' ideas on types of schools are given in Article IV of the 1958 law, reproduced below as it was given in a press release of January 7, 1959:

The following basic types of schools giving a full secondary education shall be established:

a. Schools for young workers and the rural youth — evening secondary general-educational schools where persons who have finished the eight-year school and are working in a branch of the national economy receive a secondary education and raise their professional qualifications. The term of study at these schools shall be three years.

To provide the necessary conditions for the pupils of the evening secondary general-educational schools, the USSR Council of Ministers shall establish a shorter workday or a shorter work week for those who study successfully in their spare time.

b. Secondary general-educational labor polytechnical schools giving production training where persons who have finished the

---

[10]Nikita Khrushchev, "On Strengthening the Ties of the Schools with Life and on Further Developing the Country's Public Education System," *Pravda*, September 21, 1958. (Embassy of the Union of Soviet Socialist Republics, Press Release No. 506, October 1, 1958).

eight-year school in the course of three years receive a secondary education and professional training for work in a branch of the national economy or culture.

The ratio of theory to practice in productive training and the sequence of the periods of training and work shall be established, depending on the specialty and local conditions. In the rural schools the academic year should be arranged according to the seasonal character of agriculture work.

Production training and socially useful work may be pursued at instructional and production shops in nearby enterprises, in pupil teams on collective farms and state farms, at instructional experimental farms, at school and inter-school instructional production workshops.

c. Secondary vocational and other specialized educational establishments where persons who have finished the eight-year school receive a secondary general and a secondary specialized education.[11]

This new law calls for an increase in the number of boarding schools in order that families may be helped in bringing up their children. The law states that these will enhance "the role of society." This aspect of the law suggests (1) that these schools will be used for more indoctrination into the mysteries of communism and (2) that certain families are failing in child training or are not providing a suitable home environment for children.

Comparison and contrast

The Soviets have a strong central system. Secondary education in the Soviet Union is not offered in schools similar to comprehensive high schools in the United States. Instead, at least an eight-year general education is first offered to all, and specialized education is offered beyond this level. Students in Russian schools must wear uniforms, provide their own textbooks, and provide many of their own supplies. Oral examinations are used at many levels, and some type of state examination is required for future advancement at all levels. Vocational education is stressed to a much greater degree than it is in the secondary schools of this country. Course work in science, mathematics, and languages is stressed. Compulsory education above the eight-year general educational polytechnical school has been abolished.

The Communist party controls the schools, the teachers, the curriculum, and the students. The organizational structure used

[11]"Law on Strengthening the Ties of School with Life and on Further Developing the Public Educational System in the USSR" (Embassy of the Union of Soviet Socialist Republics, Press Release No. 5, January 7, 1959).

before 1958 was a four-year elementary school and four to seven years of secondary school, followed by higher education for the academically talented and various forms of vocational training for those who were not so talented academically. The new organizational structure calls for four years of elementary education and four to six (usually four) of secondary education, followed by higher education of an academic nature for some and various forms of vocational training for others.

Secondary education in West Germany

Since the end of World War II Germany has been divided into two parts: East Germany, under Soviet control, and West Germany. The German schools suffered many setbacks as a result of the war. School buildings were in ruin, and there was a great shortage of teachers. Before education could once more function in a normal way, buildings had to be repaired or constructed, and teachers had to be evaluated along political lines to determine whether previous Nazi party connections would interfere with their teaching in the postwar era.

The purpose of the present discussion will be to describe briefly the development of secondary education throughout Germany before the Nazis took over, to discuss secondary education under the Nazis, and to give some information about secondary education in West Germany since World War II.

Secondary education before the twentieth century

After the Protestant Reformation education in the German states was left in the hands of various church groups. As early as 1648 the Prussian government affirmed its ownership of the schools, but the church continued to control them. Between 1713 and 1740 some elementary schools and two institutions for the training of teachers were established by the Prussian government, and in 1736 a compulsory attendance law was passed, requiring children between the ages of six and twelve to attend school. However, the Prussian government was not financially able to provide schools for all these children. In 1763 Frederick the Great issued the *General School Regulations*, which required school attendance by children between the ages of five and fourteen or until they had made sufficient progress in writing, reading, and religion to satisfy school authorities. Prussia at this time also required teachers to pass an examination and have a state license before they could teach. In most cases the local church pastors were to serve as the inspectors for the government. Frederick the Great also specified the tuition figure, allowing poor students to have their fees paid out of a fund-raised by the churches. Similar developments took place in other German states.

Frederick William II was responsible for a general codification of Prussian basic laws in 1794. This codification stated that schools belonged to the state, that new schools could not be established unless they were first approved by the government, and that the state could examine and supervise schools at any time.

Frederick William III viewed education as an indispensable tool in building the power of a strong state, and after the defeat of the Prussians by Napoleon at Jena in 1806, he called for a greater effort in the area of education. Military training and education were seen as means of improving the morals of the masses. Frederick William III denounced individualism and pointed to it as a national curse responsible for Prussia's defeat; he insisted that the individual should live not for himself but for Prussia.[12] By 1840 Prussia had a state system of elementary (folk) schools.

Before the close of the eighteenth century there were two types of secondary schools in Prussia—the *Gymnasium* and the *Realschulen*, often called the *Burgerschulen*. The *Gymnasium* offered a highly academic program built around the classics, while the *Realschulen* put more emphasis on science and modern languages. After 1788 students were required to pass an examination before they were graduated from the *Gymnasium*. Students were then given a certificate which served as admission to the various universities. Graduates of the *Realschulen* who sought admission to the universities were required to take an examination given by the universities themselves. Other German states followed this example.

About 1890 a movement known as Neo-Humanism began in secondary education in the German states. Neo-Humanists advocated more emphasis on the study of man through a study of literature, philosophy, art, history, Greek, Latin, and religion. Educators felt that an intense study of these subjects by students in the secondary schools and universities would advance the progress of humanity and the nation.[13] Scholars backed this movement because they felt it would free the individual spirit of the German scholar and, at the same time, free the German states from domination by foreign culture, especially the culture of France. In fact, German leaders felt not only that they could free themselves from foreign

[12]Mulhern, *op. cit.*, p. 527.
[13]*Ibid.*, p. 533.

culture but also that they could assume cultural leadership in Europe.

In many ways the Neo-Humanists were successful. For example, they did revitalize the study of the classics in German secondary schools and universities, and they were responsible for the *Gymnasium's* gaining respect and eminence in the field of secondary education.

The Neo-Humanists, however, were gradually forced into the background in the nineteenth century. In their place came proponents of extreme nationalism and militarism, which after 1848 dominated all the German educational systems below the university level. This shift in philosophy resulted from a series of military defeats and the conservatism of the German rulers in the various states. By 1855 the government in Prussia was prescribing the curriculum of the teachers' seminaries and many other schools in an effort to avoid a broad cultural education; henceforth, the government declared, the elementary and secondary school curriculums were to be instruments in developing loyal, submissive citizens.

The Franco-Prussian War, which in 1871 brought about the unification of all German states with the exception of Austria, made the king of Prussia the ruler of a German empire. In 1872 Bismarck was able to obtain legislation which forced the Jesuits out of Prussia and suppressed the influence of Catholics in the ministry of education. He also withdrew all schools from church control and appointed nonclerical officers of the state to inspect all schools.[14]

Other legislation concerning education was designed to produce citizens who would be orderly and efficient in their work, content with their position in German society, and loyal to the Fatherland. Soon Germany became a leader in vocational education, with many towns developing their own vocational schools. After 1872 part-time vocational schools were established throughout Germany.

Three types of secondary schools had developed in Germany by the end of the nineteenth century. All were secondary schools for boys. Coeducation was not practiced in Germany at this time, and those schools for girls which did exist were not considered secondary schools. The secondary schools for boys offered a nine-year course of study, after completion of which students could enter the universities automatically.

The oldest secondary school was, of course, the *Gymnasium*. A second type, the *Realgymnasium*, was a Latin-scientific school

[14]H. G. Good, *A History of Western Civilization*, 2nd ed. (New York: The Macmillan Company, 1960), pp. 325–327.

which stressed modern foreign languages instead of Greek, although Greek was sometimes offered as an elective. The *Realgymnasium* was more popular in southern Germany than in Prussia. In Germany as a whole, its curriculum was considered intermediate between the *Gymnasium*, which stressed classical studies, and the *Oberrealschule*, a third type of secondary school in which no classical languages were studied. Science, mathematics, and modern languages were emphasized in the *Oberrealschule*. Actually, this type of school can be traced back to 1747, when a *Realschule* was opened in Berlin as a six-year school; when it was made a nine-year school, the term *ober*, meaning "higher," was prefixed to its name.[15]

All these schools existed as six-year, as well as nine-year, schools, since many towns were too small or too poor to support a nine-year school, and because many students were too poor to go on to a university after secondary education. It was felt that for this group of students a nine-year school was not necessary. Also, there was a general feeling on the part of some German educators that while many of the students did not have the ability to profit from a nine-year course and a university education, they could profit from a six-year school.

Students started their secondary education at the age of nine after three years in a public or private elementary school. At the age of eighteen, students were supposed to be ready for the universities. Secondary school students were required to study ten or twelve subjects each year, the major ones being German, foreign languages, mathematics, and science. They also studied religion, history, singing, handwork, and physical education, attending about thirty-three class periods per week. While some of the subjects required no outside preparation, the major ones did require homework. The course of study was much more difficult than the curriculum of most American high schools. All subjects were required, and although some electives could be taken, they were not counted toward graduation. Most German boys were required to spend two or three years in military service, but those who finished at least six years of secondary education were required to spend only one year in the armed forces. Only a small percentage of German adolescents received a secondary education.

After 1880 the curriculum of the *Realgymnasium* became very similar to that of the *Gymnasium* because greater emphasis was placed on the study of Latin and mathematics. Extreme radicals

[15]*Ibid.*, p. 331.

and many conservatives criticized this change within the *Realgymnasium*. Conservatives considered it a threat to the high esteem of the *Gymnasium*; radicals looked upon it as an attempt to create more schools of the *Gymnasium* type, which they considered a useless luxury. They called for the abolishment of the *Realgymnasium*. In 1890 a conference called by the Kaiser did abolish it, but it was reinstated by law in 1892. At the same time, the *Gymnasium* changed its curriculum by reducing the emphasis on Latin and Greek, thus reducing the difference between the two schools. A decree issued in 1900 declared all secondary schools to be of the same value for general culture, but all schools did not, nor were they required to, have the same curriculum.[16]

One can get an insight into the philosophy that was prompting these changes in secondary education by considering the words of Kaiser William II:

> The national basis is lacking. We must take German as the foundation for the Gymnasium; we ought to educate national young Germans and not young Greeks and Romans. . . . The German exercise must be the central point about which all turns. I am looking for soldiers; we wish to have a robust generation, who can serve the Fatherland also as intellectual leaders and as officials.[17]

Despite the fact that in 1900 all secondary education offered in the three official secondary schools was declared to be of equal value, the universities continued to receive almost all of their students from the *Gymnasiums*, which continued to outnumber the other two types of nine-year schools.

As was pointed out earlier, most secondary schools were for boys only; however, girls were given some very limited educational opportunities beyond elementary schools. The traditional philosophy was that girls were to have children, to cook, and to be good housewives. Most opportunities for girls in secondary education before the twentieth century were provided by private secondary schools, but in 1872 some ten-year schools for girls were established. Girls entered these schools at the age of six. The curriculums offered were modified to such an extent that by 1894 their offerings were essentially equivalent to those provided in the secondary schools for boys; yet none of these schools, which were called *Lyzeums*, were given the recognition and privileges accorded

---

[16]Bossing, *op. cit.*, p. 83.

[17]J. L. Kandel, *History of Secondary Education* (Boston: Houghton Mifflin Company, 1930), pp. 257–258.

to secondary schools for boys. Some of the more gifted girls were admitted to the universities after 1895, but for thirteen years they were accepted only as auditors. After 1908 they were admitted as regular students. Though much more liberal opportunities for secondary education were given to girls under the Weimar Republic, the universities remained reluctant to increase the small privileges already accorded the females.[18]

Secondary education in the twentieth century

World War I accelerated the nationalistic movement in Germany and led to the extremes brought about under the Nazi regime. Greater demands were made by the people for more educational opportunities. The constitution adopted in 1919 called for a system of compulsory education which would offer eight years of elementary education in a *Volksschule* and further work in a vocational school. In 1920 the first four years of the *Volksschule* were required of all children, and the special preparatory elementary schools were abolished. Henceforth the first four years of the *Volksschule* were to be called the *Grundschule*. Upon completion of these first four years in a *Grundschule*, students had three possible choices: to continue their education in a *Volksschule*, to enter a *Mittelschule*, which offered some general education and some vocational education, or to enter one of the major secondary schools discussed earlier.

In 1920 a new type of secondary school, called the *Deutsche Oberschule*, was established. It was not designed to replace any of the older institutions but rather to make secondary education more German—to stress German life and culture.

In the late 1920's another type of secondary school, the *Aufbauschule*, was established. This school developed mainly in the smaller cities, and students were permitted to enter it at the end of the sixth grade or at about twelve years of age.

When the Nazis gained power, they changed not only the government but also the educational system. In fact, they provided another classic example of how a political party can use education to further its own cause.

The drastic reorganization of the almost hopelessly diversified array of secondary schools inherited by the National Socialist government had much to commend it. In 1937 the Reichsminister issued a decree which (1) reduced the number of secondary schools to three

[18]Mulhern, *op. cit.*, p. 538.

major types; (2) made English the important foreign language of the schools; and (3) reduced the time for preparation for the Leaving Examinations from thirteen to twelve years. The new schools created by the Republic, which emphasized German culture, were the *Deutsche Oberschule*, now made the principal secondary school, the *Aufbauschule*, and the *Gymnasium*. But the glory that was for centuries centered in the *Gymnasium* was not removed; it was reduced to the least consequential of the schools. Henceforth it was to be limited in numbers and restricted to the cities. The *Oberschule* was made the standard secondary school of eight years; all other schools were to be patterned after it. The *Aufbauschule* was retained as a six-year school to follow a six-year elementary program. It was to be restricted to rural districts and made largely a boarding school to give rural children an opportunity to prepare for the university.[19]

The forms of organization, the types of schools, and the curriculums were changed. Religion was almost completely removed from the course of study. Great emphasis was placed on the study of German nationalism, and very few electives were allowed. Two programs could be elected by boys, one emphasizing natural science and mathematics and the other stressing languages; however, the real difference in the two programs was not in subject matter but in the amount of time spent on various subjects. Physical education was considered a major subject, and much time was devoted to it.

In general, girls were allowed to attend only two types of secondary schools—the *Oberschule* and the *Aufbauschule*; however, it was possible to obtain special permission to attend a *Gymnasium*. With few exceptions, girls were not permitted to go to school with boys; their curriculums emphasized home economics, physical education, German culture, and family life. Under the Nazis they could not prepare for the universities in the typical secondary school for girls.

The aims and values of Nazi secondary education were designed in such a way that all schools and educational agencies would attempt to bring every individual into complete harmony with the will of the state. In 1938 the Minister of Education stated that the "common goal" of all efforts in education is that "of forming the National Socialist Man."[20]

The Nazis thought that character building and intellectual training were important, but not so important as physical educa-

[19]Bossing, *op. cit.*, p. 87.
[20]Mulhern, *op. cit.*, p. 670.

tion. Intellectual training was considered to be anything which helped to develop an individual in relation to his opportunities to serve the Fatherland. Above all, education was to stress devotion to the Fatherland. Love of Germany was the basis of all character. The scholars of the traditional schools were denounced because they had not been concerned with the life of the people and the welfare of the state. Hitler thought the supreme goal of women's education was motherhood.

Students were to study not for knowledge alone; they were to be pragmatic in their approach to learning so they could produce for the Fatherland. A great youth movement was organized to supplement the work of the schools along nationalistic lines. Great stress was placed on such activities.

Teachers who were Jews were dismissed because they were not of "pure" blood, and other teachers were required to accept Nazi doctrines or go to the concentration camps. In Nazi Germany the teacher was considered a little *Fuehrer*. Students were supposed to obey him without questioning his authority. Government officials considered education a physical, moral, and mental discipline, and the German people were urged to view it the same way. The lecture method in teaching received high official praise, and directed student activity was emphasized. The Minister of Education declared that it was harmful for students to have freedom to discuss topics in the classroom and to question teachers.[21]

Education in Germany since World War II
In 1945 the victorious Allied Powers drew up the famous Potsdam Agreement, which stipulated that the Nazi political and militaristic doctrines be eliminated from the German educational system. Over two thirds of the German elementary school teachers were disqualified from teaching in the American zone, and their places, in some cases, were filled by retired or poorly trained teachers. While most of the older teachers had little use for democracy, they were required to help make German education more democratic.

Some writers say that very little progress has been made. For example, Mulhern points out that the Allies tried for some years to re-educate the Germans and to impose their own educational traditions upon them. He feels that it was juvenile on the part of the Allies to think that they could change the minds and customs of so great a nation in a few short years. Nazi nationalism, imperial-

[21]*Ibid.*, p. 672.

ism, militarism, and authoritarianism were only an intensification of traditional Prussianism, according to Mulhern, who emphasizes the point that Prussianism always stood opposed to popular government and always insisted upon the idea of German racial and cultural superiority.[22]

Other writers say there have been great reforms in German education since 1945. In 1963 Plant expressed the belief that a definite change has taken place in the West German schools. He set forth the idea that the old, rigid, authoritarian patterns of secondary education are slowly giving way to more flexible approaches, that the secondary school teachers are using an approach that represents a compromise between the strictness of past teachers and the permissiveness of many American teachers. The class structure of old Germany, which had persisted during the Weimar Republic, is disintegrating, according to Plant, and many students from lower class homes are now attending the *Gymnasium.*[23]

Many technical difficulties were faced in setting up postwar schools. For example, Nazi school books were filled with propaganda and could not be used, yet the process of securing new books took time and money. As a result, photographic reproductions of many pre-Nazi textbooks were used. School facilities were sadly lacking: in some cities 80 to 90 per cent of the schools were badly damaged or destroyed. When the schools opened, they were hopelessly overcrowded. The average class size was seventy. Yet despite such difficulties, schools in the British zone were reopened in July 1945, and those in the American zone were reopened the following October. However, according to Good, children were listless and purposeless. He states that the children, like the older people, lacked power of concentration and decision.[24]

The schools in West Germany are today, in many ways, similar to the schools in Germany after World War I, but they are changing. The *Grundschule* is the first phase of the elementary school; although its course of study is still four years in most cases, as it was in the 1920's, it may be six years. The second phase of education for those not attending a secondary school is offered in *Volksschules,* which in most cases is a four-year continuation of elementary and general education. This school offers much work that Americans would consider secondary education. Conservatives want to limit this school to four years, while liberals want it to

[22]*Ibid.*, pp. 680–681.
[23]Richard Plant, "West German Education in Transition: Schools at the Crossroads," *Saturday Review,* July 20, 1963, pp. 49–51.
[24]Good, *op. cit.*, p. 546.

extend over a five-year period. Over two hundred *Volksschules* have been established in postwar Germany, offering an education which consists of academic and vocational subjects. There are many vocational schools that children can attend after completing their elementary education. Since some young people go to work at an early age, they attend vocational schools on a part-time basis.

The *Gymnasium* has regained its former position of respect in the secondary field, but because most Germans today are more concerned with modern subjects than with Greek or Latin, the modern secondary school, or *Realschule*, greatly outnumbers the *Gymnasium*. The *Realschule* offers courses in modern languages, science, history, German, mathematics, and electives of various kinds — what Americans refer to as a general education.

Examinations are still used by most of the secondary schools as the basis for admission. Today, however, if a vocational school student decides that he wants a university education, he can take special courses that will enable him to attend a *Gymnasium* and then a university.[25] Most students attend the *Volksschule* and then continue their work in a vocational school or a *Realschule* on a part-time basis.

Education in West Germany today is the responsibility of the various *Länder* (states) rather than of the federal government. The concept of high centralization, which many individuals associate with things German, does not apply to education. Within broad limits each *Land* controls its own educational system. Although there are similarities in the school policies of the *Länder*, as there are in the state systems within the United States, there is no national system of education in West Germany. In an attempt to bring about some uniformity, there has been established a *Standige Konferenz der Kultusminister der Länder*, an organization similar to an association of chief state school officers. This organization works for voluntary agreements which are adopted only by unanimous vote. Even when so adopted, however, the agreements have no legal force except as they are officially enacted in the individual *Länder* by the educational authorities.

A German child enters school at six years of age and spends four years in a primary school. In most cases he has one teacher for all his classes and often the same teacher for four years. At the conclusion of these four years, a decision is made as to the type of schooling the student should follow, starting with the fifth grade. This decision is based upon teacher recommendations, examina-

[25]Plant, *op. cit.*, p. 50.

tions, and the desires of the pupil's parents. Three teachers are required to give an opinion as to the student's aptitude for further schooling. The regular teacher does so on the basis of his past experience with the youngster; another primary teacher takes over the class for at least part of the day for two weeks and makes a judgment about the pupil's aptitude for secondary education; and a teacher from one of the secondary schools (*Mittelschule* or *Gymnasium*) teaches for two weeks and makes a similar judgment.[26]

The student may then transfer to the university preparatory *Gymnasium*, go into the technical school (*Mittelschule*), or continue in the elementary school (*Volksschule*). The *Mittelschule* (not meaning "middle" in terms of years but in the sense of being between the *Volksschule* and the *Gymnasium* in academic rigor) places less emphasis on languages than does the *Gymnasium* and leads to technical training in industry and business. Those who continue in the elementary school or *Volksschule* usually attend for four or five years more and then, at fourteen or fifteen years of age, go into some type of apprenticeship training. The technical school extends for six years beyond the primary school and may also lead to various types of apprenticeship training; the *Gymnasium* curriculum involves nine years of study and prepares students for the universities.

Of the German students who complete the four years of primary education, about 18 per cent enter the *Gymnasium*; 12 per cent, the *Mittelschule*; and 70 per cent, the *Volksschule*.[27]

Failures and transfers cause considerable attrition during the period of secondary education so that only 5 to 8 per cent of this group earn the *Abitur* and eligibility for university entrance. Of those who enter the university, perhaps a third never finish; consequently, no more than 4 or 5 per cent of primary graduates eventually complete their university studies.[28]

A graduate of any *Gymnasium* is eligible to enroll in any university. Whereas in this country there is widespread graduation from high school and selective admission to college, the opposite is true in West Germany, where there is selective graduation from the *Gymnasium* but completely open admission to the university. Once admitted to a German university, the student is free to stay so long as he behaves himself. No one is expelled for lack of academic progress.

[26]John R. Beery, "Teacher Education in West Germany," *The Journal of Teacher Education*, XVI (March 1965), 61.
[27]*Ibid.*, p. 64.
[28]*Ibid.*, p. 65.

Although many changes have been made in German education since World War II and although there is currently some tendency toward incorporating new ideas, tradition is still a very strong factor. The three types of university preparatory secondary schools (the classical, the modern language, and the mathematical and scientific) are distinguished primarily by their relative emphasis on languages. In the classical *Gymnasium* all students start Latin at the age of ten and study it for seven periods per week for the first two years. At the age of twelve, students add English or French, and at the age of thirteen everyone starts studying Greek.[29]

Comparison and contrast

Germany has a system of secondary education that is more selective than the American secondary school system; but secondary educational opportunities are no longer limited by class lines, and some of the secondary schools are now coeducational. German secondary education is beginning to stress education for citizenship just as American schools do.

It looks as if in education the United States and the countries of Western Europe are drawing closer together and yet remaining different in certain distinctive features and predispositions. They are coming closer together because of very broad social trends — essentially the "democratization" of European society — and certain broad economic trends — essentially the movement toward a more highly technological and more affluent society. There will be a natural temptation for Americans, powerful in the sense of their country's influence in the world and at the same time generous and well-meaning in their outlook, to suppose that American type education having been on the whole good for America will be good for Europe. There will also be a natural disposition for Europeans to be more receptive of American ideas than they have been in the past. At the same time many Americans who are doubtful and critical of certain trends in American education will continue to feel that Europe still holds more surely than the United States to the intellectual virtues in school and college; and there will still be Europeans who will insist that as between the two giants, the U.S. and the U.S.S.R., there is Europe with its own distinctive virtues and its way of life which they are indeed ready to modify but not to see go down.[30]

[29]*Ibid.*, p. 69.
[30]Lionel Elvin, "Reform in West Europe's Post-Primary Education," *Phi Delta Kappan*, XLIII (November 1961), 53.

Selected references

ALEXANDER, WILLIAM M. AND J. GALEN SAYLOR. *Modern Secondary Education*. New York: Holt, Rinehart & Winston, Inc., 1959.

BEERY, JOHN R. "Teacher Education in West Germany," *The Journal of Teacher Education*, XVI (March 1965), 61.

BEREDAY, GEORGE Z. F., WILLIAM W. BRICKMAN, AND GERALD H. READ, EDS. *The Changing Soviet School*. Boston: Houghton Mifflin Company, 1960.

COUNTS, GEORGE S. *The Challenge of Soviet Education*. New York: McGraw-Hill Book Company, Inc., 1957.

CRAMER, JOHN FRANCIS AND GEORGE STEPHENSON BROWNE. *Contemporary Education: A Comparative Study of National Systems*. New York: Harcourt, Brace & World, Inc., 1956.

DERTHICK, LAWRENCE G. "The Frightening Challenge of Russia's Schools," *Look*, XXII (October 14, 1958), 38–40.

Foreign Education Digest (See current issues of this publication for contemporary developments in these and other countries).

GOOD, H. G. *A History of Western Education*, 2nd ed. New York: The Macmillan Company, 1960.

KING, EDGAR A. "Features of Russian Education We Might Emulate," *The Clearing House*, XXXVIII (February 1964), 365–367.

KOROL, ALEXANDER G. *Soviet Education for Science and Technology*. Technology Press Book of Massachusetts Institute of Technology. New York: John Wiley and Sons, Inc., 1957.

SCHLESINGER, IRA. "Moral Education in the Soviet Union," *Phi Delta Kappan*, XLVI (October 1964), 74.

WEEKS, ALBERT L., JR. "Brain Surgery on Soviet Society," *Phi Delta Kappan*, XLIII (February 1962), 206.

Problems and progress
in secondary education

PART V

Critics, criticisms, and accomplishments in secondary education

chapter **17**

Criticisms of education and educational institutions are nothing new. Written records in the form of clay tablets several thousand years old show that people in ancient times were critical of schools and educators. Confucius, Socrates, St. Augustine, and Rousseau all reveal that people are quick to criticize both established institutions and practices and new movements and institutions.

During the past fifteen years American secondary education has been severely criticized in newspapers, magazines, and books. The criticisms are not restricted to any one area of education or any particular level. In many cases they are contradictory in nature. For example, some critics insist that the programs offered in the school are not so concerned as they should be with a challenging academic program; others insist that the curriculum is too academic when it should be more practical. Many believe that the education of students could be greatly improved if the schools would concentrate on the fundamentals and drop what they term the unessentials. Others say that the curriculum is altogether too narrow and should be enlarged to provide more subjects in areas that deal with citizenship and earning a living. The school should place more emphasis on college preparation, certain educators say, while others want more vocational and general education courses.

The man in the street, the college professor, the physician, the legislator—all have their conceptions of what the school should and should not do. Their opinions and convictions, of course, are the result of their experiences and backgrounds, which often inculcate respect for tradition and fear of change. Although some criticisms are shallow and ill-founded, many are based on research, facts, and changed conditions.

At the present time the anxiety and fear of many Americans as a result of the cold war and the space race have led not only to an increase in the volume of criticism of the schools but also to much that must be labeled *attacks* on the schools. There is a difference between criticism and attacks. Criticism is an attempt to identify weaknesses in order that they may be remedied, while attacks are designed to destroy or cripple. Attacks on the school and its program generate fear and suspicion, destroy public confidence and support, and undermine the efforts of teachers and administrators.

Despite the fact that some criticisms of the school are based on misconceptions, fear, hate, prejudices, and vested interests, criticism of a responsible nature paves the way for progress. Thoughtful attention to education is indispensable to improvement, because it leads to refinement in what is being practiced. Therefore, individuals concerned with secondary education should carefully examine the most common criticisms of the schools. Such examination can lead to greater appreciation of the schools, their functions, problems, purposes, and importance, and can help identify weaknesses and ways to improve schools and their programs.

Critics of secondary education

Who are the critics? What view do they represent? A brief discussion of some of the major types of critics should be helpful.

Partisans of higher education

The first secondary schools in this country, the Latin grammar schools, were designed primarily for the preparation of students for college. Soon academies were established to provide a more practical form of secondary education as well as to prepare students for college. The first high schools were established to prepare students for life. It was not long, however, before the traditional high school was also very much concerned with college preparation. It is evident, historically, that the secondary schools of this nation have served as feeders for the institutions of higher learning. It is only natural then that, with an increasing number of students going to college, more concern over college preparation should be expressed by the people in general and college educators in particular. The increased complexity of society; the demand for more training in mathematics, science, and foreign languages; the urgent need for more professional people; and the crucial position of the United States in world affairs add to this concern for greater academic preparation of secondary school students.

Many, therefore, insist that programs in secondary education should concentrate on producing the academic man. Such a course of action, they feel, will develop the best minds and produce leaders capable of coping with the problems of the space age. Some of these critics look to the European academic schools as models which this nation should follow.[1] "Return to the home and other social agencies some of the responsibilities that have been thrust upon the schools," they say. Yet they are often very indefinite as to which responsibilities they would remove from secondary education. Carried to logical conclusions, their recommendations for such things as nationalized standards, separate academic schools for the academically talented, and terminal vocational schools for the students of average or less-than-average ability would end the present system of secondary schools.

Supporters of vocational education
Less than half of all secondary school students attend college, and in many rural areas, small towns, and city slums the percentage is much smaller. In light of these conditions, some critics suggest that more vocational subjects and more general education be taught; they insist that the high schools not forget their original purpose, which was preparation for life. These individuals would not eliminate academic programs, but they ask that the school provide appropriate programs for all. Often they demand community colleges at public expense. They point out that the school must provide more technical education for a technical society. "Give us special facilities and special teachers," they say.

Parents
Frequently, conscientious parents feel that secondary education is not what it should be. Some are interested in better academic programs that will challenge the gifted; others want quality education for students of all ability levels. Some demand more national support of education, while others, seeing in this a danger of national control, instead seek more effort at the state and local levels.

[1] Frederick Mayer, "Education and the Crisis of Our Time," *Phi Delta Kappan*, XLIII (April 1962), 300–302.

Among the most consistent, but more friendly, critics of the school must be listed the parents of the students. Two standards in particular govern the nature of the parental criticisms of the school. The first is derived from the ambition of the typical parent that his child have the best possible educational advantages. The second is the measure of similarity between the program the school is offering the child and what was available to the parents, or what the parents think was available, in their day; unfortunately, it is a general tendency for adults to idealize the education they experienced.[2]

Groups with vested interests

Some individuals promote their own selfish interests at the expense of the schools. In fact, they often want the school to promote their causes for them; and when it fails to do so, they then become very vocal in criticisms. For example, groups selling worthless or low-quality books, materials, or equipment resort to smear campaigns or to unjustified criticisms of the school and its program when their products are rejected. In recent years there have also been individuals who have made much money from irresponsible publications that criticize the schools.

Unfortunately, some school systems have been victimized by such vested-interest groups, which are essentially hate-mongers and rabble-rousers. This happens when the rest of the community does not evaluate criticisms and the sources of criticisms.

Tradition-worshipers

To a certain extent most people fall into this group. While there is value in cherishing that which has been proved to be good and effective, is it not foolish to cling to that which is inappropriate, wasteful, and ineffective simply because it has been handed down through the years? Many teaching practices and many elements in school organization and administration are wasteful and inefficient.

Worshipers of tradition find their major values in some distant past. They look upon that which existed in "the good old days" as superior to anything in existence today. They lament the lack of teaching of the so-called fundamentals, and they like to complain about progressive education or the evils of life-adjustment education.

Employers

When employers get employees who are not as proficient in the fundamental skills as the employers would like them to be, the

[2]Nelson L. Bossing, *Principles of Secondary Education* (Englewood Cliffs, N.J.: Prentice-Hall, Inc., 1955), p. 8.

schools are quickly criticized for failing to produce the type of employees needed by business and industry. This does not mean that all students leave the secondary school proficient in the fundamental skills and general education. Rather, it means that the entire process of secondary education is often criticized because of the mistakes of a few clerks, secretaries, or other employees.

Taxpayers

In some communities the quickest way for the school superintendent to get fired is for him to suggest that the tax levy be raised; yet many school officials are aware of the necessity for securing more support from local taxes or bond issues. It is not unusual to find communities in which the taxpayers have organized movements to resist any efforts to raise additional taxes. It is true that the real estate owners have been overburdened in some communities, while other, more equitable, sources of revenue have been neglected. However, homeowners and real estate investors often fail to realize how little they are paying for schools as compared with their expenditures for tobacco, liquor, cosmetics, or fishing trips. Some of these people have three or four children in public schools, but their total school tax bill would not be adequate to pay for one child's education. Those taxpayers who have no children in school must consider the cost and danger of living in a society of uneducated and ignorant citizens. They must realize the high correlation between low educational levels and crime, and they should be aware of the cost of ignorance to the taxpayer in terms of relief funds. It would be wise for the person who resents paying for public education to investigate what it costs his state to support a criminal in a penal institution or to keep one family on public welfare lists.[3]

Public schools represent the largest single item on the local tax bill, at times amounting to more than 80 per cent of the local tax. The major public criticism on school costs, however, usually emanates from tax leagues and realty boards, organizations that represent the business interests in a community. The public secondary school has been the favorite target of such groups.[4]

Backers of special ideologies

Supporters of special ideologies often direct their attacks at the instructional program of the school, attacks sometimes aimed at

[3]*Schools for the Sixties,* The Project on Instruction, National Education Association (New York: McGraw-Hill Book Company, Inc., 1963), pp. 36–37.

[4]For an excellent treatment of some of the major viewpoints on taxation and public education, see the October 1960 issue of the *Phi Delta Kappan.*

what is being taught but more often at what is not being taught. These individuals have convictions concerning materials or ideologies which they feel the school should support. Some of these deal with health, religion, patriotism, communism, or the United Nations. (Publications such as the *Phi Delta Kappan* will give the reader some examples of extremist groups that are angry at the schools.)

While most educators agree that the schools should be concerned with moral and spiritual values and love of country, very few, if any, want the schools to be used by left-wing or right-wing radicals to obtain a captive audience. It is a responsibility of the public to stand by the school officials subjected to unjust criticism simply because they refuse free use of the schools for these doctrinaires to promote their convictions.

Students in the secondary schools

Young people who are enrolled in, who have recently been graduated from, or who have dropped out of the secondary schools frequently voice criticisms of secondary education. Publications such as *Youth Tell Their Story* attest to the value as well as to the volume of such criticisms. Dr. James B. Conant, in his studies of secondary schools, found it necessary and valuable to get the students' opinions on the value of their educational experiences. But though student evaluations are derived from their own recent observations and experiences and may be more objective and discerning than those of adults, it is well to remember that their criticisms may not be well founded and that their observations may be distorted by close personal involvement. Unfortunately, all remarks by these young people are often taken at face value by their parents and friends.

Responsible laymen and educators

Much of the criticism of secondary education comes from intelligent and responsible critics, and it reflects objective and sincere evaluation. They set forth the types of criticism that will lead to action for improvement. Examples of such criticism are found in the writings of James B. Conant, Walter Lippmann, James R. Killian, Jr., and Benjamin S. Bloom. The schools in general and conscientious school personnel in particular profit from this type of criticism because it helps point the way to quality in education.

As is evident from this brief discussion, it is difficult to classify the schools' many critics. This need not be a discouraging discovery, however. Most of the educational leaders in this country are intelligent and responsible, dedicated to their work and to attempts to improve secondary education. Good teachers are concerned with the quality of education but are also willing to devote time, money, and effort to its improvement.[5]

The student of secondary education might well devote some serious thought to such questions as the following: What are the major issues in secondary education today and where do I stand on these issues? Why do I have the opinions I hold? What course of action would I follow in my teaching as my work relates to these issues?

Specific criticisms of secondary education

It seems appropriate to consider not only the critics but also their specific criticisms of secondary education. Often their criticisms are very general, but the following discussion will attempt to pinpoint several shortcomings in secondary schools as seen by many critics.

Criticisms of the curriculum

The term *curriculum* can be used to mean the entire educational program, one course, or any part of either. Here it refers to the total instructional program organized and offered by the school. Because there has been such a great increase in the amount of knowledge and in the complexity of that knowledge during the past few decades, schools are now facing a most difficult task in selecting the materials, concepts, understandings, and skills which must be taught. They must also attempt to find the best ways to teach the new material so that it will be retained by the students. Some of the major criticisms of the curriculum are as follows:

1. Basic education—the social studies, languages, mathematics, science, the humanities—is not taught as it should be taught.

2. Schools should stress subject matter and not try to master current economic-political-social issues.

3. Schools should study current economic-political-social issues as well as basic subject matter.

4. Schools do not challenge gifted students, nor do they provide proper academic preparation for college.

5. Schools are too concerned with academic areas and too unconcerned with trade and vocational areas.

[5]Vernon E. Anderson and William T. Gruhn, *Principles and Practices of Secondary Education.* Copyright © 1962, The Ronald Press Company, p. 4.

6. Schools are not doing enough to teach esthetic appreciation in art, music, and literature.

7. Schools should eliminate music, art, and other "frill" subjects and concentrate on basic subject matter.

8. Schools do not provide enough "depth" education in all subject areas.

9. Schools do not provide a sufficient number of elective subjects for the many students of varying ability.

10. Schools offer too many electives in the form of frills and impractical subjects.

11. Schools fail to teach students how to study.

12. Schools fail to teach students how to solve problems and how to think.

13. Schools do not uphold high standards; they pass too many students, permitting the academically unfit to remain in school.

It is very evident that some of these criticisms are contradictory. To determine the value of any of them, one would find it necessary to study specific schools and their programs. The criticisms do, however, point up the fact that the overpowering amount of knowledge to be taught presents a great problem in the matter of selection.[6]

Despite the fact that there are areas of disagreement regarding the curriculum, there are also great areas of agreement. Pierce, in sampling the views of ten leaders in the area of curriculum, found general agreement on such elements as the need for general education and special education, the desirability of so-called extraclass activities, the teaching of social amenities, attention to individual differences, and the necessity of constant evaluation of the curriculum.[7]

Criticisms of the school's objectives

The objectives of the secondary school are often criticized. Examples of such criticisms are given below:

1. Schools do not know what they are attempting to do; they have not properly identified their basic purposes.

2. Schools spend too much time studying the needs of students and what the goals of education should be and not enough time teaching students.

3. Schools have taken over responsibilities that properly belong to the home, religious groups, or community agencies.

[6]*Schools for the Sixties*, pp. 49–50.
[7]Paul R. Pierce, "Agreements on Curriculum," *Phi Delta Kappan*, XLI (March 1960), 265–269.

4. Schools should be concerned with the preparation of students for life, not simply with an academic program. We need a curriculum designed to meet the needs of youth.

The following quotations give some insight into the wide range of criticisms of the school's role or function:

Is it any wonder that in this suddenly expanded realm of secondary education, where from time immemorial the liberal arts have had to prove themselves in competition with utilitarian education of all kinds — where they have always had to make a case for themselves or give ground — they gave ground? They did not give it in an objective test of merit or by decision of policy. They gave it by default.[8]

All except the academic subjects are of the kind which we might term "know-how." They have nothing to do with the school's primary task, which is to teach young minds to think and to train them in the elementary tools of learning. This task can be performed only by the school. Vocational, recreational or life-adjustment training can be and should be obtained elsewhere.[9]

On the other hand, there seems to be general agreement that the school must have objectives that relate to programs of general education for all students and to vocational education and specialized academic programs.[10] These objectives should give direction to curriculum planning and teaching as the school adds content, eliminates content, or changes the emphasis on various topics and courses of study. In other words, what are proper objectives for schools and what is a good high school education are meaningless questions unless a critic specifies the student, his environment, his abilities, and his goals.[11]

Criticisms of teachers

Criticism of teachers is often general and unqualified, as is evident from the following examples:

1. Teachers are often unsympathetic toward their students.

2. Teachers are often not good "explainers"; thus students do not know what the teacher wants done or how to do it.

3. Teachers are not paid enough to attract and hold good ones in the profession.

[8]A. Whitney Griswold, "What We Don't Know Will Hurt Us," *Harper's Magazine*, July 1954, p. 80.

[9]Rear Admiral Hyman G. Rickover, "Let's Stop Wasting Our Greatest Resource," *Saturday Evening Post*, March 2, 1957, p. 109.

[10]*Schools for the Sixties*, pp. 50–51.

[11]Frank L. Steeves, *Readings in the Methods of Education* (New York: The Odyssey Press, 1964), pp. 326–331.

4. Teachers need more work in academic areas.

5. Teachers are not professional enough.

6. Teachers are overly concerned with professional groups and professionalization.

7. Teachers are not fair in the evaluation of students. They do not have uniform standards.

8. Teachers adhere to rigid standards in grading and fail to consider individual differences.

9. Teachers try too many "progressive methods."

10. Teachers are using too many antiquated procedures.

No one denies the fact that the demand for qualified teachers exceeds the supply. One valid reason for criticism of schools springs from this unmet need in the United States. Criticism of teachers in general, however, should not obscure the fact that there are many excellent ones. Many know their subjects well, have good liberal educations, and are dedicated; they are people of ability who work hard. They make wise decisions as they teach, and they help their students grow and develop in many ways.[12]

Concerning teachers, the important questions can be summed up as follows: How can the schools attract more of the ablest individuals into the teaching profession? How can these individuals be provided with the best preparation for the important task they are to do? How can schools utilize their skills and abilities most effectively, and how can they be retained in the profession in the face of competition from business, industry, and other professions?[13]

Unfortunately, in many cases there is little difference between present-day teaching methods and those used a generation or more ago. In the better schools and in the classrooms of effective teachers everywhere, there have been changes—changes that were necessary in order to keep all educable adolescents in school and to provide meaningful instruction for a wide variety of scholastic aptitudes.

Trump and Baynham provide pertinent statements that apply to some of the criticisms of teachers:

Professional teachers need greater opportunity to use professional skills. Typically, they work an average forty-eight-hour week. They meet five classes a day, five days a week, for a minimum total of twenty-five hours a week with students. In addition, they supervise

[12]Henry Ehlers and Gordon C. Lee, *Crucial Issues in Education*, 3rd ed. (New York: Holt, Rinehart & Winston, Inc., 1964), pp. 304–306.

[13]Paul Woodring, *New Directions in Teacher Education* (New York: Fund for the Advancement of Education, 1957), pp. 8–14.

study halls, grade papers, keep records, collect money, sponsor student activities, and perform a host of other tasks. Not enough time remains to do what professional teachers should do: Keep up with developments in individual subject fields, plan and prepare lessons, develop imaginative instructional materials, and improve evaluation of student work.

Lack of time for professional work damages professional pride. About a third of a teacher's day goes to clerical and subprofessional tasks, another third to work which could just as well be done by various kinds of automated devices. A situation that provides only a third of a day for performance of work he is trained to do—and finds satisfaction in doing—contributes little to the morale of a talented, conscientious teacher.

Teachers need an appropriate place to perform the professional work that underlies professional teaching. Space needs to be arranged for instructional conferences between teachers, and between teachers and administrators, for the pooling of ideas which focus on educational goals and measure educational achievement.[14]

Criticism of the school's organization and administration

The school's organization and administration are frequently criticized. Organizing and managing a school system is a complex responsibility. Some of the major criticisms in this area are as follows:

1. School administrators are too autocratic; school adminstrators do not make enough decisions of their own.

2. Students do not have enough freedom in helping run the schools.

3. Classes are too large.

4. Students do not have the electives they desire.

5. Students have too many electives.

6. The athletic program is overemphasized.

7. There is not enough discipline in schools today.

8. School administrators have allowed the schools to accept responsibilities and roles that are not consistent with the school's proper function.

9. Schools and their programs are so organized that the rate of attrition in secondary education is too high.

10. The methods of organizing the school's program and the methods used in teaching do not make use of what is well known about the psychology of learning and human motivation.

[14]J. Lloyd Trump and Dorsey Baynham, *Focus on Change* (Chicago: Rand McNally and Company, 1961), p. 8.

11. Provisions for advancement of school personnel within the system are poor.

12. School schedules are too rigid.

13. Class loads are too heavy.

14. Clerical help is not provided.

Here, again, one can see that many of these criticisms are very general, and the importance of examining a particular school or school system is evident. Administrators are aware of great problems in school administration. The work of the National Association of Secondary School Principals and the Staff Utilization Studies is only one example of their efforts to improve the schools.

Criticisms of school buildings and facilities

School buildings and facilities often reflect the school's instructional program. For instance, the objective of equal-sized classes has determined the type of classrooms found in most schools. Also the general form of laboratory experiments has led to the standard design for science laboratories.

Many critics feel that the present physical facilities restrict the school's educational program. They believe that more adequate and more flexible buildings would enable the schools to offer many more avenues to knowledge, understanding, and appreciation.[15] They urge educators to provide buildings that will permit the use of television, recordings, video and audio tape recordings, films and slides, models, mock-ups, and many types of electronic teaching machines.

Instructional films and tapes will originate from a central studio and full cable installations will channel television and other audio or video facilities into school rooms where needed. No longer will it be necessary to move projectors, screens, and tape and record equipment from room to room. Automated and other programmed instruction devices will be standard equipment in laboratories and available for use in student cubicles and other independent study areas.

The building will be completely air conditioned for summer and winter use. It may be windowless, except for offices, faculty work rooms, and possibly some laboratory areas, and air control to produce a sense of well-being. Acoustical controls will reduce noise.

Reflecting the flexible school program and schedule, building spaces will be varied in size and planned specifically for large-group instruction, small-group discussion, and independent study. . . .

[15]Robert N. Bush and Dwight W. Allen, *A New Design for High School Education* (New York: McGraw-Hill Book Company, Inc., 1964), pp. 118–159.

Large-group instruction will call for an auditorium capable of seating 600 students and divisible at will into four smaller spaces, each seating 150, or any combination totaling 600. In addition, two other spaces about 1500 square feet each will be arranged to seat 150 students in tiered semi-circles for large-group presentations. Each area will be furnished with chairs with tablet arms, a speaker's platform, a screen for overhead and other projectors, and television receivers.

For small-group instruction, . . . rooms of several possible shapes — rectangular, square, five- or six-sided — each measuring 200-250 square feet, will provide desirable spaces. These rooms will contain a table large enough to accommodate the chairs for 12 to 15 students, their teacher, and one or two guests. The room will be equipped also with a portable blackboard and a bulletin-flannel-board-screen.[16]

The major criticisms of secondary school buildings and facilities deal with the following elements:

1. Lighting, heating, and ventilation often leave much to be desired.

2. Science and library facilities are inadequate.

3. Buildings are not planned for modern instructional programs.

4. Lunchrooms, shops, etc., are generally inadequate.

5. Equipment in shops, laboratories, gymnasiums, and classrooms is often not of sufficient quality or quantity.

Such criticisms would not apply in the many schools where excellent facilities and buildings are provided and in others where efforts are under way to provide the needed buildings and equipment. Nevertheless, there are cases where the criticism is justified, and something should be done.

In the face of all these criticisms, several comments by Taylor, McMahill, and Taylor may be reassuring to a prospective teacher:

Americans have seldom hesitated to criticize their presidents, congresses, and Supreme Courts, and frequently they have been highly critical of their ministers, schoolmasters, local politicians, newspapers, neighbors, wives, and husbands. Censure is a part of the American culture, and it reaches full force when the umpire calls Willie Mays "out on second!" Criticism, then, does not necessarily mean that any ethical code has been violated; it is merely a way of expression in this land.[17]

---

[16]Trump and Baynham, *op. cit.,* pp. 35–39.

[17]L. O. Taylor and others, *The American Secondary School* (New York: Appleton-Century-Crofts, 1960), p. 47.

Are these criticisms valid?

Are these criticisms of secondary education well founded? Most educators will probably say that in many cases they are. Some schools do not provide for the individual differences of their students; others neglect gifted students and provide little help for slow learners. Many school buildings are inadequate. Teachers who should not be in the profession are sometimes employed. There are many areas where improvements are needed.

On the other hand, there is much that is good in secondary education—a fact that is evident to any interested individual visiting secondary schools. But because there are millions of people involved in secondary education, one can easily find reasons for criticism. In an effort to be objective in one's evaluation of education, it is important to classify the sources of criticisms, for often such a classification will reveal that certain criticisms merely reflect the opinions of special groups. Often, too, the criticisms contradict each other. This is frequently the result of conflicting views on the role our schools should play.

Where criticisms tend to contradict each other, one may suspect an issue involving educational policy or even a basic one of educational philosophy. The criticisms that our secondary schools do not properly prepare youth for college and that too much attention is given to college preparatory courses suggest a probable issue. The implication is that the two criticisms represent divergent points of view on the purpose and function of secondary education in America. Certainly the acceptance or rejection of either criticism must be based upon a primary consideration of what should be the purposes and functions of public secondary education in a democratic society.[18]

Evaluating the critics

Anderson and Gruhn discuss critics and criticisms of secondary education:

The important questions are: By what criteria did they arrive at their recommendations? Were they qualified to decide what the secondary school should do? One might ask the same questions concerning any so-called expert.[19]

In other words, these men are calling for evaluation of secondary education based on objective evidence. It is important then that

[18]Bossing, *op. cit.*, p. 11.
[19]Anderson and Gruhn, *op. cit.*, p. 475.

the individual who would know the facts consult research studies. Since the days of William James, more than a half-century ago, men of scholarly integrity and intellectual eminence have experimented, conducted research, and made known their findings in the field of education. They have not hesitated to publish all of their findings in order that the truth might be known.

It has been noted that constructive criticisms could help the schools, but it should also be emphasized that irresponsible attacks by special interest groups can severely cripple the schools' effectiveness. These groups are willing to exploit parents and children to gain profits, avoid necessary taxes, and achieve narrowly conceived goals. At the same time, they may mouth meaningless phrases about thrift, tradition, the little red school house, and democracy. In the sixties many extreme radical groups have appeared, demanding that the school emphasize dozens of "isms" and movements. The majority of their demands are concentrated on limiting academic freedom, censoring textbooks and curriculum offerings, imposing loyalty oaths on teachers, and releasing students from needed class time to receive religious instruction. Of course, they are happy to furnish speakers and materials for assembly programs and units of study.

These critics do not hesitate to attack, defame, and seek to have expelled any administrator, school board member, or teacher who does not support their position. Their tactics are at times as unethical as those used by the Nazis in Germany when Hitler was attempting to gain power.[20]

The major forces represented by special interest groups are often classified as follows:

Political influences
Religious influences
Self-appointed guardians of the Constitution
Truly subversive influences
Big business and unions
One-way press

Americans tend to think about their schools just as the special-interest propagandist would have them think—in terms of stereotypes. These images are formed through use of time-honoured techniques that include name-calling, generalities, letters to the editor, and outright manipulation of the truth. It is amazing that despite all such efforts to harass and harness the public schools so much real prog-

[20]For an example of such criticisms and methods, the reader should see the February 1962 issue of the *Phi Delta Kappan*.

ress has been possible. The profession of education, we must remember, is the youngest of them all, and perhaps therein it has great strength and the ability to rise far above the levels to which special-interest groups would reduce it.[21]

Weighing the criticisms

Criticisms concerning such things as the preparation of teachers or the construction of school buildings must be carefully considered in light of specific situations. Some teachers are not well prepared to teach anything, while others are forced to teach out of their fields. Still others are well prepared to teach and are doing a good job.

Many communities do not have adequate school buildings, while others have provided the necessary buildings and equipment to house a good educational program. Some communities do not have secondary education programs that stress quality in either academic or vocational programs. It is also true that many secondary school teachers find it very difficult to interest their students in any type of education because of a lack of concern on the part of parents and the community. Very often one finds parents who want their children to be graduated from high school but who are relatively unconcerned with the quality of education they are receiving. It is not unusual, however, to find communities which have secondary schools that are stressing quality and in which a great majority of the parents are vitally concerned with a good educational program.

Most critics sooner or later get around to stating what they believe should be the purposes and values stressed in education.[22] But often the values and beliefs they hold are not acceptable to the general public. For instance, when critics advocate sweeping changes in secondary schools that would result in the selective policies of the European schools, they are setting forth convictions — no doubt sincere ones — which are not shared by the majority of the American people.

Students of secondary education must remember, when evaluating the schools, that young people differ greatly in their abilities, interests, and needs. This means that it would be the height of stupidity to provide only a difficult, European-style academic program and thus to eliminate from school all students who could not master such a program — especially in light of the fact that young people are required by law to remain in school until age

[21]Taylor and others, *op. cit.*, p. 57.
[22]Ehlers and Lee, *op. cit.*, pp. 207–210.

sixteen or eighteen and that industry and most business concerns are prevented from employing adolescents by present labor laws.

The schools must offer general education and appropriate special education for American youth. The secondary schools today reflect modern society and its goals. Certainly much that was valuable in the past has great value today; and, as was acknowledged in Chapter 15, European education has implications for secondary education in this country. But the United States must have schools designed to serve its youth today. If this means using much that is traditional, and it does, the traditional should be used. If practices and policies used in other countries can help, and they have in the past and will in the future, they should be evaluated and used.

In the modern secondary school, students participate in a greater variety of learning experiences than they did in the past, and they spend more time in meaningful activities that involve the use of various resource materials rather than the memorizing of textbook content. Books are used to a far greater extent than they have ever been, but they are utilized in a different way — to provide a common basis for class discussion and to supply information that will help students master specific skills or solve special problems. Many more research projects are undertaken by today's students. Group work, visiting speakers, and community resources are used. Many aids and materials are available to help make the curriculum and teaching more meaningful and more functional.

But do modern approaches work? The evidence indicates that they do. Tests show that secondary school students can write and spell better today than they ever could.

In 1955 Benjamin S. Bloom, the college examiner at the University of Chicago, renormed the secondary school tests used by the United States Armed Forces Institute in mathematics, English, social studies, and science. He administered the tests to twelfth-grade students in a 5 per cent sampling of all public high schools in the United States, exactly the same procedure that had been used in 1942 to secure the original norms on the same tests. Bloom's study revealed that the seniors of 1955 made higher average scores on all tests than did the seniors of 1943. Interestingly enough, he found that the greatest superiority of the 1955 students was in mathematics.[23]

Studies by Bernard Schwartz made in Pennsylvania and reported in the December 1949 issue of *The Journal of Educational*

[23]Benjamin S. Bloom, "1955 Normative Study of the Tests of General Educational Development," *School Review*, LXIV (March 1956), 110–124.

Research and studies involving large-scope comparisons of test results in 1957 with those of the late 1940's and early 1950's made in Kalamazoo, Kansas City, and New York City and reported in the Summer 1957 issue of *School Review* show that the secondary schools of today are doing a better job of educating more students than has ever been done before. More recent studies can also be found in the 1960 *Encyclopedia of Educational Research*.

These studies show many of the important accomplishments of today's schools and the increased emphasis on quality in American schools. Terry Ferrer, educational editor of the New York *Herald Tribune*, writing in 1963, spotlighted much of the evidence of improvement.[24] These important advances cut across the very fabric of education in the United States—the curriculum and teaching, reading, English, mathematics, science, social studies, foreign languages, and vocational subjects. Miss Ferrer points out that students are learning more and faster in modern American schools. They are doing this through better instruction on the part of better prepared teachers, through programmed textbooks and teaching machines, through language laboratories, through new courses in the curriculum such as new physics, biology, English, mathematics, and social studies courses, and many new vocational courses.

She specifies where and how many of the improvements came into existence. For example, she explains the work of the Physical Science Study Committee started by Dr. Jerrold R. Zacharias, a professor at the Massachusetts Institute of Technology, in developing new physics courses. Over 30 per cent of all high school students taking physics in the United States in 1963 were using these courses. New reading programs and reading laboratories have become a part of secondary education, and these are discussed by Ferrer. She shows how foreign language teaching has been improved and how important the work of the Modern Language Association of the United States has been in securing better teaching and better learning in the secondary school. Many other examples of attempts to improve the curriculum and some of the results of these attempts are documented in the areas of mathematics and social studies.

Professional educators and the general public should be concerned with constant evaluation of the schools, but any evaluation should be conducted in an objective way, using sound criteria. Effective evaluation must be conducted on the following principles:

[24]Terry Ferrer, *Classroom Revolution* (Pleasantville, N. Y.: Guidance Associates, 1963), pp. 1–20.

1. Written criteria that will provide objective information should be used.

2. Cooperative evaluation by the school staff, parents, students, and at times special consultants is desirable.

3. Evaluation should be comprehensive in that it should be concerned with academic achievement and social and personal development.

4. Evaluation should involve research, not just opinion.

5. Evaluation should not be limited to grades, number of diplomas, and scholarships given. It must be primarily concerned with behavior changes in the students themselves, such as the ability to solve problems, acquire new information, use one's native language effectively in speaking and writing, and use and understand mathematical processes.

6. Evaluation should be continuous, not a hit-and-miss process.

The following significant statements on the topic of evaluation are worth remembering when one is seeking to evaluate the secondary school's program:

One promising direction being taken by forward-looking secondary schools is the focus of attention on the individual, his uniqueness, his talents whatever they may be, his peculiar contribution, and what makes him capable or incapable of learning. This is one direction in which teachers should not waver in spite of the demands of certain groups for education of an elite at the expense of others. One of the significant contributions of American secondary education is the concept that each child is entitled to a high school education at public expense. As Robert M. Hutchins, former chancellor of the University of Chicago, has stated, "The concept of a people all devoting the early years of their lives to study with a view to attaining the maximum development of their highest powers is surely one of the grandest that history can show."[25]

The increased interest in the study of the student and his development is one of the important trends in education. It is not just for the purpose of finding out what he is but also to discover what he is capable of becoming and to assist him in making the most of his abilities.

In the educator's anxiety to achieve quality, he must face the difficult question, "Who are to be the chosen ones?" Ability is only one of the factors that enter into performance. Motivation, interest,

[25]Anderson and Gruhn, *op. cit.*, p. 491.

and purpose may be equally important. The fact that leaders in the arts, science, and industry are not always those who rank in the highest percentiles in academic ability indicates that more ingredients than one contribute to creativity and inventiveness. Even the experts are still a long way from knowing enough to select those who are destined to be outstanding. A genuine respect for individual differences and a regard for personal worth cannot be equated with selection for instructional grouping.[26]

Dealing with criticism

In the above discussion some general suggestions were made and others implied as to how a teacher, parent, or school administrator could deal with criticisms of secondary education and the secondary schools. These included the following:

1. Evaluate the criticisms carefully.

2. Identify the critics and study their positions, qualifications, and interests.

3. Get the facts on the schools in your locality.

4. Study the issues in secondary education.

5. Treat all criticisms with respect.

6. Formulate your own opinions in light of the evidence.

Today, with so much criticism prevalent, the individual educator must be sure of his own convictions concerning the goals of secondary education and the nature of the instructional program. Teachers, especially, who are in a position to exert positive leadership for improvement, need to have faith and purpose in their work.

Local faculties and schools should have a written philosophy of education, based on sound educational principles and the American way of life. Teachers, parents, students, and administrators should have a part in its formulation, and copies should be placed in the hands of all teachers and interested citizens.

The common and conservative nature of such a platform allays the fears of some parents who have been reading about these "terrible leftist" schools. In helping parents to understand that much of the propaganda about schools originates from persons with axes to grind, a teacher helps himself to win acceptance as a dependable leader. He thereby reduces tensions within his own classroom. An educational platform would include such topics as:

1. New and increasing demands on the school.

2. Purposes of education: preparation for citizenship in its broadest sense.

[26]*Ibid.*, pp. 492–493.

3. Responsibilities of the school: it has primary or chief responsibility for some phases of education, partial or shared responsibility for other phases, some responsibility for educational leadership in the community.

4. How students are classified and assigned to classes and the factors that determine the teachability of a class.

5. Instructional material: the good teacher requires and uses a variety of instructional material.

6. Moral and spiritual values: these values in the curriculum are identified and attention focused upon them.

7. Controversial issues: the American heritage is taught, while controversial issues within the heritage are analyzed and studied.[27]

How can a teacher or administrator deal with specific criticisms in his local school? A few specific criticisms and possible approaches to handling them are given below:

1. *Schools ignore the public's role in improving education.*

a. The school can provide for the public a continuous program of interpretation of its program and a running account of what is needed for improvement. It can and should maintain an "open door" policy—parents can be urged to visit the school and to make their desires known to school officials.

b. Teachers should visit, when possible, in the homes of their students.

c. Teachers should identify themselves with the local community.

d. Lines of communication should be kept open between the school and parents.

e. News of all the school events and the school's program should be made available to the press.

2. *Our high schools do not stress academic achievement.*

a. Enrich the instructional program for students planning to go to college. Insist on maintaining high standards in the academic program.

b. Encourage gifted students to seek scholarships and other opportunities which will enable them to demonstrate their abilities.

c. Let the public know of your students' successes in college and the business world.

d. Remind local citizens that their schools must provide adequate programs for all adolescents.

e. Stress the necessity of meeting the needs of all youth.

[27]Taylor and others, *op. cit.*, pp. 67–68.

3. *High school graduates today have not mastered the "fundamentals" and do not know about this country's major democratic institutions and its heritage.*

a. Show what research has revealed about such criticisms.

b. Have a continuous evaluation program in the school that makes use of standardized achievement tests.

c. Show parents how pupils' achievements compare with national norms.

d. Talk with parents about plans for improvements in the school's program.

e. If students are not achieving, find out why and suggest remedial programs that would be appropriate in light of the abilities of the students and the results of tests.

f. Provide a sound system of grouping in special electives and in the general education program.

4. *School taxes are too high.*

a. Show how the school's enrollments have grown.

b. Indicate the many additional responsibilities the schools have today.

c. Emphasize the school's attempts to stretch every dollar.

d. Show how teachers' salaries compare with salaries in other professions and in business and industry.

e. Make sure parents are aware of the fact that school buildings and facilities cost more today, just as homes and equipment in the home have become more expensive.

f. Show the importance of education to the local community and to the nation.

g. Show that education is a good investment. Use studies, such as the ones by the Chamber of Commerce, to point up how education lifts the standard of living and increases the productive power of the nation.

h. Make the public aware of the relation of education to personal income.

i. Have responsible citizens express their convictions on the cost of education as compared to the expense of ignorance.

j. Show the high correlation between crime and poor education.

5. *Students run the schools today; there is little discipline.*

a. Show parents the true role students play in the government of the school.

b. Show how and why teachers and students do plan together at times.

c. Urge parents to visit the schools and see for themselves.

d. Explain to parents how the school handles discipline problems.

e. Insist that parents cooperate in solving discipline problems.

6. *The schools do not teach moral and spiritual values.*

a. Explain to parents why public schools cannot teach sectarian religion.

b. Remind parents that most of the people who work in schools are members of active religious groups.

c. Show parents how the various areas of the instructional program such as science, history, literature, and music are used to teach these values.

d. Remind parents that homerooms, assemblies, and other student activities are used to teach moral and spiritual values.

Teachers should be informed and ready to meet criticisms of the secondary school, but actually the school board, the school superintendent, and the principals have the major responsibility for answering the critics and keeping the public informed. Teachers can cooperate, however, by assisting in the various ways mentioned in this chapter.

Accomplishments in secondary education

In 1945 the Harvard Committee on General Education made the following report:

We are stating the simple fact that in an industrial age, no alternative exists to the widespread unemployment of minors except some concept of schooling which meets the vast differences among students. . . . Unlike the old high school in which no one was compelled to stay if he could not or did not wish to do the work, the modern high school must find a place for every kind of student whatever his hopes and talents. It cannot justly fail to adapt itself, within reason, to any.[28]

The public secondary school has accepted this challenge, and it has also made great progress toward meeting the implications. Today's schools are designed to serve the needs of all educable youth. In summary, the major accomplishments of the secondary schools have been as follows:

1. Effective adaptation and adjustment to tremendous growth in the number of schools and the school enrollments.

[28]*General Education in a Free Society,* Harvard Committee (Cambridge, Mass.: Harvard University Press, 1945), p. 9.

2. Necessary reorganization in the forms of secondary education, such as the junior high school, comprehensive high school, and community college, in light of increased demands on education.

3. Greater provision for special education, such as education for slow learners, gifted students, and handicapped children.

4. Encouraging increased interest and participation by the general public in the support and improvement of secondary education.

5. Provision of more special services, such as guidance and counseling, health services, and placement services.

6. Use of better instructional materials in the form of textbooks, library materials, audio-visual aids, resource units, and current materials.

7. Hiring better teachers who are better educated and who understand youth.

8. Better buildings and facilities.

9. Better and more properly organized curriculum.

10. A well-balanced program of student activities consisting of student government, homerooms, clubs, etc., which are well correlated with, and which are indeed an important part of, the school's curriculum.

As he was about to finish one of his books, Hand wrote:

If the more extreme academic critics of an earlier day had succeeded, our public secondary school pupils would have been deprived of the benefits of English, mathematics, modern foreign languages, science, history, and the other social studies. If the more extreme among the present-day academic critics succeed, these will be about the only subjects in the curriculum, and there will be no important modifications to suit these offerings to the full range of aptitudes. It requires no great power of divination to prophesy that if this happens the public high school, like the Latin grammar school and the academy, will be supplanted by a protest institution which promises to accommodate itself to the full range of the capacities and educational needs of the youths of America. And, in all likelihood, this protest institution will be federally supported and controlled.[29]

Since 1957 Dr. James B. Conant has been engaged in a study of secondary education in the United States. His research has resulted in three major publications in book form and numerous

[29]Harold C. Hand, *Principles of Public Secondary Education* (New York: Harcourt, Brace & World, Inc., 1958), pp. 348–349.

articles in popular and professional publications. His findings have great significance for education, and his writings will prove to be valuable to the student of secondary education who will take time to explore them. The focus of his study of the high school was on the "comprehensive" school. Dr. Conant set forth the following statements:

No radical alteration in the basic pattern of American education is necessary in order to improve our public high schools. If all the high schools were functioning as well as some I have visited, the education of all American youth would be satisfactory, except for the study of foreign languages and the guidance of the more able girls. Most of the schools which I found unsatisfactory in one or more respects could become satisfactory by relatively minor changes, though I have no doubt that there are schools even of sufficient size where major improvements in organization and instruction would be in order. . . .

This can only be done, however, if the citizens in many localities display sufficient interest in their schools and are willing to support them. The improvements must come school by school and be made with due regard for the nature of the community. Therefore, I conclude by addressing this final word to citizens who are concerned with public education: avoid generalizations, recognize the necessity of diversity, get the facts about your local situation, elect a good school board, and support the efforts of the board to improve the schools.[30]

Selected references

ANDERSON, VERNON E. AND WILLIAM T. GRUHN. *Principles and Practices of Secondary Education*. New York: The Ronald Press Company, 1962.

CONANT, JAMES B. *The American High School Today*. New York: McGraw-Hill Book Company, Inc., 1959.

———. *Education in the Junior High School Years*. Princeton, N.J.: Educational Testing Services, 1960.

———. *Slums and Suburbs*. New York: McGraw-Hill Book Company, Inc., 1961.

DOUGLASS, HARL R. *Secondary Education in the United States*, 2nd ed. New York: The Ronald Press Company, 1964.

[30]James B. Conant, *The American High School Today* (New York: McGraw-Hill Book Company, Inc., 1959), pp. 40 and 96.

EHLERS, HENRY AND GORDON C. LEE. *Crucial Issues in Education*, 3rd ed. New York: Holt, Rinehart & Winston, Inc., 1964.

FORD, EDMUND A. *Rural Renaissance: Revitalizing Small High Schools*. U.S. Office of Education Bulletin 1961. No. 11 (Washington, D.C., 1961).

GALL, MORRIS AND WILLIAM V. HICKS. *Modern Secondary Education*. New York: American Book Company, 1964.

JOHNSON, MAURITZ, JR. *American Secondary Schools*. New York: Harcourt, Brace and World, Inc., 1965.

JOHNSTON, BERNARD, ED. *Issues in Education*. Boston: Houghton Mifflin Company, 1964.

The Junior High School We Need. Association for Supervision and Curriculum Development, National Education Association. Washington, D.C.: NEA, 1961.

Labels and Fingerprints. American Association of School Administrators, National Education Association. Washington, D.C.; NEA, 1960.

The Pursuit of Excellence: Education and the Future of America. Special Studies Report V. Rockefeller Brothers Fund. Garden City: Doubleday & Company, Inc., 1958.

Schools for the Sixties. Project on Instruction, National Education Association. New York: McGraw-Hill Book Company, Inc., 1963.

Index